Lecture Notes in Computer Science 12983

More information about this subseries at http://www.springer.com/series/7409

Yuhua Luo (Ed.)

Cooperative Design, Visualization, and Engineering

18th International Conference, CDVE 2021
Virtual Event, October 24–27, 2021
Proceedings

 Springer

Editor
Yuhua Luo (iD)
University of the Balearic Islands
Palma, Mallorca, Spain

ISSN 0302-9743   ISSN 1611-3349 (electronic)
Lecture Notes in Computer Science
ISBN 978-3-030-88206-8   ISBN 978-3-030-88207-5 (eBook)
https://doi.org/10.1007/978-3-030-88207-5

LNCS Sublibrary: SL3 – Information Systems and Applications, incl. Internet/Web, and HCI

This Springer imprint is published by the registered company Springer Nature Switzerland AG
The registered company address is: Gewerbestrasse 11, 6330 Cham, Switzerland

Preface

Welcome to the proceedings of the 18th International Conference on Cooperative Design, Visualization, and Engineering (CDVE 2021). The COVID-19 pandemic situation during 2021 made our choice of conference format very limited. We were planning to hold it physically in Bangkok, Thailand, but instead the conference was held virtually and online during October 24–27, 2021.

However, our research was not stopped by the pandemic. Our researchers and graduate students kept their work going as normally as possible. The wonderful set of papers presented in this proceedings book is a culmination of the research and development results obtained under our new way of working. It contains a collection of the accepted papers for CDVE 2021.

The papers of this volume cover a wide range of application areas. Both the breadth of the topic coverage and the depth of the research are encouraging.

In the area of cooperative application, applying concepts in other domains, such as applying gamification to cooperative team-member management, can have a positive effect. One of the papers addresses the introduction of a points system to create a competitive environment. This results in motivating the team members to take action faster and be more productive, thus improving the performance of the whole team.

Studying crowd behavior was the focus of a couple research projects reported at the conference. Polling is one of the typical processes for crowd decision making. One project studied the sincerity of the participants in polling. Such user behavior in polling can substantially affect the crowd decision making results.

The study of crowd behavior in disaster management is another topic our researchers are working on. This is very important for risk management actions such as evacuating a big crowd in a disaster situation. According to the authors, crowd cognitive modeling is a vital approach to represent typical crowd behavior. Correct management actions can then be taken to guarantee better results.

In the field of cooperative visualization there is a relatively new finding about the role of visualization in the cooperative digital humanities area. Digital humanities scholars increasingly adopt visualization approaches to enrich their research. They find that visual interfaces create new modes of knowledge generation which can facilitate more effective discovery and new observations. Cooperative visualization should be considered as a research process in its own right, which has led to multiple interdisciplinary collaborations between the digital humanities and visualization communities. The authors present their methodological workflow by applying the visualization element as a vital working process.

Cooperative engineering is becoming a common practice in the AEC industry to a certain degree. However, the sector is facing a lot of challenges. At the stage of creating building designs, mistakes are often made which are costly for the building process. The authors of one paper point out that the BIM-based model checking can help to identify errors in the design. Among them rule translation is key. To analyze this key process, they performed some detailed interviews in two different teams from Demark and Singapore. The advantages and problems of rule translation systems are identified.

Authors working in the airspace craft design field proposed to use ontologies to maintain product descriptions. They believe that this can mitigate the heterogeneity problem by providing semantic descriptions and supporting different vocabularies for a single concept. To obtain information from documents that contain tables, lists, and text, they developed an ontology-based information extraction tool which can manually or automatically extract the ontology information.

Papers involving basic methods and technologies for cooperative applications also presented some work about embedded systems and software-defined networking to mitigate the impact of anomalies on cooperative cloud.

In this volume, collaborative film making and collaborative learning are among the popular topics of cooperative application. Remote laboratory building, remote guidance on physical tasks, online cooperative calligraphic drawing, etc. are areas where our researchers have obtained convincing results.

The COVID-19 pandemic has lasted longer than we expected. In this difficult time in human history, the motivation and the efforts to develop better technology, better life did not stop. I would like to express my sincere thanks to all the authors for submitting their papers to the CDVE 2021 conference. My thanks also go to all our volunteer reviewers, Program Committee members, and Organization Committee members for their contribution. The success of this year's conference would not have been possible without their support.

October 2021   Yuhua Luo

Organization

Conference Chair

Yuhua Luo   University of the Balearic Islands, Spain

International Program Committee

Program Chair

Thomas Tamisier   Luxembourg Institute of Science and Technology, Luxembourg

Members

Conrad Boton	Université du Québec, Canada
Jose Alfredo Costa	Federal University, Brazil
Philipp M. Fischer	German Aerospace Center, Germany
Sebastia Galmes	University of the Balearic Islands, Spain
Gilles Halin	School of Architecture of Nancy, France
Figen Gül	Istanbul Technical University, Turkey
Shuangxi Huang	Tsinghua University, China
Tony Huang	University of Technology Sydney, Australia
Claudia-Lavinia Ignat	Inria, France
Ursula Kirschner	Leuphana University Lüneburg, Germany
Jean-Christophe Lapayre	Centre National de la Recherche Scientifique, France
Pierre Leclercq	University of Liege, Belgium
Jang Ho Lee	Hongik University, South Korea
Jaime Lloret	Polytechnic University of Valencia, Spain
Kwan-Liu Ma	University of California, Davis, USA
Manuel Ortega	University of Castilla–La Mancha, Spain
Juan Carlos Preciado	University of Extremadura, Spain
Niko Salonen	Rolls-Royce Oy Ab, Finland
Chengzheng Sun	Nanyang Technological University, Singapore
Nobuyoshi Yabuki	Osaka University, Japan
Xinwei Yao	Zhejian University of Technology, China

Organization Committee

Chair

Chakkrit Snae Namahoot   Naresuan University, Thailand

Co-chair

Sebastia Galmes   University of the Balearic Islands, Spain

Members

Michael Brückner	Naresuan University, Thailand
Kanokkarn Snae Namahoot	Naresuan University, Thailand
Sanya Khruahong	Naresuan University, Thailand
Chayan Nuntawong	Nakhon Sawan Rajabhat University, Thailand
Kitkawin Aramrun	Office of Atoms for Peace, Thailand
Sakesan Sivilai	Pibulsongkram Rajabhat University, Thailand
Naruepon Panawong	Nakhon Sawan Rajabhat University, Thailand
Takayuki Fujimoto	Toyo University, Japan
Pilar Fuster Parra	University of the Balearic Islands, Spain
Alex Garcia	University of the Balearic Islands, Spain
Tomeu Estrany	University of the Balearic Islands, Spain
Guofeng Qin	Tongji University, China
Linan Zhu	Zhejiang University of Technology, China

Additional Reviewers

Ortega Cantero
Supannada Chotipant
Caslon Chua
Pilar Fuster-Parra
Ewa Grabska
Weidong Huang
Manuel Ibarra
Tao Lin

Guofeng Qin
Frode Sandnes
Barbara Strug
Christian Stummer
Philemon Yalamu
Didry Yoann
Li-Nan Zhu

Contents

Gamification and Application Features for Collaborative Environments

Gabriele Kotsis[1]([✉]) [iD], Alexander Paschinger[1], and Christine Strauss[2] [iD]

[1] Johannes Kepler University Linz, Linz, Austria
gabriele.kotsis@jku.at
[2] University of Vienna, Vienna, Austria
christine.strauss@univie.ac.at

Abstract. Gamification has been adopted for various environments by applying design elements typically used within games onto a non-gaming context. In this paper we introduce a detailed concept for collaborative, team-oriented work that utilizes positive effects of gamification from a practical perspective. The integration of selected gamification features enhances functionality and usability of tools and collaborative applications. From detailed concept and implemented prototype, we demonstrate selected features, where gamification has been implemented to support interaction among team-members and improve overall team-productivity within collaborative, communicative and cooperating environments.

Keywords: Gamification · Team interaction · Team management · Collaboration · Teamwork · Player types

1 Introduction

Gamification not only has proven to be a high-potential phenomenon, but has also shown its applicability in various contexts in the computer science domain [5]. Various applications use gamification concepts and implemented components to motivate users with design elements typical for games [4]. However, the integration of gamification elements into a certain application implies the fulfillment of (i) requirements stemming from the application itself, and (ii) requirements from gamification principles. Collaborative settings need system's support with components, which fuel motivation and productivity of users on the one hand, and which at the same time decrease organizational overhead and communication frictions on the other hand [1]. Many applications support team-organization, team-management, and team-work in general providing many features for enhancing the communication or organization within teams, but fail to offer any motivational elements to nudge users being productive and cooperative. Most apps are designed to support long-established teams. Nevertheless, since

Y. Luo (Ed.): CDVE 2021, LNCS 12983, pp. 1–12, 2021.
https://doi.org/10.1007/978-3-030-88207-5_1

project implementation cycles are getting shorter and shorter, due to rapid developments of technology, companies, groups, and teams in collaborating environments need short-term team formation to make different specialists from various domains working together [9]. This calls for a mobile and agile application with a motivational component for both, long-established teams and ad-hoc groups with people new to each other. Many gamification-related applications either provide professional team-management strategies or gamification aspects, but not both. Furthermore, systems providing gamification aspects often concentrate on perfecting one single feature, rather than combining or providing various gamification components. Several tools with conceptional gamification features have been developed to encourage and motivate users [14]. However, in our approach we focus on the possibility to extend the system for a usage in productive and professional environments, and thus also incorporates practices to ensure proper functionality including the software development process. This paper aims at showing the specific integration of gamification elements into a team management tool for collaborative, communicative and cooperating environments. The support, motivation and productivity of individuals operating within a team represents the main focus of this contribution. Collaborative settings need system's support with components, which fuel motivation and productivity of users on the one hand, and which at the same time decrease organizational overhead and communication frictions on the other hand.

The remainder of the paper is structured as follows: Sect. 2 provides related work covering gamification, pitfalls of gamification, and Bartle's Player Types [2]. Section 3 discusses the conceptualization and selected implementation details of the prototype and shows exemplary the look-and-feel. Section 4 introduces four feature-sets with 11 features, which were implemented into the prototype. Detailed explanations on gamified features, components and gamification mechanisms are given. A synoptic view on the gamification effects in terms of feature and player type wraps up this core section, before we present a conclusion with an outlook on future work in Sect. 5.

2   Gamification and Teams

Gamification can be interpreted as the process of integrating game elements and mechanisms into non-game objects, with the goal to provide gameful experiences [4,16]. Gamification relates to consolidating aspects and mechanisms of gaming, meaning that there is a distinct difference to toys, (serious) games and playful design. Based on Caillois, Deterding et al. created a two dimensional visualization for delimiting gamification as a discrete concept [3,4] alongside with playful design, toys and so-called serious games [11,16].

Hunicke et al. also state, that the actual value of a game is not the product itself, but the behavior resulting from player actions; the core value is interaction [7]. Xu states, that by combining at least three of these four keys a game-like experience may engage a wide range of people and should therefore be considered, when designing such an experience [15]. Not only the playing approach (e.g., casual, hardcore or non-gamer) can be used to differentiate gamers having fun with a task, but also the type of personality and the characteristics of the player. Bartle identified four stereotypical player types [2]: "Achiever", "Explorer", "Killer", and "Socializer". *Achievers* are motivated by goals defined by the game itself. Appropriate examples for motivational factors would be points, levels, ratings or achievements. Whereas *Explorers* are driven by exploring the simulated experience and finding out as much as possible in this regards; this may include ideologies, mechanisms or geography to name some examples. Players of the type *Killer* are driven by causing uneasiness, discomfort or stress to other players, as well as by dominating others. By contrast, *Socializers* get excited by the social and communication aspect of the game. This can be achieved by using role-play with player mates, for instance. This model has been extended by Kim to reflect the social actions corresponding to the player types. These social actions can be identified during games played by different kinds of players, where also the player can have multiple characteristics motivating their interactions [17].

A meta study of Hamari et al. examined empirical studies regarding gamification and its motivators within projects. According to this meta-analysis, gamification has yet been used in a variety of contexts ranging from commerce, education and health, to work, sharing, innovation, and data gathering. Points, Leaderboards, Achievements, Levels, Stories, Avatars and Progress are some examples of motivational features, which can be implemented to engage users in these contexts. This meta study collected results from literature, and reported positive effects in terms of outcome when using gamification elements [6,15].

Pitfalls in gamification include for example overgamification. Yohannis et al. warn about overusing gamification techniques, and distract users from the actual goal. In an educational application, gamification could tempt learners to concentrate more on game elements and use of the application for fun than the learning content [16]. All-time or long-term leaderboards may neglect their actual goal by demotivating newcomers or people whose ranks are low. These participants might be demotivated by assuming there is no possibility to catch up on the leaderboard within reasonable time. Some elements demand further mechanisms to ensure an increase in motivation for all or at least most participants [8,12].

3   Design Prototype

3.1   Design Principles

In the following functionalities of selected features are explained, as well as the look-and-feel of the desired product by implementing a design prototype. Aiming at identifying and eliminating critical pitfalls in collaborative environments, we considered established and novel gamification concepts. Basic technical and platform-dependent decisions and limitations, and the context, where the application is feasible are given. Still, this section does not go into detail of the technical aspects of the project, but rather illustrates the decisions, which arose from the prototyping phase.

In the first prototyping phase the problem definition resulted in an application, that supports day-to-day routine activities, which occur when working in a (new) team. Although the look-and-feel, color and layout of the design prototype may be subject to change, it is important to consider these aspects in the beginning of the design prototype phase [10]. This section will cover basic design decisions like colors, element arrangements, as well as the screen flow and actions, which can be taken on each stage of the application. This part is also bound to some technical foundation decisions due to platform-dependent design conventions (Android versus iOS).

Besides a practical demonstration of the design prototype, we define the sketching-platform, and illustrate the screen flow, design elements and wireframes.

3.2   Platform and Technology

The following part covers the *how* and *why* of initial technology decisions, and defines the supported platforms, as well as the dedicated reasons for limitations. Requirements called in for a mobile prototype; system-extension is possible but for now the application supports iOS only. As base technology Firebase has been chosen as the main mobile development platform, as it consists of feature modules like Cloud Database, Cloud Functions, Cloud Storage, User Authentication and many more. It supports many platforms and programming languages like Swift, Java, Javascript etc. and can be used as a library to enable the desired features within a mobile application [19].

The application is implemented as a full native mobile application for iOS mobile devices. It supports the dedicated design conventions user experience guidelines and is implemented with the integrated development environment (IDE) XCode for macOS. As a base technology, the system implements Firebase, which is used for user management (like login or authentication), as the (real-time) database and communication system (push notification, Firebase Cloud Messaging).

3.3   Design of Collaborative and Gamification-Based Features

In the following we describe the main team-related features implemented in the prototype, which should illustrate some potential feature components within a collaborative environment.

Exemplary implementation details and design decisions are given together with collaborative features implemented in the prototype. The implemented features can be distinguished into *collaborative Features* and *Gamification-Based Features*. Several collaborative features have been inspired by groupware patterns and by theoretical concepts suggested by Schümmer [13].

Furthermore, design details and decisions made during prototyping are outlined for each feature. The prototype has been designed and drafted for iOS mobile devices. First and foremost, the support for the iOS-platform constraints the prototype to be conform to the appropriate iOS-design conventions and usability-guidelines. Therefore, the prototype is designed with a typical iOS-like design, including reduced color usage, appropriate fonts and dominant use of flat design. The prototype also considers system level widgets (like typical boolean-toggles or listings), as well as the usage of tab menus and navigation controllers.

To support the creation of teams and the management of users, the prototype provides basic functionality, including *Register/Login of a User*, *User Profile Management*, *Creating a Team*, *Accept/Deny Team invitation*, or *Leaving a Team*. Registration ensures, that a user is uniquely identified within the application. Firebase-Authentication has been defined as the registration platform, which also allows for the definition of roles, e.g. a creator of a team, who automatically embodies the role of an administrator. In the *Team-Member Management System* participants within the team are to be managed and modified. Team members, who should leave the team immediately, can be removed by the administrator, new members, on the other hand, can be invited to a collaboration within the team. It also covers the profile details, where the spoken languages or social network settings of a specific team member are accessible. The *Team-Dashboard* indicates new invitations, where a user can accept or deny a team invitation. After rejection an invitation disappears, an acceptance results in adding the team to user's list of active teams. The profile management system covers the modification of the user's name, the language preferences and spoken languages, as well as available social networks. In a future version, profile management will also be used to record gamification types and preferences of the user.

Another group of functions is related to team awareness and communication, implemented features include a *Team-News Tab*, *Team-Chat*.

Collaboration within the group is supported by *Team-Events*, where the planning of meetings or events relevant to the team is manageable through a synchronized calendar. The *Team-Task Management System* provides a basic planning system containing the actions in the collaboration. The actions can be estimated and ranked with some points corresponding to the effort of the tasks. The tasks also contain some basic description, member assignment and illustrate a finished or in-progress state. The task backlog furthermore is separated into a Todo and History Tab. During collaboration, there are often questions, which arise while collaborating on specific tasks. Team members can use the *Team-Question Board*, where they can state questions regarding a topic, where there is uncertainty. The question board should also motivate introvert team members to ask questions anonymously. Similar to the questions, surveys can be used to quickly obtain the team's opinion regarding a specific topic using the *Team-Survey Board*, with the addition that a survey is marked with an expiration date and relates to a specific topic with predefined answers; surveys should help to make democratic decision regarding a specific topic.

Whereas the above-mentioned features belong to the category of collaborative features, the feature *Team-Highscore* is a gamification-based feature, that embodies one of the core functionalities of the application. However, in the prototype *Team-Highscore* represents function and visualization of the performance of the team members regarding their actions within the Team-Space. It introduces a points system, which brings in a competitive component in order to motivate team members to take action and to be productive.

3.4   Implementation of the Design Prototype

This section introduces the tool used for creating the designs and presents the actual outcome. It introduces the prototyping tool, along with its workflow, and provides insights into the design and screen-flow of the application.

The prototype was created using the free, browser-based design engine Marvelapp - an online tool for creating design prototypes and wireframes [18]. When creating a free-tier account, Marvelapp provides essential features for creating prototypes and design screen-flows, but limits the user to a maximum of two Marvelapp-projects. This tool offers predefined, high-quality skeleton designs and powerful features including easy screen flow definitions, transition animations, and deployment options. Marvelapp can be used in the web-browser or via dedicated mobile apps, available for Android and iOS. The prototype can be used on a real-world device, reacts to touch inputs, and demonstrates the prototype in a realistic look-and-feel. Nevertheless, as the prototype only focuses on the screen flow and design, it demands the designer to implement many screens, when designing a realistic application prototype - every single action claims a unique screen and proper management for each of the available screen transitions. This resulted in more than 100 screens for the iOS design prototype of the application for gamified collaboration. Figure 1 shows exemplary screenshots

Fig. 1. Exemplary screenshots showing the look-and-feel of three features.

of three features of the design prototype, i.e., Member Profile, Highscore, and Rewards to provide insights into the look-and-feel.

4   Gamified Collaborative Features for Team Management

In the following we provide details on the gamified collaborative features and the underlying mechanisms implemented in the prototype. For each feature we determine its attractiveness per player type. For reasons of completeness we briefly mention general application features, and explain team-relevant and gamification-relevant features in more detail.

4.1   Team Management

Team Management refers to the core of the entire feature-sets, embodied by general management of teams and team members. Besides moderation, the possibility to create, join or leave a team are basic functionalities. The function "Creating teams" represents a basic and essential element to provide contextual separation of collaborative environments within the application. To provide this function users are to be identified uniquely; for this we integrated Firebase, a service by Google, which enables a simple user management system out of the box [19]. Besides the role of administrator, other roles such as *Moderator*, *Newbie* or *Banned* can be created with appropriate functionalities.

4.2   Team Interaction

Interaction within a team between its members requires communication, organization and collaboration of the various team members. *Team-Chat* allows to communicate in a simple text-based way within the group - it provides the possibility for team members to interact with each other directly regardless their memberships in social media or communication platforms. This feature appeals the player types Socializers and Killers. Whereas Socializers may get to know other team members better and even make friends, Killers may use it as an arena for conflicts or boast within the chat. *Member Profiles* supports personalization, the feature consists of a two-factor architecture (i.e., a modifiable personal preference area and a read-only public area). This feature may provide information on the user's player type profile. Socializers may be more motivated by this feature than others. As also implicit interaction may affect cooperation between team members, the feature *Endorsement* allows endorsing team members for positive actions, sympathy or diligence in an anonymous way, direct or accompanied by rewards to amplify a positive excitement of the feedback receiver. This idea emerged a feedback and endorsement system coupled to a rewarding system for cooperative and accommodating team members. *Endorsement* is most appreciated by the player type Socializer. Anyhow, also Killers and Explorers may be motivated by this feature, because of the exploratory nature of this feature.

4.3   Team Competition

This subsection refers on elements regarding the competitive interaction between team members - this includes competition, as well as the individual comparison Observing activities and rewards from fellow team members may be a motivator in a collaborative environment; it might spur the ambition to catch up with team members. Such a feature is based on a reporting option on activities to provide transparency, and support coordination by tracking individual work progress. For this we implemented in the prototype a *Task System*, *Team Highscore*, and a *Level System*.

Task System. The *Task System* contains all task assignments in a team. As tasks may differ substantially regarding workload, complexity, priority and/or importance tasks need to be rated with *Points*, which are distributed to the assignees of the task if it is marked as completed by every team member who contributed to its completion. Points are then awarded and documented in the *Team Highscore*. As Highscore might have demotivating effects on individuals (for e.g. team members at the bottom of the league) the prototype provides a long-term motivational system, *Level System*, which is independent from specific teams. This feature-set covers these coherent features and explains all the details regarding the Team Competition and comparison.

Highscore. The feature *Team Highscore* is a tool to allow for competition among teams and provides comparability of the individual team members' contributions. Highscores are an established gamification feature, often used in projects [14]. However, internal rankings may not be sufficient as a single gamification feature, therefore functionality and long-term motivation needs to be supported. Team Highscore provides a simple tool to compare the members' performance within the team, but also provides personal benefits, which should be independent from the team environment. The feature is connected to the *Task System* and adopts the points received from completed tasks as a comparison reference. Completed tasks increase the points of a team member in a one-to-one ratio, and rank the members according to their points. The highscore is permanent; it is used as a documentation tool and indicates a persons' performance compared to other team members. Individual team members should be clickable to instantly receive a report of the appropriate completed tasks in temporal descending order.

The following rule set has been implemented: When a member is first (or performs well in comparison to the other team members) the color is green, yellow indicates mid performers and red low performers (see Figure The color of the comparison bar in the highscore always refers to the points of the first team member in the highscore and calculates the percentage to the points of the leader in the highscore. The coloring of the progress bar fulfills the following rules - members with points greater than 66% (compared to the leader) are colored green, members who obtained more points than 33%, compared to the leader, are colored yellow, low performers with points below 33%, in reference to the first member in the highscore, are marked as red. The detailed report of the points of a specific team member also indicates the sequence of the completed tasks and the exact timestamp of completion.

To ensure motivation within the Team Competition and comparison, under-performers should have the possibility to catch-up with leaders. However, in turn this would result in penalizing really diligent team members by solely reducing their advantage, and in sophisticating their genuine contribution within the col-laborative environment. For that reason, the highscore needs to be expressed in different highscore modes (weekly reset, monthly reset), which can be chosen by each team individually.

Due to the competitive nature of a leaderboard, this feature will intrigue first and foremost Achievers, but also Killers as they can outplay fellow team members. The Highscore System will also resonate with Explorers because they can find out how the system works, how to optimize a strategy to get points, and find out the coherence between the Task System, Team Highscore and the Level System.

Level System. The *Task System* and the *Team Highscore* open out into a long-term *Level System*, which purpose is to provide a realistic progression throughout the application experience with motivational rewards on increasing the own level. Therefore level progression should follow a specific pattern, which is high in the beginning and keeps on increasing while levelling up. The detailed formula of the Level System should not be transparent to the user (at least initially), it should motivate the user by being explorable. At specific level milestones, users are able to unlock rewards.

Formally a regression could be employed for a *Level System*, that allows for easy earnings in the lower levels for unexperienced and new team members and makes it more difficult to rank up in upper levels.

The *Level System* attracts Achievers, because the mechanisms of the progress in ranking up, the achieving of specific milestones and the unlocking of rewards are perfectly suited in regards to the definitions of the driving force in respect to Achievers [2]. Explorers might be inspired to understand and reveal the mecha-nisms of the *Level System* and the interdependencies between the features within the *Team Competition* feature-set.

4.4 Reward System

The feature-set *Individualization* is gamification-specific and covers the entire *Reward System*. The reward system and its corresponding elements are user-centered and support individual accomplishments, prizes, and rewards. The feature-set covers diverse rewards, collectibles, and achievements within the application, which are appealing for many Player Types, and which may motivate either situational or long-term. To provide motivation for different player-types different collectibles are available: (i) *Achievements* are accomplished for fulfilled challenges or tasks defined in the Reward System in the UserDashboard, (ii) *Avatar Badges* are obtainable for TeamTactics Coin in the appropriate Reward System in the UserDashboard, (iii) *Backgrounds* are unlocked when levelling-up by receiving experience points, (iv) *Experience Points* are received when individuals are contributing to team-tasks and completing them, (v) *Highscore Points* are received when contributing to tasks of a team and completing them, and (vi) *TeamTactics Coins* are granted for a visit a day or for getting endorsed by another team member.

Color Scheme. Instead of a plain white background and black font on the display color-schemes can be utilized to improve team-members' engagement and personalization. The choice of backgrounds and wallpapers are stepwise unlocked via the Level System when pre-defined milestones are reached. As the rewarding system primarily consists of collecting and unlocking rewards, Achievers are motivated by this feature. Nevertheless, it is appealing for Explorers too as wallpaper rewards are only revealed when unlocked, this keeps new rewards surprising and engaging.

Avatar Badges. The *Avatar Badge* Other than the backgrounds, which are not visible to other team members team members may choose an avatar they identify with, visible for other team members. This feature is implemented by Avatar Badges, which enables the user to unlock and choose an avatar badge, which decorates the avatar picture in the personal profile and in the team member management profile. The prototype offers almost 100 different avatar badges, which can be unlocked by investing TeamTactics Coins, gained either for being endorsed by other team members, or visiting the application regularly. Due to the numerous and different avatar badges, Achievers could be engaged by encouraging their drive for completing this collection. Socializers also might heavily like this feature, because they could get to know their fellow team members better. If a team member for example equips a dog as avatar badge, this potentially implies, that this person has a dog as a pet (or at least likes these kinds of animals).

Achievement System. The component *Achievement System* relies on the achievement definition of inspirational games, especially World of Warcraft. Achievements embody small tasks or quests obtainable and collectable by team-members; they may or may not have rewards when completed. It consists of two dimensions, *Achievements* as the encapsulating object and *Achievement Properties* containing all the requirements to obtain the achievement.

We have implemented multidimensional dependencies enabling multiple achievements with the same property requiring different activation values. The Achievement System demanded a profound modification of many different classes with a framework to increase achievement properties where necessary. Achievements are visible only for the owner, team members cannot see the current achievement state of other users. Nevertheless, to furthermore motivate the user and celebrate an unlocked achievement, a popup informs the user about the new accomplishment and illustrates a confetti animation until the popup is dismissed. Some of the achievements furthermore act as a tutorial (if the user did not realize a specific feature or ignored it so far).

Achievers are obviously the prioritized target Player Type for this specific feature, the collection and completion of the achievements should be the perfect motivation. Explorers also might like the Achievement System, due to the nature of the designed achievements within the application - they introduce to the application and help to explore and navigate through all the different features offered by the application. Killers might also be attracted by this feature, when comparing different obtained achievements to the ones of their friends.

Table 1. Attractiveness of gamification features for each player type.

		"Achiever"	"Explorer"	"Socializer"	"Killer"
Team mgmt.	Team moderation	M	L	H	L
	Member admin	L	L	M	L
Team interaction	Team chat	L	M	H	H
	Member profile	M	M	H	M
	Endorsement	L	L	H	M
Team competition	Task system	H	M	M	L
	Highscore	H	H	M	H
	Level system	H	H	M	M
Reward system	Background	H	H	M	L
	Avatar badges	H	M	H	L
	Achievement	H	H	M	M

Table 1 summarizes team-relevant features of the implemented prototype and provides for each feature and each player type (achiever, explorer, socializer, killer) an estimated attractiveness (high, medium, low) of the gamification elements.

5   Conclusion

This paper has introduced a prototypical implementation of a team management application providing several mechanisms of gamification aiming at improving individual performance and collaboration-experience of team members, as well as the overall team performance in temporary, project-related teams in educational and professional context. The gamification portfolio of the presented prototype includes collectibles, currencies, avatar badges, wallpapers, and scoring. Future work includes testing of the prototype with independent test persons in heterogenous groups containing different player types. These test are expected to reveal to what extent motivation and productivity is affected by gamification elements within collaborative settings.

References

1. Al Zubaidi-Polli, A.M., Anderst-Kotsis, G.: Conceptual design of a hybrid participatory IT supporting in-situ and ex-situ collaborative text authoring. In: Proceeding of the 20th IIWAS Conference, pp. 243–252. ACM, New York (2018)
2. Bartle, R.: Hearts, clubs, diamonds, spades: players who suit MUDs. J. MUD Res. **1**(1), 19 (1996)
3. Caillois, R.: Man, Play, and Games. University of Illinois Press, Champaign (2001)
4. Deterding, S., Dixon, D., Khaled, R., Nacke, L.: From game design elements to gamefulness: defining gamification. In: Proceedings of MindTrek 2011, pp. 9–15. ACM, New York (2011)
5. Groh, F.: Gamification: State of the Art Definition and Utilization. In: Asaj, N., et al. (eds.) 4th Seminar on Research Trends in Media Informatics, pp. 39–46. Ulm University, Ulm (2012). https://doi.org/10.1145/1979742.1979575
6. Hamari, J., Koivisto, J., Sarsa, H.: Does gamification work? - a literature review of empirical studies on gamification. In: Proceedings of the 47th Hawaii International Conference on System Sciences (HICSS), pp. 3025–3034. IEEE, New York (2014)
7. Hunicke, R., LeBlanc, M., Zubek, R.: A formal approach to game design and game research. In: AAAI Workshop - Technical Report 1, p. 1722 (2004)
8. Ipeirotis, P.G., Gabrilovich, E.: Quizz: targeted crowdsourcing with a billion (potential) users. In: Proceedings of the 23rd International Conference on World Wide Web (WWW 2014), pp. 143–154. ACM, New York (2014)
9. Koehler, A., Mladenow, A., Strauss, C.: Collaboration and co-creation in a general engagement platform to foster organizational benefits during a post-project-phase. In: Luo, Y. (ed.) CDVE 2019. LNCS, vol. 11792, pp. 209–218. Springer, Cham (2019). https://doi.org/10.1007/978-3-030-30949-7_24
10. Leitner, M.-L., Strauss, C., Stummer, C.: Web accessibility implementation in private sector organizations: motivations and business impact. Univ. Access Inf. Soc. **15**(2), 249–260 (2014). https://doi.org/10.1007/s10209-014-0380-1
11. Michael, D.R., Chen, S.L.: Serious Games: Games that Educate, Train, and Inform. Muska & Lipman/Premier-Trade, Boston (2005)
12. Morschheuser, B., Hamari, J., Koivisto, J.: Gamification in crowdsourcing: a review. In: Proceedings of the 49th Hawaii International Conference on System Sciences (HICSS), pp. 4375–4384. IEEE, New York (2016)
13. Schümmer, T., Lukosch, S.: Patterns for Computer-Mediated Interaction. Wiley, Hoboken (2013)
14. Singer, L., Schneider, K.: It was a bit of a race: gamification of version control. In: Second International Workshop on Games and Software Engineering (GAS), pp. 5–8. IEEE, New York (2012)
15. Xu, Y.: Literature review on web application gamification and analytics. In: CSDL - Technical Report, pp. 1–33 (2012)
16. Yohannis, A.R., Prabowo, Y.D., Waworuntu, A.: Defining gamification: from lexical meaning and process viewpoint towards a gameful reality. In: Conference on Information Technology Systems and Innovation (ICITSI), pp. 284–289. IEEE, New York (2014)
17. Designing the player journey. https://www.slideshare.net/amyjokim/gamification-101-design-the-player-journey. Accessed 7 June 2021
18. Marvelapp. https://marvelapp.com/. Accessed 7 June 2021
19. Google firebase. https://firebase.google.com/. Accessed 7 June 2021

Questions of Sincerity in Cooperative Polls

Barbara M. Anthony[✉], Miryam Galvez, and Chris Ojonta

Southwestern University, Georgetown, TX 78626, USA
{anthonyb,galvezm,ojontac}@southwestern.edu

Abstract. Online tools like Doodle polls are frequently used for meeting coordination and other decentralized cooperative decision-making. Since Doodle polls are a form of approval voting, theoretical results from voting theory often underpin work in this area. Sincerity, where a voter never says yes to a less-preferred option without saying yes to all more preferable choices, is a common assumption in approval voting. However, that does not take into account cooperative behavior sometimes exhibited by users when others' responses are known. We conduct a user study investigating the extent to which college-student participants in Doodle-style polls were sincere, reporting on responses from one institution.

Keywords: Approval voting · Doodle polls · Sincerity

1 Introduction

Doodle polls (www.doodle.com) are a widely-used tool for cooperative scheduling of meetings at convenient or desirable times. A poll organizer selects a set of potential time slots for a meeting; participants can then view those time slots on a calendar, putting a checkmark in a box to indicate availability at a given time or leaving it blank if unavailable. Doodle polls are a form of approval voting, though few users think of them in those terms.

Approval voting has been well-studied and it is often accepted in the literature that voters are *sincere* [4–6], i.e. if a participant says yes to a time slot that they value at some amount v, then they must also say yes to any slot that they value more than v. Nothing is stipulated about slots with value equal to v.

Prior research on large sets of actual Doodle polls has revealed some insights into participants' behavior. Zou et al. [9] showed evidence of strategic voting, presenting a theory of "social voting" that suggests a tendency of voters to say yes to popular slots. In addition, Proposition 2 in [9] confirms that said social voting is sincere when participants can have what are called preference levels. Studying numerous Doodle polls from hundreds of countries Reinecke et al. [8]

A Sam Taylor Fellowship Fund grant compensated study participants. Southwestern University's High-Impact Experience Fund supported student research assistants.

Y. Luo (Ed.): CDVE 2021, LNCS 12983, pp. 13–19, 2021.
https://doi.org/10.1007/978-3-030-88207-5_2

observed behaviors that align with countries' cultural norms, such as collectivist cultures saying yes to fewer time slots.

These analyses have led to further theoretical work that attempts to explain the observed behavior. Obraztsova et al. [7] proposed an equilibrium strategy model where voters obtain a small bonus for additional time slots that they approve up to a certain limit that aligns with the observations of [9]. Anthony et al. [2,3] used a game-theoretic approach to determining the existence of Nash equilibria in Doodle polls under the assumption of sincerity. Alrawi et al. [1] showed that when voters deviate from their true availability, the quality of the selected time slot can be greatly impacted: supposedly helpful behavior of indicating greater availability can lead to worse outcomes, while being more restrictive about when one indicates availability can yield better results.

While prior analyses of actual Doodle poll data provide some insights, Doodle data is limited to user-submitted responses submitted and general web traffic information, which enabled country-specific analysis. It inherently lacks details about schedules and criteria participants were considering in making their decisions. We seek to determine how theoretical results about Doodle polls, including assumptions of sincerity, align with human behavior. As algorithms and online mechanisms are relied on more extensively for consensus-building and cooperative decision-making, it is important to understand the underlying assumptions.

2   Research Methods

Since real Doodle poll data contains information only about the time slots selected, not the individual's schedules or other considerations, we provided volunteer participants with hypothetical schedules and scenarios, asking them to fill out Doodle-style polls based on those schedules and scenarios. All data collection was done with the Qualtrics online survey tool due to the pandemic, and approved by the Southwestern University Institutional Review Board. A $10US Amazon gift card was provided to all participants unless they specifically declined it. All participants were college students at United States institutions.

Survey and Scenarios. Participants were given a week-long hypothetical schedule with 40 h of pre-scheduled classes, labs, and work, and asked to respond based on that schedule in all four scenarios. Each scenario had 126 distinct hour-long time slots, daily from 8am to 1am the next morning. In the first scenario, participants were asked to consider their availability for a group project meeting with three other students for a class in their major, rating it on a scale of 1 to 5, with 5 indicating a least desirable time or one at which the person was unavailable. In the second scenario, they were asked to respond with a yes or a no, as in a Doodle poll, rather than the numerical rating. The third scenario again asked for yes/no responses and had the same schedule, but now participants were provided with the number of other group members who reported being available for each time slot, which allowed for evaluation of the extent to which a desire to be or appear cooperative influenced responses. In the final scenario, instead of considering a class project, participants now had a hypothetical, conveniently-located, zero-travel time, local grocery store job. Their manager was asking about their availability to work five additional hours that week, and participants were told that their yes/no answers should reflect that they did want to work more hours.

Participants were then asked which scenario they found most difficult to complete, followed by free response questions of *why?* and if there was *any additional information you want to provide about what you were considering while completing these activities.* The survey concluded with optional demographic questions, and providing a .edu email associated with a United States college to receive a $10US Amazon gift card. Attention checks were embedded into the Qualtrics questions to ensure a high quality of responses. For example, participants were instructed to rank Thursday at 6pm as a 2, which was enforced by the survey software in order for them to continue to subsequent steps. Naturally, the Thursday at 6pm time slot was then excluded in response analysis. Participants who failed attention checks were routed out of the study.

Python Code to Evaluate Sincerity. While a response is either sincere or not, when a participant has to indicate their availability on over 100 time slots, the potential for human error or inattention is large. Thus, rather than merely reporting if a user is sincere, we consider how many responses would have to be changed in each of scenarios 2, 3, and 4 to then be sincere based upon the availability reported in scenario 1.

Fundamentally, a sincere participant has a threshold (a rating value from 1–5) for which they should say yes to all ratings above their threshold, no to all lower ratings, and either yes or no to ratings matching their threshold. Since we do not inherently know a participant's threshold, we determine the number of insincere responses for each possible threshold, and take the minimum over said values; for a sincere participant, that minimum will be 0. Though unlikely and rather contrived, knowing the theoretical maximum contextualizes the results: a sincerity score as large as 62 is possible if, after excluding slots with values specified by attention checks, participants rated half of the slots as 5, the other half as 1, said no to all slots rated 1, and yes to all others.

```python
import numpy as np
def calc_sincerity_for_threshold(rating, yes_no, thresh):
    adjust=np.asanyarray(rating.apply(lambda x: x-thresh))
    adjust[74] = 0    # Ignores Thursday 6pm slot
    decision = {'y': 1, 'n': -1}
    yes_no_val = np.asanyarray(yes_no.map(decision))
    sincerity_product = np.multiply(adjust, yes_no_val)
    result = np.sum(sincerity_product > 0)
    return result
```

Code Block 1: Python function to calculate a sincerity score for a given threshold

Code Block 1 illustrates the Python function used to determine if participants' responses are sincere, taking as input the numerical ratings provided in scenario 1, the yes/no responses from a later scenarios, and a threshold value ranging from 1 to 5. First, we decrease all provided ratings by the threshold, so that ratings less than 0 are now ones to which a sincere participant should say yes, while the sincere response to positive values is no, and ratings of 0 could receive either a yes or a no from a sincere respondent. We then set the time slot whose value was mandated to be 2 by the attention check slot (slot 74 is Thursday at 6pm) to be 0, so that it does not impact calculations of sincerity. We next convert yes and no values into ± 1, respectively. A sincere respondent will now have $+1$ (from a yes) in the array positions corresponding to negative values in the adjusted ratings array, and -1 (from a no) in the array positions corresponding to positive values in the adjusted ratings array. A sincere participant could have ± 1 in the array positions corresponding to 0s in the adjusted rating arrays. Thus, if we multiply the corresponding positions in the two arrays, a sincere participant has only negative or 0 values for each component. Thus, we perform that multiplication, and determine the number of positive entries in the array, which is the sincerity score for that participant for the provided threshold.

3   Results from Participants at One College

In this work in progress, we analyze the responses from students at Southwestern University (SU), a small private liberal arts college in the US. Future work will contain data from all study participants. Table 1 provides summary statistics about the sincerity scores from the 34 SU participants, calculated as described in Sect. 2. Some results are broken down by gender, with 20 female, 11 male, and 3 nonbinary participants. The age breakdown was 5 participants who were 18 years old, 11 who were 19, 12 who were 20, 5 who were 21, and 1 who was 25 or or older. Approximately one-quarter ($n = 9$) of the respondents indicated a Hispanic ethnicity, and six different racial identities were provided. While the college has a more balanced male/female gender distribution than the respondents, many other demographics are comparable to those of the entire college. Given the size of the sample, analysis was not done on the responses grouped by race, ethnicity, or age, but that information is retained for use in analyzing the responses from all participants, beyond SU.

Table 1. Statistics on sincerity scores.

	Min	Max	Average				Median				
			Female	Male	Nonbinary	All	Female	Male	Nonbinary	All
Scenario 2	0	13	4.90	5.09	2.67	4.76	5.5	3	0	4.5
Scenario 3	0	25	12.20	9.54	9.67	11.12	12.5	10	9	11
Scenario 4	0	35	11.15	7.09	6.00	9.38	9.5	7	6	7.5

Table 2 indicates which scenario participants found most difficult to complete. (Percentages may not add to exactly 100.0 in each column due to rounding.) The word cloud in Fig. 1 highlights commonalities in the responses to the open-ended questions. Note that the word *work* could mean many things, including group work (with *group* a frequent term), homework (another frequent term), or job (a term that did not appear as such).

Table 2. Percentage of participants by gender and overall who indicated a particular scenario was the most difficult to complete.

	Female	Male	Nonbinary	All
Scenario 1 (numerical rating)	70.0	36.4	66.6	58.8
Scenario 2 (yes/no, class project)	0	18.2	33.3	8.8
Scenario 3 (yes/no, know group members' availability)	25.0	36.4	0	26.5
Scenario 4 (yes/no, picking up work shifts)	5.0	9.1	0	5.8

Fig. 1. Word cloud of words and phrases used in responses to the open-ended questions. The larger a word or phrase is, the more often it occurred.

4   Discussion

It is perhaps unsurprising that the majority of participants found the scenario where they had to give numerical ratings rather than yes/no answers the most difficult, because the numerical ratings required more granularity. Scenarios 2 and 4 differed only in whether the availability was for a class project or a job:

the data does not provide clear support for which was perceived as harder, but it will be interesting to see if that changes with the data from institutions throughout the country, as different communities may prioritize class projects or paid employment in different ways. While participants did not have to consider the availability of others in Scenario 3, the reported difficulty suggests that information impacted how people responded.

The change in sincerity scores from Scenario 2 to Scenario 3 suggests some participants were ostensibly willing to go against their preferences to some degree to be cooperative and more available at times that many of their group members had indicated availability. There were 3 participants whose sincerity scores were unchanged from Scenario 2 to 3, 26 who were less sincere (a *larger* sincerity score), and 5 who became more sincere in Scenario 3. From viewing the individual responses, some were quite willing to disregard their preferences if the rest of their group members were available, while others seemed to be adamant about rules like *no meetings past 10pm* even if the rest of their group was available. Participants often confirmed such behavior in the free-response questions.

In this analysis, indications are that participants rarely meet the formal definition of sincerity, but that many of their responses are consistent with sincerity. One possible explanation is that participants generally are sincere, but that it is difficult to retain all of that information mentally and to respond consistently. Participants may tend toward sincerity but make some choices that either align with personal preferences that they value (knowingly or unknowingly) more than sincerity, or that they are attempting to be either cooperative or restrictive, as suggested by prior theoretical work.

Naturally, with a small sample size and limited study population, this work presents a preliminary analysis. Analysis of data later collected on ≈ 200 college students throughout the United States is underway to determine if the trends in students from Southwestern University are similarly observed elsewhere. Doodle polls and other cooperative tools for decision-making that have comparatively large numbers of options may show different patterns than what is common or expected in situations with a far more limited number of choices. Future work will report not only on sincerity, but also the ways in which people do or do not exhibit strategic behaviors in Doodle polls. Understanding behavior in Doodle polls can have implications for the algorithmic design, implementation, and usage of a variety of decentralized decision-making or consensus-building tools.

References

1. Alrawi, D., Anthony, B.M., Chung, C.: How well do doodle polls do? In: Social Informatics of the 8th International Conference, pp. 3–23 (2016)
2. Anthony, B.M., Chung, C.: How bad is selfish doodle voting? In: Proceedings of the 17th Conference on Autonomous Agents and MultiAgent Systems, pp. 1856–1858 (2018)
3. Anthony, B.M., Chung, C.: Equilibria in doodle polls under three tie-breaking rules. Theor. Comput. Sci. **822**, 61–71 (2020)
4. Brams, S.J., Fishburn, P.C.: Approval Voting. Birkhauser, Boston (1983)

5. Brams, S.J., Sanver, M.R.: Critical strategies under approval voting: who gets ruled in and ruled out. Elect. Stud. **25**(2), 287–305 (2006)
6. Endriss, U.: Sincerity and manipulation under approval voting. Theor. Decis. **74**(3), 335–355 (2013)
7. Obraztsova, S., Polukarov, M., Rabinovich, Z., Elkind, E.: Doodle poll games. In: 16th Conference on Autonomous Agents and MultiAgent Systems, pp. 876–884 (2017)
8. Reinecke, K., Nguyen, M.K., Bernstein, A., Näf, M., Gajos, K.Z.: Doodle around the world: online scheduling behavior reflects cultural differences in time perception and group decision-making. In: 2013 Conference on Computer Supported Cooperative Work, pp. 45–54 (2013)
9. Zou, J., Meir, R., Parkes, D.: Strategic voting behavior in doodle polls. In: 18th Conference on Computer Supported Cooperative Work, pp. 464–472 (2015)

Crowd Cognitive Modeling as a Vital Process for Collaborative Disaster Management

Therese Anne Rollan[1,2(✉)], Caslon Chua[1], and Leorey Marquez[2]

[1] Swinburne University of Technology, Hawthorn, Australia
{trollan,cchua}@swin.edu.au
[2] CSIRO Data61, Clayton, Australia
{therese.rollan,leorey.marquez}@data61.csiro.au

Abstract. Human safety is one of the most important investments of societies world-wide. Evacuation is among the preparation procedure of securely moving a crowd out of danger in the most efficient way possible. Fortunately, technology offers a great deal on significantly decreasing monetary and non-monetary operational costs and redirecting these to place more attention to details and investigation. Simulation allows users to examine, analyze and optimize evacuation schemes. What differs humans from other subjects of simulation is the complexity of modeling their characteristics and actions. This is due to cognition which governs how people think and act. In this early 20th century, the concept of cognition now involves higher brain functions and structures dedicated to processing of physical and other experiences including emotions. In this paper, the ongoing Agent-Based Modeling research is presented as well with the proposed evacuation simulation framework built from the literature review, its primary contributions, and the agent conceptual framework. We conclude that there is a need for an integrated, comprehensive and standard emergency management system regardless of disaster type, incorporating human cognitive aspects to improve realism. Further, concrete recommendations for the cognitive modeling and evacuation simulation improvements are provided. In this respect, collaboration of various disciplines such as social sciences, natural hazards and computer science professionals, and cooperation from the public through participation on surveys, interviews and other relevant data gathering methods to create well-establish cognitive models are imperative.

Keywords: Collaborative disaster management · Group behavior modeling · Agent-based methods

1 Introduction

What makes a disaster fatal is its being unprecedented. In addition to natural disasters as a safety threat, people around the globe have never been more active than today due to the increasing accessibility in travel. Thus, making public safety an utmost priority and a major day-to-day matter. Disaster management is one of the fundamental duties of a society's welfare arm. It is an interdisciplinary field which requires collaboration

© Springer Nature Switzerland AG 2021
Y. Luo (Ed.): CDVE 2021, LNCS 12983, pp. 20–31, 2021.
https://doi.org/10.1007/978-3-030-88207-5_3

of professionals from a number of fields including social sciences, natural hazards and computer science.

Prior to the actual disaster occurrence, we can only get in par with them at most by enhancing our preparedness. As a way of establishing preparedness, evacuation is a risk management process involving a movement of a large number of people to a secure place in response to a calamity [1]. A substantial improvement would be a realistic simulation of crowd movement in an evacuation. Studying crowd dynamics enables the understanding of how an individual behaves and interacts with others given an incident. In accomplishing a simulation of a phenomenon especially involving behavior and interaction, the challenge is set on the presentation of sufficient realism to which purpose it is done [2]. Among the aspects of a realistic crowd evacuation simulation are the involvement of the influences of emotions and personality traits [3–8], knowledge, and roles [9, 10] to behavior and decision-making. Customarily, cognitive science concentrates on "purely cognitive processes," such as decision-making, memory, calculation, planning, perception, problem solving, and the like [11]. In this early 20th century, Martinovski [11] claimed that the concept of "cognition" now involves higher brain functions and structures dedicated to "processing" of physical and other experiences including emotions. This paper tackles some of the core theories and recent works in cognitive modeling and its applications to disaster management with most existing works utilizing agent-based approach. It aims to assess the importance of cognitive modeling in collaborative disaster management particularly in evacuation simulation and to identify the gaps in its technical implementations through recent works. In addition, it intends to investigate the need for an integrated emergency management system within which not only the expertise of various professionals, but also the cooperation of the public are called for.

2   Emotions and Personality

Traditionally, artificial intelligence (AI) applications utilize the appraisal theory (AT) by Arnold [12] and Lazarus [13] (also known as the cognitive emotion theory). AT acts as the dominant theory in terms of causal generation and type differentiation of emotions, and has become a "central paradigm of psychological emotion research" [14]. This theory is known to be suitable for programming [11] especially in simulations. Simulation allows users to examine and visualize a phenomenon and its governing factors, and analyze the results. Optimization of crowd mobility in different types of places had drawn much interest from researchers in the early 20th century [15]. For instance, in a workplace, emotions fundamentally contribute in shaping behaviors, performance, productivity, interpersonal relationships and engagement [15]. In emergency situations, it has become a major factor in the decision-making process and behavior [4, 16]. Often we hear that panic is an emotion that significantly affect crowd movement [17]. Digging deeply, emotion states may consciously or unconsciously emanate to other people as well in the process called emotional contagion [18]. This pertains to the process wherein individuals involuntarily and constantly imitate the facial expressions, sounds, gestures, movements, and behaviors of others during their interaction with other people [19]. Consequently, controlling such phenomenon especially negative emotions is the key to emergency management [17]. In addition, personality play a role as to what particular emotions an individual may feel and how he or she will behave [4]. Thus, one's personality can greatly affect one's actions during emergency situations. Emotions and personality can be incorporated within the virtual representation of humans as agents through characteristics and actions, and within the simulation as modules containing cognitive architectures which will be discussed in the following subsections.

2.1 Agents

Agents represent the subject of the phenomenon being simulated such as a set of things or a group of people which can be provided with characteristics and actions. Representation of human as agents through attributes is vital to effectively model the cognition and their interactions. To demonstrate this, four key features were incorporated by Tsai et al. [20] namely: different agent types, emotional interactions, informational interactions and behavioral interactions. One approach that can be taken in differentiating agent types is by dividing them into three kinds specifically lead agent, ordinary agent and panic agent [21]. Another way to do this is using the categories: third-party authority agents, group leaders, members and isolated agents [8]. Additionally, Bhushan and Sarda [22] categorized the people inside a building into three types: fit evacuees, injured unfit evacuees and need help from rescuers to evacuate, and rescuers who are well-trained in evacuating people. Mao et al. [23] incorporated an emotion attribute affecting moving speed, desired goal and route planning. Furthermore, with the role of third party authorities (e.g. policemen) to the emotion of the crowd and evacuation guidance, they concluded that third party authorities can suppress negative emotions and assign suitable exits for the agents. For instance, security guards guiding individuals and teachers leading their students to safe egress and calmness [8]. A minimum ratio of 1 authority to 35 people is highly recommended to optimize emergency rescue [18].

2.2 Simulation

Simulations make use of different cognitive architectures in order to link cognition to the agents. The following are the most commonly applied cognitive architectures and their respective advantages and disadvantages. Among these is the Ortony, Clore and Collins (OCC) emotion model which is popularly used by computer scientists to build systems of reasoning and artificial characters based on emotions [24]. Empirically discovered in the early 1980s by Goldberg [25], the model of the five major personality factors, also referred to as the Big-Five or the Five-Factor Model (FFM), is a descriptive taxonomic psychological model of the five personality traits factors [26]. The model is now more popularly known as the five dimensions of Big-Five personality model or the OCEAN model [27–32] which is comprised of openness to experience, conscientiousness, extraversion, agreeableness, and neuroticism. The Alternative Five-Factor Model (AFFM) by Zuckerman *et al.* [33], a less popular personality model [34], claims that the FFM did not give enough emphasis to the biological foundations of personality. The developers defined the five factors of the AFFM as: i) impulsive sensation seeking or the tendency of taking action without thinking and planning, and the need for thrills, excitement and adventure, ii) neuroticism-anxiety or the undesirable emotions, fear and insecurity, iii) aggression-hostility or the tendency of expressing verbal aggression, anti-social behavior and impatience, iv) sociability or the delightfulness felt in interacting with people, being friendly and being uncomfortable with social isolation, and v) activity or the need for general activity, eagerness and the inclination to puzzling and tough work.

Mathematical models are often applied to obtain explicit values similar to the works of Favaretto et al. [35] on personality and culture, and Zhou et al. [3] involving emotion, personality and intimacy. Bourgais et al. [36] presented an architecture with explicitly defined elements of cognition, social relations and emotions in developing a dynamic emotional behavior capability to social agents. Liu et al. [37] chose to apply two orthogonal emotions hope and fear while Faroqi and Mesgari [18] applied six levels of emotions namely calm, alarm, fear, terror, panic, and hysteria. Zhu and Li [38] developed a multi-layer modeling method using mathematical models of emotions, personality, mood, decay and behavior, providing a learning ability to the human agents. When it comes to emotional contagion, research in crowd animation is still scarce [39]. Among these studies, Xue et al. [40] managed to examine emotional contagion in crowd queuing by utilizing standpoints in the fields of psychological and social computing. They based their emotional contagion method from Bosse's study [41] to enhance the realism of crowd simulation results. Mao et al. [42] adapted OCEAN and OCC models enriched with the cellular automaton - susceptible infected recovered susceptible (CA-SIRS) emotion contagion model to develop an emotion-based diversity behavior model. In terms of route planning process, Zhou et al. [3] showed effect of emotions in terms of time consumption for route selection with the assumption that the emotional stability and calmness an individual is inversely proportional with the route length. Additionally, they employed models of environmental familiarity as a function of spatial cognition and sense of direction. For Liu et al. [17], without incorporation of emotions, the agents will follow the geodesic path. But with emotions, agents will choose to stay away from hazards which will not necessarily be the shortest route. Though intuitively, emotion increases the disorder leading to human collisions, it can accelerate the evacuation under certain circumstances [16]. Emotional contagion may assist the evacuation process by facilitating the spread of information among the crowd and finding the right exit but at the same time may cause incorrect navigation information and congestion due to rapid spread of panic [7]. To support this, crowd interaction can facilitate uniform movement and orderliness resulting to increased successful evacuee count [43] but excessive information flow may impede its beneficial purpose to successful egress [21]. Liu et al. [39] devised a process within a simulation such that every individual's emotional value is averaged within each individual's circular perception area. The individual will be affected if his or her emotional value is lower than the calculated average.

3 Behaviors

To further improve existing disaster management strategies and communications among collaborating professionals from different disciplines, it is crucial to extend the understanding of human behavior and interactions [44]. This is in line with Feng et al. [45] that such information can contribute to the development of evacuation guidelines and practices. In normal circumstances, people maintain ample distances from each other as well as obstructions [46]. In the context of stressful situations, e.g. during evacuation, people move at higher speeds [47] and their behaviors will be unexpected and irrational [48]. Moreover, decision-making is then influenced by social factors such as emotions and emotional contagion from other evacuees [49], and physical environmental factors such as the time elapsed from the onset of the alarm [50]. One of the most well-known behavioral model is the belief-desire-intention (BDI) architecture which basically depends on human's decision-making principles [51]. It can be initially difficult to comprehend but it offers a gain in modularity, flexibility, understandability, extensibility [52] provides a high-level planning mechanism [51].

Wu et al. [53] identified human behavior in emergency evacuation as following, escaping together, pathfinding, avoiding the obstacles, overcrowding at the "bottleneck", back for rescuing, and panic. Generally, an evacuee may opt to move along the shortest path, and avoid danger and the crowd, or join a group and follow the leader [17]. Ríos and Pelechano [54] observed that humans consistently tend to go along the majority irrespective of their stress level. This trend was seen by Haghani and Sarvi [55] as potentially detrimental to the evacuation process and would pose greater risk of casualty. Although, they added that the factor of familiarity with escape routes would avoid the blind following tendency. Such following behavior is called herd mentality in which at low crowd density it can be expected that an individual will perform in accordance with his or her belief through the perceived information and current state [43]. Otherwise, with the rising density, each person unfamiliar with the place will feel stressed, nervous, or even confused [56]. From a questionnaire survey, researchers found out that 82.5% of the population left upon witnessing others evacuating due to absence of official warning prior to the arrival of the tsunami [57]. Hence, the social trigger of seeing other resident flea played a significant role in initiation of the evacuation and consequently decreasing the number of casualties. One of the causes of inappropriate or irrational evacuation behaviors is the so-called herd behavior which is a cognitive bias in humans [58]. Taking for instance the work of Şahin et al. [59], the said behavior was observed from conducting a series of evacuation simulations in which cramming at an exit occurred due to excessive following of the crowd despite the presence of a more convenient gate. A reasonable assumption on herd behavior by Tsurushima [58] debates that leaders and followers comprise a herd. In this assumption, the leaders' behaviors are determined by their own intentions and the followers' behaviors are determined by the behaviors of other leaders or followers, because without a leader, no one would be able to behave. However, the assignment of the roles of leader and follower is left unclear and thus called the "leader and follower problem" [58]. Feng et al. [45] show that the participants tended to be influenced by others, especially those in authority and who are willing to accompany other people while evacuating. Not only that the authorities can provide physical assistance but also the control of the increase in negative emotions of the crowd and prevention from plunging into the negative state [23]. Once public information regarding evacuation become well-disseminated, evacuees will then follow the majority [60]. Tytko et al. [47] observed two threatening effects called "faster-is-slower" and "freezing-by-heating". The first one happens when the increase in movement speed becomes counterproductive due to surge in physical interactions and pressure. On the other hand, the second effect takes place when the pressure completely reduced the motion of the crowd. In addition, Şahin and Alhajj [51] have observed that in each of their experiments there is a certain portion of the population that are slow-moving and thus, affects the total evacuation duration for all evacuees to completely get off an establishment. Nonetheless, if accomplished immediately and with enough time, effective communications will promote procedural efficiency and reduce the associated physical and mental burden [61].

Emergency behaviors can be distinguished in two stages namely normal (NS; pre-emergency activities) and response (RS; response to emergency by investigating or evacuating) [62]. Lovreglio et al. [63–66] implemented a three-stage process of hierarchical decision-making: 1) strategic or the choice to move to a safe place, 2) tactical or the selection of routes and exits, and 3) operational or the "short-range" alternatives with regards to interactions with other evacuees and obstacles. Initially, all agents are randomly distributed in the "world and are randomly walking in the initial "quiet" state in the "world" in the absence of interaction with other agents [38]. Evacuation time is comprised of the response time, decision time, notification time (in the case of mandatory evacuation) and preparation time in accordance with the Sorensen evacuation behavior model [67].

Despite the limitations on existing studies and regarded as being overlooked, Haghani [68] proposed that behavioral modification approach has a great potential in offering new possibilities in evacuation management in terms of practicality and possibility of implementation as compared to architectural and path/schedule planning solutions. He also emphasized that with this approach, people are viewed as the solution and not as burden that can cause chaos. It is also important to note that group differences of evacuation behavior are brought about by differences in age, gender, level of education, level of familiarity with the environment, and length of stay in a place (e.g. duration of residency) [69]. Aside from these mentioned personal factors, Pan [61] added the external factors of safety, short distance and familiarity in the decision-making of an evacuee.

4 Discussion and Contribution

The presented literature review in this paper laid a foundation in an ongoing research with the main objective is to develop an evacuation simulation framework (Fig. 1) using agent-based modeling (ABM). This aims to provide guidance to DRM researchers and decision-making authorities. Its significance lies on the timeliness and the capability of the framework to be a standard guide of which components are user-customizable. In addition to this, the research site is a crucial setting for a case study which is a university campus located in Sampaloc, Manila, Philippines. It is situated within 8.4 km from the West Valley Fault with a student population of around 8000, rendering it highly vulnerable to earthquake.

Figure 1 is comprised of two main framework components 1) the database and 2) the simulation engine. Within the database are spatial data from which 3D environment will be built, and non-spatial data (e.g. class schedule). Inputs to the simulation engine include evacuation scenarios, perception and navigation methods, the agent model and the planning and intervention decision support model. The agent model involves emotion model, personality model, behavior set and decision-making model. The simulation engine will then produce evacuation plans, data statistics, tables, graphs and maps.

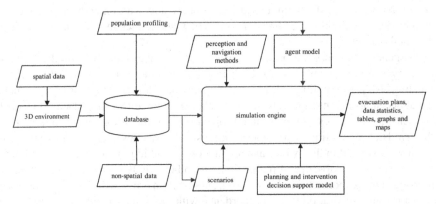

Fig. 1. The evacuation simulation framework that will be developed by this study

The contributions of this study include i) a detailed agent representation following the agent conceptual framework in Fig. 2 which mainly suggests (to be further established in the future work) the influence of demographical information and disaster-related experiences to one's personality, personality and situation to one's emotions, and personality, situation and emotions to behavioral decision-making ii) the exploration of the behavioral modification approach introduced in Sect. 3 [68] as among the main solutions to efficient evacuation which will pave way to the review and improvement of safety protocols and practices, and iii) the expansion of the evacuation simulation application through incorporation of a multi-storey 3D environment and a decision support tool.

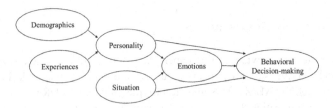

Fig. 2. The conceptual framework for the agent model (Fig. 1) during a disaster

5   Conclusion and Recommendations

Crowd cognitive modeling is a vital process for collaborative disaster management. With regards to the technical recommendations, aside from increasing the number of considered emotions, correlations among them [3] can deepen the understanding of simulation outcome. Based on the conducted series of interviews with key stakeholders of Shipman and Majumdar [70], they have established the lack of appropriate models for states of fear during extreme emergency situations. Further rules to ensure sample representativeness and definition of sufficient sample size is imperative [61]. Inclusion of in-depth information regarding the evacuees' demographics, characteristics, previous disaster experiences, [50] and social relationships [3, 71] can help extract more details that will open new perspectives. Focusing on social relationships means more concentration on the interactions between agents and the resulting group dynamics [20, 59]. Well-trained third party authorities who are guaranteed to smoothly and calmly manage emergency situations [59] should be predefined and consistently undergo training. Mechanism of emotional contagion for positive emotional climate, not only the usual negative, [15, 51] can extend the evacuee behavioral modification approach [68] for enhancing evacuation efficiency, guidelines and case-specific training programs.

There might be several studies available but most of them are just small portions of a very large work. There is a need for an integrated emergency management system, regardless of disaster type, which can be properly developed through the in-depth investigation and understanding of relationships among these disasters [72]. Formolo and van der Wal [73] have already taken the initial steps in filling the huge gap in defining which are the required and the desired features. According to Wu et al. [53], the need for some knowledge of psychology and sociology is inevitable in studying evacuation. However, the authors believe that not all human behavioral characteristics can be included and therefore, evacuation simulations should be more comprehensive and more standard. Thus, the collaboration of various professionals, and the cooperation of the public through participation on surveys, interviews and other relevant data gathering methods to create well-establish cognitive models are imperative.

References

1. Siyam, N., Alqaryouti, O., Abdallah, S.: Research issues in agent-based simulation for pedestrians evacuation. IEEE Access, 1 (2019)
2. Bourgais, M., et al.: Emotion modeling in social simulation: a survey. J. Artif. Soc. Soc. Simul. **21**(2), 5 (2018)
3. Zhou, R., et al.: An emergency evacuation behavior simulation method combines personality traits and emotion contagion. IEEE Access **8**, 66693–66706 (2020)
4. Belhaj, M., Kebair, F., Ben Said, L.: Emotional agent model for simulating and studying the impact of emotions on the behaviors of civilians during emergency situations. In: Hanachi, C., Bénaben, F., Charoy, F. (eds.) ISCRAM-med 2014. LNBIP, vol. 196, pp. 206–217. Springer, Cham (2014). https://doi.org/10.1007/978-3-319-11818-5_18
5. Belhaj, M., Kebair, F., Ben Said, L.: A computational model of emotions for the simulation of human emotional dynamics in emergency situations. Int. J. Comput. Theor. Eng. **6**, 227–233 (2014)
6. Dionne, S.D., et al.: Decision making in crisis: a multilevel model of the interplay between cognitions and emotions. Organ. Psychol. Rev. **8**(2–3), 95–124 (2018)
7. Liu, T., Liu, Z., Chai, Y., Wang, J., Lin, X., Huang, P.: Simulating evacuation crowd with emotion and personality. Artif. Life Robot. **24**(1), 59–67 (2018). https://doi.org/10.1007/s10 015-018-0459-5
8. Mao, Y., et al.: Personality trait and group emotion contagion based crowd simulation for emergency evacuation. Multimedia Tools Appl. **79**(5), 3077–3104 (2020)

9. Chu, M.L., Law, K.H.: Incorporating individual behavior, knowledge, and roles in simulating evacuation. Fire Technol. **55**(2), 437–464 (2018). https://doi.org/10.1007/s10694-018-0747-6

10. Pelechano, N., et al.: Crowd simulation incorporating agent psychological models, roles and communication. In: First International Workshop on Crowd Simulation (2005)

11. Martinovski, B.: Role of emotion in group decision and negotiation. In: Kilgour, D.M., Eden, C. (eds.) Handbook of Group Decision and Negotiation, pp. 157–192. Springer, Cham (2021). https://doi.org/10.1007/978-3-030-49629-6_5

12. Arnold, M.B.: Emotion and Personality: Neurological and Physiological Aspects, vol. 1 & 2. Columbia University Press, New York (1960)

13. Lazarus, R.S.: Psychological Stress and the Coping Process (1966)

14. Reisenzein, R.: Cognitive theory of emotion. In: Zeigler-Hill, V., Shackelford, T.K. (eds.) Encyclopedia of Personality and Individual Differences, pp. 723–733. Springer International Publishing, Cham (2020)

15. Lejmi-Riahi, H., Belhaj, M., Ben Said, L.: Studying emotions at work using agent-based modeling and simulation. In: MacIntyre, J., Maglogiannis, I., Iliadis, L., Pimenidis, E. (eds.) AIAI 2019. IFIP Advances in Information and Communication Technology, vol. 559, pp. 571–583. Springer, Cham. https://doi.org/10.1007/978-3-030-19823-7_48

16. Nguyen, V.T., et al.: Integration of emotion in evacuation simulation. In: Hanachi, C., Bénaben, F., Charoy, F. (eds.) First International Conference, ISCRAM-med 2014, vol. 196, pp. 192-205. Toulouse, France. Springer International Publishing (2014). https://doi.org/10.1007/978-3-319-11818-5_17

17. Liu, B., et al.: An evacuation route model of crowd based on emotion and geodesic. Math. Prob. Eng. (2018)

18. Faroqi, H., Mesgari, M.-S.: Agent-based crowd simulation considering emotion contagion for emergency evacuation problem. Int. Arch. Photogrammetry Remote Sens. Spat. Inf. Sci. **40**(1), 193 (2015)

19. Hatfield, E., Cacioppo, J.T., Rapson, R.L.: Emotional contagion. In: Studies in Emotion and Social Interaction. Cambridge University Press, Cambridge (1994)

20. Tsai, J., et al.: ESCAPES: evacuation simulation with children, authorities, parents, emotions, and social comparison. In: The 10th International Conference on Autonomous Agents and Multiagent Systems. International Foundation for Autonomous Agents and Multiagent Systems (2011)

21. Chen, Y.-X.: Agent-based research on crowd interaction in emergency evacuation. Springer Cluster Comput. **23**(1), 189–202, 1–14, 10 (2020)

22. Bhushan, A., Sarda, N.L.: Indoor evacuation planning. In: Sarda, N.L., Acharya, P.S., Sen, S. (eds.) Geospatial Infrastructure, Applications and Technologies: India Case Studies, pp. 107–119. Springer, Singapore (2018). https://doi.org/10.1007/978-981-13-2330-0_9

23. Mao, Y., et al.: An emotion based simulation framework for complex evacuation scenarios. Graph. Models **102**, 1–9 (2019)

24. Steunebrink, B., et al.: The OCC Model Revisited (2009)

25. Goldberg, L.R.: From ace to Zombie: some explorations in the language of personality. Adv. Pers. Assess. **1**, 203–234 (1982)

26. Goldberg, L.R.: The structure of phenotypic personality traits. Am. Psychol. **48**(1), 26 (1993)

27. Costa, P.T., McCrae, R.R.: Professional manual: revised NEO personality inventory (NEO-PI-R) and NEO five-factor inventory (NEO-FFI). Odessa, FL: Psychological Assessment Resources, **61** (1992)

28. Digman, J.M.: Personality structure: emergence of the five-factor model. Annu. Rev. Psychol. **41**(1), 417–440 (1990)

29. Goldberg, L.R.: An alternative description of personality: the big-five factor structure. J. Pers. Soc. Psychol. **59**(6), 1216 (1990)
30. John, O.P.: The Big Five factor taxonomy: dimensions of personality in the natural language and in questionnaires. Handb. Pers. Theor. Res. (1990)
31. McCrae, R.R., John, O.P.: An introduction to the five-factor model and its applications. J. Pers. **60**(2), 175–215 (1992)
32. McCrae, R., Costa, P.: Toward a new generation of personality theories: theoretical contexts for the five-factor model. Five-Factor Model Pers. Theor. Perspect. (1996)
33. Zuckerman, M., et al.: A comparison of three structural models for personality: the big three, the big five, and the alternative five. J. Pers. Soc. Psychol. **65**(4), 757 (1993)
34. Sârbescu, P., Boncu, A.: The resilient, the restraint and the restless: personality types based on the alternative five-factor model. Pers. Individ. Differ. **134**, 81–87 (2018)
35. Favaretto, R.M., Musse, S.R., Costa, A.B.: Simulating personality and cultural aspects in crowds. In: Emotion, Personality and Cultural Aspects in Crowds, pp. 141–158. Springer, Cham (2019). https://doi.org/10.1007/978-3-030-22078-5_11
36. Bourgais, M., Taillandier, P., Vercouter, L.: Enhancing the Behavior of Agents in Social Simulations with Emotions and Social Relations. Springer International Publishing, Cham (2018)
37. Liu, B., et al.: An optimization-driven approach for computing geodesic paths on triangle meshes. Comput. Aided Des. **90**, 105–112 (2017)
38. Zhu, Y.-B., Li, J.-S.: Collective behavior simulation based on agent with artificial emotion. Clust. Comput. **22**(3), 5457–5465 (2017). https://doi.org/10.1007/s10586-017-1288-3
39. Liu, T., et al.: Modeling Emotional Contagion for Crowd in Emergencies. Springer International Publishing, Cham (2019)
40. Xue, J., et al.: Crowd queuing simulation with an improved emotional contagion model. Sci. China Inf. Sci. **62**(4), 44101–44111 (2019)
41. Bosse, T., et al.: Agent-based modeling of emotion contagion in groups. Cogn. Comput. **7**(1), 111–136 (2015)
42. Mao, Y., Li, Z., Li, Y., He, W.: Emotion-based diversity crowd behavior simulation in public emergency. Vis. Comput. **35**(12), 1725–1739 (2018). https://doi.org/10.1007/s00371-018-1568-9
43. Qing, Y., et al.: MAS-based evacuation simulation of an urban community during an urban rainstorm disaster in china. Sustainability **12**(2), 1–19 (2020)
44. Mancheva, L., Adam, C., Dugdale, J.: Multi-agent geospatial simulation of human interactions and behaviour in bushfires. In: International Conference on Information Systems for Crisis Response and Management. Valencia, Spain (2019)
45. Feng, Z., et al.: How people make decisions during earthquakes and post-earthquake evacuation: using verbal protocol analysis in immersive virtual reality. Safe. Sci. **129**, 104837 (2020)
46. Porzycki, J., et al.: Velocity correlations and spatial dependencies between neighbors in a unidirectional flow of pedestrians. Phys. Rev. E, **96**(2), 022307 (2017)
47. Tytko, K., et al.: Simulating Pedestrians' Motion in Different Scenarios with Modified Social Force Model. Springer International Publishing, Cham (2020)
48. Adam, C.: Human behaviour modelling for crisis management: an overview of MAGMA projects applied to 3 different disasters (bushfires, floods, earthquakes) (2018)
49. Sharpanskykh, A., Zia, K.: Understanding the role of emotions in group dynamics in emergency situations. In: Nguyen, N.T., et al (eds.) Transactions on Computational Collective Intelligence XV, 2014, Springer Berlin Heidelberg: Berlin, Heidelberg. pp. 28–48 (2014). https://doi.org/10.1007/978-3-662-44750-5_2

50. Zhao, X., Lovreglio, R., Nilsson, D.: Modelling and interpreting pre-evacuation decision-making using machine learning. Autom. Constr. **113**, 103140 (2020)
51. Şahin, C., Alhajj, R.: Crowd behavior modeling in emergency evacuation scenarios using belief-desire-intention model. In: Kaya, M., Birinci, Ş., Kawash, J., Alhajj, R. (eds.) Putting Social Media and Networking Data in Practice for Education, Planning, Prediction and Recommendation. LNSN, pp. 1–14. Springer, Cham (2020). https://doi.org/10.1007/978-3-030-33698-1_1
52. Adam, C., et al.: BDI vs FSM agents in social simulations for raising awareness in disasters: a case study in melbourne bushfires. Int. J. Inf. Syst. Crisis Response Manage. **9**(1), 27–44 (2017)
53. Wu, X.-M., Wang, J., Guo, X.-H.: Personnel Behavior and Modeling Simulation in the Emergency Evacuation. Atlantis Press, Paris (2015)
54. Ríos, A., Pelechano, N.: Follower behavior under stress in immersive VR. Virtual Reality **24**(4), 683–694 (2020). https://doi.org/10.1007/s10055-020-00428-8
55. Haghani, M., Sarvi, M.: Imitative (herd) behaviour in direction decision-making hinders efficiency of crowd evacuation processes. Sci. Direct Safe. Sci. **114**, 49–60 (2019)
56. Treuille, A., Cooper, S., Popović, Z.: Continuum crowds. ACM Trans. Graph. **25**(3), 1160–1168 12 (2006)
57. Harnantyari, A.S., et al.: Tsunami awareness and evacuation behaviour during the 2018 Sulawesi earthquake tsunami. Int. J. Disaster Risk Reduction, **43**, 101389 (2020)
58. Tsurushima, A.: Modeling Herd Behavior Caused by Evacuation Decision Making Using Response Threshold. Springer International Publishing, Cham (2019)
59. Şahin, C., Rokne, J., Alhajj, R.: Human behavior modeling for simulating evacuation of buildings during emergencies. Phys. Stat. Mech. Appl. **528**, 121432 (2019)
60. Tong, W., Cheng, L.: Simulation of pedestrian flow based on Multi-agent. Procedia Soc. Behav. Sci. **96**, 17–24 (2013)
61. Pan, A.: Study on the decision-making behavior of evacuation for coastal residents under typhoon storm surge disaster. Int. J. Disaster Risk Reduction, **45**, 101522 (2020)
62. Reneke, P.A.: Evacuation decision model. US Department of Commerce, National Institute of Standards and Technology (2013). http://dx.doi.org/10.6028/NIST.IR.7914
63. Lovreglio, R., Fonzone, A., dell'Olio, L.: A mixed logit model for predicting exit choice during building evacuations. Transp. Res. Part Policy Pract. **92**, 59–75 (2016)
64. Lovreglio, R.: Data-collection approaches for the study of the decision-making process in fire evacuations. In: 1st SCORE@ POLIBA Workshop. Bari (2014)
65. Lovreglio, R., Ronchi, E., Nilsson, D.: A model of the decision-making process during pre-evacuation. Fire Saf. J. **78**, 168–179 (2015)
66. Lovreglio, R., Ronchi, E., Nilsson, D.: Calibrating floor field cellular automaton models for pedestrian dynamics by using likelihood function optimization. Phys. **438**, 308–320 (2015)
67. Sorensen, J.H., Vogt, B.M., Mileti, D.S.: Evacuation: an assessment of planning and research. Oak Ridge National Lab., TN (USA). p. Medium: X; Size, p. 234 (1987)
68. Haghani, M.: Optimising crowd evacuations: mathematical, architectural and behavioural approaches. Saf. Sci. **128**, 104745 (2020)
69. Chen, C., Cheng, L.: Evaluation of seismic evacuation behavior in complex urban environments based on GIS: a case study of Xi'an, China. Int. J. Disaster Risk Reduction. **43**, 101366 (2020)
70. Shipman, A., Majumdar, A.: Fear in humans: a glimpse into the crowd-modeling perspective. Transp. Res. Rec. **2672**(1), 183–197 (2018)
71. Sharma, S., Singh, H., Prakash, A.: Multi-agent modeling and simulation of human behavior in aircraft evacuations. IEEE Trans. Aerosp. Electron. Syst. **44**(4), 1477–1488 (2008)

72. Chen, N., Liu, W., Bai, R., Chen, A.: Application of computational intelligence technologies in emergency management: a literature review. Artif. Intell. Rev. **52**(3), 2131–2168 (2017). https://doi.org/10.1007/s10462-017-9589-8
73. Formolo, D., van der Wal, C.N.: An Adaptive Simulation Tool for Evacuation Scenarios. Springer International Publishing, Cham (2017)

Animated Transitions for Multi-user Shared Large Displays

Yu Liu[1,2(✉)], Paul Craig[1,2], and Fabiola Polidoro[1,2]

[1] Xi'an Jiao-tong Liverpool University, Suzhou, China
[2] Liverpool University, Liverpool, UK
Yu.Liu@xjtlu.edu.cn

Abstract. This study looks at the optimal duration for animated transitions between different views selected by different users operating a shared information visualization interface on a large display. In collaborative environments with a shared large screen both users are able to interact with the interface with users tending to alternate between the role of active-user and observer. This can cause problems if view updates are observed by users that do not trigger the updates themselves. These inactive users are more easily disoriented and confused by changes in the display that they themselves did not initiate. In order to reduce this sense of disorientation, animation can be used to smooth the transition between views. This study looks at the effect of different shared screen sizes on the optimal transition time. The results showed the best time for a shared large screen and a shared normal PC are both around 1000 ms. This is significantly longer than the best time on a single-user device which is in the range of 300 ms.

Keywords: Information visualization · Animated transitions · Shared large displays

1 Introduction

Large displays are becoming increasingly affordable and popular peripheral devices and large display centered multi device environments are increasingly being used to support group collaboration [7]. This is primarily because a large screen display has more space and a wider viewing angle to support larger numbers of users [26,27]. When combined with handheld devices, large screen environments can also afford users their own individual space to explore information without interruption. For instance, meeting rooms can be fitted with large displays on the walls to support multiple groups' data exploration. Group members do not have to continuously guess and ask their partners for information about what they are looking at on the screens of handheld devices. Instead, they can easily share information on the large screen. They can also be aware of the actions of their partners and group members can use a shared display to actively participate in the sharing of activities in a process of mutual collaboration.

© Springer Nature Switzerland AG 2021
Y. Luo (Ed.): CDVE 2021, LNCS 12983, pp. 32–43, 2021.
https://doi.org/10.1007/978-3-030-88207-5_4

Despite the advantages of shared large display environments, the instantaneous update of the view, i.e. visual elements moving abruptly, appearing or disappearing, has been shown to produce a disruption in the users' mental map, which in turn negatively affects the users' performance [11,25]. This especially affects users to a greater extent when the update is not directly triggered by the user themselves. Cognitive psychology [10] named this phenomenon as "cognitive destabilization", which means users' are mentally destabilized when facing with unexpected or unpredicted contents. Users in this stage need a while to re-stabilization.

Animation can be used to reduce this effect making changes smoother and easier to follow with less disorientation for the user [19]. The users attention can be guided by the movement [6,32] and the animation also even act to help users build mental map of the data space [2]. However, while the usefulness of animation is well established, there is little in the way of guidelines relating to *how* it should be used in collaborative setting and it is difficult to know how we should configure the style or duration of the animation to best improve the interface usability.

Implementing animated transforms in a collaborative environment can also have challenges distinct from those of a single user environment. For example, we need to consider how non-interacting users are affected by transitions triggered by other users. In this paper, we investigate the use of animations to support users to follow the changes happening on the shared large displays. Specifically, we investigate the impact of different sizes of shared screens on transition time under different operations.

2 Related Work

The work described in this paper stands between the field of computer-supported cooperative work (CSCW) and visualization technology to support data exploration. In this section, we review some of the most relevant related work in these areas.

2.1 Computer-Supported Cooperative Work

The work we present in this paper belongs to a particular branch of CSCW, that of co-located collaboration [5] of a group of users on a shared task. In our experiments, we chose a configuration combining a mobile device and a fixed display, which allows users to move objects between a personal view on a personal device (e.g. a smartphone) and a collaborative view on a shared display (e.g. a wall-mounted screen) [22]. This configuration overcomes some of the common problems affecting the adoption of alternative configurations with a single display shared by all participants, such as frustration when multiple users try to interact with the screen at the same time [31].

When it comes to computer-supported collaborative work, it is of utmost significance that participants are aware of the changes that are taking place in the workspace. Awareness is thought to hold promise for significantly improving the efficiency of groupware [13]. There are a number of established methods to help users maintain awareness of the actions and intentions of other participants involved in computer-supported collaborative work. These methods include the use of multiple cursors and multi-user scrollbars [14].

Given that we are focusing on a geo-information exploration task, we have adopted a method of copying individual view boxes to the shared screen to support group awareness. Also, to support real-time contextual information, our large screen will always have a smallest rectangle to include all users' views to show contextual information and information about the user's exploration area. This will cause the view of the large screen to be updated as the user's individual view changes. So for users whose personal perspective has not changed, sudden changes in perspective are unpredictable and can feel disoriented. The next session will explore how to use animation reduce disorientation.

2.2 Animated Transitions

Human beings are by nature attracted to motion. This makes animation a great tool to direct the users' attention where needed [28] and to explain the cause-and-effect relationship [24], e.g. like spatial relations between views [2].

When animation is applied to an interface, its advantages are twofold. Firstly, animation can help the user perceive and understand how objects move across the screen [1] and smooth the transition between screen updates by establishing a visual connection. Secondly, it can be highly useful in helping to mask latency times caused by processing or network delays so that the user does not perceive it [16].

Despite their advantages, animations need to be carefully designed, otherwise they can cause problems [1,2]. This is because in some cases animation can be effective in holding the user's attention, while in other places it can cause distraction. For example, when animation is used carelessly in presentation design, data flying around the display without any clear purpose can cause confusion and disorientation. Configuring animations with inappropriate durations can also cause problems. If the animation is too long it can make the application seem too slow to respond, and too short it can make the user feel dizzy or even disorientated as it disrupts her mental map [1].

Extensive research has explored various techniques to better design animated transitions. Heer [15] contributes design considerations for crafting animated transitions, which extended the design principles proposed by Tversky [32]. Heer [15] also introduced staged transitions to statistics data graphics to help users follow changes. Chevalier et al. [3] studied staggering, where the start time of elements is delayed incrementally, but found it had a negligible impact on users' performance. Dragicevic et al. [8] investigated different conditions of temporal distortion, including constant speed, slow in/slow out, fast in/out, and adaptive speed, and found slow in/out outperformed other techniques. Wang et al. [34] proposed a vector field design approach for non-linear transitions. Du et al. [9] indicated that bundled trajectories were useful when tracking more targets.

Existing research also recognises the critical role played by animation. Lasseter [19] proposes 11 principles for animation design and pointed out that the timing is crucial to making ideas readable. Studies on object tracking in perceptional psychology also revealed that speed was one of key factors for people's performance in object tracking [12,21,29,35]. Although the speed of animation has not received much attention thus-far in the empirical testing of collaborative information visualisation interfaces [15,20,33], it is clear that it plays an important role in the user's understanding of actions, especially in a collaborative environment in which users share a large display where some people have no idea what is about happen.

To our knowledge, at the moment, there are no guidelines for coping with states and view updates in multi-user applications running on shared displays, although a lot of attention has been paid to single-user applications, both on mobile and desktop environments. Users in a collaboration environment, compared to the situation of a single person and a single device, are in a passive state and are hard to predict the data changes. In this paper we did the user studies on animated transitions on two different sized shared screens to support shared-view changes, in order to possibly guide designers of multi-user shared interfaces in designing appropriate animations.

3   Pilot Study

Our evaluation was carried out with the help of a prototype application, named TravelPlanner we designed and developed specifically for this study. The geographical data used in the experiments were all taken from Baidu Map. Our software is simulating a collaborative team exploration of geographic data. Our design follows the three design guidelines proposed by Yuill, Nicola and Rogers [23], which are "high awareness of others' actions and intentions, high control over the interface and high availability of background information".

Our prototype assumes that in a multi-device environment with mobile devices and shared display space. The large displays contain a shared state and the mobile provide an individual state that respond to the interaction of a single user. All participants can see (and typically interact with) the shared display through mobile devices. Meanwhile, all participants also have a private mobile screen that shows the visual representation and supports interacting with the data.

In the shared large display, different users are encoded with different colors to distinguish contribution and status, similar to Isenberg et al.'s Cambiera [17] and Chung et al.'s Narges [4]. The large display always uses the smallest rectangle to include all users' mobile devices. This ensures that users can keep track of each other's progress and understand the background information around their focus. Animated transitions are used to help users track the changes triggered by personal devices as they take effect on the the shared display.

This pilot test described involved eight expert users using TravelPlanner to identify factors that possibly affect the duration of animated transitions between views and collected users' feedback on our user tasks and questionnaires. We asked the users to track the changes happening on the large displays when we operated our individual device. We also investigated the appropriate transition time based on user feedback and previous work.

There have been many studies involving appropriate transition times. Benjamin et al. [2] pointed out that 0.5–1 s was appropriate. Robert [30] reckoned that 1 s may be more appropriate, but it may take a shorter time for smaller movements. Christan [2] recommends 300 ms in scroll-based applications. In Heer et al. 's work [15], animation were lengthened to 1.25 and 2 s for staged animations. We reckoned that the basic animation used in large shared display may be longer than that of the normal desktop and mobile devices. After 8 expert users' test, we chose transition times of zero (no animation), 300 ms, 1000 ms, 1500 ms, and 2000 ms as test times.

The study also helped us to find some factors that influence users' performance of following the view changes, which were the map data we use, the gap time between each operation and the colour of the view ports which the participants intended to follow. Based on these factors, we used two different city maps on two screens. Before the experiment, we asked users how familiar with the map to make sure it was a city they were unfamiliar with.

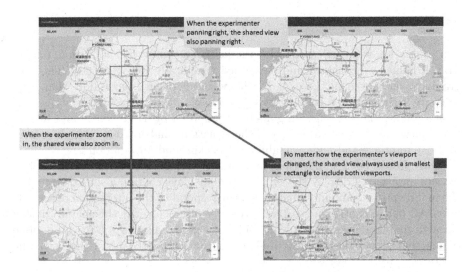

Fig. 1. The interface for the large display when two users, A and B, are collaborating on a map. The orange and green rectangles represent the current viewport of A and B's mobile devices, respectively, and the circles indicate the selections made by such users. (Color figure online)

4　User Study

In this section, we present experiments that assess the effect of time duration on shared displays. We describe our experimental designs and present the results. We have chosen a normal size PC as our baseline, to compare with a large screen.

4.1　Participants and Apparatus

The experiment was carried on with a group of 24 participants (9 females and 15 males), ranging from 22 to 33 (M = 24, SD = 2.5). All of them hold a bachelor or above degree and were all studying computer. All of participants had normal vision and 90% of them hardly used large displays in collaboration.

The experiments were conducted using one desktop PC (23.6″, 1920 * 1080 pixel resolution, 60 Hz refresh), one large display (65″, 1920 * 1080 pixel resolution, 60 Hz refresh) and one mobile phone (6.39″, 2340″1080 resolution).

4.2　Procedure

The experiments was designed to test the effects of the different duration of animated transitions on shared displays. Subjects were asked to pay attention to the view changes happening on the shared display. The two different sized shared displays were arranged in randomly balanced order (half PC first, the half large displays first). To reduce the possible learning, the different duration were presented in a Latin Square order across the subjects. At the same time, in order to prevent the psychological hint after knowing the length of the transitionthe participants were blind to which duration they were currently testing.

The experiments had the following design: 24 participants * 2 displays * 4 operations (panning horizontally/vertically, zoom in/out) * 2 scales (small, large) = 2304 trials.

View tracking performance was determined by objective and subjective measures. The participants were asked to record the changes after each trials. After all trails of each duration, users were asked to rate at each timing on two aspects, effectiveness and efficiency.

Prior to formal test users were given brief introduction of the software and tasks, and performed a short practice session (2 min) to familiarize themselves with the two sized screens and the software. A brief interview was conducted at end. The experiment lasted average 30 min for each participants.

At the beginning of the formal experiment, participants were asked to fill in basic information (age, gender, major, familiarity with the big screen) and asked if they were familiar with the map area tested by default. According to the feedback from the participants, none of the test map areas we selected was familiar to the participants.

Our test environment was in a simulated collaborative environment. When the tested user was in a non-active state (passive listening) and the viewing of the shared device was changed by the operation of experimenter on the personal device. At this time, they lacked the ability to predict the possible changes in the shared screen. Animated transitions can be helpful for them to track the change.

Our developers triggered the update of the big screen by panning and zooming the map on the personal mobile phone (one operation per time), because the shared views used the smallest rectangular to include the current viewports of the user (indicated by rectangle), seen at Fig. 1. Such a view was helpful for further communication by letting other users understand his/her focus area when working closely together. The participants were asked to record the changes happened after each operation we did. The operation included panning up, down, left, and right and zooming in, out. The zoom and pan were also in two different ranges, small and large. The zoom scale of a small area only increased or decreased by one level, and a large area increases or decreases by 3 levels. The left and right panning in a small range did not exceed one-third of the width of the mobile phone screen, and the wide range was close to the width of the entire screen. The small range of up and down panning did not exceed one-third of the length of the mobile phone screen, and the large range was close to the length of the entire screen. Each time included eight operations, four zooms, and four pans. Half of them were small-scale operation and half were large-scale.

After all operations on each duration, participants were asked to evaluate the effectiveness of the each timing on a 5-point Likert scale. Also they need to rated the efficiency of the each duration on zooming and panning using a 5-point Likert scale. For each trial, if it was right or not was recorded. In order to avoid a low accuracy resulting from tiredness, participants were allowed to take a short break after test each screen.

5   Results

In this section, we report the study results. Both quantitative and qualitative analyses are employed to evaluate and compare the effectiveness and efficiency of different animation duration on understanding view changes. A 2 (screen size) * 6 (animation speed) RM-ANOVA was performed for the accuracy rate. Pairwise comparisons were conducted using a Bonferroni adjustment for multiple comparisons. All results are summarized in Fig. 4.

5.1   Comparison Between Normal Sized PC and Large Displays

The accuracy rate refers to the number of times the users' correct judgments on the changes on the shared display divided by the total number of operations. Analysis found no substantial differences in accuracy rate between two sized screens on every transition duration.

5.2   Comparison Among Different Animation Duration

Animation speed had a significant effect on accuracy, both PC ($F(2.286) = 44.29$, $p < 0.001$) and large displays ($F(2.286) = 27.73$, $p < 0.001$). Specifically, mean

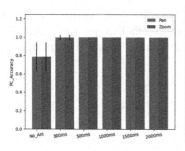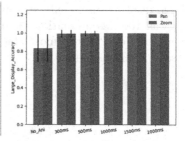

Fig. 2. The mean accuracy of two operations on large displays and PC.

accuracy for 0 and 300 ms were significantly different, both on large displays ($p = 0.000055$) and PC ($p = 0.000005$). But there were no significant difference between other animation duration.

5.3   Comparison Between Zooming and Panning

There were statistically different between panning and zooming on PC ($p = 0.017$), not on large displays, seen at Fig. 2.

Animation Speed(ms)	Large Displays				PC			
	Effectiveness	Efficiency		Accuracy	Effectiveness	Efficiency		Acuracy
		zoom	panning			zoom	panning	
0	2.86	-1.5	-1.27	0.82	3.55	-1.36	-1.14	0.85
300	4.32	-0.73	-0.5	0.99	4.59	-0.55	-0.36	0.99
500	4.77	-0.41	-0.36	0.99	4.59	-0.45	-0.5	1
1000	4.95	-0.27	-0.36	1	4.86	-0.32	-0.32	1
1500	4.95	-0.55	-0.55	1	5	-0.45	-0.5	1
2000	4.95	-0.91	-0.91	1	4.81	-0.77	-0.77	1

Fig. 3. Summary results: mean effectiveness, efficiency, accuracy rate. Best results of each columns are highlighted.

5.4   Subjective Preferences

Our study questionnaire contained three questions for each duration in which the participants responded on a 5-Likert scale. The first is about effectiveness, how easily you can follow the view changes on the shared display (1 = very hard, 5 = very easy). The results are shown in Fig. 4. The second and third is about efficiency, how efficient of the transition for zoom and for panning (1 = very slow, 2 = a little bit slow, 3 = moderate, 4 = a little bit fast, 5 = very fast). When calculating the efficiency score, we recorded -2 if it was very fast or very slow, recorded -1 if it was a little bit slow/fast, and recorded 0 if it was moderate.

On average, with animated transitions, users found it was greatly easier to follow the view changes on both screens. There was a significant difference between the subjective effectiveness scores of those without animation and those with animation ($p < 0.001$). However, once the animation transition time reached 500 and above, there was basically no difference in effectiveness on both screens.

For large displays, users subjectively believed that the most efficient zoom transition was 1000 ms animation. The most efficient panning transition was 500–1000 ms. As for PC, the most efficient animation and panning transition were the same, 1000 ms animation.

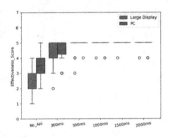

Fig. 4. The results of subjective rating of effectiveness on large display and PC.

6 Discussion

According to our experiment, there was no much difference in accuracy between ordinary-size personal computers and large screens. This may seem counter-intuitive, but as users were allowed to freely adjust the distance between the seat and the screen, they tended to choose the most comfortable distance so PC users could become more accurate by moving closer to the screen. PC users also had the option to adjust the monitor and become more comfortable this way. We presumed that as long as the distance and angle were appropriate, the difference between an ordinary screen and a large screen was not a significant factor for our users. Future work may involve some proper experimentation to test this conjecture.

The difference in subjective rating between large screens and ordinary computers may be due to the user's familiarity with devices of different sizes. 80% of the users participating in the test rarely used big screens for teamwork or personal work. The frequency of use by all users of ordinary screens was more than 5 days a week. In the final interview, many users also mentioned that if they were familiar with the big screen, they should do better.

Regarding that there was a significant difference between the zoom and panning error rates on the PC side, many users mentioned in the interview after the test that the changes caused by zoom was more abrupt than the panning under the same transition time, especially when the transition time was 0 and 300 ms. However, the reason for the insignificance on the large screen, we speculated that the user concentrated more in front of the unfamiliar screen, so there was no difference in the accuracy rate. The difference between the two operations still needs further study to explore.

During the interview with respondents after tests, many users asked whether the current general map application had added animation, and they thought it can greatly help them understand the transition. At the same time, some users said that as they became more familiar with the data, the transition can actually become shorter, but it cannot be reduced to zero. For the large screens that were not too familiar for them, many users believed that increasing the use of it for a certain period of time would have a need for faster transitions.

7   Conclusion

In this paper, we have explored the animated transitions on shared displays between view changes. The experiments found that animation significantly improves both accuracy and user satisfaction on effectiveness and efficiency. This result corroborates the findings of several previous studies in this field [18, 32].

We also found that the users performance on following the changes on two sized shared screens is basically similar. Given all the results, we can recommend implement 1000 ms animations in any shared application that is dominated by zooming and panning interactions. This is significantly longer than the best time for scrolling tested by [2] on a single-player device. Therefore, we can conclude that in the shared screen, users who passively accept changes need to longer animated duration to follow view changes.

Overall, subjects were enthusiastic about animated transitions on shared displays, and felt it facilitated both improved understanding and increased engagement. The majority of participants expressed that they realized the importance of animated transitions in data exploration type activities.

In conclusion, we believe our results can inform other scholars on designing animated transitions for shared displays. Since our study is an initial work in CSCW and InforVis, and there are number of promising future directions to pursue. Our future will include design adaptive animated transitions for visualization systems that gradually shorten the time as users become more familiar with the interface data.

Acknowledgements. This project is supported by Key Program Special Fund XJTLU project KSF-E-10 and XJTLU Research Development Fund project RDF-14-03-22.

References

1. Baudisch, P., et al.: Phosphor: explaining transitions in the user interface using afterglow effects. In: Proceedings of the 19th Annual ACM Symposium on User Interface Software and Technology, pp. 169–178 (2006)
2. Bederson, B.B., Boltman, A.: Does animation help users build mental maps of spatial information? In: Proceedings 1999 IEEE Symposium on Information Visualization (InfoVis 1999), pp. 28–35. IEEE (1999)
3. Chevalier, F., Dragicevic, P., Franconeri, S.: The not-so-staggering effect of staggered animated transitions on visual tracking. IEEE Trans. Visual. Comput. Graph. **20**(12), 2241–2250 (2014)

4. Chung, C.W., Lee, C.C., Liu, C.C.: Investigating face-to-face peer interaction patterns in a collaborative Web discovery task: the benefits of a shared display. J. Comput. Assist. Learn. **29**(2), 188–206 (2013)
5. Ellis, C.A., Gibbs, S.J., Rein, G.: Groupware: some issues and experiences. Commun. ACM **34**(1), 39–58 (1991)
6. Cooper, A., Reimann, R., Dubberly, H.: About Face 2.0: The Essentials of Interaction Design. Wiley, New York (2003)
7. Divitini, M., Farshchian, B.A.: Shared displays for promoting informal cooperation: an exploratory study. In: COOP, pp. 211–226. Citeseer (2004)
8. Dragicevic, P., Bezerianos, A., Javed, W., Elmqvist, N., Fekete, J.D.: Temporal distortion for animated transitions. In: Proceedings of the SIGCHI Conference on Human Factors in Computing Systems, pp. 2009–2018 (2011)
9. Du, F., Cao, N., Zhao, J., Lin, Y.R.: Trajectory bundling for animated transitions. In: Proceedings of the 33rd Annual ACM Conference on Human Factors in Computing Systems, pp. 289–298 (2015)
10. Durrani, S., Durrani, Q.S.: Applying cognitive psychology to user interfaces. In: Tiwary, U.S., Siddiqui, T.J., Radhakrishna, M., Tiwari, M.D. (eds.) Proceedings of the First International Conference on Intelligent Human Computer Interaction, pp. 156–168. Springer, New Delhi (2009). https://doi.org/10.1007/978-81-8489-203-1_14
11. Eades, P., Lai, W., Misue, K., Sugiyama, K.: Preserving the mental map of a diagram. In: Technical Report IIAS-RR-91-16E, Fujitsu Laboratories (1991)
12. Feria, C.S.: Speed has an effect on multiple-object tracking independently of the number of close encounters between targets and distractors. Attention Percept. Psychophys. **75**(1), 53–67 (2012). https://doi.org/10.3758/s13414-012-0369-x
13. Gerrard, S.: Book reviews: Adams, j. 1995: Risk. london: Ucl press. xii + 228 pp. £35.00 cloth, £12.95 paper. isbn: 1 85728 067 9 cloth, 1 85728 068 7 paper. Prog. Hum. Geogr. **20**(1), 133-134 (1996). https://doi.org/10.1177/030913259602000110
14. Greenberg, S.: Building real time groupware with GroupKit, a groupware toolkit. Acm Trans. Comput. Hum. Interact. **3**(1), 66–106 (1998)
15. Heer, J., Robertson, G.: Animated transitions in statistical data graphics. IEEE Trans. Visual. Comput. Graph. **13**(6), 1240–1247 (2007)
16. Huhtala, J., Sarjanoja, A.H., Mäntyjärvi, J., Isomursu, M., Häkkilä, J.: Animated UI transitions and perception of time: a user study on animated effects on a mobile screen. In: Proceedings of the SIGCHI Conference on Human Factors in Computing Systems, CHI 2010, pp. 1339–1342. Association for Computing Machinery, New York (2010). https://doi.org/10.1145/1753326.1753527
17. Isenberg, P., Fisher, D.: Collaborative brushing and linking for co-located visual analytics of document collections. In: Computer Graphics Forum, vol. 28, pp. 1031–1038. Wiley Online Library, Oxford (2009)
18. Klein, C., Bederson, B.B.: Benefits of animated scrolling. In: CHI 2005 Extended Abstracts on Human Factors in Computing Systems, pp. 1965–1968 (2005)
19. Lasseter, J.: Principles of traditional animation applied to 3D computer animation. In: Proceedings of the 14th Annual Conference on Computer Graphics and Interactive Techniques, pp. 35–44 (1987)
20. Lind, M., Kjellin, A.: Faster is better: optimal speed of animated visualizations for decision makers. In: Ninth International Conference on Information Visualisation (IV 2005), pp. 896–900. IEEE (2005)
21. Liu, G., Austen, E.L., Booth, K.S., Fisher, B.D., Argue, R., Rempel, M.I., Enns, J.T.: Multiple-object tracking is based on scene, not retinal, coordinates. J. Exp. Psychol. Hum. Percept. Perform. **31**(2), 235 (2005)

22. Luff, P., Heath, C.: Mobility in collaboration. In: CSCW, vol. 98, pp. 305–314 (1998)
23. Maceachren, A., Brewer, I.: Developing a conceptual framework for visually-enabled geocollaboration. Int. J. Geograph. Inf. Sci. **18**(1), 1–34 (2004). https://doi.org/10.1080/13658810310001596094
24. Michotte, A.: The Perception of Causality. vol. 21, Routledge, New York (2017)
25. Misue, K., Eades, P., Lai, W., Sugiyama, K.: Layout adjustment and the mental map. J. Visual Lang. Comput. **6**(2), 183–210 (1995)
26. Morris, M.R., Morris, D., Winograd, T.: Individual audio channels with single display groupware: effects on communication and task strategy. In: Proceedings of the 2004 ACM Conference on Computer Supported Cooperative Work, pp. 242–251 (2004)
27. Paek, T., et al.: Toward universal mobile interaction for shared displays. In: Proceedings of the 2004 ACM Conference on Computer Supported Cooperative Work, pp. 266–269 (2004)
28. Palmer, S.E.: Vision Science: Photons to Phenomenology. MIT Press, Cambridge (1999)
29. Pylyshyn, Z.W., Storm, R.W.: Tracking multiple independent targets: evidence for a parallel tracking mechanism. Spat. Vis. **3**(3), 179–197 (1988)
30. Robertson, G., Cameron, K., Czerwinski, M., Robbins, D.: Animated visualization of multiple intersecting hierarchies. Inf. Visual. **1**(1), 50–65 (2002)
31. Sugimoto, M., Hosoi, K., Hashizume, H.: Caretta: a system for supporting face-to-face collaboration by integrating personal and shared spaces. In: Proceedings of the SIGCHI Conference on Human Factors in Computing Systems, pp. 41–48. ACM (2004)
32. Tversky, B., Morrison, J.B., Betrancourt, M.: Animation: can it facilitate? Int. J. Hum. Comput. Stud. **57**(4), 247–262 (2002)
33. Wallace, A., Savage, J., Cockburn, A.: Rapid visual flow: how fast is too fast? In: Proceedings of the fifth conference on Australasian user interface, vol. 28, pp. 117–122. Australian Computer Society Inc. (2004)
34. Wang, Y., Archambault, D., Scheidegger, C.E., Qu, H.: A vector field design approach to animated transitions. IEEE Trans. Visual. Comput. Graph. **24**(9), 2487–2500 (2017)
35. Yantis, S.: Multielement visual tracking: attention and perceptual organization. Cogn. Psychol. **24**(3), 295–340 (1992)

A 360-Degree Video Shooting Technique that Can Avoid Capturing the Camera Operator in Frame

Tianyu Zhu$^{(\boxtimes)}$ and Takayuki Fujimoto

Graduate School of Information Sciences and Arts, Toyo University, Tokyo, Japan
fujimoto@toyo.jp

Abstract. In this research, we propose a shooting method and video processing method that uses two fisheye cameras to avoid capturing the camera operator in frame. 360-degree video is rapidly becoming widespread with it being supported on YouTube since 2015. In the future, 360-degree videos are expected to be used in all parts of society. However, when a camera operator usually shoots while holding a 360-degree camera, they themselves will unavoidably by captured in frame. This is a crucial problem with 360-degree cameras. Of course, some techniques have been proposed to avoid this, but all of them are limited and impractical. In this research, in order to solve this problem, we will refer to the conventional methods and then propose a new technique.

Keywords: 360-degree video · Fisheye camera · Video editing

1 Purpose

The Coronavirus, which started in 2020, has changed our lives and our society, forcing us to do everything online. Now, virtual communication and activities using video are becoming more widespread. Among them, the need for digital cameras that can shoot 360-degree videos is rising rapidly. The possibility of virtual travel through video—where physical access to remote areas, or gatherings at facilities or sites has become difficult—is also drawing attention.

However, 360-degree cameras have a fatal flaw that it is impossible to avoid. That is, the camera operator themselves are captured in frame. Although there are methods such as trying to minimize this unwanted element as much as possible during shooting, or processing the image after shooting through sequential image processing, there are still no definitive solutions. Although virtual travel features '360-degree viewing angles', many users are not satisfied with the fact that the above problem remains: the camera operator is visible. Therefore, in this study, we design a 360-degree video shooting system, which solves the problem with 360-degree cameras and avoids capturing the camera operator in frame. And as Fujimoto mentioned (2021), 360video has problems in real experience. This study attempts to solve that by the method proposed next.

Y. Luo (Ed.): CDVE 2021, LNCS 12983, pp. 44–52, 2021.
https://doi.org/10.1007/978-3-030-88207-5_5

2 Background

With the launch of 5G high-speed communication, the demand for high-resolution, wide-angle video is soaring in all aspects of society. In particular, the use of 360-degree video is expected to increase rapidly in the future. For instance, the act of 'actually going to the place', such as overseas travel, has become difficult due to the Coronavirus, both in and outside of Japan. Now, there is an increased demand for 'virtual travel' and 'online tours' using 360-degree video, with a great expectation for wide-angles and high-resolution quality. In addition, for the inspection of remote sites and event grounds, internal observation of real estate, archiving of historic ruins and buildings, the active use of 360-degree video is expected to increase dramatically. However, although the problem with capturing the camera operator in the frame of 360-degree videos has been pointed out so far, it has not been adequately addressed. There is no '360-degree video shooting technique that completely avoids the camera operator', and in most cases, all that can be done is an attempt to minimize the unwanted element. If you try to google "how to remove yourself from 360 video", you will find that there are so many people in need of this matter.

In this study, authors propose the Dual Hemisphere Integration (DHI) video generation method, in which the camera operator is not captured in 360-degree videos, and implement the dedicated software.

Using the DHI video generation method, it is possible to shoot omnidirectional videos with commonly used consumer-marketed 360-degree cameras, without capturing the camera operator in frame. As far as the authors are aware, this kind of technique and system does not already exist, and the idea can be said to be extremely original. And now, with increasing societal expectation and demand for 360-degree videos, this method for generating videos without capturing the camera operator solves the fatal flaw of 360-degree cameras, and offers a great contribution to society.

3 Mechanism for Generating 360-Degree Videos Using the DHI Method

In this study, a practical system based on the DHI video generation method, in which the camera operator is not visible in 360-degree video, is developed. In the DHI method, a 360-degree video is generated by stitching together two 180-degree fisheye videos—back and front (or left and right).

The basic mechanism of the DHI method is achieved by simultaneously using two consumer 360-degree cameras to shoot, then from the two sets of fisheye videos that are generated, the 180-degree side where the camera operator is not visible is extracted, and the two are composited together. Usually, 360-degree cameras are shot with fisheye lenses, and it is physically impossible to prevent the camera operator from being captured in frame. Therefore, in the DHI method developed by the authors, two consumer 360-degree cameras with common fisheye lenses are used, and by using the application, the captured videos are composed together to achieve a 360-degree video without the camera operator being visible.

The system we are aiming to develop in this research topic consists of a T-shaped adapter with a grip that horizontally connects two consumer 360-degree cameras at appropriate positions, as well as two applications that automatically avoid the camera operator when composing the 360-degree video captured by the two fisheye lenses. For a summary of the mechanism, refer to the Fig. 1 below:

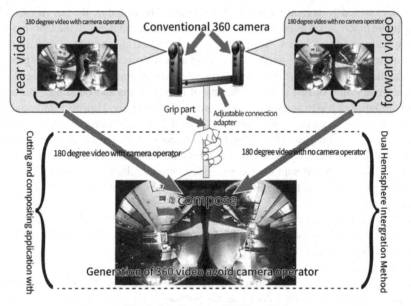

Fig. 1. Mechanism of DHI method

4 Dual Hemisphere Integration and Video Composition Application

In this paper, we describe the implementation of an application that splices the 360-degree videos taken by two fisheye cameras (where the camera operator is visible) to stitch together a 360-degree video without the camera operator.

4.1 Application Design Overview

The application designed in this research will be prototyped as an automatic video composition application for macOS on Apple's iMac or MacBook using the integrated development environment Xcode. The application automatically stitches two 360-degree videos imported by the user and exports the composite video. Specifically, based on the framework: AVFoundation built in Xcode, this application edits a video with the subclass: AVMutableVideoComposition and exports the composite video with the subclass: AVAssetExportSession. Figure 2 shows the execution screen of the prototype application.

As shown in Fig. 2, the interface is simple. Clicking on the two graphic buttons imports the videos. The names of the imported video files are also indicated below. Then, clicking the "Stitch it" button starts the composition. We designed it so that users can quickly understand the operation of the application as soon as they see the interface.

Button to add video file

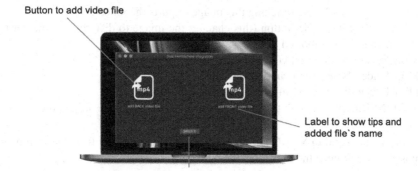

Label to show tips and
added file's name

Button to merge the video side by side

Fig. 2. Execution screen

4.2 The Development Process of the Application

a) User Interface

Figure 3 shows the user interface for the prototype application. Because the interface is designed using a storyboard, the UI elements can be configured with drag-and-drop actions.After configuration, adding a Constraint will stop the layout from changing when zooming in or out.

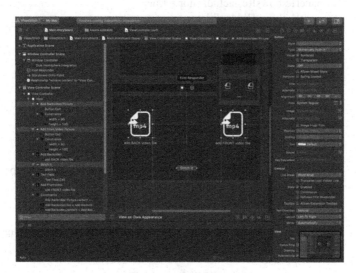

Fig. 3. User interface

b) Connection

Regarding this application, it is necessary to connect the following 7 items to connect the UI elements on the storyboard and the Swift code. addFrontvideo:NSTextField (this shows the imported file's name)

- addFrontvideo:NSButton (clicking this image imports the video file)
- addFrontvideoPicture:NSButton (this changes the image to distinguish whether the video file has been imported or not)
- addBackvideo:NSTextField (same as above)
- addBackvideo:NSButton (same as above)
- addBackvideoPicture:NSButton (same as above)
- StitchIt:NSButton (pressing this final button will start the composition process)

These are declared in ViewController.swift, and by connecting from the storyboard it is possible to organize the user interface with code.

c) **File Open and Save Dialogs**

To compose videos, the paths of the two videos you want to combine are needed. Therefore, the File Open and Save dialogs are implemented. There are several types of dialogs, and here we use a function called NSOpenPanel. This shows the Finder where the user can directly select the video file. Although this code sets the action for all three buttons—addFrontvideo, addBackvideo, and StitchIt—one example is shown below.

```
@IBAction func addBackvideo(_ sender: Any) {
    let panel1 = NSOpenPanel();
    panel1.message = "Choose a video file";  //windows message
    panel1.showsResizeIndicator = true;
    panel1.showsHiddenFiles = false;
    panel1.allowsMultipleSelection = false;
    panel1.canChooseDirectories = false;
    panel1.allowedFileTypes = ["mp4","MP4"] //limit file type
    if (panel1.runModal() == NSApplication.ModalResponse.OK) {
        let result1 = panel1.url
        if (result1 != nil) {
            path = result1!.path
            videoUrl1 = result1 //backup    the path
            // get the filename from path
            theBackFileName = (path as NSString).lastPathComponent
            // change the text to filename
            addBackvideo.stringValue = theBackFileName
            // change the picture of button
            addBackvideoPicture.image = NSImage(named: "Drag2")
        }
    } else {
        return  // close if click cancel
    }
```

Clicking the button showed in Fig. 4 will bring up the screen to call Finder. According to the setting of the code, only files in MP4 format can be selected. The window has the title "Choose a video file." Then, by clicking the Open button, the application's image and the text below will change to show that the video has been imported.

Fig. 4. Screen to call finder by NSOpenPanel

d) **Video Composition**

In Swift, video editing inevitably requires AVComposition, so we start with the basics. 'Composition' is one video project. 'Track' is the sound track of the videos or sounds that make up the project. Each track is dealt as 'Asset'. The final composited video is exported using AVAssetExportSession. As for the video composition in this study, since the two videos have the same size, time length and roughly the same sound, the composition is carried out as shown in Fig. 5.

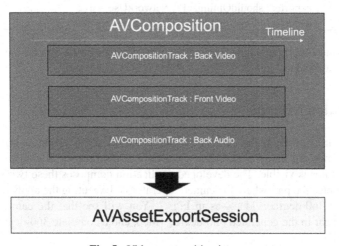

Fig. 5. Video composition image

Part of the code for composition is shown below.

```
func VideoStitch(videoSize: CGSize) {
    if videoUrl1 == nil || videoUrl2 == nil {
        return
    }         // return if one of videourl is nil
    let asset1: AVAsset = AVAsset(url: videoUrl1!)      //set Asset
    let asset2: AVAsset = AVAsset(url: videoUrl2!)
    var
layerInstructionArray:[AVMutableVideoCompositionLayerInstruction] = []
                     . . . .
    videoComposition.renderSize = CGSize(width: videoSize.width*2,
height: 1000)      //change the width
    let composition = AVMutableComposition.init()
    let mainInstruction = AVMutableVideoCompositionInstruction()
                     . . . .
    let firstTrack = composition.addMutableTrack(withMediaType: .video,
preferredTrackID: kCMPersistentTrackID_Invalid)  //add into track
    guard let videoAssetTrack = videoAsset.tracks(withMediaType:
AVMediaType.video).first else { continue }
                     . . . .
    let path = NSTemporaryDirectory().appending("Output.mp4")
    let exportURL = URL.init(fileURLWithPath: path)
    let exporter = AVAssetExportSession.init(asset: composition,
presetName: AVAssetExportPresetHighestQuality)     //set exporter
    exporter?.outputURL = exportURL
    exporter?.outputFileType = AVFileType.mp4
    exporter?.shouldOptimizeForNetworkUse = true
    exporter?.videoComposition = videoComposition
```

Setting the export path and running the above function of the StitchIt button exports the composited video.

5   Execution Example

An execution example of the application implemented in this article is shown below. Figure 6 shows the 360-degree video taken by a common fisheye camera where the camera operator is visible. The developed application composes these two videos in a way that deletes the part where the camera operator is. Executing the application shows the resultant 360-degree video—as in Fig. 7. You will see that the camera operator does not appear in the generated 360-degree video, and a complete 360-degree video is generated.

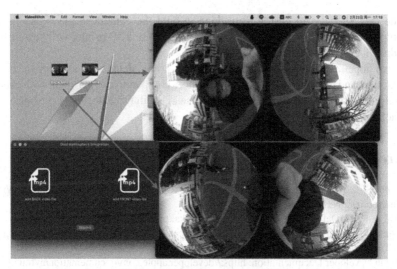

Fig. 6. Video before composition

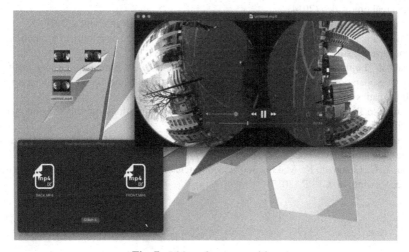

Fig. 7. Video after composition

6 Conclusion and Future Work

In this paper, we have designed a 360-degree video shooting system that avoids capturing the camera operator in frame, and have developed a related application for macOS.

Since panoramic photo appeared, 360-degree video has also gradually gained popularity. However, it is not a mature market and fails to meet all the users' demands. We believe that a camera system that avoids capturing the camera operator in 360-degree videos is one of these demands.

This study will support camera operators who have 360-degree cameras, and aims at the proposed method's popularization.

The task ahead is to design a machine to hold the camera in place and make a prototype using a 3D printer. We expect that anyone with a 3D printer will be able to do reproduce it easily with the shared model data.

I also hope that this research can be used in various fields such as tourism, facility introduction, and cultural exchange. At that time, a comparative experiment with existing methods and tools will be launched, and the research will be evaluated according to user satisfaction and actual use experience.

References

1. Chen, S.E.: Apple Computer, Inc. QuickTime VR – An Image-Based Approach to Virtual Environment Navigation (1995)
2. Dai, J., et al.: Deformable convolutional networks. In: ICCV (2017)
3. Apple Developer Documentation: https://developer.apple.com/documentation/avfoundation/avcomposition
4. Apple Developer Documentation: https://developer.apple.com/documentation/avfoundation/avassetexportsession
5. Fujimoto, T., Fujita, K.: Development of scale processing method to fuse background image and real time video (2014)
6. Munechika, N.: Why we should separate VR video and 360-degree video (2020)
7. Fujimoto, T., Ogawa, R.: The possibility of 3D-origmi system as a tourism promotion tool for Japan. J. Adv. Res. Soc. Sci. Hum. 3(1), 1–10 (2018)
8. Fan, Z., Fujimoto, T.: Proposal of a disposable camera app providing sensory reality of analog operation on smartphone. In: 2019 8th International Congress on Advanced Applied Informatics (IIAI-AAI), pp. 1001–1006 (2019)
9. Fujimoto,T., Fujita, K.: Eigo Ito A proposal of communication-type broadcasting system which can share pictures in real time (2011)
10. Jeon, Y., Kim, J.: Active convolution: learning the shape of convolution for image classification. In: CVPR, pp. 4201–4209 (2017)
11. Su, Y.-C., Grauman, K.: Making 360° video watchable in 2d: learning videography for click free viewing. In: CVPR (2017)

Cooperative Digital Humanities:
A Methodology

Mohammad Alharbi[1](✉), Tom Cheesman[1], and Robert S. Laramee[1,2]

[1] Swansea University, Swansea, UK
{m.alharbi.508205,t.cheesman,r.s.laramee}@swansea.ac.uk
[2] University of Nottingham, Nottingham, UK
robert.laramee@nottingham.ac.uk

Abstract. Researchers in the digital humanities use visualization with ever increasing frequency to address their cultural data challenges. However, interdisciplinary and collaborative projects with visualization researchers are associated with various and common research challenges, such as cooperative communications and methodological differences. A number of strategies have been proposed to guide and steer general cooperative projects to realize the common team objectives. In this paper, we propose a methodological workflow for interdisciplinary digital humanities and visualization research based on our previous work and experience. Our methodological workflow consists of three spaces, three channels, and three criteria. The three spaces feature the main collaborative entities: problem, task, and solution spaces. The three channels illustrate the connections between spaces and include communication, previsualization, and evaluation channels. The three quality criteria include expressiveness, purposefulness, and trustfulness. These three criteria are included to ensure useful outcomes from each space. In each section of the workflow, we draw from our previous cooperations to demonstrate the effectiveness of the workflow.

Keywords: Visualization · Digital humanities · Interdisciplinary framework

1 Introduction and Motivation

Digital humanities scholars increasingly adopt visualization approaches to enrich their research. They find that visual interfaces create new modes of knowledge generation and facilitate more effective discovery and new observations [1,12,14]. Hinrichs and Forlini [12] claim that visualization should be considered not just a means to an end but as a research process in its own right, which has led to the development of multiple interdisciplinary collaborations between the digital humanities and visualization communities. These collaborations have also been studied and discussed in both communities in order to identify means to enhance the collaborations and discuss the challenges encountered [10,14,25].

© Springer Nature Switzerland AG 2021
Y. Luo (Ed.): CDVE 2021, LNCS 12983, pp. 53–62, 2021.
https://doi.org/10.1007/978-3-030-88207-5_6

We believe that cooperation ideally follows a conceptual workflow that considers all aspects of collaboration if possible. Without this, collaboration may develop in undesirable directions due to the different perspectives each stakeholder brings to the project.

In this paper, based on our previous collaborative work, we contribute a methodological workflow of the collaboration between interdisciplinary projects. The goal of this workflow is to guide the collaborative work between digital humanities and visualization. The workflow also aims to foster more effective interdisciplinary research which integrates all of the discipline involved in a balanced manner. The workflow via the quality criteria ensures the usefulness of the results obtained in each space.

The rest of this paper is organized as follows: In Sect. 2, we present previous research related to digital humanities collaborative research. Section 3 introduces our proposed conceptual workflow based on our collaborative experience. Finally, Sect. 4 concludes our paper and points our future directions.

2   Related Work

Collaboration between the visualization team and digital humanities for interdisciplinary visualization projects has been the subject of significant discussion. Recent developments in interdisciplinary research highlight challenges in digital humanities projects and encourage research to propose a collaborative framework to address these challenges [9,11,28]. Munzner [20] proposes a general nested model that guides the process of design and evaluation of visualization projects, while Kath et al. [16] propose a methodological framework supporting knowledge generation of collaborative projects using visualizations. Simon et al. [26] suggest the liaison role shares knowledge and language with both domains to foster collaborative communication. El-Assady et al. [10] present a conceptual workflow of the problem-solving process and collaboration in digital humanities projects with visual text analytics. Jänicke et al. [14] discuss collaboration themes, including the initial start of projects, development iterations, and evaluation methods. Roberts et al. [22] discuss a similar process on the collaboration between academia and industry in visualisation projects, discussing the nature of such projects and how knowledge transfers between the two parties throughout an interview study. Most recently, Schetinger et al. [24] introduce a re-purposed framework of the Data-Users-Tasks triangle [19] to overcome limitations in the context of digital humanities.

In this paper, we provide a methodological workflow based on our previous collaboration with digital humanities. The approach combines the three most important aspects: domain, tasks, and design spaces. It also integrates quality criteria to ensure useful outcomes.

3   Collaborative Workflow

The proposed workflow is a conceptual workflow (Fig. 1) to inform the collaboration and design of interdisciplinary visualization projects. It features three

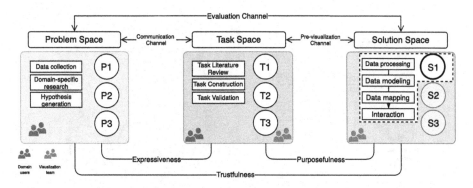

Fig. 1. Our proposed methodological and interdisciplinary workflow. The workflow consists of three main components: the domain, task, and solution spaces. The tasks are informed by a communication channel between the two users' groups. A pre-visualization channel is attempted between the task and solution spaces to prepare for implementation. In the solution space, one or multiple solutions are implemented to address the predefined tasks. The terms expressiveness, purposefulness, and trustfulness indicate the quality criteria that need to be fulfilled to obtain useful outcomes (Sect. 3.2).

spaces, three channels, and three criteria. The following section discusses the workflow components and how they complement one another.

3.1   Three Spaces and Three Channels

This section consists of a discussion of our workflow. The word *"channel"* is used to illustrate the connective phases between spaces as they usually involve communication between the two users in the workflow.

Problem Space: The problem space is the starting point of the workflow. It essentially resembles the domain users, the data, and more likely a set of challenges. For example, in the TransVis project [4], a collection of German translations of Shakespeare's *Othello* was curated by the domain expert in order to be analyzed and visualized. Exploring and examining the collection without computational and visual aids is a laborious and challenging process for digital humanities scholars. The domain users are usually interested in studying how existing approaches can solve their problems, and they generate hypotheses to be confirmed and evaluated based on their data. In this space, the domain problems are clearly identified. Each problem statement needs to be unambiguous, focused, concise, complex, and arguable [10].

Communication Channel: This channel plays a vital role when collaborating on interdisciplinary projects. In our collaboration, we think of this communication as an educational experience for both domain scholars and visualization teams. The domain scholars strive to understand computational and visual tools

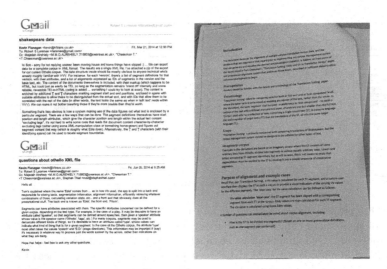

Fig. 2. On the left, email that was exchanged in the early stages of the collaboration to enable sufficient understanding of domain-specific terminology. On the right, a screenshot of a formal document that explains the dataset components and terminology.

as much as possible. This understanding and awareness increase the chances of designing helpful solutions. This means that the visualization team explains the fundamentals and does not assume that they are self-explanatory. The visualization team also strives to understand the domain data and problems, and is encouraged to participate in domain readings and discussions which can help discover relevant mutual problems [1]. The development of such common knowledge can be complex, and we suggest constructive regular meetings at the early stages of collaboration to bridge the differences between the two domains. Simon et al. [26] propose a liaison role in the workflow who shares sufficient knowledge in both disciplines to foster more effective interdisciplinary communication and contributes to the project by capturing the problem complexity or mental model. We also suggest documenting a glossary of terminology that define the key terms in the domain area. In the early stages of our collaboration, various email was exchanged and sessions were held to create sufficient understanding of the dataset element and its associated terminology (Fig. 2).

In this communication phase, flexibility is an essential skill as the discussions strive for balance between the two disciplines. If the visualization team focuses more on the implementation and computational side, it might result in failure to deliver useful solutions. Additionally, what each discipline considers a contribution may vary and this could take the project in an undesired direction if the initial communications and discussions are not balanced [24].

Task Space: In this space, the tasks are formulated based on the research problems (gaps) and interdisciplinary discussions, and are expressed differently between domains. One problem could result in one or more tasks to be solved.

Table 1. Example representatives of the results of the implementation stages in the solution space that correspond to our contributions, TransVis [4], AlignVis [2], and VNLP [3].

	TransVis [4]	AlignVis [2]	VNLP [3]
Data processing	Data cleaning, integration, tokenization, normalization, feature extractions		
Data modeling	Eddy and Viv analysis	Similarity computation	Embedding analysis, similarity computation
Data mapping	Segments colors	Segments and edges colors	Histogram, bar charts, etc.
Interaction	Multiple sorting options, Filtering and selection	Confidence threshold, Filtering and selection	Overview similarity results, Customizable pipeline items

The domain scholar might have broad, high-level tasks, such as close or distant reading, while the visualization team is responsible for transferring these tasks into more technical, well-expressed tasks. The tasks are complete, discriminative, objective, and measurable [29]. Although this is not always achievable, it is nevertheless attempted. In a previous collaboration [4], we adapted the detailed Brehmer and Munzner [7] typology of visualization tasks, which can be communicated to the domain scholar in order to abstract user tasks.

Pre-visualization Channel: This channel is usually where the visualization team parts ways with the domain scholars. The main goal of this channel is to study user tasks and data and begin implementing visual solutions. Here, the visualization team surveys the design space of existing approaches in order to explore potential design solutions and carefully study their advantages and limitations [29]. It is also beneficial to study the domain specific tools because the use of visualization is becoming an essential element of research [12]. The main properties of the activities in this channel are that they involve iterative sketching and trials, and it is crucial to communicate the results to the domain scholar and validate appropriateness against the tasks specified.

Solution Space: Implementing a visual solution starts with data transformation. Often, the data that comes from the domain suffers from a number of problems and may come from a variety of sources with different formats or conventions. Therefore, the data must be preprocessed in order to be cleaned, integrated, and prepared for the next stage. In data modeling, the data is analyzed and interesting meta-data derived, such as Eddy and Viv [4], alignment detection [2], and embeddings generation (VNLP). In data mapping, the abstracted data is mapped to visual encodings. Lastly, user interaction is implemented to aid exploratory analysis. Table 1 shows example representatives of the results of the implementation stages that correspond to our contributions, TransVis [4], AlignVis [2], and VNLP [3].

Based on our previous collaborations, we recommend implementing prototypes iteratively with a subset of the data and presenting the results to the domain scholars. Such frequent presentations and discussions help satisfy the

Fig. 3. Samples of different recordings of our domain expert feedback sessions.

user tasks, obtain intuitive results, and increase the domain scholar's engagement [15].

Evaluation Channel: Evaluating the efficacy and usability of the visual solution is an essential goal of any interdisciplinary project. However, many visualization approaches lack an in-depth, effective quantitative or qualitative evaluation [5]. Furthermore, humanities scholars tend to doubt and question computational, qualitative evaluation. A lack of ground truth is one of the most common challenges in digital humanities [28]. Jänicke et al. [14] report that there are more visual approaches for text analysis tasks published in digital humanities than in the visualization communities due to the usual demand of quantitative evaluations which are challenging to incorporate as a result of the limited number of collaborators from the humanities. Munzner [20] provides guidance on evaluation methods for different design choices. Lam et al. [17] provide a scenario-based method to study evaluation for information visualization. They introduce seven scenarios derived through an extensive literature review of over 800 visualization publications. There has also been work on evaluating visualization which guides users on how to carry out an evaluation for information visualization [8,18,21,27].

In our collaboration with the domain scholar, we evaluate our project usability obtaining domain expert feedback and conducting use cases. The domain expert feedback is based on regular sessions to demonstrate the design features. All of the sessions are video-recorded for post-analysis and archiving. Figure 3 shows a selection of feedback session recordings of our collaboration with the domain expert. Semi-structured interview questions are planned and guided by Hogan et al. [13]. The early sessions usually consist of mock-ups, sketches, or software demonstrations to guide the development of features, and gradually become active hands-on use of the software by the domain expert. During the sessions, the software evolves due to feature demands. During the face-to-face feedback sessions, patterns can be observed, such as the discovery of software bugs and data-level errors.

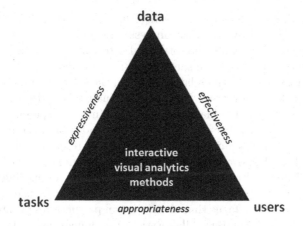

Fig. 4. The design triangle by Miksch and Aigner [19]. They include factors to be considered during the design and implementation of interactive visualizations. Image courtesy of Miksch and Aigner [19].

3.2   Quality Criteria

The design triangle (data–users–tasks) (Fig. 4) methodological approach to inform the design of interactive visualizations suggests three quality criteria that need to be fulfilled in order to obtain useful outcomes [19]. Expressiveness refers to the requirement of conveying the information contained in the data, effectiveness concerns the degree to which the visualization addresses the cognitive capabilities of the human visual system and the context of the user, and appropriateness quantifies the cost-value ratio of the benefit of the visualization process with respect to achieving the intended task. Schetinger et al. [24] repurpose the design triangle and propose three quality criteria that take into consideration the context of digital humanities. Trustfulness reflects the degree to which it can provide guarantees of faithfulness within the epistemological framework of its domain, purposefulness is similar to appropriateness and represents the relation between users and tasks, and meaningfulness expresses the potential value of the custom-made visualization software in terms of generating new insight from the data.

Our workflow consists of domain, task and solution spaces. We adopt similar quality criteria that need to be satisfied in order to obtain the most useful results: expressiveness, purposefulness, and trustfulness (Fig. 1).

Expressiveness refers to the relation between the problem space and task space. It has general and specific aspects. The general aspect is that interdisciplinary exchange and communication can be challenging [10,26], so a glossary of terminology can be adopted and all researchers involved are clearly established. In the specific aspect, the tasks must be well-expressed. Different well-established typologies of task abstractions [6,7] can be utilized to establish a well-defined and expressed task and requirement analysis.

Purposefulness refers to evaluating the visualization against the given tasks. If the requirement and task analysis are optimally defined, this criterion can be quantified. It also important also to consider alternative solutions and how they would achieve the same tasks if they could.

Trustfulness refers to the relation between the solution and the expert user and to what extent they trust the result. Visualizations designed for digital humanities tend to exhibit black-box behavior (not transparent). Rieder and Röhle [23] define transparency as "our ability to understand the method, to see how it works, which assumptions it is built on, to reproduce it, and to criticize it". Based on this, overcoming the lack of transparency is a challenge. The results of modeling and machine learning algorithms are often difficult to interpret and backtrace. Additionally, visualization tends to reduce informational dimensions to produce a focus that shows certain perspectives or interpretations of the data [28]. Based on our collaboration, the domain users do not appreciate this and struggle to trust such results until they understand how they are derived, which is in most cases very difficult. In our collaboration, we keep a close connection with the domain user in the early stages and validate the visual approach with a subset of the data that they know. The user evaluates the result based on the input data. If this visual approach is deemed faithful to the data and domain knowledge, we test the tool with a larger subset of the data.

4 Conclusion

This paper propose a methodological workflow for collaborative research with digital humanities, introducing three spaces, three channels, and three criteria to guide the collaboration in order to produce visualization solutions. The spaces characterize the domain, task, and solution aspects of the project. The channels illustrate the three communicative means between spaces: the communication channel between the problem space and the task space, the pre-visualization channel between the task space and the solution space, and the evaluation space between the solution space and the problem space. The three criteria (expressiveness, purposefulness and trustfulness) are essential to obtain useful outcomes between each space. For the future work, we would like to apply our methodological workflow to other real-world interdisciplinary research projects.

References

1. Abdul-Rahman, A., et al.: Rule-based visual mappings-with a case study on poetry visualization. In: Proceedings of the 15th Eurographics Conference on Visualization (EuroVis), pp. 381–390 (2013). https://doi.org/10.1111/cgf.12125
2. Alharbi, M., Cheesman, T., Laramee, R.: AlignVis: semi-automatic alignment and visualization of parallel translations. In: 24th International Conference on Information Visualisation (IV), pp. 98–108 (2020). https://doi.org/10.1109/IV51561.2020.00026
3. Alharbi, M., Cheesman, T., Laramee, R.: VNLP: visible natural language processing (2020, submitted)

4. Alharbi, M., Cheesman, T., Laramee, R.S.: TransVis: integrated distant and close reading of Othello translations. IEEE Trans. Vis. Comput. Graph. 1 (2020). https://doi.org/10.1109/tvcg.2020.3012778

5. Alharbi, M., Laramee, R.S.: SoS TextVis: an extended survey of surveys on text visualization. Computers **8**(1), 17–35 (2019)

6. Amar, R., Eagan, J., Stasko, J.: Low-level components of analytic activity in information visualization. In: IEEE Symposium on Information Visualization. INFOVIS 2005, pp. 111–117 (2005). https://doi.org/10.1109/INFVIS.2005.1532136

7. Brehmer, M., Munzner, T.: A multi-level typology of abstract visualization tasks. IEEE Trans. Vis. Comput. Graph. **19**(12), 2376–2385 (2013)

8. Carpendale, S.: Evaluating information visualizations. In: Kerren, A., Stasko, J.T., Fekete, J.-D., North, C. (eds.) Information Visualization. LNCS, vol. 4950, pp. 19–45. Springer, Heidelberg (2008). https://doi.org/10.1007/978-3-540-70956-5_2

9. Deegan, M., McCarty, W.: Collaborative Research in the Digital Humanities: A Volume in Honour of Harold Short, on the Occasion of His 65th Birthday and His Retirement, September 2010. Ashgate Publishing Company, USA (2012)

10. El-Assady, M., Gold, V., John, M., Ertl, T., Keim, D.A.: Visual text analytics in context of digital humanities. In: 1st IEEE VIS Workshop on Visualization for the Digital Humanities as part of the IEEE VIS 2016 (2016). https://scibib.dbvis.de/publications/view/686

11. Gold, M.K.: Debates in the Digital Humanities. University of Minnesota Press, Minneapolis (2012)

12. Hinrichs, U., Forlini, S., Moynihan, B.: In defense of sandcastles: research thinking through visualization in digital humanities. Digit. Sch. Humanit. **34**(1), i80–i199 (2018). https://doi.org/10.1093/llc/fqy051

13. Hogan, T., Hinrichs, U., Hornecker, E.: The elicitation interview technique: capturing people's experiences of data representations. IEEE Trans. Vis. Comput. Graph. **22**(12), 2579–2593 (2016). https://doi.org/10.1109/TVCG.2015.2511718

14. Jänicke, S., Franzini, G., Cheema, M.F., Scheuermann, G.: Visual text analysis in digital humanities. Comput. Graph. Forum **36**(6), 226–250 (2017). http://doi.wiley.com/10.1111/cgf.12873

15. Jänicke, S., Geßner, A., Franzini, G., Terras, M., Mahony, S., Scheuermann, G.: TraViz: a visualization for variant graphs. Digit. Sch. Humanit. **30**(suppl_1), 83–99 (2015). https://doi.org/10.1093/llc/fqv049

16. Kath, R., Schaal, G.S., Dumm, S.: New visual hermeneutics. Zeitschrift für germanistische Linguistik **43**(1), 27–51 (2015)

17. Lam, H., Bertini, E., Isenberg, P., Plaisant, C., Carpendale, S.: Empirical studies in information visualization: seven scenarios. IEEE Trans. Vis. Comput. Graph. **18**(9), 1520–1536 (2012). https://doi.org/10.1109/TVCG.2011.279

18. Laramee, R.S.: How to write a visualization research paper: a starting point. Comput. Graph. Forum **29**(8), 2363–2371 (2010). https://doi.org/10.1111/j.1467-8659.2010.01748.x

19. Miksch, S., Aigner, W.: A matter of time: applying a data-users-tasks design triangle to visual analytics of time-oriented data. Comput. Graph. **38**, 286–290 (2014). https://doi.org/10.1016/j.cag.2013.11.002, http://www.sciencedirect.com/science/article/pii/S0097849313001817

20. Munzner, T.: A nested model for visualization design and validation. IEEE Trans. Vis. Comput. Graph. **15**(6), 921–928 (2009). https://doi.org/10.1109/TVCG.2009.111

21. Plaisant, C.: The challenge of information visualization evaluation. In: Proceedings of the Working Conference on Advanced Visual Interfaces. AVI 2004, pp. 109–116. Association for Computing Machinery, New York, NY, USA (2004). https://doi.org/10.1145/989863.989880

22. Roberts, R., Laramee, R., Brookes, P., Smith, G.A., D'Cruze, T., Roach, M.J.: A tale of two visions - exploring the dichotomy of interest between academia and industry in visualisation. In: Proceedings of the 13th International Joint Conference on Computer Vision, Imaging and Computer Graphics Theory and Applications - Volume 2: IVAPP, pp. 319–326. INSTICC, SciTePress (2018). https://doi.org/10.5220/0006635803190326

23. Röhle, B.R.T.: Digital Methods: Five Challenges, pp. 67–84. Palgrave Macmillan UK, London (2012). https://doi.org/10.1057/9780230371934_4

24. Schetinger, V., Raminger, K., Filipov, V., Soursos, N., Zapke, S., Miksch, S.: Bridging the gap between visual analytics and digital humanities: Beyond the data-users-tasks design triangle, Eingeladen; Vortrag. In: 4th Workshop on Visualization for the Digital Humanities, Vancouver, Canada (2020)

25. Silvia, S., Etemadpour, R., Abbas, J., Huskey, S., Weaver, C.: When the tech kids are running too fast: Data visualisation through the lens of art history research. In: Proceedings of the Workshop on Visualization for the Digital Humanities. IEEE, Berlin, Germany, October 2018

26. Simon, S., Mittelstädt, S., Keim, D.A., Sedlmair, M.: Bridging the gap of domain and visualization experts with a liaison. In: Bertini, E., Kennedy, J., Puppo, E. (eds.) Eurographics Conference on Visualization (EuroVis) - Short Papers. The Eurographics Association (2015). https://doi.org/10.2312/eurovisshort.20151137

27. Tory, M., Moller, T.: Human factors in visualization research. IEEE Trans. Vis. Comput. Graph. **10**(1), 72–84 (2004). https://doi.org/10.1109/TVCG.2004.1260759

28. Van Den Berg, H., et al.: A philosophical perspective on visualization for digital humanities. In: Proceedings 3rd Workshop on Visualization for the Digital Humanities (VIS4DH) (2018)

29. van Wijk, J.J.: Views on visualization. IEEE Trans. Vis. Comput. Graph. **12**(4), 421–432 (2006). https://doi.org/10.1109/TVCG.2006.80

GBMVis: Visual Analytics for Interpreting Gradient Boosting Machine

Yulu Xia[1], Kehan Cheng[1], Zhuoyue Cheng[1], Yunbo Rao[2], and Jiansu Pu[1(✉)]

[1] VisBig Lab, Department of Computer Science amp, University of Electronic Science and Technology of China, Chengdu, Sichuan, China

[2] School of Information and Software Engineering, University of Electronic Science and Technology of China, Chengdu, Sichuan, China

Abstract. The gradient boosting machine (GBM) composed of multiple weak learners is an efficient and widely used machine learning method. As a key factor in the prediction process of the gradient boosting machine, feature affects the performance of the gradient boosting machine when splitting nodes. The idea of GBM gives it a natural advantage to discover a variety of distinguishing features and feature combinations. Once the gradient boosting machine has the correct features, other factors play a relatively weak role. However, the GBM is a complicated and tedious process with diverse structure and attributes of decision tree, leading the model to be less interpretable, especially for high risk areas such as medical diagnosis and financial analytics that require transparent prediction. To tackle this issue, we have proposed an interactive visual analytic system, GBMVis, to help experts quickly analyze and of the gradient boosting machine. In addition to providing information about the features, we have also provided a visualization of the structure of boosting trees, which aims to display the major data flow in the gradient boosting machine. We have demonstrated the effectiveness of our system in a real dataset.

Keywords: Gradient boosting machine · Boosting tree · Feature · Prediction · Visualization

1 Introduction

Gradient boosting machine (GBM), an ensemble machine learning model that consists of many independent weak learners, has been proved to be widely utilized in different areas, such as regression methods and classification [20]. GBM is one of the best traditional machine learning algorithms for fitting real distributions. It is an algorithm that classifies or regresses data by using an additive model (i.e., a linear combination of basic functions) and continuously reducing the error generated by the training process [9]. Due to its effectiveness, GBM is applied to commercial tasks. Before deep learning was a big deal, GBM was a big hit in various competitions because of its stable performance, diverse applications and the function of filtering features. For example, GBM appears in the solution of the champion team at KDD Cup in 2016 [17]. Besides, gradient boosting

© Springer Nature Switzerland AG 2021
Y. Luo (Ed.): CDVE 2021, LNCS 12983, pp. 63–72, 2021.
https://doi.org/10.1007/978-3-030-88207-5_7

machine has been adopted by 9 of the first 14 teams in Kaggle competition since 2016 [21].

Despite the wide use and high efficiency, the GBM still meets the function flaw and the performance limitation in the practical application. The first comes from the complex structure of the GBM model and its algorithm. Although GBM has the advantage of stable performance, it also has some limitations. For a large number of identity features, GBM cannot store them effectively due to the tree depth and tree limitation (to prevent overfitting). The second challenge is the output of features engineering. Compared to deep learning models, GBM lacks a certain encoder capability, which is a different feature point organization method that gives flexibility in constructing the network, and corresponding network is usually constructed to better encode the features according to the specific problem [16]. Therefore, to generate useful features is a difficult work with manually selecting process. The third issue stems from the need to interpret the GBM model completely and intuitively. One of the drawbacks of GBM algorithm is that it requires careful tuning of parameters, and the training time may be longer owing to confusing information, which affects performance analysis.

To tackle challenges mentioned above, we develop GBMVis, an interactive visualization system, to help users and machine learning experts interpret gradient boost machine from different perspectives. Specifically, our contributions in this paper are summarized as follows:

- An interactive visualization system, GBMVis, that assists users in interpreting gradient boost decision tree models and predictions through three levels: overview level, feature level and prediction level.
- A combination of diverse feature bar chart design that explain the relationship between feature and prediction.
- A usage scenarios and qualitative user research, which proves the effectiveness and usefulness of GBMVis on incomplete data sets.

In this paper, the prediction model is from the GBM plus logistic regression (LR) model adopted by He et al. in 2014 [9]. It is a hybrid model with input features transformed by boosted decision tree method and output of each tree treated as categorical input to a linear classifier, respectively. We choose boosted decision tree approach due to its high effectiveness in feature transform. The algorithm we use in this article is Lightgbm [1], which is a specific implementation of the GBM model.

2 Related Work

In this section, we review existing work on tree-based model and model prediction visualizations.

2.1 Visualization of Tree-Based Model

Feature Interpretation. Feature interpretation methods are mainly divided into 2 categories: feature importance and partial dependence plots.

Feature importance calculates a score for each feature to reflect its impact on model predictions [2, 3, 8]. Common criteria for evaluating the feature importance are Mean Decrease Accuracy (MDA) [2] and Mean Decrease Impurity (MDI) [3]. In this paper, the result of feature importance calculation contains numbers of times the feature is used in a model. We rank the features according to their importance in predictions to find appropriate split values for each node, so that effectively boosting trees.

Another approach to reveal the relationship between features and predictions is the partial dependence plots (PDPs) [6, 7], which reflects how features affect predictions. PDP is generally visualized with a line chart, where the x-axis represents the value range of the feature, and the y-axis represents the predicted probability [13]. Due to the intuitiveness of the line chart, we also use it to describe the partial dependence information.

Data Flow Interpretation. Zhao et al. [20] proposes a visual analytic system, iForest, to interpret random forest models and predictions. iForest designs a pixel-based bar chart, which summarizes the decision paths to reveal the underlying working mechanism of random forest. Unlike boosting trees, decision trees used in random forest are classification trees, while boosting trees are regression trees. In this paper, we focus on the decision path of the regression tree, including feature discretization.

In order to display the tree structure more intuitively, BOOSTVis [15] uses the node link tree visualization, and also considers the visualization of the tree as a whole. In this paper, we pay more attention to the interpretability of the boosting tree and reveal its influence on the prediction results through visualization techniques, rather than the structural details of the tree.

2.2 Visualization for Model Prediction

INFUSE [12] proposes a visual design, which assist experts in understanding how predictive features are ranked across feature selection algorithms, cross-validation folds, and classifiers. Each visual object represents a feature, and the information obtained from the algorithm can be reflected in its design and layout. To help data scientists to understand their models, EXPLAINEXPLORE [5] supports a variety of different data sets and machine learning models. Experts could use explanations to diagnose the model and find problems. In this paper, diagnosing and improving the model is not our main purpose. We propose an interactive visual analytic system, which can reflect the model prediction results, and analyze the features used in model prediction through visualization. We also show the structure of trees in GBM.

3 Design Goals

After a comprehensive summary of papers collected from machine learning, visualization and human-computer interaction fields, we propose the following design goals.

G1: Uncover the Relationship Between Features and Model Prediction. In order to better understand GBM, users should first understand the general knowledge of the model and be able to evaluate the predictions of the model [14]. During the training process, GBM learns the mapping between features and predictions, which reflects the model behaviors. Displaying input features and their relationships with model predictions enables users to understand and measure the impact of features on prediction results. For example, users may want to know which features are important in the prediction, or which minor changes in feature values will not significantly affect the prediction results, so that users can modify the model or delete unnecessary features. Therefore, uncovering the relationship between features and predictions is helpful to explain GBM.

G2: Reveal the Internal Mechanism of the Model. Making GBM transparent not only needs to reveal the relationships between features and predictions, but also reveals the internal mechanism of the model [14]. Experts should be able to review the model prediction to ensure the correctness of the decision process. For example, Data scientists working in banks may need to understand the model predictions of loan applications to assess whether the loan applicants are in good standing, so that they can decide whether to apply for loans for them. The working principle of GBM can be described by the structure and decision path of the boosting tree. For example, the information gain of each branch node of the tree describes its splitting performance. Analyzing the decision path from root to leaf can help explain the rules of certain features and the prediction process of GBM. Therefore, displaying boosting trees can help experts understand the underlying working mechanism of GBM.

G3: Provides Case-Based Analysis. Case-based analysis is the most effective part of the decision-making program [10]. Its idea is to extend the solution of similar problems to new problems [11]. When interpreting GBM, users can compare new cases with similar cases in the training data to evaluate predictions [4]. However, there are multiple measures for calculating the similarity of GBM. For example, the similarity can be measured by calculating how many common leaf nodes reach [18]. Therefore, providing different similar cases is helpful for users to evaluate predictions from various angles.

4   Analytical Tasks

T1. Encode Feature Importance. Feature importance helps users build an understanding of the model (G1). Users may not be interested in the internal mechanism and structure of the model, but are more familiar with the features. Feature importance reflects the impact of a feature on the prediction result, which is consistent with the user's subjective perception and can increase the user trust in the model.

T2. Encode Partial Dependence Information. Feature importance refers to the influence of a certain feature on model prediction, which is a numerical value, and partial dependence information can reflect how this feature affects prediction (G1). Partial dependence information can be used to answer similar questions as follows: If all other features remain unchanged, what effect does latitude and longitude have on housing prices? In the two different groups of people, is the difference in health predicted by the model caused by their debt level, or is there another reason? What partial dependence information reflects is the change of the mean value. If the features of some training data increase the prediction probability, and some decrease, they may cancel each other out. Therefore, in practical applications, users need to be patient to observe and interpret.

T3. Encode Split Point Distribution. The split points distribution is another key clue to reveal the relationship between features and predictions (G1). In this paper, we use histogram algorithm to split features. The basic idea of the histogram algorithm is to discretize the continuous feature values into k integers, and then construct a histogram with a width of k. When traversing the data, the discretized value will be used as an index to accumulate statistics in the histogram. After traversing the data once, the histogram accumulates the required statistics. Then the algorithm traverses to find the optimal split point according to the discrete value of the histogram.

T4: Review Training Data Value Distribution. Reviewing this distribution is useful for both feature (G1) and case-based analysis (G3). The training data value distribution can also be used as evidence when partial dependence information and the split point distribution cannot correctly reflect the relationship between features and predictions. For example, if there is interaction between variables, it is possible that the partial dependence plot is completely flat, but the feature importance is very large. Furthermore, examining the distribution of similar training data is also helpful to check the model predictions.

T5: Analyze Prediction Errors. During the inspection process, the user may need to check whether the test data is correctly predicted. If a set of data is incorrectly predicted, they can check the feature values and distribution of the test data to determine which features caused the error (G1). Understanding the prediction error of the model allows users to improve model inputs and parameters.

T6: Encode Structures of Tree. Each tree's structure is unique, including the depth of the tree, the number of branches of the tree, the features that appear on the path from the root to the leaves, and the segmentation threshold of the features in each node. These structures can give users a deeper insight into the underlying working mechanism (G2) of GBM.

T7: Provide Interactive Inspection of the Model. GBMVis provides interactive inspections of the three design goals listed above. Users may want to know the impact of different input features on the prediction results (G1). They may also be interested in a single tree in GBM (G2), or interactively analyze similar cases (G3). Therefore, interactive inspection can help users better understand the model.

5   Visual Design

As shown in Fig. 1, we use GBMV is to interpret GBM with student card records dataset. GBMV is contains three main views: (A) Data Overview, which shows the training data after dimensionality reduction. The visual encoding of the Data Overview are a) general data information viewing b) feature values of a single data. We provide a search function that allows users to understand a single piece of data and view its features. By entering a single data in the search box, the upper and lower parts of the data respond simultaneously; (B) Feature View, which describes the relationship between features and prediction results from multiple perspectives. The visual encoding of the Feature View are a) feature importance, b) partial dependence information, c) training data value distribution, d) split point distribution, e) prediction errors; (C) Data Flow Path, which aims to enable users to observe the flow of data during the prediction process by showing the structure of the boosting trees, and understand GBM more intuitively. The visual encoding of the Data Flow view is the structure of boosting trees. In addition, users can explore the working mechanism through multi-graph interactions.

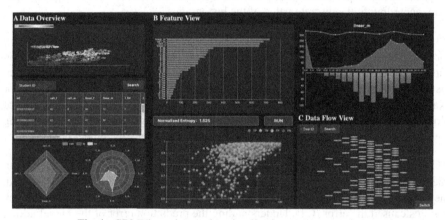

Fig. 1. GBMVis, an interactive visualization system overview.

5.1 Data Overview

Data overview summarizes data information in order to give users a comprehensive grasp of all data. The data we use is multidimensional data. If we visualize it directly, it not only reduces the response efficiency of the system, but also makes it difficult to display all the data on the visual charts. Therefore, according to the amount and type of data we have, we use the t-SNE dimensionality reduction technique for multidimensional data [19]. t-SNE uses Principal Component Analysis (PCA) to reduce multidimensional data to two dimensions and then maps it to the visualization chart. The t-SNE enables the user to visualize the distribution of the data. The objective function of t-SNE used to can be expressed as:

$$C = \sum_i KL(P_i \| Q_i) = \sum_i \sum_j p_{j|i} \log \frac{p_{j|i}}{q_{j|i}} \tag{1}$$

As in Fig. 1A., we show a data table that allows users to easily browse information about the data by searching. The features of a single piece of data are displayed using a radar chart. The radar chart shows a particular data more clearly than the traditional display of values. The user can modify the data displayed in the radar chart by searching.

5.2 Feature View

In Feature View, users can see the values of individual features to analyze the relationship between features and predicted results. This helps users to understand the model. For example, the user may want to know which features are most important for model learning (T1) and how the features affect the prediction (T2). In addition, split point distribution for each feature (T3) and training data value distribution (T4) reflect the relationship between features and predictions. Therefore, we designed Feature View to interpret such information to help users understand the model.

In Fig. 1B., we visualize the three plots showing the feature information as one graph. From top to bottom, they are the line plot, area plot, and histogram, which represent the partial dependence information, training data value distribution, and split point distribution, respectively. The line graph represents the partial dependence information. For a feature $f^m \in F = \{f^1, f^2, \ldots, f^M\}$, let $C = F - \{f\}$ to be the complement set of f, and the partial dependence can be calculated as:

$$PDP_{f^m}(\alpha) = \frac{1}{N} \sum_{i=1}^{n} GBM \left(x_i^C, x_i^m = \alpha \right) \tag{2}$$

where N denotes the size of the training data and the function $GBM(x)$ denotes the GBM models, which takes the training data as input and outputs the probabilities. Partial dependence calculates the average value of the prediction f, x_i^C is fixed and the value of feature m for each data is set to α. In this figure, the y-axis indicates the prediction of the model. In Fig. 1B., we use area plots to show the distribution of the training data values. The x-axis represents the feature values within a certain range represented by each bin, and the y-axis represents the number of data items within a certain range of feature values. We use histogram algorithm to count the number of split points of feature.

5.3 Data Flow View

In the Data Flow View, we present the structure of the boosting trees to allow users to gain a clearer understanding of the data flow in the GBM model during construction and prediction. The structure of the boosting tree is designed to reveal the structure and properties of the decision paths, which allows users to examine the order in which features appear in different decision paths. This is crucial for measuring the importance of features. As shown in Fig. 1C., the depth of the tree increases from left to right.

In addition, we provide a switch button to change the growth direction of the tree, from left to right to top to bottom, to suit different users' habits. Users can also zoom in or out of the diagram by dragging and dropping the mouse to enable users to observe the structure of the tree more clearly. The details of the Data Flow View are shown in Fig. 2.

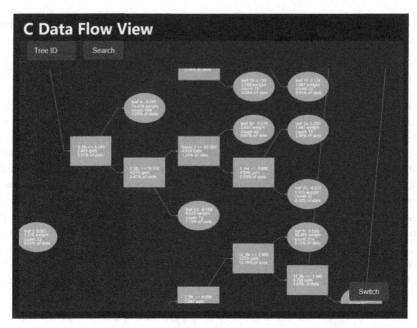

Fig. 2. Data flow view's visual encoding for structure of boosting trees.

6 Case Study

In this section, we describe a usage scenario and a qualitative case study that demonstrate the effectiveness of GBMVis. The data set we use comes from the behavior and score of students at the University of Electronic Science and Technology of China.

The dataset is the four-year student card records of the students who enrolled in the University of Electronic Science and Technology of China in 2009 and 2010 (9,457 in total), and the scores of all the students' courses. There are about 3 million records, including hot water in the teaching building and access to the library. We think that the more times a student goes to the library or teaching building, the more time he spends on studying. The score data includes mid-term and final scores. We first process the training data and simplify the model by combining similar or redundant features. Finally, we generated the following features: the mid-term and final scores of calculus and linear algebra in the first semester, and the number of access to the library and hot water in the teaching building in the first twelve months. The reason why we only choose the first year's math courses scores and behaviors as input features is that the first year is a critical period, which largely determines the student's final GPA. Math is also a key course, which widens the gap between students' scores. The label to be predicted is whether the student's grade point average (GPA) reached 60 points at graduation. This is a binary variable, where 60 points or less are marked as positive.

First, we find that the mid-term contribution score of linear algebra in the first semester (linear_m) ranked top by observing the Feature View, so linear_m is the most important feature related to prediction (T1). Then we check the split point distribution

(T3) and training data value distribution (T4). We find most data are distributed over 50, of which 60 have the highest statistic. This is consistent with the fact that students with good math scores have a higher GPA when they graduate. But in partial dependence plot (T2), the change of linear_m did not have much impact on the prediction result. Since the PDP curve has been fluctuating in a relatively stable interval, we need to examine the reason in conjunction with the analysis of prediction errors (T5).

Through the scatter chart, we observe that the linear_m of the students in the TN group (GPA higher than 60) are all concentrated above 60, while the students in the TP group (GPA lower than 60) are almost below 60. However, the FN group (which is incorrectly predicted to have GPAs higher than 60) has a similar score distribution to the TP group, but the prediction results are different. In order to check the model further, we click on a certain point (T7) in the FN group to view other feature values of the student. We first check the feature values of the student whose student ID is 292311017, and find that the student's math score is above 60 three times, but linear_m is less than 60. It can be seen that although linear_m has the highest importance, other math scores still affect the prediction. Then, we choose the student whose student ID is 2901304009. His math scores are all below 60. By observing his behavior data, we find that he went to the library 6 times in the fourth month (4_lib). And the final exam was held that month. This shows that the model mistakenly believes that the student spends more time studying, so his GPA is high. Understanding the prediction errors of the model can help users improve the model. If users, especially machine learning beginners, are interested in the working mechanism of the model, they can view the structure of the boosting tree (T6). But if users do not understand machine learning, they can also understand the prediction through the previous steps.

7 Conclusion

In this paper, we have presented an interactive visualization tool, GBMVis, that helps users and machine learning experts interpret gradient boosted machine model. The tool first assists analyze the input feature automatically, hence boosting the feature engineering process. In addition, the main decision path is visualized to display the data flow in gradient boosting machine, which clearly show the basic mechanism of GBM procedure. The result of the visualization indicates that our tool can effectively explain the relationship between the input feature and the prediction result and demonstrate all key feature combination and decision path intuitively.

For future work of GBMVis system, there are two aspects to be improved. One is that we are going to expand the dataset and use another set of data for case study to further validate the effectiveness of our tool. The other is based on the experimental results of He et al. [9], in addition to using GBM, we also use logistic regression for feature classification, and this part should be visualized and added to GBMVis to completely explain the feature processing process.

References

1. Microsoft LightGBM. https://github.com/Microsoft/ LightGBM. Accessed 31 Mar 2017

2. Breiman, L.: Random forests. Mach. Learn. **45**(1), 5–32 (2001)
3. Breiman, L.: Manual on setting up, using, and understanding random forests v3. 1. Statistics Department University of California Berkeley, CA, USA 1 58 (2002)
4. Caruana, R., et al.: Case-based explanation of non-case-based learning methods. In: Proceedings of the AMIA Symposium. American Medical Informatics Association (1999)
5. Collaris, D., van Wijk, J.J.: Explain explore: visual exploration of machine learning explanations. In: 2020 IEEE Pacific Visualization Symposium (PacificVis). IEEE (2020)
6. Friedman, J.H.: Greedy function approximation: a gradient boosting machine. Ann. Stat. 1189–1232 (2001)
7. Friedman, J., Hastie, T., Tibshirani, R.: The Elements of Statistical Learning, vol. 1, no. 10. Springer Series in Statistics, New York (2001)
8. Genuer, R., Poggi, J.-M., Tuleau-Malot, C.: Variable selection using random forests. Pattern Recogn. Lett. **31**(14), 2225–2236 (2010)
9. He, X., et al.: Practical lessons from predicting clicks on ads at facebook. Proceedings of the Eighth International Workshop on Data Mining for Online Advertising (2014)
10. Kim, B., Rudin, C., Shah, J.: The Bayesian case model: A generative approach for case-based reasoning and prototype classification. arXiv preprint arXiv:1503.01161 (2015)
11. Kolodner, J.: *Case-based reasoning*. Morgan Kaufmann, 2014.
12. Krause, J., Perer, A., Bertini, E.: INFUSE: interactive feature selection for predictive modeling of high dimensional data. IEEE Trans. Vis. Comput. Graph. **20**(12), 1614–1623 (2014)
13. Krause, J., Perer, A., Ng, K.: Interacting with predictions: Visual inspection of black-box machine learning models. In: Proceedings of the 2016 CHI Conference on Human Factors in Computing Systems (2016)
14. Lipton, Z.C.: The mythos of model interpretability: in machine learning, the concept of interpretability is both important and slippery. Queue **16**(3), 31–57 (2018)
15. Liu, S., et al.: Visual diagnosis of tree boosting methods. IEEE Trans. Vis. Comput. Graph. **24**(1), 63–173 (2017)
16. Ng, A.: Machine Learning and AI via Brain simulations. Accessed May 3 2013: 2018
17. Sandulescu, V., Chiru, M.: Predicting the future relevance of research institutions-The winning solution of the KDD Cup 2016. arXiv preprint arXiv:1609.02728 (2016)
18. Tan, S., et al.: Tree space prototypes: another look at making tree ensembles interpretable. In: Proceedings of the 2020 ACM-IMS on Foundations of Data Science Conference (2020)
19. Van der Maaten, L., Hinton, G.: Visualizing data using t-SNE. J. Mach. Learn. Res. **9**(11) (2008)
20. Zhao, X., et al.: iForest: interpreting random forests via visual analytics. IEEE Trans. Vis. Comput. Graph. **25**(1), 407–416 (2018)
21. No free hunch–the official blog of kaggle.com. http://blog kaggle.com/category/winners-interviews/. Accessed 31 Mar 2017.

Improvement for Time Series Clustering with the Deep Learning Approach

Do Quang Dat and Phan Duy Hung$^{(\boxtimes)}$

FPT University, Hanoi, Vietnam
`dat18mse13010@fsb.edu.vn, hungpd2@fe.edu.vn`

Abstract. Clustering methods, especially time series clustering, are increasingly interested in and applied in many fields such as finance, risk management, forecasting, etc. This work performed various time series clustering approaches to analyze their effectiveness. In particular, the study proposes a method to increase clustering efficiency by combining clustering results from different methods. The entire research is evaluated on an actual dataset of bank account balances. The results are analyzed in detail for each technique, and the different methods are compared.

Keywords: Data mining · Big data processing - fusion · Time series clustering · Auto encoder · Variation auto encoder · Long short-term memory auto encoder

1 Introduction

With the development of computing technology and systems, time series clustering methods are increasingly developed in different ways. For traditional ways, the most commonly used distances are Euclidean, DTW, etc. At the same time, more modern methods apply Deep Learning technology to represent latten features of string data such as Auto Encoder (AE), Variation Auto Encoder (VAE), or Long Short-Term Memory (LSTM) Auto Encoder.

The authors use the time series clustering based on DTW distance in [1] for model-based sequence clustering that addresses several drawbacks of existing algorithms. The approach uses a combination of Hidden Markov Models (HMMs) for sequential estimation and Dynamic Time Warping (DTW) for hierarchical clustering. For accelerating DTW clustering, the authors in [2] propose a novel pruning strategy. The authors in [3] present an efficient implementation of anytime K-medoids clustering for time series data with DTW distance. And the authors in [4] confirm the improved DTW distance method as a powerful one compared to the classical way, Euclidean.

The deep learning algorithms are also applied for finding latten features of time series data. These latten features are input for the clustering process. A two-stage deep learning-based methodology for clustering time-series data is introduced in [5]. In work, an AE based on a deep learning model is built to model both known and hidden non-linear features of time series data. The authors in [6] propose Donut, an unsupervised anomaly detection algorithm based on VAE. The authors in [7] present cyber-attack anomaly

Y. Luo (Ed.): CDVE 2021, LNCS 12983, pp. 73–83, 2021.
https://doi.org/10.1007/978-3-030-88207-5_8

detectors based on VAEs and investigates their detection performance. The authors in [8] use multilayer LSTM networks to learn representations of video sequences. Their model uses an encoder LSTM to map an input sequence into a fixed-length representation. The authors in [9] utilized LSTM AE networks to distinguish a particular speaker from the rest of the speakers in a single channel recorded speech.

The above studies have suggested many solutions for clustering, but no solution combines the advantages of the methods.

This study uses an actual data set to find groups of users who share similar behavior. Time-series clustering uses traditional methods and encoder neural network technology. By analyzing, comparing various ways, and proposing to improve clustering efficiency based on a combination of clustering methods.

The remainder of the paper is organized as follows. Section 2 describes the collected actual dataset. The methodology is explained in Sect. 3. Section 4 includes experiments, analysis, and suggestions for improvement. Then, conclusions and perspectives are illustrated in Sect. 5.

2 Data Description

The data set is taken from a bank's deposit account information. For each account, there is data about balance history in 48 months from January 2013 to November 2017.

The total number of accounts collected is 976,289. However, 95% of the accounts are no longer active or the balance is very low, under 350 USD, and will not be used in this study because of their low significance. The number of remaining accounts with high balance is 5,869. These accounts represent only 0.6% of the total but they contain 46.55% of the total balance of all deposit accounts.

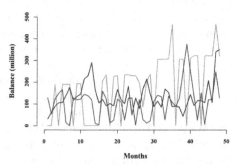

Fig. 1. Balance history of ten customers.

For privacy reasons, all customer information and bank information have been discarded. Only the account balance details remain. Hence, the data for each customer is a sequence of 48 values, each being the balance at the beginning of the month. Figure 1 shows the balance history of ten customers.

3   Methodology

3.1   Proposed Method

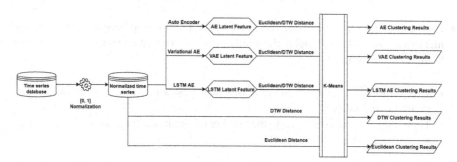

Fig. 2.   Clustering.

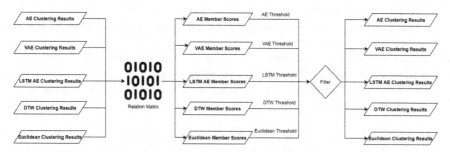

Fig. 3.   Filtering out members from clusters.

The study proposes two main stages: implementing clustering algorithms (Fig. 2) and filtering out members from clusters (Fig. 3).

In stage 1, deep learning techniques are used to learn latent features. These features are input parameters for clustering methods. Deep learning architectures used include Auto Encoder, Variational Auto Encoder and LSTM Auto Encoder.

Stage 1 - clustering includes the following steps:

- Time – series normalization: this step normalizes time series to the interval [0, 1] to focus on grouping time series by shape.
- Calculate latent features of time series based on Auto encoder (AE), Variational Auto Encoder and LSTM Auto Encoder (LSTM AE) methods.
- Calculate distances according to each type of distance are Euclidean and DTW.
- Perform time series clustering with the K-Means algorithm.
    Stage 2 – "Cluster filtering" includes the following steps:
- Calculate the relational matrix of points (members)
- Calculate the member score for each cluster for each method
- Filter out members from the above clusters

3.2 Cluster Filtering

In stage 2, the proposed new points are as follows:

The Relational Matrix

The relational matrix is a square matrix of size NxN where:

- Each cell (i, j) contains a value representing the relationship between member i and member j. This value is equal to the number of methods that i, j members are assigned to the same cluster:

  - This value has the minimum value of 0 when both i and j are never in the same group in all methods.
  - This value is maximum equal to the number of combined methods (ie i and j always go together in the same cluster).

- Cells (i, i) have a value of 0.

Calculating Member Score

For each method, the score of member i in each cluster is calculated as follows:

- Consider all pairs (i, j) in the cluster, ie i will not change and j runs in the entire cluster.
- The score of member i will be added an amount which is the value of the cell (i, j) in the above relational matrix. This value is normalized by dividing by the number of members in each cluster.

With the above proposal, members frequently in the same cluster in all methods will result in high values (i, j). These points are considered to be core cluster members. Conversely, the cluster boundary points will usually have low (i, j) values.

From the relational matrix, an appropriate threshold or an appropriate core members ratio to filter out the boundary members to increase clustering efficiency.

4 Experiments

This study implemented the following time series clustering methods:

4.1 Auto Encoder Training

The data reduction methods used are AE, VAE and LSTM AE. Training loss of the methods is shown in Figs. 4 and 5.

The results from Figs. 4 and 5 show that:

- The compression methods have mostly converged
- The compression methods according to AE and LSTM have the best loss results. VAE's loss is many times larger than other methods.
- Loss decreases when increasing the number of features from 2, 3 to 4.

Table 1. Time series clustering methods

Data	Number features	Distance		K-Means clustering	Symbol
		Euclidean	DTW		
Auto Encoder (AE)	2	x	x	x	ae_2 ae_dtw_2
	3	x	x	x	ae_3 ae_dtw_3
	4	x	x	x	ae_4 ae_dtw_4
Variational Auto Encoder (VAE)	2	x	x	x	vae_2 vae_dtw_2
	3	x	x	x	vae_3 vae_dtw_3
	4	x	x	x	vae_4 vae_dtw_4
LSTM Auto Encoder (LSTM)	2	x	x	x	lstm_2 lstm_dtw_2
	3	x	x	x	lstm_3 lstm_dtw_3
	4	x	x	x	lstm_4 lstm_dtw_4
RAW	48		x	x	dtw
RAW	48	x		x	euclidean

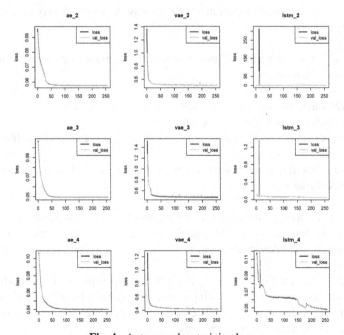

Fig. 4. Auto encoders training loss.

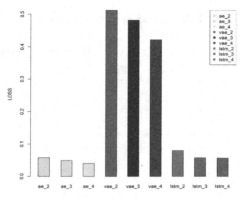

Fig. 5. Auto encoders training loss (in bar chart).

4.2 Clustering

Clustering data by different methods and evaluating them through the silhouette value. The result in Fig. 6 indicates that:

- The silhouette value in most methods decreases gradually as the number of clusters increases.
- VAE data reduction method gives unstable results compared to other methods at both Euclidean and DTW distance.
- The optimal number of clusters for most methods can be chosen is 4. The reason is that the methods have "broken" silhouette value curve at 4 (trend: curves decrease sharply, then decrease slowly from 4; or the curve decreases slowly to 4, and then it decreases sharply).

In addition, comparing the silhouette values between methods with 4 clusters, the results in Fig. 7 show that:

- The LSTM methods gave the best results out of all the methods.
- The VAE methods gave the worst results.
- Small numbers of data dimensions provide better clustering efficiency, although there will be greater data loss.
- Combining data dimensional reduction with DTW distance is not really effective in time-series clustering problem.

Thus, by evaluating all the above clustering results, the conclusion here that the data dimension reduction method is not suitable with time series clustering. Therefore, in the next analysis, the VAE method will be discarded and the number of clusters for all methods is fixed to 4.

We analyse the trend in each group and filter out all values equal to 1 which is the result of a similar time series correlating with itself. The results in Fig. 8 show that the LSTM methods are dominant with the density graphs deviating much to 1, meaning that the time series in the clusters have the same trend.

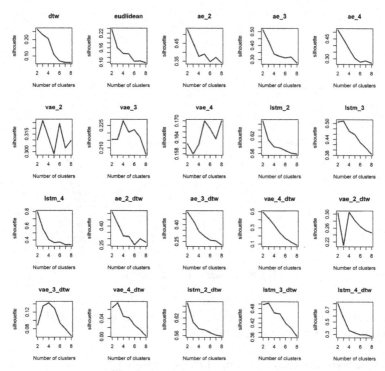

Fig. 6. Clustering silhouete values.

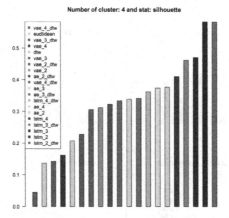

Fig. 7. Silhouete values between methods.

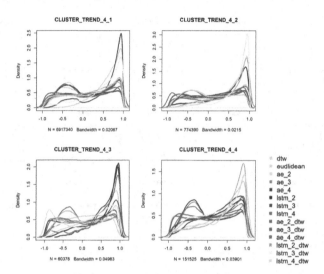

Fig. 8. Cluster trend correlations.

The mean of the trend correlation value in each cluster is represented as a bar chart as shown in Fig. 9. Some results are following:

- LSTM methods give good clustering efficiency, proved by the tendency in clusters.
- DTW distance also attests efficiency, especially when combined with the LSTM method.
- The AE method does not yield significant results from the analysis of trend results.

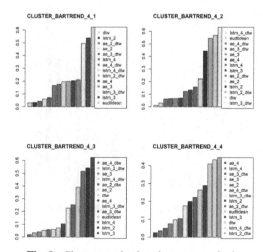

Fig. 9. Cluster trend values between methods.

4.3   Cluster Filtering and Analysis

From the analysis and evaluation in Sect. 4.2, eight clustering methods selected to perform "cluster filtering" include: dtw, euclidean, lstm_2, lstm_3, lstm_4, lstm_dtw_2, lstm_dtw_3, lstm_4. Relational matrix of 8 methods in Fig. 10.

	1	2	3	4	5	6	7	8	9	10
1	0	3	4	2	2	3	3	2	1	2
2	0	0	6	3	3	8	8	0	0	0
3	0	0	0	3	5	6	6	1	0	1
4	0	0	0	0	6	3	3	3	2	3
5	0	0	0	0	0	3	3	3	0	3
6	0	0	0	0	0	0	8	0	0	0
7	0	0	0	0	0	0	0	0	0	0
8	0	0	0	0	0	0	0	0	5	8
9	0	0	0	0	0	0	0	0	0	5
10	0	0	0	0	0	0	0	0	0	0

Fig. 10. Relational matrix of 8 methods.

Filter out 20% of the members in the clusters with the lowest scores. Compare silhouette values before and after the filter, the results are obtained in Fig. 11:

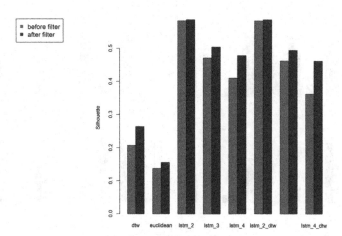

Fig. 11. Silhouette values after filter.

The increased silhouette value with all methods proves that the cluster filtering has significantly improved clustering efficiency.

Data are reduced to 2 by PCA method and shown in Fig. 12. Clusters are now more concentrated, members at the cluster boundary have been filtered out.

EUCLIDEAN   LSTM_2_DTW

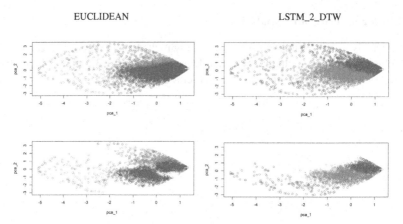

Fig. 12. PCA 2 dimentions before and after filter.

The trend correlation in the pre- and post-filter cases is compared in Fig. 13. The results show that the trend correlation values are significantly improved in most methods and in some clusters. However, this value also decreased in a small number of methods and in some clusters. Except for the LSTM_4_DTW method, it is inefficient when combining multiple clustering results.

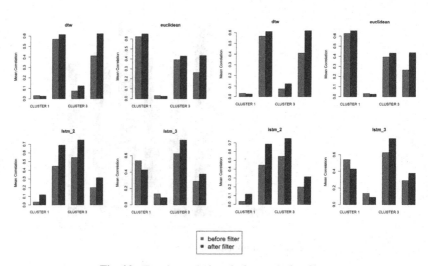

Fig. 13. Trend correlations before and after filter

Some conclusions drawn from the analysis above:

- The VAE and AE methods are not suitable for the data set to yield good clustering results.
- The LSTM methods have good results, shown in the clustering results, especially when combined with the DTW distance.

- Combining clustering results improves clustering efficiency. This conclusion is confirmed in this study's scope with the collected data.

5 Conclusion and Perspectives

The paper offers improvements to time series clustering based on deep learning techniques. First, based on clustering efficiency, the best time series clustering methods will be chosen from which to construct the relational matrix. Next, the point of each member is calculated. Finally, filter out the components at the edge of the clusters, keeping the core components of the cluster. The study is evaluated on a real dataset of bank account balances. This result will be evaluated and analyzed on larger data and other actual time series data to draw conclusions with higher universality.

References

1. Hu, J., Ray, B., Han, L.: An interweaved HMM/DTW approach to robust time series clustering. In: Proceedings of the 18th International Conference on Pattern Recognition (ICPR'06), pp. 145–148 (2006). https://doi.org/10.1109/ICPR.2006.257
2. Nurjahan, B., Liudmila, U., Jun, W., Eamonn, K.: Accelerating dynamic time warping clustering with a novel admissible pruning strategy. In: Proceedings of the 21th ACM SIGKDD International Conference on Knowledge Discovery and Data Mining (KDD '15). Association for Computing Machinery, New York, NY, USA, pp. 49–58 (2015). https://doi.org/10.1145/2783258.2783286
3. Huy, V.T., Anh, D.T.: An efficient implementation of anytime k-medoids clustering for time series under dynamic time warping. In: Proceedings of the Seventh Symposium on Information and Communication Technology (SoICT '16). Association for Computing Machinery, New York, NY, USA, pp. 22–29 (2016). https://doi.org/10.1145/3011077.3011128
4. Puspita, P.E., Zulkarnain: a practical evaluation of dynamic time warping in financial time series clustering. In: Proceedings of the International Conference on Advanced Computer Science and Information Systems (ICACSIS), pp. 61–68 (2020). https://doi.org/10.1109/ICACSIS51025.2020.9263123
5. Tavakoli, N., Siami-Namini, S., Adl Khanghah, M., Mirza Soltani, F., Siami Namin, A.: An autoencoder-based deep learning approach for clustering time series data. SN Appl. Sci. 2(5), 1–25 (2020). https://doi.org/10.1007/s42452-020-2584-8
6. Haowen, X., Wenxiao, C., Nengwen, Z., et al.: Unsupervised anomaly detection via variational auto-encoder for seasonal KPIs in web applications. In: Proceedings of the 2018 World Wide Web Conference (WWW 2018). International World Wide Web Conferences Steering Committee, Republic and Canton of Geneva, CHE, pp. 187–196 (2018). https://doi.org/10.1145/3178876.3185996
7. Takiddin, A., Ismail, M., Zafar, U., Serpedin, E.: Variational auto-encoder-based detection of electricity stealth cyber-attacks in AMI networks. In: Proceedings of the 28th European Signal Processing Conference (EUSIPCO), pp. 1590–1594 (2021). https://doi.org/10.23919/Eusipco47968.2020.9287764
8. Nitish, S., Elman, M., Ruslan, S.: Unsupervised learning of video representations using LSTMs. In: Proceedings of the 32nd International Conference on International Conference on Machine Learning - Volume 37 (ICML'15). JMLR.org, pp. 843–852 (2015)
9. Rahmani, M., Razzazi, F.: An LSTM auto-encoder for single-channel speaker attention system. In: Proceedings of the 9th International Conference on Computer and Knowledge Engineering (ICCKE), pp. 110–115 (2019). https://doi.org/10.1109/ICCKE48569.2019.8965084

Practitioner Experiences and Requirements for Rule Translation Used for Building Information Model-Based Model Checking

Peter Nørkjær Gade[1]([✉]), Rasmus Lund Jensen[2], and Kjeld Svidt[2]

[1] University College Northern Denmark, Sofiendalsvej 60, 9200 Aalborg SV, Denmark
pega@ucn.dk
[2] Aalborg University, Thomas Manns Vej 23, 9220 Aalborg, Denmark

Abstract. Creating building designs is difficult for the designers, and mistakes that are costly for the building process are often made. The technology BIM-based Model Checking can help the designers identify errors in the design so they can correct them. BIM-based Model Checking systems uses translated rules that specify how errors are identified; in this sense, it is how the rules are identified that are the most important. Therefore, translation of the rules is a key to how successful a BIM-based Model Checking systems perform. However, there is not an agreed-upon method of translating such rules from, for example, building codes, and poorly translated rules often cause problems and has been identified as a key to better adoption of BIM-based Model Checking systems in building design practices. In this study, we investigated the experiences of practitioners whose work is either supported or unsupported by checking systems. The challenges were related to the translation of rules used in the assessment because such rules become more explicit and thereby reduce the designer's interpretative flexibility.

Keywords: BIM-based model checking · Rule translation · Practitioner inquiry · Activity theory checklist

1 Introduction

BIM-based Model Checking (BMC) is an umbrella concept for the myriad of terms used to describe the process of checking BIM-based models, and is also known as rule checking or automated compliance checking [1]. The automation of assessments using BMC-systems can potentially improve the speed, consistency, and precision of the assessment building designs [2, 3]. Eastman et al. [4] categorised the process into four classes: (1) Rule Interpretation, (2) Building Model Preparation, (3) Rule Execution, and (4) Reporting Checking Results (see Fig. 1). Rules are translated from natural languages (e.g., building codes into computer executable code). The BIM-models are prepared for the checks by validating the required information needed for the checks. The information is then checked to assess the conformity with the translated rules, which then communicate the checking results. The foundation of BMC consists of the rules that embed how the BIM models are checked; therefore, proper handling of the rules

© Springer Nature Switzerland AG 2021
Y. Luo (Ed.): CDVE 2021, LNCS 12983, pp. 84–96, 2021.
https://doi.org/10.1007/978-3-030-88207-5_9

is essential to proper checking. Handling the rules includes inventing and/or translating existing rules into computer-executable code to perform the checking mechanism.

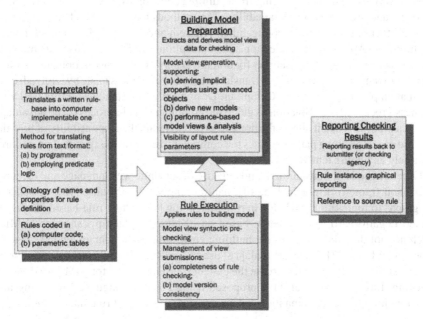

Fig. 1. The four classes of functionality a rule checking system should support rule derivation, building model preparation, rule execution, and rule reporting, and their needed internal capabilities [4].

While there is a general optimism in research regarding BMC [5], the technology is yet to become an integrated part of building design practices. Few commercial and often monopolized BMC systems exist, and only a few companies have integrated them, mainly for limited geometrical collision checking or information validation [6, 7]. In regard to national initiatives, some have been created to develop and implement BMC systems to assess rules such as building codes; however, none have been successful and no national BMC system has been adopted [7]. One of the more significant national BMC initiative was the Singaporean ePlanCheck project, which regrettably encountered significant challenges in the attempt to integrate a BMC system into practice [8–10], and has now been discontinued [7]. The challenges for successfully adopting BMC into the construction industry are numerous and multifaceted. However, it has recently been indicated that the most significant current issue is regarded as the lack of "precise digitizable regulations" [7]. To achieve precise digitizable regulation rules, a better method for translation is needed. Amor and Dimyadi [5] argue that there is not yet a sufficient method of translation that is exact enough. The lack of precision and exactness stems from the vague and imprecise way in which the rules are formulated in the code and standards. The formulations used are often not enough for computers to express and must be extended through interpretation.

1.1 Existing Methods for Translating Rules

A study by Ismail, Ali, and Iahad [11] identified 23 methods for rule translation to translate various regulations ranging from building code topics (accessibility, fire safety, and occupant circulation) to sustainability. The methods have a different emphasis, and some are focused on practical applicability. Hjelseth and Nisbet's [12] method, named Requirement, Applicability, Selection, and Exception (RASE), was used to translate rules focusing on improving usability for domain experts in the construction industry and providing a range of steps in order to translate. A similar effort was made by Dimyadi et al. [13] that emphasized the use of Compliant Design Procedure that was formalised with Business Process Model Notation to guide the compliance audit process. The advantage of such a process is that it allows the domain expert to retain the responsibility of how the rules are executed along paths and uses the computer to execute the specified procedures accurately and consistently.

Other methods of translation include the use of semantic web language and resource description framework graphs [15, 14], natural language processing [16], or conceptual graphs to represent knowledge in rule translation [17]. Other rule-based languages include LegalRuleML and RuleML based on eXtensible Markup Language (XML), which are not directly related to the building environment but contain a wide range of resources and tools [3]. Ghannad et al. [18] used LegalRuleML and visual programming to reduce the complexity and increase the ease of translating rules for BIM-based Model Checking. Lastly, Song et al. [19] proposed using Natural Language Processing and Deep Learning to enable semantic analysis processes to support rule interpretation.

1.2 Normative and Deterministic Rule Translation

The existing methods do not emphasise practitioner inquiry as a foundation of how the translation methods were developed; rather, they are predominantly built on a "normative" perspective of understanding the rules and are used in practice. This perspective is typically dominated by a top-down or rule enactor hierarchy that entails a deterministic view that separates the translation of rules and their use. So, when a rule regarding space requirements is translated, it is done solely by a designated "specialist" that must accommodate all potential use-cases of how the translation is used and not by the actual uses of the translation. Such a perspective can be problematic because it neglects the context of the practices and causes the practitioners to often either misuse or reject the BMC systems that use the translations. An example of the "normative" perspective is noticeable in Ismail et al.'s [11] study where it was concluded that the reviewed methods' functionality was sufficient enough for the proper translation of rules for BMC systems. Nevertheless, none of the reviewed methods made an explicit effort to include practitioner inquiry. The study concluded that the reason why translation issues continued to persist was a mere matter of implementation, which was thereby deemed to demonstrate a deterministic view of translating rules. Another example of the "normative" approach can be found in Hjelseth and Nisbet's [12] RASE methodology that emphasises using rules as "normative texts," which are considered universally valid.

In general, BMC-systems research has practitioner inquiry been neglected, and the few studies that exist are very limited. This is a bit surprising when it has been recognised that the technology is mature and available, but it is the soft human aspects of organization, culture, and adoption of the technology that are the real challenges [9, p. 58]. However, the notions of "the soft human aspects of organization, culture, and adoption" have received very little attention. This could be the reason why many studies regarding BMC-systems superficially note issues related to the practitioner's environment due to "Cultural resistance to accepting automated compliance checking" [7]. However, as Orlikowski [20] argued, the deterministic way of looking a technology was incomplete and limited to how we understand people and their relationship with technology.

1.3 Aim of This Paper

The rejection of many of the translation methods might not be due to ill will from the practitioners, but rather an inevitable result of the methods' inability to accommodate the users and their environment in which the practices are taking place. This paper hypothesises that by exploring the socio-technical aspects of BMC systems used, the user's environment can be better accommodated, which can improve the translation of rules and therefore aid in the successful use and implementation of BMC. This paper is not concerned with the technical aspects of BMC systems, but rather the socio-technical aspects; it aims to explore the practitioner's environment to create better methods of translation for BMC systems.

2 Methodology

To explore the practitioner's environment to create better translation methods for BMC systems, this article investigates different settings qualitatively using semi-structured interviews that are theoretically founded in activity theory using the activity theory checklist. This is done to explore assisted and unassisted practitioners' experience working with design and related rules. These insights are categorised and discussed in terms of how we can improve the current translation methods for rules used in BMC systems.

2.1 The Danish and Singaporean Rule Environments

In this article, two different national building design environments were explored via semi-structured interviews. The first environment explored was based in Singapore, where a BMC system supports companies. Singapore was chosen because of its efforts in the development and implementation of BMC. The second environment focused on traditional practices in Denmark that are unsupported by BMC systems and are challenged by the complexity of rules from sustainability assessment methods. Denmark was chosen because of its sustainability efforts in the construction industry and because the interviewees are subject to issues related to how rules derived from sustainability.

Background on the Traditional Sustainability Assessment Practice in Denmark.
In Denmark, DGNB-DK, a building sustainability assessment method, is typically used in the construction industry to specify and assess buildings' sustainability. The method vastly increases the design complexity and contains multiple rules [21]. DGNB-DK

covers six areas of quality: environmental, economic, social, technical, process, and location. The exact number of criteria varies depending on the specific scheme (i.e., office buildings or low-rise housing). The method is very complex because it has been estimated to contain more than 2000 atomic rules [21]. In practice, it is difficult to as-sess the impact of one decision against another, and currently, the designers are rela-tively unsupported by any technology besides, spreadsheets or similar means.

Background on the BMC-Supported Practice in Singapore. In Singapore, many building design companies have successfully integrated a BMC system that automates the assessment of a building design's buildability. In collaboration with the BCA, Sin-gapore's Institute of Architects has developed a BMC solution known as the electronic Buildability Design Appraisal Score (eBDAS) BIM system, which automates the assess-ment of the Bscore using BIM-models. The Building and Construction Authority (BCA) in Singapore specifies the measurement of buildability of newly constructed buildings using the metric Buildable Design Score for the building (Bscore). The build-ability score is based on quantities from the building design combined with a labour-saving index (LSI). The LSI is a parameter that determines the labor intensiveness of building objects such as walls and floors [22]. The eBDAS (not BIM) started as an expert system in 2004 that was able to electronically understand building designs from 2D computer-aided design (CAD) data submitted by architects and engineers [23]. Later, eBDAS was developed to support BIM, and then became known as eBDAS BIM. This system uses quantities from the BIM model that can be transferred through either a plug-in or man-ually. The objects' LSI information can either be typed into the BIM model manually from the authoring system or in the eBDAS BIM system.

2.2 Semi-structured Interviews

Semi-structured interviews were used for inquiry of the practices experienced in a nat-ural setting. The semi-structured interviews were carried out according to the theories by Barriball and While [24] and were conducted with both individuals and groups. This method helps the interviewer understand the respondents' perception and opinions regarding complex topics by exploring their attitudes, values, beliefs, and motives while simultaneously supporting comparability between the respondents [24], thus allowing for subjective ideas. Semi-structured interviews allow for "probing" when answers are vague, which can be defined as asking follow-up questions in responses not fully under-stood by the interviewer or to obtain more in-depth information [25]. The interviews were primarily conducted face to face and were one to two hours in length.

2.3 Interviewee Selection

The interviewees were chosen from the two design environments, as previously stated. The first environment represented nine designers from four companies working with a building design that is subject to accommodating complex rulesets like the DGNB-DK set in Denmark. The interviews focused on the role of systems in the respondents' work and how the design's creation is mediated. The interviewees were selected to represent a traditional design environment and included representatives from architectural and engineering businesses working with DGNB-DK. The second design environment represented four designers, two rule enactors, and four BMC/BIM-systems developers from six Singapore companies. Table 1 gives an overview of the interviewees, their role, company type, and size.

Table 1. Background of the 19 interviewees.

	Role	Company type and size according to the European Commission (2003)
Denmark (n=9)	Design practitioner and DGNB Consultant – MSc	Large engineering company
	Design practitioner and DGNB Consultant – MSc	Medium sized architectural company
	Design practitioner and DGNB Consultant – MSc	Medium sized architectural company
	Design practitioner and DGNB Consultant – BSc	Medium sized engineering company
	Design practitioner and DGNB Consultant – Construction Architect	Large architectural company
	Design practitioner and DGNB Auditor – Construction Architect	Large architectural company
	Design practitioner and DGNB Auditor – MSc, PhD	Medium sized engineering company
	Design practitioner – Construction Architect	Medium sized engineering company
	Design practitioner – Construction Architect	Medium sized engineering company
Singapore (n=10)	BIM manager	Large consultancy company
	BIM manager	Small BIM consultancy company
	Design and BMC practitioner	Large consultancy company
	Design and BMC practitioner	Large consultancy company
	BMC developer	Small developer company
	BMC developer	Small developer company
	Rule enactors	Large public institution
	Rule enactors	Large public institution
	BIM developer	Large BIM developing company
	BIM developer	Large BIM developing company

2.4 Activity Theory Checklist

The interviews with the 19 practitioners were conducted according to the Activity Theory Checklist [26]. The Activity Theory Checklist is a method for investigating user interaction with technology or the lack thereof [27]. The method provides a framework for understanding human relations with technology built on psychological and sociological theories [26]. The Activity Theory Checklist provides a set of "skeleton" questions that interviewers can apply to investigate the interviewee's interaction with technology. The questions are modified to suit the interviewer's research topic and seek to ensure that the interviewees are questioned according to the aspects that according to the aspects that enable an exploration of the challenges they experience with the technology. Kaptelinin et al. [26] argued that by having a predetermined set of questions built on this method, the interviewer's objectivity would increase. Without this approach, the interviewing process would be more random, which can lead to missing critical aspects in understanding the use of technology [27]. The use of technology is not only a matter of input-output between a user and the machine: it also requires a rich depiction of the user's environment [27]. The theoretical framework of Activity Theory (AT) provides theories for describing human activities [27]. The Activity Theory Checklist uses the AT concept of tool mediation (Kaptelinin, Nardi, and Macaulay, 1999; Quek and Shah, 2004). Tool mediation concerns the human use of tools, both material (computer) and immaterial (routines), to transform objects. Objects represent everything objectively represented in the world, from the object of teaching children mathematics to the creation of a building. The use of the checklist assists the interviewers in exploring critical aspects such as the use of technology, and in this case, how complex rules are supported or unsupported by BMC systems.

3   Results

The results are presented in two sections: the first from the Danish interviews and the second from the Singaporean interviews. The results were transcribed and analysed through categorizing and organizing the results with affinity diagramming. Affinity diagramming is a method that can be applied for organizing qualitative data in complicated domains [29].

3.1   Results from the Traditional Danish Sustainability Assessment Practice

The interviewees expressed various characteristics related to the use of rules in the traditional design practice, which identified both how they accommodated the rules in creating the building design and why they often rejected systems that potentially could automate and assist their work. An essential aspect for the interviewees was the need to ensure certainty in processing the design information according to the rules. Using systems to automate their work moved tasks away from them and thus made their work more efficient; however, involving such systems meant that the interviewees needed to fully understand how the system would automate their work, i.e., how the rules were formulated and executed in the systems. To obtain certainty, the interviewees expressed that they required transparency of the systems they used.

Transparency of a system would allow the designers to scrutinise how the systems interpreted the rules and embedded them into the automation, an approach which has two advantages. First, it would assist users and their organization in establishing certainty. Second, it would help the users understand the consequences of their design choices according to the system. Often, the interviewees argued that it could be challenging to predict the consequences of their design choices if they lacked transparency. Therefore, improving the transparency could also improve the designer's ability to predict their design's consequences according to the automation. The interviewees argued that their experience with many systems often lacked transparency because the automation (i.e., information processing) was hidden in unformalised rules embedded in the complex code. They argued that, while most of the systems that could automate and assist in their tasks were rejected, the systems lacked transparency. They were thus unable to establish enough certainty and trust in how rules were interpreted in the system and how it was applied in their context. One interviewee gave a concrete example regarding the calculation of the Life-Cycle Cost (LCC). The interviewee had reviewed several potential systems, but none of them provided the ability to ensure that the automation was aligned with the interviewee's context. While the systems could automate the developer's interpretation of rules derived from LCC-based sustainability assessment methods, the interviewee was unsure if the results were valid according to the interviewee's project, company, or regional and national standards. This prompted a dilemma regarding whether or not a system could be trusted in terms of the developer's interpretation and be deemed suitable for use by the interviewee; unfortunately, however, the system was ultimately rejected. Therefore, they still relied on self-made ad-hoc spreadsheets to assist in their LCC assessments.

The interviewees also voiced that the rejection of a certain system was related to a lack of adaptability. While transparency would allow the interviewees to understand how the systems processed the information, the adaptability would allow the interviewees to change the processes. Some systems only allowed for minor adaptions, which required the interviewees to manually conduct comprehensive post-editing of the results and minimise the automation benefits. It was important for the interviewees that the system would allow them to adapt the information processing according to their contexts, both in regard to the business and the project; in essence, interviewees wanted translations of the rules that were easily adaptable to their context. The interviewees explained that they were often required to spend a great deal of time altering the calculations' results. For example, the company for which the interviewees worked used a solar performance system to assess rooms' solar performance. Using this system required the users to make manual calculations of the system's results to make them usable for their national context. This would only be possible if the system was sufficiently transparent and allowed the users to identify what adaptions of the results were required to be made.

The interviewees explained that the systems first needed to be adaptable to national contexts (i.e., national standards) and then business contexts. The business contexts affect the information processing quality level, which is assessed according to the strategy and values for the business. Also, the project context often requires the systems to be adapted due to unique characteristics. For example, systems can make it challenging to understand a design manifested in a BIM model. Here, rooms can overlap due to the possibility of rooms being embedded in other rooms (a service kitchen room can be embedded in a break room), making it difficult for a system to recognise air circulation calculation, for example. In this case, either the design or the system must be adapted to the purpose of automating the task. This requires that the designers steer the system and take such characteristics into account to produce relevant results. The interviewees argued that the transparency of the rules was essential for establishing certainty and trust through the ability to scrutinize the automation. Interviewees argued that a lack of transparency and the inability to obtain trust often resulted in a rejection of systems.

3.2 Results from the BMC-Supported Assessment Practice

The interviewees in Singapore expressed overall satisfaction with the eBDAS BIM system. By using the BMC system, developers could provide the designers with an effective system that helped the designers assess the Bscore of their building designs and helped the rule enactors receive more consistent evaluations of the Bscore. Moreover, the use of eBDAS BIM fits into the business's use of BIM, according to BIM managers and developers. The interviewees in Singapore expressed that the Bscore assessment automation vastly increased the speed of the designer's buildability assessment process. One interviewee expressed that it reduced the workload of one person from two weeks to half an hour and increased the assessment's consistency and precision. The main issue encountered in using eBDAS BIM was ensuring the consistency between the correct object types (e.g., roofs are modelled with roof objects and not floor objects) and LSI values (e.g., the brick walls are assigned the brick wall LSI value). The calculation itself was conducted in seconds.

The use of the eBDAS BIM system transformed the division of labour related to the assessment process. Previously, there was a more significant separation between the designers and the Bscore assessors, but they have since merged. The designer is now creating the BIM models responsible for ensuring consistent object types and LSI values in the model. Previously, this was located beside the actual creation of the design. The use of eBDAS BIM now requires that the designers know the consequences of their design decisions related to the eBDAS BIM because the BIM model's information is directly used in the automation of assessing the Bscore. This adjustment to the labour divide required BIM-modellers to foresee how their design choices would affect the results from eBDAS BIM. However, this contradicts the interviewees' explanation that the system is primarily black-boxed (when the information processes are hidden) and hard-coded (with limited possibility of adapting the information process). This restriction was a design choice made by SIACAD to ensure a degree of consistency in the calculation of the Bscore. However, the interviewees argued that this was not considered a problem because SIACAD rapidly and frequently updated eBDAS BIM according to any general changes in the designers' environment, such as updates to the building codes.

The interviewees argued that the reason why this approach worked was related to how the rules were translated. The rules were translated with the intent that they would be suitable for automation, potentially negating the designers' contextual requirements. One interviewee (Architect) criticized the negation of the contextual requirements, arguing that the rules' transformation has led to severe architectural issues. Arguing it would remove the designer's ability to interpret what constitutes buildability in the specific project. Before the rule was made explicit, buildability could be assessed using the designer's expert knowledge of various contextual aspects, and they would know it was formulated into the exact value of the LSI score. The explication allowed for a more consistent and straightforward assessment of the Bscore, but it was considered highly constraining in terms of the designer's ability to affect the building designs' buildability. A concrete example was mentioned regarding the LSI score and bricks: the low LSI score of using bricks in the building designs restricted bricks' use by disregarding any other possibility of using bricks in a more buildable manner. The interviewee (Architect) argued that this disregard would lead to less innovation regarding buildability, which negatively affects the construction industry that is subject to these rules.

4 Discussion and Conclusion

This article explored the practitioner's experiences regarding the use of rules in building design in Denmark and Singapore in order to contribute one of the first dedicated practitioner inquiries on BMC. Using semi-structured interviews and the Activity Theory Checklist helped cover broad qualitative socio-technical aspects and rules regarding BMC in building design, which showed a need for transparency, flexibility, and recognition of unique, situated requirements in project contexts. In addition, the exploration of Singaporean practices indicated existing challenges regarding the consequences of normative translations of rules that led to the design's unwanted restrictions.

The findings highlight several dilemmas in formalising rules used for BMC-systems that are relevant in other domains, namely the representation of knowledge. Rules themselves and the application of rules embed knowledge that is represented in a system like BMC. The current approach relies on a predominantly normative perspective where the translation is done by "experts." These experts then envision the best translation for the users, which would often not embed necessary localized knowledge. The deterministic view of translating rules is still prevalent in much of the research concerning BMC systems where the main solution is to solve perceived issues of missing consistency and exactness using technological solutions like NLP or AI [5]. Yet, Sydora and Stroulia [30] acknowledge that it is unlikely that relevant stakeholders will ever be able to agree upon a set of rules.

Amor and Dimyadi [5] suggested that an effort to harmonise terms and reduce inconsistencies in rules is necessary. This view is substantiated by a survey done by Beach et al. [7] who found that the main obstacles for rule checking was a lack of precise digital regulations and standards for data regarding rule checking compliance. However, while some standardization and harmonisation are possible, these findings highlight the need to accommodate situated realities from situated terms. This means that a model of translation must provide a clear and understandable taxonomy of the translation process, and its results must allow everyday and non-programmer users to fully understand how the rule was interpreted. Numerous research studies call for better usability with regard to understanding and manipulating the rules, the majority of which focus on visual programming solutions or other graphical notation solutions like Business Process Management Notation 2 [31]–[34]. Amor and Dimyadi [5] also found that "white-box" approaches to show rule translations are necessary because they allow for the further adaption of user input when the automated rules are executed in a specific context.

However, the normative translations can never represent the natural complexities of the practices and often become restrictive and problematic, as seen in the Singaporean example regarding buildability. Demaid and Quintas [35] noted that failing to understand the tacit knowledge needed for translating the rules into the necessary contexts potentially leads to easy solutions for ill-structured problems and that we must leave the notion that rules can and must be normatively translated by experts alone. A situated component is needed where users can understand and adapt the rules to their needs and requirements. The fundamental role of rules in construction industry practices and their transformation through digitalization is rarely mentioned in the domain of research. However, as Nawari [36] highlighted, it is the fundamental questions of how such knowledge is and can be represented that will pose the real issues. Problematic representation of rules can potentially lead to rejection and misuse of the systems that will be reported as "soft" or cultural issues [9] Aligned with this paper's findings, further work is needed to ensure user understanding and the ability to change rules must ensure contextual adaptions.

References

1. Hjelseth, E.: Classification of BIM-based model checking concepts. J. Inf. Technol. Constr. **21**(July), 354–370 (2016)
2. Beach, T.H., Rezgui, Y.R., Li, H., Kasim, T.: A rule-based semantic approach for automated regulatory compliance in the construction sector. Expert Syst. Appl. **42**(12), 5219–5231 (2015). https://doi.org/10.1016/j.eswa.2015.02.029
3. Solihin, W., Dimyadi, J., Lee, Y.: Advances in Informatics and Computing in Civil 12 and Construction Engineering. Springer International Publishing (2019)
4. Eastman, C., Lee, J., Jeong, Y., Lee, J.: Automatic rule-based checking of building designs. Autom. Constr. **18**(8), 1011–1033 (2009). https://doi.org/10.1016/j.autcon.2009.07.002.
5. Amor, R., Dimyadi, J.: The promise of automated compliance checking. Dev. Built Environ. **5**,100039 (2021). https://doi.org/10.1016/j.dibe.2020.100039.
6. Hjelseth, E.: Foundations for BIM-based model checking systems. Norwegian University of Life Sciences (2015)
7. Beach, T.H., Hippolyte, J.L., Rezgui, J.L.: Towards the adoption of automated regulatory compliance checking in the built environment. Autom. Constr. **118**, 103285 (2020) https://doi.org/10.1016/j.autcon.2020.103285.
8. Khemlani, L.: AECbytes, *Q4* (2015)
9. Refvik, R., Skallerud, M., Slette, P.A., Bjaaland, A.: ByggNett - Status survey of solutions and issues relevant to the development of ByggNett (2014). https://doi.org/10.1017/CBO978 1107415324.004
10. Khemlani, L.: Automated code compliance updates, AECbytes Feature (2017)
11. Ismail, A.S., Ali, K.N., Iahad, N.A.: A Review on BIM-based automated code compliance checking system. Int. Conf. Res. Innov. Inf. Syst. ICRIIS (2017). https://doi.org/10.1109/ICR IIS.2017.8002486
12. Hjelseth, E., Nisbet, N.: Capturing Normative Constraints by Use of the Semantic Mark-up RASE Methodology. In: Proceedings of 28th International Conference CIB W78, pp. 1–10, 2011, [Online]. http://202.154.59.182/ejournal/files/Capturing normative constraints by use of the semantic mark-up (RASE) methodology.pdf.
13. Dimyadi, J., Clifton, C., Spearpoint, M., Amor, R.: Computerizing regulatory knowledge for building engineering design. J. Comput. Civ. Eng. **30**(5), C4016001 (2016) https://doi.org/10.1061/(asce)cp.1943-5487.0000572.
14. Zhong, B.T., Ding, L.Y., Luo, H.B., Zhou, Y., Hu, Y.Z., Hu, H.M.: Ontology-based semantic modeling of regulation constraint for automated construction quality compliance checking. Autom. Constr. **28**, 58–70 (2012). https://doi.org/10.1016/j.autcon.2012.06.006

15. Bouzidi, K.R., Fies, B., Faron-Zucker, C., Zarli, A., Le Thanh, N.: Semantic web approach to ease regulation compliance checking in construction industry. Futur. Internet **4**(3), 830–851 (2012). https://doi.org/10.3390/fi4030830
16. Zhang, J., El-Gohary, N.M.: Semantic NLP-based information extraction from construction regulatory documents for automated compliance checking. **30**(1), 1–5, (2016). https://doi.org/10.1061/(ASCE)CP.1943-5487.0000346
17. Solihin, W., Eastman, C.:A knowledge representation approach in BIM rule requirement analysis using the conceptual graph. J. Inf. Technol. Constr. **21**, 370–402, (2016)
18. Ghannad, P., Lee, Y.C., Dimyadi, J., Solihin, W.: Automated BIM data validation integrating open-standard schema with visual programming language. Adv. Eng. Inform. **40**, 4–28 (2019) https://doi.org/10.1016/j.aei.2019.01.006.
19. Song, J., Kim, J., Lee, J.K.: NLP and deep learning-based analysis of building regulations to support automated rule checking system. In: ISARC 2018 - 35th International Symposium Automation Robotic Construction International AEC/FM Hackathon Future Build Things, no. Isarc, (2018)
20. Orlikowski, W.J.: The duality of technology: rethinking the concept of technology in organizations. Organ. Sci. **3**(3), 398–427 (1992). https://doi.org/10.1287/orsc.3.3.398
21. Gade, P., Svidt, K., Lund Jensen, R.: Analysis of DGNB-DK criteria for BIM-based Model Checking automatization (2016). http://vbn.aau.dk/da/publications/analysis-of-dgnbdk-criteria-for-bimbased-model-checking-automatization%28df19474a-0594-43ad-b41f-5785d2155da8%29.html.
22. Building and Construction Authority, Code of practice on: Buildability (2015)
23. Wittkopf, S.K., Hee, H.: Design by grading? electronic buildability design appriasal score (eBDAS) as a major design consideration in architectural design in Singapore. In: eCAADe 21, no. 1, pp. 111–116 (2003)
24. Barriball, K.L.: and a While, collecting data using a semi-structured interview: a discussion paper. J. Adv. Nurs. **19**(2), 328–335 (1994). https://doi.org/10.1111/1365-2648.ep8535505.
25. Legard, R., Keegan, J., Ward, K.: In-depth interviews. Qual. Res. Pract. Guide Soc. Sci. Stud. Res. 138–169 (2003). https://doi.org/10.4135/9781452230108
26. Kaptelinin, V., Nardi, B.A., Macaulay, C.: Methods & tools: the activity checklist: a tool for representing the 'space' of context, interactions. **6**(4) 27–39 (1999). https://doi.org/10.1145/306412.306431.
27. Nardi, B.: Activity theory and human-computer interaction. Context Conscious. Act. Theor. Hum.-Comput. Interact. 7–16 (1996)
28. Quek, A., Shah, H.: A comparative survey of activity-based methods for information systems development. In: ICEIS 2004 Proceedings International Conference Enterp Information System, pp. 221–232 (2004)
29. Beyer, H., Holtzblatt, K.: Contextual Design, 1st edn. Morgan Kaufmann, San Fransisco (1997)
30. Sydora, C., Stroulia, E.: Towards rule-based model checking of building information models. In: Proceedings of 36th International Symposium Automation Robotic Construction ISARC 2019, no. Isarc, pp. 1327–1333 (2019). https://doi.org/10.22260/isarc2019/0178.
31. Solihin, W., Dimyadi, J., Lee, Y.: In search of open and practical language-driven BIM- based automated rule checking systems. Adv. Inform. Comput. Civ. Constr. Eng. (2019). https://doi.org/10.1007/978-3-030-00220-6
32. Preidel, C., Borrmann, A.: Automated code compliance checking based on a visual language and building information modeling. In: Proceedings International Symposium Automation Robotic Construction, June 2015. https://doi.org/10.13140/RG.2.1.1542.2805
33. Häußler, M., Esser, S., Borrmann, A.: Code compliance checking of railway designs by integrating BIM, BPMN and DMN. Autom. Constr. **121** (2021). https://doi.org/10.1016/j.autcon.2020.103427

34. Kim, H., Lee, J.-K., Shin, J., Choi, J.: Visual Language approach to representing KBimCode-based korea building code sentences for automated rule checking. J. Comput. Des. Eng. (2018). https://doi.org/10.1016/j.jcde.2018.08.002
35. Demaid, A., Quintas, P.: Knowledge across cultures in the construction industry: sustainability, innovation and design. Technovation **26**(5–6), 603–610 (2006). https://doi.org/10.1016/j.technovation.2005.06.003.14
36. Nawari, N.: The challange of computerizing building codes in BIM environment. Comput. Civ. Eng. **1** (2012). https://doi.org/10.1017/CBO9781107415324.004.

Automatic Data Sheet Information Extraction for Supporting Model-Based Systems Engineering

Kobkaew Opasjumruskit[(✉)] [ID], Sirko Schindler[ID], and Diana Peters[ID]

German Aerospace Center, Institute of Data Science, Mälzerstraße 3,
07745 Jena, Germany
{kobkaew.opasjumruskit,sirko.schindler,diana.peters}@dlr.de

Abstract. To describe modeling objects in Model-Based Systems Engineering (MBSE) tools, physical properties of these objects are often provided only in data sheets, which are not truly machine-readable. Previously, we proposed a product data hub to exchange spacecraft product information between manufacturers and various MBSE tools. However, issues with heterogeneous structures and semantics of information, such as differences in data format and vocabularies, persist. Using ontologies to maintain product descriptions can mitigate the heterogeneity problem by providing semantic descriptions and supporting different vocabularies for a single concept. To automatically and semantically obtain information from documents that contain tables, lists, and text, we developed an ontology-based information extraction tool. We present how to use the Data Sheets Annotation Tool (DSAT) for, either manually or automatically, extracting information from data sheets, and populating a database with the obtained data. Particularly, we emphasize on the usage of DSAT as a user interface for improving ontologies, which, in turn, are used for a (better) information extraction from the data sheets. Although DSAT is initially created for supporting collaborative systems engineering, it is not limited to the domain of spacecraft design. It can also be applied to other domains, where information needs to be extracted from a multitude of heterogeneous sources.

Keywords: Semantic technologies for information-integrated collaboration · Ontology for information sharing · Web based cooperation tools

1 Introduction

According to INCOSE [9], MBSE has been created with the vision of using models instead of documents as the formal resource for system engineering activities. It aims on the one hand to integrate different models, and on the other hand to link them with a coherent digital system model, which serves as the single and controlled source of information about the system. These models consist of many

© Springer Nature Switzerland AG 2021
Y. Luo (Ed.): CDVE 2021, LNCS 12983, pp. 97–102, 2021.
https://doi.org/10.1007/978-3-030-88207-5_10

parts, each selected out of multiple products provided by different suppliers. The current practice is that engineers manually enter information about components based on the suppliers' PDF data sheets, manually maintained spreadsheets, and their implicit knowledge [11].

To close the gap between these scattered sources of information, in [15], we introduced the idea of a product data hub that enables up-to-date product information to be digitally exchanged between all stakeholders. However, there are heterogeneity issues in terms of data presentation and semantics. For example, the information is sometimes provided in multi-column text with images and graphs, or with tables or lists, and oftentimes mixed. Additionally, the vocabulary used for the same concept can vary substantially, which may lead to ambiguities and requires experts' clarification. Instead of resorting to these manual efforts over and over again, this knowledge can be captured inside a semantic knowledge base. Such a knowledge base needs to be constantly updated to keep up with new developments in the field.

Ontology-Based Information Extraction (OBIE) is one information extraction approach to mitigate these issues as proposed and discussed in [11,17,20]. Most OBIE tools are tailored to extract entities and their relationships but fall short when it comes to extracting literal values, which are the crucial information in the data sheets. They often appear in the form of key-value(-unit) tuples, like weight-200-grams. Furthermore, the vocabulary used in data sheets is highly domain-specific and not consistently used. For example, an attribute of a star sensor, *sun exclusion angle*, is also called *sun angle*, *sun avoidance*, *sun exclusion*, or *sun keep out*. This can be confusing, even for engineers who are familiar with the domain. Missing to detect information can have fatal and costly consequences in the later phases of design and production.

In DSAT-demo [12] we presented a system which provides a human-in-the-loop interface for the automatic extraction of technical properties from data sheets based on an OBIE-pipeline. This paper is a continuation of our aforementioned contribution by providing a graphical user interface. We enhanced the tool DSAT by providing an intuitive user interface so that domain experts, who are not necessarily familiar with ontologies, can suggest the previously undetected attributes or provide corrections to incorrectly identified ones.

2   Related Work

Since most data sheets are provided in PDF format, the text extraction is the first step. Yet, the task is not trivial and there are many solutions available. *PDFminer.six* [14] is an open-source and actively maintained PDF Parser library in Python. It offers an extraction with customizable parameters, such as a page to extract, or coordinations on the page. *Textricator* [18] is an open-source tool to extract data from PDFs and can also handle scanned documents using Optical Character Recognition (OCR), but requires consistently formatted inputs. *Camelot* [4] is and open source software tool to extract tabular data from PDF files. For an extensive review of tools for extracting data and text from PDFs, please refer to [16].

Text, table layouts, and schematic drawings are equally important in technical data sheets. However, most of the existing tools focus on either text or tables, and, to the extent of our knowledge, there is no unified solution that tackles all of these. To achieve the best result, we use a combination of techniques, i.e. using *PDFminer.six* to extract text, and *Camelot* to detect tables.

Once the raw text is extracted, we use entity recognition tools to detect important keywords and their associated information, particularly, product properties and their values. *Amazon Comprehend* [1] can extract property names and values with their unit, although the relation between them is lost. *DBpedia Spotlight* [6] can detect nouns, pronouns, or specific names with a corresponding entry in DBpedia. However, it extracts words without considering the particular domain, therefore, the results are often associated with unrelated concepts due to similar names. *Intelligent Tagging* [10] extracts names and their surrounding text, which likely contain a corresponding value, but its results tend to be too generalized towards the news domain. *GATE-ANNIE* [8] detects words and recognizes their syntax and category. It is possible to define a custom dictionary for *GATE-ANNIE* to tailor its results to a specific domain.

The aforementioned approaches can detect individual properties, but the customization is not intuitive. Moreover, they detect entities and values separately, so the required relations between them are lost. One approach to detect entities with their relations is Ontology-Based Information Extraction (OBIE).

Baclawski et al. [2] summarize the current trends that combine Machine Learning (ML), information extraction, and ontology techniques to solve complex problems, such as OBIE. Here, the unstructured or semi-structured text is processed using ontologies to extract information. Barkschat [3] exploits technical data sheets to populate ontologies using a classifier model and regular expressions. Likewise, *Smart-dog* [11] extracts data from data sheets of spacecraft parts to populate an ontology. It features an ontology enrichment step but relies extensively on ontology knowledge. Rizvi et al. [17] include irrelevant terms and probably-relevant terms in their ontology to calculate the confidence score of the extracted information.

Based on the lessons learned, we implement OBIE to not only populate and enrich ontologies but also to improve information extraction workflows.

3   System Overview

An overview of our system architecture is shown in Fig. 1. The main inputs are data sheets obtained from various sources including websites of manufacturers and retailers. *Continuously Trained Ontologies (ConTrOn)* [13] enables the extraction of information from data sheets and stores the results to a database. The extraction relies on domain-specific ontologies that are constantly adapted using generic, semantic knowledge bases, such as Wikidata [19].

The initial, local ontologies were based on satellite component data derived from an MBSE tool (*Virtual Satellite* [7]), European Cooperation for Space Standardization (ECSS), and feedback from domain experts. The ontologies include

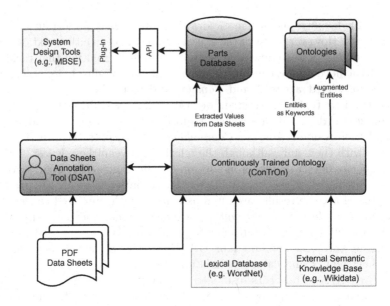

Fig. 1. System overview

a core ontology covering concepts common to most satellite parts as well as specialized ontologies specific for the different categories of satellite parts. All ontologies are publicly available from ConTrOn's ontologies [5].

Meanwhile, *Data Sheets Annotation Tool (DSAT)* [12] is not only a standalone tool assisting users for manually annotating data, but is also used as a user interface connecting users to ConTrOn. We use DSAT to review ConTrOn's extracted information and to manually correct any mistake made by the system. Finally, the extracted data is made available to external components or modeling tools, such as MBSE tools via the Parts Database [15].

DSAT displays the information extracted by ConTrOn and allows for user-review before storing them into a database. This web-based application allows users to upload and select their data sheets (see Fig. 2-I). Then, the selected data sheet is displayed and essential properties can be highlighted on the left panel (II). Data sheets can be processed by ConTrOn, via the Auto-Detect feature to automatically highlight properties in the data sheet. The highlighted text can be categorized as a key, value, or remark (III). Users can also add custom text in a comment box. One set of a key, a value, a remark, and a comment is denoted as an annotation. All annotations created for the currently selected data sheet are summarized on the bottom right panel (IV). Users can add, edit, or delete the annotations afterwards. The ontologies' classes used for the (automatic) information extraction can be individually reviewed and edited (V). If an attribute (key) is incorrectly identified, e.g. DC Voltage is identified as Hardware Interface instead of Supply Voltage, users can suggest the correct description (class), or even suggest a new description. Such feedback from users

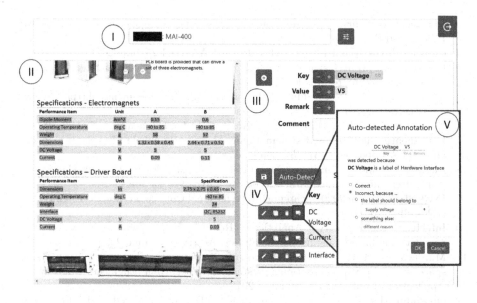

Fig. 2. Data Sheets Annotation Tool interface allows domain experts to review annotations in a data sheet.

will be used to update the ontologies in order to assure the correctness of the semantic information. Currently, all the corrections and suggestions must be reviewed by domain experts before applying them to the ontologies. Since we are sharing the ontologies with other systems, the automatic update at this point is not recommended. Eventually, the OBIE process gets improved as well as the quality of information extraction.

4   Conclusion and Future Work

In this paper we presented an integrated system consisting mainly of DSAT and ConTrOn to support engineers in extracting technical information from PDF data sheets. A feedback feature on DSAT enables users to change the key's concept (class) or suggest a new class to our ontologies. The feedback for incorrectly extracted data can be specified either as a class suggestion or as a comment in free-text form. Next, we plan to conduct a user study to evaluate DSAT whether the feedback form is intuitive to use and if the feedback can help improve the quality of the extracted information as well as the ontologies.

References

1. Amazon Comprehend - Natural Language Processing (NLP) and Machine Learning (ML). https://aws.amazon.com/comprehend/. Accessed 25 June 2021
2. Baclawski, K., et al.: Ontology Summit 2017 communiqué - AI, learning, reasoning and ontologies. Appl. Ontol. **13**, 3–18 (2017)

3. Barkschat, K. Semantic information extraction on domain specific data sheets. In: ESWC (2014)
4. Camelot. https://camelot-py.readthedocs.io/ Accessed 25 June 2021
5. ConTrOn. Contron - spacecraft parts ontology - dsat demo, September 2020. https://zenodo.org/record/4034478
6. DBpedia Spotlight - Shedding light on the web of documents. https://www.dbpedia-spotlight.org/. Accessed 25 June 2021
7. Fischer, P.M., Lüdtke, D., Lange, C., Roshani, F.-C., Dannemann, F., Gerndt, A.: Implementing model-based system engineering for the whole lifecycle of a space-craft. CEAS Space J. 9(3), 351–365 (2017)
8. English Named Entity Recognizer. https://cloud.gate.ac.uk/shopfront/displayItem/annie-named-entity-recognizer. Accessed 25 June 2021
9. INCOSE SE Vision 2020. techreport, International Council on Systems Engineering (INCOSE) (2007)
10. Intelligent Tagging & Text Analytics — Refinitiv. https://www.refinitiv.com/en/products/intelligent-tagging-text-analytics. Accessed 25 June 2021
11. Murdaca, F., et al.: Knowledge-based information extraction from datasheets of space parts. In 8th International Systems & Concurrent Engineering for Space Applications Conference, September 2018
12. Opasjumruskit, K., Peters, D., Schindler, S.: DSAT: ontology-based information extraction on technical data sheets. In: SEMWEB (2020)
13. Opasjumruskit, K., Schindler, S., Thiele, L., Schäfer, P.M.: Towards learning from user feedback for ontology-based information extraction. In: Proceedings of the 1st International Workshop on Challenges and Experiences from Data Integration to Knowledge Graphs co-located with the 25th ACM SIGKDD, vol. 2512 of CEUR Workshop Proceedings, CEUR-WS.org (2019)
14. PDFMiner - a tool for extracting information from PDF documents. https://github.com/pdfminer/pdfminer.six. Accessed 25 June 2021
15. Peters, D., Fischer, P.M., Schäfer, P.M., Opasjumruskit, K., Gerndt, A.: Digital availability of product information for collaborative engineering of spacecraft. In: Luo, Y. (ed.) CDVE 2019. LNCS, vol. 11792, pp. 74–83. Springer, Cham (2019). https://doi.org/10.1007/978-3-030-30949-7_9
16. Pollock, R.: Tools for extracting data and text from pdfs - a review. April 2016. https://okfnlabs.org/blog/2016/04/19/pdf-tools-extract-text-and-data-from-pdfs.html
17. Rizvi, S.T.R., Mercier, D., Agne, S., Erkel, S., Dengel, A., Ahmed, S.: Ontology-based information extraction from technical documents. In: Proceedings of the 10th International Conference on Agents and Artificial Intelligence, SCITEPRESS - Science and Technology Publications (2018)
18. Textricator. https://textricator.mfj.io/. Accessed 25 June 2021
19. Vrandečić, D., Krötzsch, M.: Wikidata: a free collaborative knowledgebase. Commun. ACM 57(10), 78–85 (2014)
20. Wimalasuriya, D.C., Dou, D.: Ontology-based information extraction: an introduction and a survey of current approaches. J. Inf. Sci. 36, 306–323 (2010)

Integrating 4D Simulations and Virtual Reality Environments: An Innovative Prototype

Yacine Mezrag$^{(\boxtimes)}$ and Conrad Boton

LaRTIC – Research Laboratory on Information Technology in Construction, École de Technologie Supérieure, 1100, rue Notre-Dame Ouest, Montréal, Canada
`yacine.mezrag.1@ens.etsmtl.ca`

Abstract. 4D simulation based on immersive Virtual Reality-based collaboration can be a great help in constructability studies and in detecting spatiotemporal interference. Recent publications propose some methods and frameworks to support collaboration centered on 4D BIM models in Virtual Reality (VR) environments. However, the existing VR systems and platforms remains poorly suited to the task of integrating the data libraries generally conveyed by 4D models. In the context of the multiplication of platforms and the increased need for interoperability, it will be essential to develop interoperable solutions, based on OpenBIM formats. However, to date, there is no framework based on open interoperable formats to guide experts and users through the steps necessary for effective VR-based 4D simulation. This work proposes a new method to improve the integration of 4D simulations in virtual reality environments. The method is centered on the use of OpenBIM standards, uses a normalized and structured workflow on three main phases that correspond to different work environments, and considers a two-way data exchange mechanism. In order to evaluate and validate the proposed method, a prototype was developed, adopting the same workflow and using a suitable software ecosystem.

Keywords: 4D simulation · Virtual reality · Constructability · Building information modeling · Common data environment

1 Introduction

In the construction industry, Building Information Modeling (BIM) is a catalyst for a broad digital transition, with the objective of best responding to the major challenges of the sector. Each construction project is unique, and the construction process evolves in a constantly changing environment. Construction planning itself becomes a complex activity that is critical to the good management of a project. This planning is carried out under different methods and generally uses several tools.

In the BIM approach, 4D models are used to simulate the construction process, by a combination of a 3D model and a construction schedule. Using specific software, the objective is to generate a virtual model that can simulate construction activities. This type of simulation has become a communication tool very much appreciated by general

© Springer Nature Switzerland AG 2021
Y. Luo (Ed.): CDVE 2021, LNCS 12983, pp. 103–114, 2021.
https://doi.org/10.1007/978-3-030-88207-5_11

contractor and execution teams, especially because it allows all parties to have a visual perspective of the evolution of the site as a way to better understand the extent of the work to be done [1]. However, the collaborative use of 4D simulations remains under-exploited by project teams and is often reduced by the capacity of the tools being used, compounding the difficulties faced by teams in their efforts to interact collectively with 4D simulations [2]. Recent research by Boton [2] and Sampaio [3] has suggested the use of virtual reality to optimize the use of 4D simulations. Known for its immersive and interactive nature, this booming technology in the construction industry opens up new dimensions for exploring space and other perspectives of group work. Indeed, the immersion and the feeling of presence that virtual reality provides can be of great value as it allows users to explore and inspect all the aspects of a construction site model, as a team in a virtual dynamic is brought closer to reality. In addition, interactive and intuitive functioning in a collaborative framework makes it possible to make the decision-making process more efficient thanks to the exchanges of ideas that this new work environment offers, with the objective of considering the most fluid sequencing for construction work.

Although the advantages of using virtual reality to optimize the planning process and address the limitations of current simulation tools are foreseeable [4], the integration of 4D models in virtual reality environments remains technologically difficult, given the rigidity of existing software and the exchange formats lack of adaptation to the libraries of information conveyed by 4D models [5]. On the other hand, we note that the use of OpenBIM standards (IFC-BCF) has proven its effectiveness in supporting the metadata of 3D models and in supporting a data exchange consisting of virtual reality support software, specifically for game engines [6]. From this perspective, introducing 4D models in virtual reality environments using OpenBIM standards is a promising option.

The objective of this research is to explore this opportunity as a way to propose a new method to improve the integration of 4D simulations in virtual reality environments. This article is structured in five sections. After the first section has introduced the problem, a literature review is proposed in section two. The third section presents the research methodology in the context of Design Science. In the fourth section, a prototype to foster the integration of 4D simulations in Virtual Reality environments is presented. The fifth section concludes the paper.

2   Related Work

The literature review focuses first on the use of 4D BIM models, to define their different aspects and discover recent advances. This section then explores virtual reality and the known practices around this technology in the construction industry. Finally, with the objective of linking the two themes of BIM 4D and virtual reality, recent developments are presented in order to explain the limits and issues that hinder this link. This section ends with a summary of the potential needs and objectives justifying the research approach.

2.1   4D BIM Models in Construction

The planning of construction activities is one of the most important processes in construction management; this process includes the definition of activities and the estimation and programming of resources by identifying the interrelationships between the different tasks of a project [7, 8]. Construction schedules are prepared based on quantities, available resources and other constraints related to project management. The construction activities are then organized according to a work breakdown structure (WBS) to represent a hierarchical breakdown of the construction work to be carried out by the teams in order to achieve the projects objectives [9]. The arrival of BIM has transformed planning and project management practices. By moving from a traditional 2D representation, today's construction schedules can be completed as 4D BIM models [10]. A 4D BIM model is produced by linking the elements of a threedimensional model to the activities of a construction schedule.

The added values of using 4D simulations lie in how they ease the process of communicating ideas and support collaborative work in the context of project reviews and on-site meetings [11]. This technology can also support various practical uses, including studies and analyses of constructability, the detection of spatio-temporal interference, simulation and management of logistics and resources, the planning of excavations, and on-site health and safety management [2]. Aware of the need for collaboration, Boton [2] found that 4D simulation is very useful for carrying out constructability studies. This practice brings actors together very early in a project, in order to analyze and evaluate several construction scenarios and sequences, based on their experience, in order to choose the best construction alternative and validate the feasibility of the schedule. Going beyond other modes of representation such as diagrams and two-dimensional visualization supports, 4D simulation considers the spatial aspect of the construction and becomes a powerful tool for analyzing and anticipating dangerous situations on site, as well as organizing and promoting health and safety on site [12].

The adoption of 4D simulations faces several obstacles, and the technological tools must adapt to the real needs of practitioners. Studies show that current 4D simulation practices are still too limited to support all the suggested options and meet the real needs of the construction industry [13]. Among the technological limitations of 4D simulation tools, Mazars and Francis [14] evoke the problems related to the interoperability of data and the incompatibility between 3D BIM software and 4D simulation. This gap leads to the need for repetitive and redundant processes in order to perform modifications on the model during spatio-temporal conflict detection, among other actions.

With the aim of automating and optimizing the production of construction schedules, Mazars and Francis [14] propose a new method of chronographic modeling of 4D simulations based on the interoperability between the 3D modeling software Revit and the 4D simulation in Navisworks. This interoperability can be exploited to integrate an iterative process to edit data in both software applications as well as to improve the activity of spatio-temporal conflict detection. In the same perspective, Elghaish and Abrishami [18] present an innovative solution in Navisworks using a genetic multicriteria optimization algorithm to automate the production of 4D models and improve the process of selecting construction alternatives. Indeed, to a large extent these works contribute to the integration of a unique and dynamic platform to optimize the production of 4D models. Hakkarainen et al. [19] propose an Augmented Reality-based integration system to consult and compare in real time the progress of the work on a construction site with the data related to its 4D simulation. Ratajczak et al. [20] developed an AR application in the form of a site manager connected to a database that integrates a management system based on the location-based management system (LBMS) using the coding of a location breakdown structure (LBS).

As stated by Boton [2], 4D simulations with today's tools are not able to meet the challenge of adequately representing the collaboration between stakeholders, especially in terms of visualization and interaction. As a way to address this lacuna, Boton evokes the concept of integrating virtual reality technology to support collaboration during constructability analysis meetings.

2.2 Virtual Reality (VR) Systems in the Construction Industry

The use of virtual reality in the construction industry is not new. In 1996, Bouchlaghem and Liyanage [21] were already exploring the potential use of this technology in design processes to provide layout ideas, to approve the ergonomics of future living spaces in relation to several factors, and to assess the risks associated with fires. The use of virtual reality can also be applied in education: to help students understand the essence of different architectural concepts, to conduct more in-depth architectural studies, and to learn how to solve problems with greater openness to new ideas and innovation [22].

Li et al. [23] strongly recommend virtual reality for health and safety training. Studies and tests have shown that through the VR medium, users are more motivated, attentive and remain focused on the subjects in immersive environments. Virtual reality provides an effective visual support that helps to better understand and identify complex engineering problems and thus improve the management of the risks and uncertainties of a future site. With the objective of integrating virtual reality into BIM processes and to support emerging practices, several large software and IT content publishing companies such as Autodesk, Trimble and Unity have embarked on the development of VR solutions and plug-ins to create links with the BIM models.

The work of Huang et al. [24] presents a comparative review of the most popular solutions in the construction industry, based on the features and capabilities they provide to users in an immersive experience, including navigation techniques, annotations, interaction-objects and interaction-data, as well as some criteria related to the communication and collaboration of users. Several of these plug-ins and game engines were tested during this research, using the Oculus Quest and HP Reverb headsets to closely assess the BIM models' integration capabilities.

Overall, the integration of BIM models and data is done according to two methods, either through a transfer flow using exchange formats, or by using an API connection from BIM software (which is the case with most VR plugins). However, we can see that the workflow offered by most of these solutions still does not allow a two-way connection between the VR environment and the BIM software to be integrated so as to synchronize changes in both directions and thereby support a complete process. The exception appears to be the UnityReflect extension, which despite being still in development, is likely to support a two-way data connection from the VR environment to Revit and Navisworks.

2.3   Linking 4D Simulation and Virtual Reality

Some research works [2, 3, 25] have studied the difficult question of the integration of 4D simulations in virtual reality environments. Yerrapathruni [26] conducted multiple experiments to test the application of 4D models in an immersive virtual environment (IVE) and determined that students quickly managed to acquire the experience and instincts related to choosing construction methods, activity sequencing logic, site planning and logistics. The IVE has been a very promising tool, helping practitioners identify and resolve critical issues related to job planning in order to collaboratively develop and generate more realistic and consistent installation sequences. According to Sampaio [3], the combination of 4D models with VR technology makes it possible to explore a construction site virtually, on a real-life scale, to inspect each corner of a model and determine the quantities of materials relating to each construction task. Virtual reality is an effective medium for improving the perception of practitioners and to foster the level of collaboration required to support constructability analysis meetings. The intuitive interaction on the 4D simulation could allow users to develop a much better understanding of the problems and conflicts of a projects schedule in order to generate more realistic construction scenarios [2].

Two approaches are generally used to connect 4D simulations and VR environments. The first approach uses a pipeline connection with BIM software APIs and VR support software in order to visualize and manipulate the 4D model in an immersive environment. Kuncham [27] proposes an application that uses the APIs (.NET) of the Navisworks software to project the 4D simulation in a CAVE system. However, this application is limited by the capacity of Navisworks' APIs; it does not accept the integration of new interactions to perform advanced manipulations on 4D simulation in the virtual reality environment, and so it is mainly used just for visualization purposes. The second approach is better known among developers and consists of integrating BIM data into game engines. We highlight the work of Bourlon and Boton [5], who propose an application for integrating 4D simulations in the virtual environment of the Unity3D game engine to be experimented with the Valyz immersive system. The workflow uses the FBX format to manage the 3D model separately from the construction schedule, which is attached from the Excel software in .CSV format to be integrated and then linked into the Unity3D game engine. The application thus makes it possible to link the temporal data to the elements of the 3D model. In immersion, we can interact with the 4D simulation and visualize the different activities of the calendar. However, the workflow adopted during the preparation and integration of the data remains tedious and does not allow the metadata of the 3D model to be preserved. In addition, the quality of the graphics rendering is not optimal and needs improvement.

Each of the two approaches has their advantages and disadvantages. Nevertheless, the use of game engines as a support for the virtual reality environment is an unlimited resource in terms of the development of interactions and connections, and the quality of the graphics is much more accomplished than the other software and systems. Moreover, in order to capitalize on the value of these experiments, ensure the conditions for inter-action and extend collaboration in the practices, it is necessary to use an interoperable system as described in step 4 of the framework proposed by Boton [2]. However, to develop such a mechanism, the incompatibility of the software and exchange formats remains a formidable challenge.

3   Research Methodology

This research is anchored in the field of Design Science insofar as the objective is to propose a method for integrating 4D simulations in virtual reality environments and to validate it through the development of a prototype. Inspired by work in this field [28, 29], this research approach is organized around the seven guidelines proposed by Hevner and Chatterjee [30] to build and evaluate the artefact: to relate to the design as an artefact, emphasize the relevance of the problem, evaluate the method, assess its contribution to research, ensure research rigor, design as a research process and clearly communicate the research.

Considering that design is both a process and a product, March and Smith [29] identi-fied two complementary and interdependent processes in design science: the construction and evaluation of an artefact. Among other things, an artefact is defined for a particular context, and when that context changes, the artefact can become obsolete. With the aim of bringing the artefact to life, the research approach is based on an evolutionary and incremental process. This process is evolutionary, as it considers the evolution of poten-tial needs and specifications to improve and readjust the prototype to new features, and it is incremental, because it can be iterated multiple times at defined locations, resulting in a new prototype or a working product at the end of each iteration, thereby promoting the continuous improvement of the artefact.

The literature review made it possible to identify and define the research question, and to define and characterize the key concepts of the research. Next, we compared the solutions and evaluated the existing practices, which allowed us to refine the research question and reposition it accordingly. This step involved the identification of the poten-tial needs and target goals of the artefact, and also allowed us to define the criteria for evaluating the proposed artefact. The third step then prioritizes and specifies a set of characteristics and functions elementary to the construction and evaluation of the arte-fact. An artefact in the form of a method is proposed to integrate 4D simulations in a virtual reality environment following an OpenBIM approach based on IFC in step four. Finally, with the objective of evaluating the proposed method, a prototype is developed in the last step using a specific ecosystem of software and tools, which is then validated according to the criteria identified in the second step.

The objective is to develop a complete method suitable for existing systems, which meets the need to optimize the integration and handling of 4D simulations in VR envi-ronments. The method is designed to respond to the work process explored by Boton [2], and is carried out with particular attention to recent developments in BIM-VR, in partic-ular the work of Nandavar et al. [6]. The workflow presented by the method covers three work environments identified as key concepts (Pre-VR, VR and Post-VR) and triggers an iterative integration mechanism structured over six steps. To divide the main issue into several questions, the three concepts are represented by work environments in the rest of the document. This subdivision strategy makes it possible to delineate the systems in order to easily materialize and characterize the design, to bring together the relevant elements and to identify the critical aspects of each work environment to advocate the best possible connection between them.

In addition to the virtual reality (VR) environment that remains at the heart of this project, a Pre-VR environment is represented as a workspace for the preparation of the 4D simulation. Moreover, to integrate a BIM philosophy and incorporate part 4 of the "feedback" mentioned in the framework proposed by Boton [2], it is essential to introduce the concept of a Post-VR environment. This Post-VR environment refers to the definitions of Common Data Environments (CDE) presented in the literature review and requires a complete process.

In order to facilitate its applicability and generalizability, it was necessary to adopt a certain rigor in order to standardize the process and to formalize all the activities. The activities are identified as the critical elements of each step; they are characterized and then analyzed by input and output data with the aim of highlighting the prerequisites and the target objectives to be achieved through the various developments. Subsequently, a set of rules and conditions are generated to support good practices around each activity.

4 Development of a Prototype to Foster the Integration of 4D Simulations in Virtual Reality Environments

4.1 The Prototype

The power and efficiency of this prototype are based primarily on how it simplifies the manufacture and assembly of a WBS, using a new communication strategy that exploits the functionalities of the Tridify tool to automate the integration of PBS entities into WBS planning activities. The simplicity of the development method uses the technique of quickly creating simulations in a VR environment adopted from the work of Lucas [32]. Figure 1 summarizes the prototype development process.

We chose to work with Revit Architecture to model and configure the data, then transfer and integrate them into the Unity3D game engine using the Tridify extension. Given that the motivation for creating a 4D model is to link the WBS elements with a corresponding PBS, it is therefore important to prepare a WBS from the Product Breakdown Structure corresponding to the breakdown of the model once downloaded in Unity3D. The Hierarchy window of the Unity3D engine interface contains a tree structure arranged by level, and each level contains the elements in the entities of the IFC diagram that are dedicated to them.

The code for performing the animation sequencing of WBS activities in the VR environment is in part adopted from recent work by Lucas [32]. It uses an array (Array) to contain the activities of the WBS in their Gameobject forms and has a container to serve as a countdown (increasing from zero) mechanism to trigger the tasks at each defined interaction.

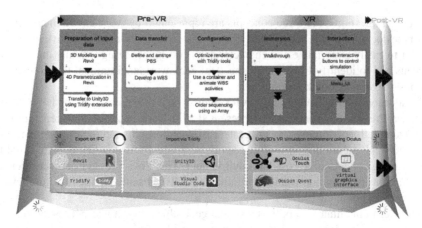

Fig. 1. Summary of the prototype development process

The virtual reality experience was performed using an Oculus Quest headset. Unity3D in its recent versions offers an integration package for Oculus tools. These packages have been particularly useful in the modeling of the virtual character and accessories to build an immersive and intuitive experience. In order to conduct immersive constructability studies, it is useful to provide users with effective navigation techniques so that they can comfortably inspect different aspects of a changing construction site. To this end, the (walkthrough) mode seems to offer a fairly natural navigation compared to other modes such as the (flyover). To achieve this, we used the "OVR Player Controller" from the Oculus integration package. For additional character control and to adjust the camera easily during immersion, we added the possibility of manual rotation via the "SnapRotation" controllers to the automatic tracking that is already done on 6DoF (six degrees of freedom) with the Oculus headset. To achieve walkthrough experience in the VR environment, it is necessary to add collision property to the model elements, including the floors, walls and stairs.

After modeling the virtual character and arranging the immersive environment, the experience must be made interactive. Unity3D offers several packages with the accessories and toolkits necessary to develop the interactions sought by the user in a virtual environment. We used the "XR interaction toolkit" package to develop some interactive functions and capabilities. Beforehand, a Laser Ray (Raycaste) was added to the Oculus controllers to extend the range of user interactions. In order to control the simulation in the immersive environment, we added two arrow buttons to the UI to call the functions "construct the next task" and "deconstruct the existing task". A UI menu in the form of a dashboard was created and attached to one of the user's controllers to accompany him during the immersion. This menu offers as shortcuts giving access to the available functions and interaction capabilities. We also connected the container numbers to a text space in the UI Menu (Fig. 2) in order to simultaneously generate and view the sequence number corresponding to each of the WBS activities triggered in the VR environment.

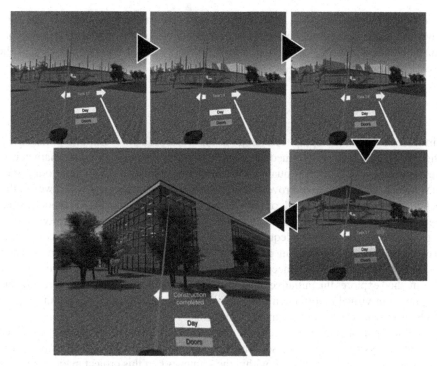

Fig. 2. UI-menu that gives access to VR control functions

4.2   The Validation

In this step, we verify the applicability of the proposed method through the experimentation and the tests carried out on the prototype (the product of the method) and based on the criteria developed in the context of Design Science. The development of the prototype requires the selection of an ecosystem composed of suitable software and tools in order to perform the activities of the process under the best conditions. We validated the performance of the prototype and the effectiveness of the proposed method by testing the prototype. According to the criteria suggested by Hevner and Chatterjee [30] in the context of evaluation by experimentation, we verified the completeness (To what extent does the proposed method meet the integration objectives?), consistency (How does the method adapt to different contexts and under what conditions does it respond to challenges?), ease of use, and accuracy (A manual assessment of the accuracy of the rules that build the method).

The prototype's completeness was assessed and compared to the objectives highlighted at each step of the method. It has been noted that the rules of interactions are insufficient in relation to the convincing objectives of the mechanism. Therefore, it is not yet feasible to use the feedback step to be able to evaluate the method through this first prototype, nor for the iterative aspect of the cycle. The method's consistency was validated, as it is characterized by its ability to be reconfigurable. The formalism of activities can be remodeled and thus can accept different techniques and conditions depending on the software ecosystem. In addition, the method considers certain use ergonomics and accepts a simplified workflow at the heart of the two environments (Pre-VR and VR). Several activities can be automated, such as WBS development, rendering quality optimization and sequencing scheduling, which provides ease of use and accuracy of the results obtained.

5 Conclusion

Virtual reality is a developing technology at the crossroads of several disciplines. Identified as a remarkable visual medium with an immersive and interactive character, in the construction industry it is qualified to enrich and capitalize the value of our digital BIM models, as well as to improve and innovate the traditional practices. However, this technology still expresses a lack of integration, specifically to support 4D models, since the existing connections between 4D simulation software and VR support software such as game engines are still not adequate. The research presented in this article contributes to resolving this issue by creating an artefact in the form of a method that provides a new approach to strengthen the connection of 4D simulations to virtual reality environments. This method explores the initiative of an IFC-based 4D model to support a more efficient integration in virtual reality environments, optimizing data exchange with an iterative mechanism that accepts a two-way exchange link.

Following the hierarchical steps of the proposed method, a prototype was developed using an ecosystem of tools and software adapted to the evaluation of the method. The experimentation on this prototype within the framework of this project made it possible to simplify and standardize a number of activities for the preparation and integration of data, to identify rapid simulation techniques in the Unity3D game engine in order to explore the model in immersion in a virtual reality environment, and to control the dynamism of the 4D simulation following the succession of construction activities based on intuitive interaction.

However, this project did not make it possible to solve all the difficulties of 4D interactions in regards to composing and adjusting the sequencing and scheduling of construction activities in real time during a VR immersion and so it could not meet the challenges related to information return and data extraction. As indicated in the Discussions section, promising future work would be to focus on the aspects of data interaction, collaboration and feedback in order to provide a complete evaluation of the method and thereby develop a prototype capable of meeting the needs of future construction project management.

Funding. This study was funded by *Fonds de recherche du Québec – Nature et technologies (FRQNT), Établissement de la relève professorale* program, Project ID 2021-NC-284064).

References

1. Coyne, K.: Leveraging the power of 4D models for analyzing and presenting CPM schedule delay analyses (2008)
2. Boton, C.: Supporting constructability analysis meetings with Immersive virtual reality-based collaborative BIM 4D simulation. Autom. Constr. **96**, 1–15 (2018)

3. Sampaio, A.Z.: Enhancing BIM methodology with VR technology. In: State of the Art Virtual Reality and Augmented Reality Knowhow, pp. 59–79 (2018)
4. Van Den Berg, M., Hartmann, T., De Graaf, R.: Supporting design reviews with pre-meeting virtual reality environments. J. Inf. Technol. Constr. **22**, 305–321 (2017)
5. Bourlon, S., Boton, C.: Automating the integration of 4D models in game engines for a virtual reality-based construction simulation. In: Luo, Y. (ed.) CDVE 2019. LNCS, vol. 11792, pp. 123–132. Springer, Cham (2019). https://doi.org/10.1007/978-3-030-30949-7_14
6. Nandavar, A., Petzold, F., Schubert, G., Youssef, E.: Opening BIM in a new dimension. A simple, OpenBIM standards based virtual reality collaboration technique for BIM. In: Intelligent & Informed, Proceedings of the 24th International Conference of the Association for Computer-Aided Architectural Design Research in Asia (CAADRIA), pp. 595–604 (2019)
7. Patrick, C.: Construction project planning and scheduling. Prentice Hall, Upper Saddle River (2003)
8. Boton, C.: Conception de vues métiers dans les collecticiels orientés service: Vers des multi-vues adaptées pour la simulation collaborative 4D/nD de la construction (2013)
9. Norman, E.S., Brotherton, S.A., Fried, R.T.: Work Breakdown Structures: The Foundation for Project Management Excellence. Wiley, Hoboken (2008)
10. Tulke, J., Hanff, J.: 4D construction sequence planning: new process and data model. In: Proceedings of 24th CIB-W78 Conference "Bringing ITC Knowledge to Work", pp. 79–84, Maribor, Slovenia (2007)
11. Boton, C., Kubicki, S., Halin, G.: 4D/BIM simulation for pre-construction and construction scheduling. Multiple levels of development within a single case study. In: Creative Construction Conference, pp. 500–505 (2015)
12. Sulankivi, K., Kähkönen, K., Mäkelä, T., Kiviniemi, M.: 4D-BIM for construction safety planning. In: W099-Special Track 18th CIB World Building Congress, May 2010, Salford, United Kingdom, pp. 1–12 (2010)
13. Campagna-wilson, J., Boton, C.: Challenges related to 4D BIM simulation in the construction industry. In: Luo Y. (ed.) CDVE 2020. LNCS, vol. 12341, pp. 270–278. Springer, Cham (2020). https://doi.org/10.1007/978-3-030-60816-3_30
14. Mazars, T., Francis, A.: Chronographical spatiotemporal dynamic 4D planning. Autom. Constr. **112** (2020)
15. Pour Rahimian, F., Seyedzadeh, S., Oliver, S., Rodriguez, S., Dawood, N.: On-demand monitoring of construction projects through a game-like hybrid application of BIM and machine learning. Autom. Constr. **110**, 103012 (2020)
16. Forgues, D., Leonard, M.: Formalisation et analyse du processus de détection d''interférences spatiotemporelles. In: 4th Construction Specialty Conference, pp. 1–9 (2013)
17. Preidel, C., Borrmann, A., Mattern, H., König, M., Schapke, S.-E.: Common data environment. In: Borrmann, A., König, M., Koch, C., Beetz, J. (eds.) Building Information Modeling, pp. 279–291. Springer, Cham (2018). https://doi.org/10.1007/978-3-319-92862-3_15
18. Elghaish, F., Abrishami, S.: Developing a framework to revolutionise the 4D BIM process: IPD-based solution. Constr. Innov. **20**, 401–420 (2020)
19. Hakkarainen, M., Woodward, C., Rainio, K.: Software Architecture for Mobile Mixed Reality and 4D BIM Interaction. In: Proceedings of the 25th CIB W78 Conference, pp. 1–8, Istanbul, Turkey(2009)
20. Ratajczak, J., Riedl, M., Matt, D.T.: BIM-based and AR application combined with location-based management system for the improvement of the construction performance. Buildings **9**, 118 (2019)
21. Bouchlaghem, N.M., Liyanage, I.G.: Virtual reality applications in the UK''s construction industry. http://itc.scix.net/data/works/att/w78-1996-89.content.pdf

22. Kamath, R.S., Dongale, T.D., Kamat, R.K.: Development of virtual reality tool for creative learning in architectural education. Int. J. Qual. Assur. Eng. Technol. Educ. (IJQAETE) **2**, 16–24 (2012)
23. Li, X., Yi, W., Chi, H.L., Wang, X., Chan, A.P.C.: A critical review of virtual and augmented reality (VR/AR) applications in construction safety. Autom. Constr. **86**, 150–162 (2018)
24. Huang, Y., Shakya, S., Odeleye, T.: Comparing the functionality between virtual reality and mixed reality for architecture and construction uses. J. Civil Eng. Archit. **13**, 409–414 (2019)
25. Messner, J.I., Yerrapathuruni, S.C.M., Baratta, A.J., Whisker, V.E.: Using virtual reality to improve construction engineering education. In: American Society for Engineering Education Annual Conference and Exposition, pp. 1–8 (2003)
26. Yerrapathruni, S.: Using 4 D CAD and Immersive Virtual Environments to Improve Construction Planning (2003)
27. Kuncham, K.: Timelining the construction in immersive virtual reality system using BIM application (2013). https://oaktrust.library.tamu.edu/handle/1969.1/151003
28. Loup-Escande, É., Burkhardt, J.-M.: Évaluer l''utilité dans le contexte des technologies émergentes pour identifier des besoins latents: éléments issus d'une analyse des interactions en situation d'usage. Activités (2019)
29. March, S.T., Smith, G.F.: Design and natural science research on information technology. Decis. Support Syst. **15**, 251–266 (1995)
30. Hevner, A., Chatterjee, S.: Design science in information systems research. In: Integrated Series in Information Systems, pp. 75–105. Springer (2004)
31. Pradère, T., Gaillard, I., Pomian, J.-L.: Comprendre les pratiques de l'ingénierie: un impératif pour mieux cibler le contenu de leur formation initiale en ergonomie. In: XXIIème congrès de la Société d''Ergonomie de Langue Française. Recherche, pratique, formation en ergonomie (1997)
32. Lucas, J.: Rapid development of virtual reality based construction sequence simulations: a case study. J. Inf. Technol. Constr. **25**, 72–86 (2020)

Collective Knowledge Management in City Planning: Building Spatial-Cognition Ontologies from Literary Works

Maria Rosaria Stufano Melone and Domenico Camarda[✉]

DICATECh, Polytechnic University of Bari, Bari, Italy
domenico.camarda@poliba.it

Abstract. Due to the multiple dimensions of urban complexity, ontology-based multiagent models become widespread. These models seem to support complex relational and cognitive interactions in urban decision-making processes. In this context, simulations and experiments are today investigating ontologies applied to spatial planning, as a support in the real world.

Useful feedback can be also found in extensive narratives of some literary works. We explored spatial representations in them, aiming to investigate the complex features and attributes structuring urban spaces, and to develop ontological analyses. A multiagent experimentation was developed with university students, individually selecting extracts from relevant literary works dealing with urban environments, according to the judgment of each student.

This paper focuses in particular on the landmark of the urban square (or 'piazza'), to build an ontology of the square that includes aspects of literary semantics. The reference foundational ontology is DOLCE ontology, represented through Protégé 5.5.0 software.

Keywords: Knowledge management · Decision support · Urban planning · Ontology

1 Introduction

A consolidated scientific literature today confirms the shared awareness of the great dimensional multiplicity of urban complexity [1, 2]. This multiple dimensionality contributes to the formation of an open and very dynamic system, with many different agents, characterized by emergent properties that are the effect of this dynamism [3, p.53]. The most typically representative agents of the city are human agents. They contribute to a complex stratification of artifacts but also of relational and behavioral aspects [4, 5]. These are explicit or tacit relationships, stable or uncertain but unavoidable for the development of cities. An effective management model of such

---

The present paper is the result of a more extensive research project. It has been entirely written by the two authors together.

© Springer Nature Switzerland AG 2021
Y. Luo (Ed.): CDVE 2021, LNCS 12983, pp. 115–125, 2021.
https://doi.org/10.1007/978-3-030-88207-5_12

a complex system should therefore aim to structurally involve natural but also artificial environmental components, together with infrastructural elements or technological support and enhancement of urban dynamics.

This has led to a general reluctance to address such management problems in a systematic way, neglecting more elaborate agent-based approaches where agents are biotic but also abiotic, and the natural or built environment is itself often considered as an agent [6]. Yet in this context, multi-agent models capable of supporting complex interactions between agents, cognitive exchanges and informed decision-making seem possible system architectures [7]. In particular, technology becomes a critical support for intelligent systems to structure the problems posed by the fuzzy and dynamic uncertainty of complex environments, especially cities. This is a technological emphasis recognized today as a critical factor in characterizing a smart city as such [8]. Today, the concept of smart city suggests intelligently connecting times, spaces and agents through geographical and physical relationships but also through emotional, creative and informal trusts. In this context, the concept of smart city represents the ability of the city to exist, maintain itself, progress as a multi-agent entity (an 'agency'), intelligently interconnected in its intimate constituents.

In this approach, consciously complex, planning, policymaking, as well as dynamic decision-making actions benefit in terms of sustainability and effectiveness of urban governance. However, the operational terms of this transformation of complex knowledge into action still remain complex and 'wicked' [9]. Recently, an ontology-based approach emerged as an interesting opportunity for the analysis and understanding of such multidimensional cognitive assortment. It came out as an adequate formalization model of smart-city management architectures [10]. Some lines of research have followed, resulting in a number of explorative publications [11–14]. Currently, research activities on ontologies applied to planning have been developed by our group, on the construction of ontologies integrated by multilevel and multidisciplinary knowledge [13, 15, 16].

In particular, practical activities were developed in recent years at the Polytechnic University of Bari, Italy. They have often aimed at investigating perspectives for the evolution of research on ontologies applied to planning, in support of the activities carried out in the real field. The knowledge investigated along these experiments had to do with the concept of spatial cognition, especially with the search for material and non-material, proper and interpreted features of the relationship spaces of human agents in their mental or expressed representation activity.

In this context, interaction with the community is necessary to elicit and exchange knowledge from below, as occurring in a mutual learning environment [17]. Interaction with expert agents for formal and formalized multidisciplinary knowledge is also useful [18]. But in the field of spatial planning, a traditional social inspiration often involves aspects of storytelling and narratives [19]. In this direction, we can also note that many spatial representations can be traced in narration expressions, especially in written narrations, found in literature productions. Different literary genres have always grappled with the representation of spaces: prose, poetry, novels. Therefore, we decided to explore such representations, with the aim of investigating on features and attributes of complex urban environment spaces, and to develop an ontological analysis. In this context, a multi-agent experimentation carried out with university students of the Urban planning program aimed at identifying literary works that deal with cities and urban environments in a narrative context, identifying salient aspects of the individual contributions according to the judgment of each student. Some preliminary results of this experience have been published in the past years and constitute the first step of the entire research [20, 21].

The research work now continues exploring the potential of narration-based investigation after the previous preliminary results, in more illustrative and explanatory terms. The analysis was carried out to one of the landmarks of Lynch's renowned works: the urban square [22]. Therefore, the general objective of this work represents a second step of the entire research. That is building an ontology of the square that includes aspects of literary semantics, framed in a context of support for urban spatial organization, planning and/or design. Specifically, this paper concerns the construction, in an ontological key, of a first taxonomy of the urban square, using the results of the university experimentation on narratives and comparing it with another taxonomy of the square coming from traditional architectural/urban planning manuals [23–25]. The aim is to investigate actual differences between the two taxonomies in catching the spatial-cognition complexity. The foundational ontology of reference is DOLCE ontology, structurally represented through Protégé 5.5.0 software.

The paper consists in the following sections. After this introduction, a section deals with the methodological framework of the research, with particular reference to the planning-oriented and decision-oriented operational aspects of the city. The third section introduces the case study, analyzing the results achieved, while the fourth section comments and discusses the results in the actual research context and towards future perspectives.

2   A Background of Complex Knowledge and Ontology in Planning

Our knowledge of the city and our communication about it occurs between different human (and non-human) agents and is made of words: it mainly consists of natural language. Natural language generally uses implicit meanings and hidden semantic subtleties, so that often its reliability does not reach the level required by some particular activities -as in this case, for example, the technical activities concerning the transformation of the city. The richness of the notion of the city with its complex dynamics has always been a challenge for the planner who has only limited modelling methodologies and techniques available, while it is increasingly clear that the planner is called to identify and manage a great variety of information and points of view.

The role of formal ontology is bringing together different but coherent worldviews. It is a specification of conceptualization in a knowledge domain. Moreover, it helps in sharing disambiguated meanings. Formal ontologies allow for example to characterize the different types of agents that take part in a process, with their behaviours [26, 27].

Our knowledge of places often derives from experiences, from our feelings about them. There is, therefore, a 'subjective knowledge' of places, which is synthesized by a consonance of intentions and experiences in collective knowledge - enriched by the chorus of individuals who form it (such as the inhabitants of a city centre). It is a question of memory and perspective, but often it is also a question of intentionality, that is even able to start the knowledge of places. 'Subjective knowledge' is a kind of representation of places, and a representation varies from agent to agent and even during an agent's life. With this applied ontological base we can refer to another kind of knowledge implementation, as said previously, i.e., the one we can elicit from prose, novels, poems.

The ontological analysis is the study of what is at the center of a vision of reality. It helps our reading of a given domain. It clarifies and organizes the essential elements and characteristics, for example of places, in terms of objects, properties and processes. We have dealt with applied ontology in the domain of urban and territorial planning in previous research [10, 15, 28]. It mainly aimed to make explicit and clarify the different terminologies involved and to extract interconnections and contrasts through the agents' perspectives or in the available elicited knowledge. Then we proposed a subdivision into ontological levels (such as spatial, artefactual, cognitive, social, cultural) and process (about events over time). Explaining them through the ontological analysis method favours a new basic clarity concerning the 'real' materials with which we act and with which we interface, helping us to propose a self-aware and explicit knowledge system in its semantic-semiological levels. For example: what kind of relationship does the city have with time? Is time a kind of relationship external to the unfolding frame of the dynamics of a city? Time modelling is a special relationship in ontology and a relationship that presents a particular form of complexity in city ontology.

The method described here aims to offer a different, integrative way of supporting planning and managing the territory, that can be even more articulated and advanced in the future.

3 Ontological Support to Decision from a Literary-Based Case Study

This paper draws its materials from a collective exercise carried out with the students of the Urban planning course at the Polytechnic University of Bari. It was carried out by administering an interactive questionnaire with Google forms, through which each student was asked to select from their usual readings three literary passages that dealt with the city. The first general results of this experiment have been published. The experiment was carried out with the aim of contributing to an ontological approach to the spatial analysis of the city, populated with data taken from the literary materials themselves, for purposes of spatial decision support [20, 21]. The general organization of the research involves multi-source cognitive experiments, to be developed through interaction with urban communities, with experts, as well as through the reading of structured, textual or graphic formal data. The general layout can be summarized through a flow chart excerpted from previous papers and shown in Fig. 1.

In this framework, the present work addresses the next step of the research program. In fact, with the aim of investigating the structuring potential of an ontology starting from the experimentation on literary works, we decided to analyze the concept of square (or "*piazza*"), in the works where it is mentioned or described. We have chosen the square among the landmarks recalled by Lynch's famous work [22], as an element genetically embedded in a city (starting from the Agora of the Greeks or the Forum of the Romans)

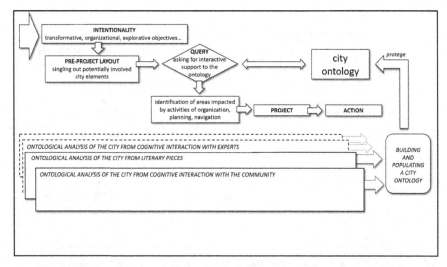

Fig. 1. Phases of ontology building for decision support . (figure taken from [20])

both from a physical, symbolic and social point of view. Therefore, in a first phase we explored the database of the answers of the 160 students to the questionnaire, consisting of 480 literary excerpts. Out of the cited excerpts, 90 contained even a minimal reference to the square, but very often the passage chosen by the students was the same (students seem to have very similar readings!). By eliminating double citations and neglecting those excerpts in which the square was cited without contextualization or description, we finally found 7 passages, including 4 passages from novels and essays, and 3 passages from poems. In relation to these 7 works, relational graphic maps have been developed to highlight the conceptual elements involved: an example of an Italian poem is shown in Fig. 2 [29]. The elements are written in Italian since all the students considered only Italian works. In the paper we have kept the original language throughout the description, to maintain consistency of meaning and of syntactic links, but the final results can be easily translated if needed.

Aiming at a final ontological formalization of the square reported in literature, we decided to create a taxonomic description of it, using DOLCE ontology, lite version, as a structure [30]. This environment was chosen because according to the literature it appears to be the most suitable ontological structure for engineering applications and is dynamically articulated both in concrete and abstract levels. This allows to include many material, immaterial and conceptual aspects, even dynamic ones, which are especially embedded in the complexity of literary representation. For the representation of the structure, we used the well-known software Protégé 5.5.0, from Stanford University, and an extract of the taxonomy of the square built on all 7 maps of the literary works is shown in Fig. 3. Please note that both Fig. 3 and subsequent Fig. 4 are not put down for the purpose of verbatim detailing all classes and subclasses. The two figures are put down with the sole purpose of showing the general articulation level of the LT and TT classifications. Obviously, such large scale limits Protégé's ability to detail mapped written texts here. However, the readability of the mapped texts is not functional in this

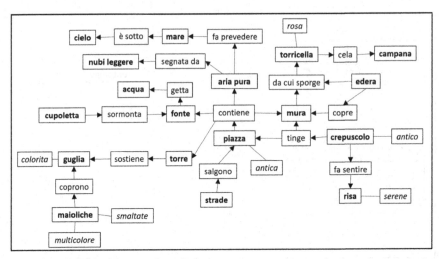

Fig. 2. Example of a relational map of the 'literary' square (bold = nouns, locutions; italic = adjectives; other = verbs)

context, and its lessening does not affect the significance of the figures. In fact, at this large scale, the visual comparison immediately supports the evidence of the significant differences in complexity and richness between the two taxonomies.

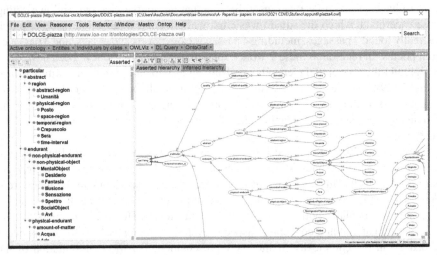

Fig. 3. Partial excerpt from the 'literary' square taxonomy on DOLCE lite ontology (screenshot from Protégé 5.5.0)

The structure of DOLCE lite has not been completed with the intrinsic and relational properties of the individual elements at this stage. However, the taxonomy thus structured allows to maintain and highlight the representative complexity of the concept of square. It is a fine representation in terms of classes - indeed subclasses, as the classes (or superclasses) are already formally defined on the ontological root of DOLCE. In this organization, the literary taxonomy (LT) contains 121 subclasses. An amount of 63 subclasses can be classified as *endurant*. This means something having no conceptually distinguishable temporal parts and thus existing in its entirety at each instant of its existence - e.g., being F at time t and *nonF* at time $t + n$ [31]. Other 51 subclasses can be classified as *perdurant*. They are entities extended in time by temporal parts, that are partially present over time but may be not necessarily present along the entire time - e.g., one phase of a whole, which is present now, may not be present in the future [32]. The rather numerous presence of the subclasses of *endurant* and *perdurant* suggests that in LT the elements of dynamism of the square (particularly *perdurant*) are fundamental to characterize its conceptualization. This seems to be in line with the role played by the square in the spatial and social organization of the city [33].

In this regard, a further parallel survey was developed in order to verify the relevance and relative importance of LT in a perspective of complexity, compared to more traditional conceptualizations of the square. In particular, a comparative analysis was developed with an ontology derived from traditional manual and didactic texts of urban architecture and planning - given the orientation of the work towards spatial planning and design objectives [23–25]. An excerpt of the 'traditional' square taxonomy (TT) is given in Fig. 4.

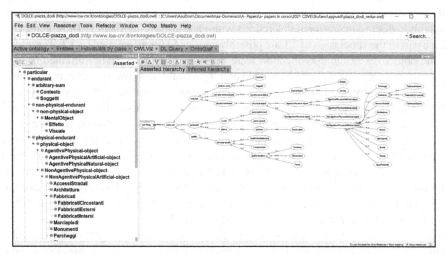

Fig. 4. Partial excerpt from the manual-based square taxonomy on DOLCE lite ontology (screenshot from Protégé 5.5.0).

Along this representation, TT contains only 23 subclasses. An amount of 17 subclasses are *endurant*, while only one is *perdurant* (namely "Observing"). *Endurant*s here are essentially physical architectures, monuments, roads, sidewalks, buildings.

Carrying out a comparison between LT and TT, an imbalance between *endurant* and *perdurant* in the two cases seems evident. Generally speaking, this at least suggests that the role of time is very limitedly considered in TT, while it seems a great value in LT. A vision of an essentially physical and static type emerges in TT, which almost shows a sort of screenshot and does not seem to include the square in the flow of life of a city. This circumstance is also confirmed by the absence of agentive components in TT (in LT they are 10) and of temporal regions in TT (in LT they are 2).

Moving forward with the comparison, we can analyze mental objects, as part of the non-physical nature of *endurants*. In literary taxonomy there are 5 mental objects, while they are 2 in TT. In LT they are perceptions, sensations, mental objects as active motions of individual agents. In TT, on the other hand, these are more general and aggregated characteristics. Again, the focus here seems to be on generalizing a subjective interpretation rather than on individual aspects of perception. This circumstance seems to confirm a limitation of TT in the representation of the intrinsic complexity of the urban 'piazza' environment and of the relationships it exerts.

The disproportion between the two taxonomies emerges in an evident way, but actually also reflects clearly intrinsic characters. In particular, the spartan TT derives from an articulation driven not by descriptive aims but by design needs. In them, much is typically left to the sensitivity of the designer and many elements of abstract characterization are considered implicit and embedded in the effect of the final composition. Yet LT has the merit of making a large part of those tacit elements explicit, limiting the interpretation of the planner or designer to a more intimately creative or 'artistic' part and therefore discretionary only to a more limited extent. However, this reduction does not appear as a burden of constraints and prescriptions, but rather an enrichment of the conceptual basis towards the achievement of more aware and informed decisions, suitably reducing operational discretions without constraining them [34]. In general, a large part of the subclasses of TT are possibly contained (or articulated) in LT. Therefore, if the objectives of the classification were the same (e.g. both design-oriented or both description-oriented), a single integrated ontology could be drawn from this perspective.

In a more implementation-oriented discourse, we can for example hypothesize that there is a need for support for the design of a square that is specifically characterized perceptually. Looking at the classes that are represented in the ontological taxonomy, we can think, for example, of a square that should arouse a sense of security in socialization during twilight ('sense', 'security', 'socializing' and 'twilight' are in fact represented classes). An ad-hoc query made on an ontological structure of the square (once the ontology is completed with properties, instances, data, etc.) could be carried out through a special function provided by Protégé. A coherently articulated result for a useful design support would be guaranteed especially referring to LT, since the use of TT alone would in any case imply a high degree of interpretative discretion on the part of the designer, which might not guarantee an adequate response to actual needs in a complex operational context.

4 Conclusions

This work is part of the search for decision support systems (DSS) for spatial planning, design or organization based on the management of multi-agent and multi-source spatial knowledge, particularly in the urban environment. In order to mirror the intrinsic complexity of urban systems, the organization of spatial knowledge should include the aspects of environmental, situational, social and dynamic complexity that characterize cities. For this reason it was decided to use the ontological analysis approach discussed above.

Our previous and still ongoing research activities refer to the management of diffused knowledge expressed from below by urban communities, or elicited among disciplinary experts, or developed within narratives - particularly those written in different literary genres. In these research areas, collective experiments have been developed in real contexts or in simulations carried out with university students. The present work sought to explore the potential for building ontologies based on literary narratives, using various conceptualizations of the urban square within an experiment conducted at the Polytechnic University of Bari.

Two simple taxonomies of the square were thus developed, grafted onto the ontological structure of DOLCE lite, and were compared. In this framework, they have shown some suggestions. In particular, the conceptual and relational analysis of the literary square has shown a fair possibility of building a coherent taxonomy, rather rich in concepts, attributes and spatial links. It contains an assortment of both concrete, abstract, situational, dynamic and agentive elements, which make it possible to interestingly represent the spatial and cognitive complexity that characterizes a square in its environmental and social role in the city.

Based on the results, it is likely that such an approach could be extended to other landmarks or important elements of the city, envisioning an extension of the approach to the city as a whole, in perspective. In addition, we are dealing with the elicitation of elements that are not always easy to draw from direct interaction with agents of a community within participatory knowledge processes from below, nor through the involvement of expert knowledge agents [35–37]. Therefore, it is reasonable to think that the construction of ontological environments to support decision-making in the urban environment can appropriately benefit from this integration made starting from literary narratives.

In this context, the work of this short study suggests that some useful follow-ups could be developed in perspective. Initially, the ontological construction of the square will be completed including properties, instances, formal relationships, thus enabling the formulation of queries, operationally coherent with an ontology-based DSS functionality. Subsequently, an attempt will be made to extend the ontological structure to other urban parts, up to targeting the entire city system if possible. The ultimate results of this formalization effort will then be further investigated and possibly structured, in order to integrate them within the process scenario indicated in the original layout in Fig. 1.

Therefore, our research activities will be oriented towards these objectives for the near future.

References

1. Lichfield, N., Barbanente, A., Borri, D., Khakee, A., Prat, A. (eds.): Evaluation in Planning: Facing the Challenge of Complexity. Springer, Dordrecht (2013). https://doi.org/10.1007/978-94-017-1495-2
2. De Roo, P.G., Van Wezemael, P.J., Hillier, P.J.: Complexity and Planning: Systems Assemblages and Simulations. Ashgate, London (2012)

3. Portugali, J.: Complexity Cognition and the City. Springer, Berlin (2011). https://doi.org/10.1007/978-3-642-19451-1
4. Simon, H.A.: Bounded rationality and organizational learning. Organ. Sci. **2**, 125–134 (1991)
5. Borri, D., Camarda, D., Pluchinotta, I.: Planning urban microclimate through multiagent modelling: a cognitive mapping approach In: Luo, Y. (ed.) CDVE 2013. LNCS, vol. 8091, pp. 169–176. Springer, Heidelberg (2013). https://doi.org/10.1007/978-3-642-40840-3_25
6. Arentze, T., Timmermans, H.: Multi-agent models of spatial cognition, Learning and complex choice behavior in urban environments. In: Portugali, J. (ed.) Complex Artificial Environments. Springer, Berlin (2006). https://doi.org/10.1007/3-540-29710-3_12
7. Pereira, G., Prada, R., Santos, P.A.: Integrating social power into the decision-making of cognitive agents. Artif. Intell. **241**, 1–44 (2016)
8. Geertman, S., Ferreira, J., Goodspeed, R., Stillwell, J. (eds.): Planning Support Systems and Smart Cities. LNGC, Springer, Cham (2015). https://doi.org/10.1007/978-3-319-18368-8
9. Rittel, H.W.J., Webber, M.M.: Dilemmas in a general theory of planning. Policy Sci. **4**, 155–169 (1973)
10. Borgo, S., Borri, D., Camarda, D., Stufano Melone, M.R.: An ontological analysis of cities, smart cities and their components. In: Nagenborg, M., Stone, T., González Woge, M., Vermaas, P.E. (eds.) Technology and the City. PET, vol. 36, pp. 365–387. Springer, Cham (2021). https://doi.org/10.1007/978-3-030-52313-8_18
11. Calafiore, A., Boella, G., Borgo, S., Guarino, N.: Urban artefacts and their social roles: towards an ontology of social practices. In: Proceedings of the 13th International Conference on Spatial Information Theory, pp. 1–13. Dagstuhl Publishing, L'Aquila (2017)
12. Bhatt, M., Hois, J., Kutz, O.: Ontological modelling of form and function for architectural design. Appl. Ontol. **7**, 1–32 (2011)
13. Borri, D., Camarda, D., Stufano Melone, M.R.: Modelling the knowledge of urban complexity: the role of ontologies in spatial design tasks. In: Ferreira, J., Goodspeed, R. (eds.) Planning Support Systems and Smart Cities (CUPUM 2015), pp. 16015–16019. MIT, Boston (2015)
14. Camarda, D., Mastrodonato, G., Patano, M.: The collective construction and management of spatial knowledge in open spaces: a pilot study In: Luo, Y. (ed.) CDVE 2019. LNCS, vol. 11792, pp. 236–243. Springer, Cham (2019). https://doi.org/10.1007/978-3-030-30949-7_27
15. Stufano, R., Borri, D., Camarda, D., Borgo, S.: Knowledge of places: an ontological analysis of the social level in the city. In: Papa, R., Fistola, R., Gargiulo, L. (eds.) Smart Planning: Sustainability and Mobility in the Age of Change, pp. 3–14. Springer, Berlin (2018). https://doi.org/10.1007/978-3-319-77682-8_1
16. Stufano, R., Borri, D., Camarda, D., Borgo, S.: Knowledge organization for community revitalization: An ontological approach in Taranto industrial city. In: Colombo, G., Lombardi, P., Mondini, G. (eds.) 2016 INPUT Conference: E-Agorà/e-ἀγορά for the Transition toward Resilient Communities, pp. 441–446. Politecnico di Torino, Torino (2016)
17. Schön, D.A., Argyris, C.: Organizational Learning II: Theory, Method and Practice. Addison-Wesley, Reading (1996)
18. Fischer, F.: Citizens, Experts, and the Environment: The Politics of Local Knowledge. Duke University Press, Durham (2000)
19. Goldstein, B.E., Wessells, A.T., Lejano, R., Butler, W.: Narrating resilience: transforming urban systems through collaborative storytelling. Urban Stud. **52**, 1285–1303 (2015)
20. Stufano Melone, M.R., Borgo, S., Camarda, D., Borri, D.: Spatial design, planning processes and literary works on cities: an ontological approach for integrating heterogeneous knowledge. In: Carlotti, P., Ficarelli, L., Ieva, M. (eds.) Reading Built Spaces: Cities in the Making and Future Urban Form, pp. 1143–1154. U+D Editions, Roma (2019)

21. Stufano Melone, M.R., Borgo, S., Camarda, D., Borri, D.: Heterogeneous knowledge for sustainable planning: notes from ontology-based experimentations. In: Yang, X.S., Dey, N., Joshi, A. (eds.) Third IEEE Conference on Smart Trends in Systems Security and Sustainablity (WorldS4), pp. 43–47. Research Publishing Services, London (2019)
22. Lynch, K.: The Image of the City. The MIT Press, Cambridge (1960)
23. Moughtin, C., Cuesta, R., Signoretta, P., Sarris, C.: Urban Design: Method and Techniques. Architectural Press, Oxford (1999)
24. Tagliaventi, G.: Manuale di architettura urbana. Pàtron, Bologna (2007)
25. Dodi, L.: Città e Territorio: Urbanistica Tecnica. Masson, Milano (1972)
26. Masolo, C., Oltramari, A., Gangemi, A., Guarino, N., Vieu, L.: La prospettiva dell'ontologia applicata. Rivista di Estetica. **22**, 170–183 (2003)
27. Guarino, N., Oberle, D., Staab, S.: What is an ontology? In: Staab, S., Studer, R. (eds.) Handbook on Ontologies, pp. 1–17. Springer, Berlin (2009). https://doi.org/10.1007/978-3-540-92673-3_0
28. Stufano Melone, M.R., Borri, D., Camarda, D., Borgo, S.: Knowledge of places: an ontological analysis of places and their semantic stratifications. Plurimondi, pp. 103–115 (2017)
29. Campana, D.: Canti Orfici e Altre Poesie. Garzanti, Milano (1989)
30. Borgo, S., Masolo, C.: Ontological foundations of DOLCE. In: Poli, R., Healy, M., Kameas, A. (ed.) Theory and Applications of Ontology: Computer Applications, pp. 279–295. Springer, Dordrecht (2010). https://doi.org/10.1007/978-90-481-8847-5_13
31. Cresswell, M.J.: Why objects exist but events occur. Stud. Logica. **45**, 371–375 (1986)
32. Gangemi, A., Guarino, N., Masolo, C., Oltramari, A., Schneider, L.: Sweetening ontologies with DOLCE. In: Gómez-Pérez, A., Benjamins, V.R. (eds.) EKAW 2002. LNCS (LNAI), vol. 2473, pp. 166–181. Springer, Heidelberg (2002). https://doi.org/10.1007/3-540-45810-7_18
33. Madanipour, A.: Public and Private Spaces of the City. Routledge, London (2003)
34. Stufano Melone, M.R.: Ontologie della creatività: Memorie e decisioni creative in architettura. FrancoAngeli, Milano (2019)
35. Pluchinotta, I., Esposito, D., Camarda, D.: Fuzzy cognitive mapping to support multi-agent decisions in development of urban policymaking. Sustain. Cities Soc. **46**, 101402 (2019)
36. Borri, D., Camarda, D., De Liddo, A.: Envisioning environmental futures: multi-agent knowledge generation, frame problem, cognitive mapping. In: Luo, Y. (ed.) CDVE 2004. LNCS, vol. 3190, pp. 230–237 (2004). https://doi.org/10.1007/978-3-540-30103-5_27
37. Gertler, M.S., Wolfe, D.A.: Local social knowledge management: community actors, institutions and multilevel governance in regional foresight exercises. Futures **36**, 45–65 (2004)

Cooperative Dynamic Programmable Devices Using Actor Model for Embedded Systems of Microcontrollers

Sylvia Encheva[1](✉) and Sharil Tumin[2]

[1] Western Norway University of Applied Sciences, 5030 Bergen, Norway
sbe@hvl.no
[2] SISINT, 5020 Bergen, Norway
sharil@trimensity.tech

Abstract. IoT devices are everywhere. Developing embedded system software is a challenge. Embedded systems are inherently event-driven and concurrent multitasks. Coroutine-based concurrency is better suited than multi-threading on microcontrollers with limited computing resources. Using higher interpreted language and a robust cooperative model will help. An Actor Model implemented in MicroPython can provide a solution for agile development and deployment of dynamically programmable devices in actor-based networks.

Keywords: Actor model · Dynamic programmable devices · Embedded system · Concurrency · Cooperative Internet of Things

1 Introduction

1.1 IoT and Programmable Devices

IoT (Internet Of Things) [1] is nothing new. But the usage of the term contributes to a lot of confusion in the industry. This is due to its usage as a marketing gimmick as something new is desirable. Not all IP (Internet Protocol) network-connected things are IoT devices. It may be even dangerous to connect certain controlling devices to the open Internet. It is much more accurate and productive to say NOD (Network Of Programmable Devices) to talk about all 'smart' devices ubiquitously around our daily life nowadays. A thing is something that exists, while a PD (Programmable Devices) is a useful thing. A network is any form of connectivity, not only an IP-based network.

Another misused word is 'smart' [2]. This is also due to marketing people. Anything which is programmable and with network capabilities is coined smart. Most of these devices can not make decisions (and we certainly will not want that at this very moment), at most what they can do is to provide us with data for our informed decision-making processes. It takes hundreds of PDs to make a 'smart' appliance. Most of these PDs are one-time programmable. The many different firmware they have were programmed at the factories to enable them with simple functional capabilities. A scriptable device is a PD capable of dynamic programmability, a new script (i.e. program) can be uploaded to the device after deployment and during its operation.

© Springer Nature Switzerland AG 2021
Y. Luo (Ed.): CDVE 2021, LNCS 12983, pp. 126–137, 2021.
https://doi.org/10.1007/978-3-030-88207-5_13

Most of the time, we are unaware of the NOD. These PDs are small and embed in our daily appliances, for example, phones, printers, coffeemakers, dishwashers, and so on. One important property all these devices have in common is that they have sensors. These sensors are designed and put in place to enable environmental sensing, collecting data for their specific functionalities. A PD with more sensors appears to be smarter than those with a few sensors. A PD with more sensors can provide developers with more sensing data to be used to program 'smart' solutions to decision problems. For example, a coffeemaker with only a temperature sensor, a timer, and a buzzer can only measure temperature and time, while another coffeemaker with a temperature sensor, a timer, a camera, and a WiFi (Wireless) can do much more 'smart' thing.

1.2 Microcontrollers in Embedded Systems

Generally, we talk about CPU (central processing unit) to mainframe computers or even PCs (personal computers). Take, for example, the new 10th generation Intel Core I9 has 10 cores with 20 MByte cache, supports 20 threads, and running at 5.3 GHz (Giga Cycles per second). Its peripheral bus runs in the order of 8 GT/s (Gigatransfers per second) or 1 GB/s (Giga Bytes per second) of raw data. A system using such a CPU can support tens of GB (Giga Bytes) RAM (Random Access Memory), I9 supports up to 128 GB of RAM. It is not uncommon that a low-end PC is equipped with at least 8 GB RAM.

The story is completely the opposite when it comes to processing units for embedded systems. In this case, we will talk about MCU (microcontrollers unit). An MCU runs at tens of MHz (Mega Cycles per second). Compared to a CPU, an MCU runs at a snail pace. Mobile embedded systems run on batteries. Power consumption is directly related to processing speed. Another important difference between CPU and MCU is that primary memory RAM and secondary memory FLASH (non-volatile memory storage medium) is usually a part of the SOC (system on chip) package. The size is fixed and in the order of hundreds of KB (KiloBytes). Obviously, the embedded system developers are working with constrained computing resources.

The developers need to have a different mindset when working on embedded system development. It was not too long time ago when developers need to program using a specific Assembly language specific to the MCU. This was too cumbersome and non-productive. By using header files where different MCU definitions are done, developers can use a higher language, like C, to program. The source code in C is compiled to machine code of a specific MCU. The compiled machine code firmware is then uploaded (burn, flash) to the flash memory of the MCU with a flashing tool. Now, it is even possible to use an interpreted language for example Basic, Lua, JavaScript, or Python on a high-end MCU. Developers can use scripts to program embedded systems rather than statically programming them based on one-time firmware. Using a script, the logic running in an interpreter-enabled embedded system can be changed dynamically. Consider PDs buried in concrete or orbiting in satellites. The ability to script, i.e. dynamically programmable will surely provide new opportunities and challenges on the way we deal with embedding 'intelligence' into our 'smart' devices.

At the edge, where software meets hardware, the behavior of an embedded system is predominately event-driven. It is no accident that JavaScript is the dominant programming language of the Web, JavaScript supports the event-driven programming paradigm naturally. It was designed for this purpose using event callbacks. JavaScript enters the main event loop implicitly. We never see forever-loop as in C programming code. We do not see threading in JavaScript either, because it runs time virtual machine runs in a single thread. Different routines get scheduled to run based on event-based logic. Developers write programs using 'on' event callbacks which wait on event 'emit' signal from system or user defines subroutines. JavaScript programming model suited embedded system development very well. Indeed, a JavaScript run-time virtual machine call Espruino [3] can be deployed on resource constrain MCU have been in the offering as an open-source project for sometimes now.

2 Concurrency

2.1 MicroPython

However, in this work, we opted for MicroPython [4]. MicroPython was a complete rewrite in C of Python 3.4 with many programming languages constructs for MCU GPIO (General Purpose Input Output), hardware peripherals like UART (Universal Asynchronous Receiver/Transmitter), SPI (Serial Peripheral Interface), I2C (Inter-Integrated Circuit), RTC (Real Time Clock), Timers and Interrupts, plus some Python 3.5 features like asynchronous coroutines. MicroPython interpreter and the run-time engine are uploaded into the flash memory of an MCU as firmware acting as OS (Operating System). It is small and efficiently designed as it can run on a low-end 32bits MCU with only 256 KB of ROM and 16 KB of RAM. An MCU with MicroPython is a NOP and can be programmed directly using REPL (Read–Eval–Print Loop), but also provide provision to run application script at boot time using editable flash storage boot.py and main.py special files. MicroPython includes *asyncio* as a Python frozen module as a standard library. A frozen module is a precompiled Python script appended to the firmware and becomes a part of it to add extra functionality. This ability to insert Python scripts into the firmware makes MicroPython adaptable, customizable, and flexible.

The standard *asyncio* provides support for non-blocking sleep, non-blocking stream IO (Input/Output), async/await coroutine programming construct. However, after having said that, we will develop a simple Actor based framework that is both transparent and easy to use. MicroPython *asyncio* has a total of 855 lines of code with 2852 words, while our *act* module has only 39 lines of code with 97 words.

2.2 Multitasking

Developing multi-threaded programs is difficult. Programmers may use sophisticated static analysis methods to weed-out problems at an early stage of development [5]. Preemptive multitasking as in time-multiplex multi-threading has its share of subtle problems that may be difficult to solve. Shared resources, for example, global scope memory storage, need protection from multiple access consequences using locking mechanism on a critical region, precise scheduling is difficult to implement due to non-deterministic of time-multiplexing interlacing with low level interrupt routines and difficulties in managing critical resources like memories and processing time. It is important to remember that each created thread consumes RAM resources to save threads contacts and states. Executing concurrent tasks in multiple threads is not scalable.

It is of paramount importance that those problems are solved due to the explosive growth of IoT in all parts of our life; health, manufacturing, business, smart cities, and homes.

Most multi-threading implementations on MCU are based on RTOS (Real-Time Operating System) running in a single core and are therefore inherently time-multiplex. This is to say, a thread will run for some time, get preempt so that another thread can run. The period and the sequence in which these threads run are controlled by the underlying RTOS, the developers have no say in these. Consider this simple example:

Example 1. Concurrency using threads.

```
import _thread as th
cnt=0
def test(w,n):
   global cnt
   for i in range(n):
      cnt+=1;print(cnt, w, i)
t0=th.start_new_thread(test, ("WWWW", 100))
t1=th.start_new_thread(test, ("XXXX", 100))
t2=th.start_new_thread(test, ("YYYY", 100))
t3=th.start_new_thread(test, ("ZZZZ", 100))
```

The excerpt from the output:

```
1 WWWW 0
2 WWWW 1
...
30 WWWW 29
31 YYYY 0
...
60 YYYY 29
61 ZZZZ 0
...
90 ZZZZ 29
91 XXXX 0
...120 XXXX 29
121 WWWW 30
...
```

Running on MicroPython v1.14-74-g1342debb9 for ESP32, we have wwww run until cnt equals 30. Next yyyy ran from cnt equals 31 until 60. Next zzzz ran at cnt equals 61 until 90. And xxxx ran at cnt equals 91 until 120. The execution pattern repeated until each reached 100 local counts. We can say that the thread system switches context every 30 iterations of the inner loop of test() (see Example 1).

The sequence order does not correlate to the sequence of adding a new thread. We see that xxxxran last in the ran sequence but was inserted 2.nd into the threading system. There is no guarantee these orders will play out again in the later invocation. What more, we have no control over scheduling, for example, what if we want to run one iteration at a time on each test()loop, i.e. wwww xxxx yyyy zzzz run order? For this case, we need a different method of running concurrent multitasking.

2.3 Actor Model

A way to solve the above-mentioned problems is to program an embedded system in terms of cooperative multitasking within an Actor Model paradigm [6] rather than deploying the time-multiplex multi-threading method of concurrency.

An Actor Model is an abstraction of how to program, and it is not new. Different programming environments implement an Actor Model framework differently. There are four fundamental properties of the Actor Model, which are:

1. An actor can create other actors,
2. Actors have addresses,
3. Actors send and receive messages,
4. All actors run concurrently.

For a single-core machine like most MCU, these concurrent executions are logical (apparent) concurrency and not physical (real) concurrency. In a traditional function call, a function calls a subroutine and waits for it to return and continue execution when the subroutine completes. In *asyncio*, *async/await* a coroutine starts another coroutine and waits asynchronously (*await*) for the other to complete. The *await* pauses the execution of the calling coroutine and return control to the *asyncio* run-loop scheduler. The scheduler will resume the suspended coroutine and provide it with the return values from the called coroutine. In the meanwhile, the scheduler will run another coroutine from its coroutines run queue.

Python language has had a long tradition in asynchronous programming. Started in 1999, Python 1.5.2 with *Asyncore*. Followed in 2001, Python 2.2 with *Generator*. The current *Asyncio* was introduced in 2014, python 3.4 [7].

Our *act* library runs on the single main thread, not unlike *asyncio*. However, our *act* library is very lightweight. It just provides a data structure, a few operational functions, and a scheduler. The implementation is based on the Python generator. Any function containing one or more *yield* statements is a generator. When *yield* statements are used to purposely suspend an executing function, to let another function resumes using a *next* or a *send* statement then generators become coroutines. These coroutines are actors in our system. The components of the *act* library (see Fig. 1) are:

1. One ring buffer for the run-queue, append to head extract from the tail.
2. Two methods to create actors; actor()to create and insert an actor to the run-queue, and actors()to create and insert multiple actors.
3. One method to delete actors and empty the run-queue, purge().

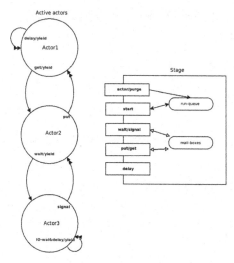

Fig. 1. Actor model run-time.

4. Two methods for sending and receiving messages from named mailboxes; put()to write a value into a named variable, and get()to read a value from the variable.
5. Two methods for registering and receiving events; wait()to register and wait, and signal()to signal events.
6. One method to non-blocking delay; delay().
7. One method to supervise scheduling and resource management; start()
8. One procedure for creating an actor at global scope; add_actor().

When an actor creates another actor within its scope, the actor()or actors()will behave as a recursive function call. However, a recursive invocation of actors will not free RAM even after the parent actors were completed. To mitigate this, we use the global add_actor()function. The add_actor()places the new actor and its resources within the global scope, thereby, resources can be reclaimed by the scheduler.

The scheduler manages active generator objects. When an active coroutine yields, the scheduler will resume the next suspended coroutine from the run queue using the *send* statement. The *yield/send* pair within the script makes logical concurrency among many actors possible. The coroutine is reinserted back into the run-queue when it yields a *None* value. The coroutine is terminated as soon as the scheduler receives a non-*None* type value, for example, a string 'Done'.

Equip with our *act* library an example (see Example 2) shows simple controlled scheduling can be easily done, where the thread concurrency failed to do so.

Example 2. Concurrency using act library.

```
from act import Stage
def test(pm):
  global cnt; w,n=pm; c=(yield)
  for i in range(n):
    cnt+=1;print(cnt, w, I);yield
  yield 'DONE'
cnt=0; s=Stage()
s.actors([test(("WWWW", 100)), test(("XXXX", 100)), test(("YYYY", 100)), test(("ZZZZ", 100))])
s.start()
```

The excerpt from the output:

```
1 WWWW 0
2 XXXX 0
3 YYYY 0
4 ZZZZ 0
5 WWWW 1
...
396 ZZZZ 98
397 WWWW 99
398 XXXX 99
399 YYYY 99
400 ZZZZ 99
```

Implementing the Actor model using the Python generator does incur time overhead. Table 1 shows the overhead comparison between _thread and act handling of sleep and delay with two concurrently running tasks. When a task goes to sleep (blocking),

```
sleep_ms(int(p*1000))
```

the _thread will not reschedule the task, not until the sleep period is over. The delay (non-blocking, pooling) will busily check for delay timeout.

```
d=p*1000;now=ticks_ms()
while c.delay(d, now): cnt+=1;yield
```

The _thread controlled by RTOS has an overhead of 10 ms. While the delay()with its busy pooling method has 90 ms overhead.

The act library was not designed for precise timing tasks. The delays in an embedded system are mostly IO-bound. The delay()method is meant for controlling timeout in an IO wait, to break out of the *yield* loop-trap after some definite time. *Actor3* in Fig. 1 hinted at such usage.

Table 1. Overhead comparison.

Concurrency type	Sleep/delay (p) ==> Total run time (msec)	Overhead (msec)
_thread	5 ==> 5	0
Act	5 ==> 100	95
_thread	500 ==> 510	10
Act	500 ==> 591	91
_thread	5000 ==> 5010	10
act	5000 ==> 5085	85

Example 3. Two actors put/get .

```
from act import Stage,add_actor
def X(pm):
    def waitval():nonlocal m;m=c.get(b);return m==None
    i=0;b,m='BOX1',None;c=(yield)
    while waitval():
      i+=1
      if i%25==0:print("X Waiting for mailbox BOX1 from Y", i)
      c=(yield)
    print("X Get BOX1", m)
    c.put('BOX2', (1,True,"OK"))
    yield 'OK'
def Y(pm):
  def waitval():nonlocal m;m=c.get(b);return m==None
  c=(yield);i=0
  while i<100:
    i+=1
    if i%25==0:print('Inside Y', i)
    c=(yield)
  c.put('BOX1', (2,"This is from Y"))
  b,m='BOX2',None
  while waitval():
    print("Y Waiting for mailbox BOX2 from X")
    c=(yield)
  print("Y Get BOX2", m)
  yield 'OK'
s=Stage()
s.actors([X(()), Y(())])
s.start()
```

The excerpt from the output:

```
X Waiting for mailbox BOX1 from Y 25
Inside Y 25
X Waiting for mailbox BOX1 from Y 50
Inside Y 50
X Waiting for mailbox BOX1 from Y 75
Inside Y 75
X Waiting for mailbox BOX1 from Y 100
Inside Y 100
Y Waiting for mailbox BOX2 from X
X Get BOX1 (2, 'This is from Y')
Y Get BOX2 (1, True, 'OK')
```

Example 4. Three actors wait/signal.

```python
from act import Stage, add_actor
def cntdown(pm):
  sk,sv,cnt=pm;c=(yield)
  while cnt:cnt-=1;c=(yield)
  c.signal(sk,sv)
  yield True
def test(pm):
  print("Waiting for event");c=(yield)
  add_actor(c, cntdown, ('CTN1', True, 1000))
  while c.wait('CTN1', True):c=(yield)
  c.signal('MSG', 'shutup!')
  print("Event happened")
  yield True
def hello(pm):
  c=(yield);i=0
  while c.wait('MSG', 'shutup!'):
    i+=1
    if i%200==0:
      print("Hello at ", i)
    c=(yield)
  yield True
s=Stage()
s.actors([test(()), hello(())])
s.start()
```

The excerpt from the output:

```
Waiting for event
Hello at  200
Hello at  400
Hello at  600
Hello at  800
Hello at  1000
Event happened
```

2.4 The *Act* Module Implementation

We use *while/yield* pattern when we pooling for an event (delay(), get(), wait()). While a wait condition is true, the running coroutine will yield a *None* value to the scheduler.

The delay()method is implemented using time.ticks_diff(), and will return a *True* value as long as delay period is less then the different between current ticks time and start ticks, t0:

$$\text{time.ticks\_diff(time.ticks\_ms(), t0)} < \text{delay}$$

The is a subtle difference between get()and wait(). These methods read and write values to a mailbox directory specified by keys. The get()method will return whatever value associated with a key as long as it is a non-*None* value. However, the wait()method returns *True* as long as the value associated with a key is not equal to the waited-for value specified in the wait()call. The get()will reset the value back to a *None* value after reading, but not the wait(). The value registered by a signal()can be read by a multiple coroutines with a wait()statement of the same key.

Both the delay()and the wait()methods return a *True* value, to be used to control the while-true loop. The get()pooling control is different, the loop is terminated when it reads a non-*None* value. To implement the while-true loop we defined a waitval()sub-routine (see Example 3).

In our simple implementation, both the put()and signal()methods simply write a value associated with a key to the mailbox directory. Any previously written value is immediately overwritten without any manner of checking.

3 Use Cases

3.1 Simple Examples

Simple examples are given above. The *put/get* construct is shown in Example 3. The *wait/signal* construct is presented in Example 4. Notice that the code blocks contain the *yield-loop*. The script yields its execution to the scheduler as long as it still has something to do or waiting for an event to happen.

3.2 WebCam Server

We use an ESP32-Camera board running a custom-designed MicroPython firmware to run as a webcam server. We start with three actors to serve three HTTP (Hypertext Transfer Protocol) on ports 1) 80 for live streaming, 2) 81 for static image captures, and 3) 82 for sending camera control. Each of these actors will wait for request connections on their respective ports. Upon getting a request a particular server will create a new actor to deal with the incoming request. Depending on what type of service was requested, a new actor will be created further on in the service-process chain.

Sending an http://10.0.0.133:82/apikey/spe/2 request, for example, will change the image capture effect to gray-scale. All these servers are running concurrently. Changing camera parameters will immediately affect the camera image capturing properties. The webcam server manages to serve multiple live streaming clients. We have tested with five clients without a problem. Of course, the frame-rate drops as we add more clients. We experienced problems with stability when using thread-based serve.

This sub-US$10 board contains an ESP32 WiFi-enabled MCU with 520 KBytes of internal SRAM to run application script, complemented with a 4 MBytes external PSRAM to provide enough memory for image capture by an OV2640, 2 million pixel CMOS Sensor digital camera module and supports TF (TransFlash a.k.a Micro SD) card for captured image storage. The actor-based script running on this board can provide us with a cheap and reliable imagery system for surveillance cameras for smart-home, smart-farming, and smart-manufacturing. A UDP (User Datagram Protocol) network of ESP32-Cam boards and powerful Linux-based servers in an actor-based collaborative framework can provide us with a smart, efficient, and secure solution to IoT.

3.3 Dynamic Scripting Over UART

AT command set, developed way back in 1981 [8], is used to communicate both commands and data between computers and modems. It is still in use today by some WiFi and Bluetooth adaptor boards, for example, ESP8285 WiFi. This sub-UD$2 ESP8285 board provides WiFi capability to the host MCU through UART. The default firmware shipped with the boards supports a set of *AT* commands. The ESP8285 integrates 1 MBytes Flash in DOUT mode with 112 Kbytes user RAM. We replaced the default firmware with MicroPython.

To save some memory space both in RAM and flash the MicroPython was built excluding some built-in libraries and GPIO pins. Furthermore, we freeze the *act* and *KA* Python libraries into the MicroPython firmware.

The *KA* library will take control and disassociate UART from the REPL 10 s after a reboot. The user can interrupt this from happening with a keyboard (control+c) interrupt within 10 s of the reboot. The main purpose of *KA* is to read code strings from the UART and execute them using exec()function. The *KA* starts the main loop as an actor that does a non-blocking wait for codes written to UART. With this setup, we replace the default *AT* commands firmware of the ESP8285 with a dynamically programmable device capable of running Python script. Since any codes send to the UART will be executed, any host MCU can use the ESP8285 as a WiFi gateway.

4   Conclusion

This work proposes and implements a style of asynchronous multi-tasking programming method, by using the Python Generator primitives *yield/next* and *yield/send*. We have shown that an actor-based model is viable for programming microcontrollers with a high-level programming language MicroPython. Our minimalistic *act* library can assist developers to program applications on a constraint execution environment of MCU with limited RAM and processing power. By using our flexible *act* library, we can develop applications in any of the following; actor-model, event-driven, data-driven, message-passing, request-response, and reactive programming styles.

MicroPython interpreter implemented in a compact and efficient virtual runtime engine makes it possible to do dynamic scripting within deployed applications. It is also feasible to install a secure update system while the applications are in a production run. The possibility of running applications with dynamically swappable scripts on remote and physically inaccessible MCUs will be a very important factor of the future of edge computing.

Standard MicroPython firmware does not support the camera module in its ESP32 port. We exclude a few standard libraries and include a few additional libraries in our modified firmware [9]. The structure and the process for building MicroPython are well designed. It is relatively easy to custom build your version of MicroPython firmware. The open-source and generous licensing term of MicroPython benefited everyone. We will see more commercial usage of MicroPython in the future as scriptable devices in NODs becomes more prevalent.

References

1. Maney, K.: Newsweek. http://www.newsweek.com/2015/03/06/meet-kevin-ashton-father-int ernet-things-308763.html. Accessed 10 Mar 2021
2. Scroxton, A.: Computerweekly. https://www.computerweekly.com/news/4500258239/Word-smart-being-abused-by-IoT-advocates. Accessed 10 Mar 2021
3. Williams, G.: Espruino. https://www.espruino.com. Accessed 15 Mar 2021
4. George, D.: MicroPython. http://micropython.org. Accessed 15 Mar 2021
5. Artho, C., Biere, A.: Applying Static Analysis to Large-Scale, Multi-Threaded Java Programs.. 68–75. https://doi.org/10.1109/ASWEC.2001.948499, (2001).
6. Agha, G.A.: Actors - a model of concurrent computation in distributed systems. The MIT Press Series in Artificial Intelligence, ISBN 0-262-01092-5 (1986)
7. Picard, R.: Hands-On, Reactive Programming with Python. Packt Publishing (2018). Figure 2.4. ISBN 9781789132755
8. Shannon, V.: International Herald Tribune. https://www.nytimes.com/1999/01/07/news/the-rise-and-fall-of-the-modem-king.html. Accessed 18 Mar 2021
9. Sharil, T.: https://github.com/shariltumin/esp32-cam-micropython. Accessed 19 Mar 2021

SMC: A New Strategy Based on Software-Defined Networking to Mitigate the Impact of Anomalies on Cooperative Cloud

Houda Guesmi[✉], Anwar Kalghoum, Ramzi Guesmi, and Leïla Azouz Saïdane

CRISTAL LAB, National School of Computer Science, Manouba, Tunisia
{houda.guesmi,anwar.kalghoum,leila.saidane}@ensi-uma.tn,
ramzi.guesmi@gmail.com

Abstract. Distributed Denial of Service (DDoS) attacks remain one of the most effective cybercriminals methods to cause significant financial and operational damage. In Cloud Computing, these attacks' goal is to shut down cloud servers, flooding them with traffic from compromised devices or networks. To address these issues, we offer SMC, a new approach to protect cloud servers against distributed denial of service attacks and mitigate their impact on network performance. SMC uses an SDN-based attack detection system to detect possible DDoS attacks and effectively mitigate their impact by rerouting malicious traffic, adjusting switch rule timeouts and aggregating these rules into SDN switch tables. Our experiments show that SMC maintains network performance during DDoS attacks. In addition, SMC significantly reduces packets' loss and their average transmission time in the network during DDoS attacks.

Keywords: Cloud · Software defined networking · Malicious flow · Anomaly detection · DDoS mitigation

1 Introduction

With the growth in information technology, there is a massive increase in Cloud Computing traffic due to a large number of connected devices and modern internet applications. Network administrators must manage a wide range of data formats, types of services, and devices, which is difficult with traditional network management tools that were not designed to cope with scalable to very high topologies on a large scale.

As Cloud Computing gains attraction and more vendors and data center administrators move to it, there is growing interest in security issues that could arise with its deployment and production. A cloud security threat investigation classifies attack such as unauthorized access, data modification, malicious applications, distributed denial of service (DDoS), and configuration issues [1]. Cloud Computing is vulnerable to DDoS attacks. This type of attack aims to overload a

© Springer Nature Switzerland AG 2021
Y. Luo (Ed.): CDVE 2021, LNCS 12983, pp. 138–149, 2021.
https://doi.org/10.1007/978-3-030-88207-5_14

targeted network or server by aggressively flooding it with a large amount of traffic until it becomes essential to serve these legitimate users. Several researchers such as [10] and [11] have shown that these DDoS attacks can have severe effects on the performance of the network. Indeed, a distributed denial of service attack overwhelms the victimized cloud server and blocks server resources such as CPU, memory and network bandwidth. Therefore, web pages that benign users want to access will not load or they will be very slow to load. This attack has direct effects like service downtime, economic loss caused by scaling up, and loss of revenue. Indirect effects include the cost of attack mitigation, the cost of power consumption, the reputation and the loss of branding.

The concept of software-defined networking (SDN) is the solution to meet users' needs of these network services and applications. The SDN architecture allows network operators to react and dynamically manage their infrastructure to traffic behavior changes in the network [7]. SDN allows the separation between the control plane, which is responsible for deciding the routing of flow in the network and the management of the services and applications offered by the latter, and the data plane, which is in charge of transmitting the data flow according to the directives provided by the control plane [3].

The paper is structured as follows. In Sect. 2, we discuss relevant work describing the main differences with our proposed approach, while in Sect. 3, we describe the architecture of SMC. Section 4 presents the implementation details and the performance evaluation experiments of the proposed anomaly mitigation mechanism on the cloud. Finally, in Sect. 5 we conclude the paper.

2 Related Work

In this section, we primarily focus on research efforts that have addressed DDoS attacks in SDN and cloud networks to mitigate their impact on network performance. First, we outline the different mitigation techniques, which are developed in various studies. Then, we end this section with a comparative study that compares our proposed solution, SMC, to those that already exist.

SLICOTS is a solution proposed in [5], to mitigate the impact of TCP-SYN flood attacks. For each TCP connection request, SLICOTS installs temporary flow rules during the TCP connection process. After validating a connection, it installs permanent flow rules between the client and the server. Additionally, SLICOTS blocks the attacker who sends a large number of half-open TCP connections. This solution offers a low response time for legitimate requests. However, during a DDoS attack, the time it takes to detect and block malicious traffic can overload the network during the detection period, given many temporary flow rules in place.

The authors in [13], offer FlowRanger, a flow tidying system that can detect and mitigate DoS attacks' impact. FlowRanger is implemented in the SDN controller. This system consists of three main components. The first is a trust value management component that calculates each packet-in message's trust value by checking its source. The second is in charge of putting the "packet-in" messages in the queue as a priority according to its confidence value already calculated by the first component. And the third represents the message scheduling component. The FlowRanger technique can reduce DDoS attacks on network performance by ensuring that legitimate flow are served first in the controller. However, this solution does not prevent overloading the controller and overloading switch routing tables.

FloodGuard is a defense platform against DoS attacks proposed in [12]. When a DoS attack is detected, the packet migration module starts redirecting them to a cache installed in the data plane. Subsequently, the Proactive Switch Rules Analysis module will generate forwarding rules according to the current state, such as the amount of data in the network and the link state. At the same time, the data plane cache begins to manage the packets already collected by sending the "packet_in" messages with a limited send rate using the round-robin algorithm as a technique of packet scheduling [9]. FloodGuard is effective in decreasing the rate of bandwidth usage. In addition, this solution avoids the saturation of the flow tables. However, FloodGuard does not prevent control plane overload because it will increase the controller level's processing load.

The autonomic management technique [6] is a solution, in which the authors exploit the centralization and programmability offered by SDN technology. The ISP and its customers are working together to mitigate the impact of DoS attacks. In this solution, the vendor collects information about customers' threats to enforce security policies and update flow tables for switches in the network. If a flow is considered legitimate by customers, the controller marks it with a high priority so that it takes a high-quality path that ensures speed is sent and guarantees receipt. However, if there is any doubt about the flow's legitimacy, the provider's controller will assign it a low priority and direct it to the designated path for malicious flow. This proposal reduces the DDoS attack on network performance at the transmission plane level by balancing the load on different paths.

SMC aims to maintain acceptable server performance during DDoS attacks. In addition, our solution aims to reduce the load on cloud servers, the bandwidth between the controller and the switch and avoid flooding the flow tables. Existing techniques have been successful in reducing the impact of these attacks on network performance. However, none of the solutions mentioned can simultaneously reduce the controller load, the congestion of the communication link between the switches and the controller, and avoid overwhelming the switch flow tables. In this work, we aim to achieve these goals simultaneously (Table 1).

Table 1. SMC approach compared to existing solutions

Approach	Minimises flow table use	Reduces Packet_in messages	Routing of false positive flow	Reduces network bandwidth use	Reduces SDN workload	Controller bandwidth use
SMC	Yes	Yes	Yes	Yes	Yes	Yes
SLICOTS [5]	No	No	No	Yes	Yes	No
FlowRanger [13]	No	No	No	Yes	Yes	No
Autonomic management [6]	No	No	No	Yes	No	No

3   SMC Approach

In this section, we present the architecture of the solution we have proposed, SMC. Thus, we discuss its components and its main design reasons. This approach aims to reduce the Cloud servers' processing load, the consumption of the bandwidth of the control plane, and avoid exceeding the storage capacity in the flow tables of the OpenFlow switches.

As shown in Fig. 1, SMC is viewed as an architecture that can be used to detect and mitigate DDoS attacks at the cloud server level. It uses the SDN architecture to analyze network traffic and generate alerts whenever a malicious traffic flow is detected. Based on alerts from the current network condition, SMC makes the appropriate decision for each flow to minimize impact of anomalies on the cloud server's performance. SMC consists of three phases that guide the controller to make the right decision for each flow and assign flow rules to the switches. These phases make sure that the network traffic is well managed and not congested during DDoS attacks.

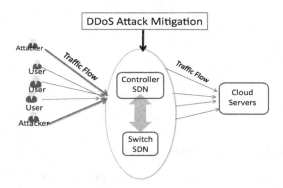

Fig. 1. SMC architecture

The SDN architecture allows us to integrate an attack traffic filter based on switches and an SDN controller. The entities of the SMC method are: the SDN switches, the SDN controller, the cloud servers and the users. The cloud server is the entity that offers a set of services and resources to legitimate users. Then, the user entity operates the Cloud services by sending one or more requests to the Switch SDN. The SDN controller is responsible for deciding each of the flow and assigns the appropriate activity timeout for its entries. SDN switches are responsible for monitoring and collecting statistics on flow such as throughput and usage of flow tables and link bandwidth in the data plane. The SDN controller will use these statistics to make its decision regarding the routing of flow.

3.1 Detection of Distributed Denial of Service Attacks

We have three phases to carry out the DDoS attack detection that are: the data collection phase, the data analysis phase and the attack flow detection phase.

In the data collection phase, the SDN switches send the attributes of new requests to the SDN controller. The latter collects the statistics of all the switches connected to it in order to store them in a global flow table which contains the Global count of incoming flow. In the data analysis phase, the controller supervises the traffic evolution using the flow count column of its global flow table. Then, it launches the attack flow detection phase based on the fast entropy algorithm [2]. If it detects attack flow, it announces this in all switches. Otherwise, it transmits the flow to the corresponding cloud server.

For each data flow, we calculate the entropy in a particular short time interval to measure the uncertainty of a connection i in future traffic (Eq. 1). An entropy noted $E(i,t)$ is calculated for a flow count noted $C(i,t)$ of a particular connection i in a time interval t. $C(i,t)$ is the number of flows calculated for connection i in a particular time interval t.

$$E_{(i,t)} = -log\frac{C_{(i,t)}}{\sum_{i=1}^{n} C_{(i,t)}} + \varepsilon_{(i,t)} \tag{1}$$

where

$$\varepsilon_{(i,t)} = \begin{cases} \left| log\frac{C_{(i,t+1)}}{C_{(i,t)}} \right|, C_{(i,t)} \geq C_{(i,t+1)} \\ \left| log\frac{C_{(i,t)}}{C_{(i,t+1)}} \right|, C_{(i,t)} < C_{(i,t+1)} \end{cases} \tag{2}$$

Next, we calculate the entropy-based variables which are:

- μt: The mean of the entropy values during the time interval t.
- α: The standard variation of the entropy values during t.
- $D(i,t) = |\mu t - E(i,t)|$: Difference between the current entropy and the mean.
- Threshold $= \beta * \alpha$, β is the threshold multiplication factor, it is updated as a function of E(i, t) and μt.
- If $D(i,t) > Threshold$, Then announce a DDoS attack detection alert.

3.2 Mitigation of Distributed Denial of Service Attacks

In the part of DDoS mitigation, the SDN controller is responsible for assigning switch rules for each of the flows and decides its timeout required for the flow rule entry to remain installed in the switch tables. The controller makes its decisions based on threat alerts sent by the SDN controller to mitigate the DDoS attack's impact on network performance.

Switches are responsible for monitoring and collecting statistics on flow and network links (for example, throughput, flow table usage, and link bandwidth in the data plane). The flow controller uses the statistics from the monitoring phase to assign the appropriate flow rules. In addition, SDN switches are responsible for aggregating malicious flow rule entries installed in switch flow tables and have shared properties (for example, source and destination TCP port, IP addresses, protocol). The purpose of flow rule aggregation is to reduce the number of entries used in switch flow tables. Therefore, it helps to avoid the SDN table's memory overflow problem.

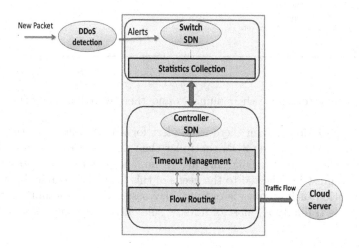

Fig. 2. DDoS mitigation phases

Subsequently, we detail the main considerations taken in designing the proposed solution to mitigate the impact of DDoS attacks on the Cloud server's performance. In SMC, flow management is based on three main points (Fig. 2): assigning and managing flow rules to switches according to the type of flow, timeout management, and aggregation of flow rules.

Routing According to the Type of Flow. Upon receiving a DDoS attack detection alert, the SDN controller decides the routing rule for each flow and assigns the appropriate activity timeout for its corresponding entries in the switch tables. Legitimate flow is always routed by the shortest paths between the source and the destination. Two cases can be identified (Algorithm 1).

- Malicious flow: Whenever the SDN controller receives a DDoS attack detection alert on a malicious flow, it assigns a high timeout value to its corresponding flow rule. This high value ensures that this rule remains in the switch flow table for a long time and avoids successive packet_in type requests sent by the switches (requesting a forwarding rule for the same flow) in the event of DDoS. In addition, SDN switches collect the most minor used links in terms of bandwidth and memory consumption from the switch's flow tables to ensure that this flow does not compete with legitimate flow and affects their performance. SDN switches analyze the rules generated for this malicious traffic and try to merge them,

---

Algorithm 1: Flow aggregation decisions

```
If Alert Then
  { Flow = Malicious_flow
    Timeout= High_time
    Path= least_used_path
    Rule= Obligatory _aggregation  }
Else
   { Flow = Legitimate_flow
    Timeout= Regular_time
    Path= Shortest_path
    Rule= Optional_aggregation  }
End.
```

---

where possible, to reduce their numbers and thereby reduce the use of switch flow tables.

- Legitimate flow: When there is no alert for a particular flow, that flow is considered legitimate. The SDN controller then directs it to the shortest path which is calculated by the Dijkstra's algorithm, and assigns it a regular timeout value which must be adapted to the needs of this legitimate traffic. In this case, the aggregation of flow rules is optional. By assigning an appropriate timeout value for this traffic type, most of its flow rule entries no longer stay in switch flow tables.

Timeout Management. The SDN controller assigns the activity timeout value for each of the forwarding rules based on the alerts. Our work focuses on the timeout value which indicates the maximum use of the forwarding rule. The entry must be deleted regardless of its activity. Whenever the timeout expires, the flow rule entry will be deleted from the switch table.

Typically, when a new flow is received, the SDN switches must communicate with the controller to request rules to forward that flow to the destination. In the event of a DDoS attack, these switches receive a large amount of traffic. This will translate into multiple rules and results in excessive communication between the controller and switches that request a new rule for the same flow. Assigning a low value to the timeout results in more communication traffic with the controller. This increases the consumption of bandwidth between the switches and the controller and the cloud server's overhead.

In order to avoid this problem, if the incoming flow is considered malicious, SMC assigns a high timeout to its forwarding rules. With this consideration, we make sure that the same flow does not trigger many communications between the switch and the controller. On the other hand, when the controller does not receive an alert concerning a flow, it considers it legitimate. It assigns an appropriate timeout value to it according to its need and its activity in the network.

Aggregation of Forwarding Rules. High timeouts are attributed to the rules for forwarding malicious flow. Thus, these flow entries will remain in the switch flow table for a long time. During a DDoS attack, this could increase the number of entries stored in switch tables and overload them.

To resolve this issue, we propose to aggregate the malicious flow rule entries for each switch. These rules are automatically aggregated if they have shared properties (for example, same source and destination, same port, etc.) and transmitted to the same output link. In the following, we present an example of the concept of aggregation.

Each entry in the flow table comprises three fields (rule, action, and statistics). The "rule" field is used to define the condition for matching a flow, the "action" field defines the action to be applied to a flow, and the last "statistics" field is used to count the occurrence of the rule for management purposes. In our example, we are focusing on the first two fields (rule and action). Table 2 shows an example of an SDN switch flow table that contains forwarding rules for different flow.

Table 2. Example of switch flow table rules

Connections	IP source	IP destination	TCP Source port	TCP Des port	Action
1	192.95.27.190	71.126.222.64	15222	60	Port 5
2	51.81.166.201	71.126.222.69	12454	60	Port 3
3	192.120.148.227	71.126.222.65	33543	25	Port 7
4	51.173.229.255	71.126.222.68	23332	60	Port 2
5	202.1.175.252	71.126.222.66	23456	25	Port 8
6	40.75.89.172	71.126.222.67	21346	60	Port 4
7	192.95.27.190	71.126.222.64	17334	60	Port 5
8	192.120.148.227	71.126.222.65	14887	25	Port 7
9	202.1.175.252	71.126.222.66	56443	25	Port 8
10	202.1.175.252	71.126.222.66	12224	25	Port 8
11	202.1.175.252	71.126.222.66	34223	25	Port 8

During a DDoS attack, switches receive an enormous number of flow from one or more sources that aim to block a specific victim (destination). These flows translate into forwarding rules that must be installed in the flow tables of the switches. The latter can thus be saturated because of the limited storage capacity of their tables. In order to minimize this storage overflow problem, the feed aggregation module will compare the information of the entries installed in the table. When it finds a match between two or more entries, it will merge them into a single entry.

Applying this principle on the switch table presented in Table 2, we obtain the aggregation result presented in Table 3. In our example, the aggregation module checks the rows' correspondence in the switch table (Table 2). Each row in this table represents a forwarding rule. When it finds two or more rules with the same properties (source IP address, destination IP address, destination TCP port, and action), it merges them into a single flow rule in the table. We notice that the number of flows has been reduced, which prevents memory overflow in the switches.

Table 3. Aggregation of switch table rules

Connections	IP source	IP destination	TCP source port	TCP Des port	Action
1	192.95.27.190	71.126.222.64	–	60	Port 5
2	51.81.166.201	71.126.222.69	12454	60	Port 3
3	192.120.148.227	71.126.222.65	–	25	Port 7
4	51.173.229.255	71.126.222.68	23332	60	Port 2
5	202.1.175.252	71.126.222.66	–	25	Port 8
6	40.75.89.172	71.126.222.67	21346	60	Port 4

4   Experiments and Analysis

We realized several simulation scenarios using a set of tools to evaluate SMC architecture. CloudSim [4] is the simulator employed to design cloud computing architecture, user nodes, SDN controllers and switches. Scapy [4] is applied to generate DDoS attacks and traffics on our cloud server.

Our experiments used a cloud server, 100 users, and a testbed SDN with 15 switches. Our proposal's main objective is to improve SDN's hold time during a DDoS attack to protect the cloud server's performance. Subsequently, we measure the holding time of malicious packets by SDN in two cases. We use the SMC mitigation technique in the first case. Thus, we test SDN's hold time without exploiting the proposed defense approach. The SDN holding time without using the proposed technique is (time1 - time0), knowing that (time0) is the time when the DDoS attack begins and (time1) is the time when the target switch becomes full. The SDN holding time using the proposed approach is (time2 - time0), knowing that (time2) is the time when all switches have become full. Our proposal's second objective is to reduce the number of packet-in messages exchanged between the controller and the switch during the DDoS attack. Therefore, we measure the number of this type of message in both cases without using the proposed approach. The Figs. 3, 4 and 5 show the results obtained through various experiments.

Figure 3 illustrates SDN holding time during a distributed denial-of-service attack, with and without using the proposed method. We notice that SMC improves the SDN uptime. In this figure's experiment, we considered a single target switch and the other switches are not intended by the attack. In addition, 30% of the switch tables' memory space is used at the switch not intended by the attack. 70% of this memory space is available for sharing. We apply this experiment several times on different switches. Indeed, we observe that the results are similar for all the repetitions.

In the experiments of Fig. 4, we measured the SDN holding time by modifying the attack rate. Therefore, we observe that the SDN holding time decreases as the attack rate increases. This is because the increase in the SDN holding time allows the DDoS defense system to mitigate the flow flooding.

Our objective was to reduce the number of exchanged packet messages between controller and switches in the SMC approach. Figure 5 shows the variation in the number of OpenFlow messages with and without using our proposal.

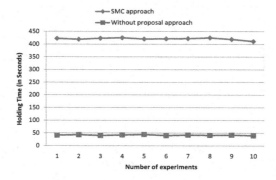

Fig. 3. Holding time of SDN with different experiments

We observe that the number of messages exchanged between controller and switches decreases significantly when we use our approach. The reason behind this result is that we increase the timeout of the attack flow.

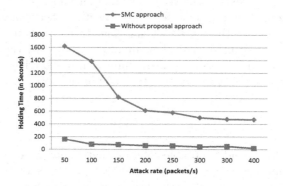

Fig. 4. Holding time of SDN by changing the attack rate

All the simulations performed show the effectiveness of using the SDN controller and the fast entropy algorithm in protecting the cloud system against DDoS attacks. In our approach, the controller plays an important role in analyzing traffic and identifying DDoS attack packets among those that are benign legitimate packets. Thus, it allows monitoring of cloud traffic by periodically analyzing the variation of flows. Then, it triggers the fast entropy algorithm in the event of an abnormal increase in traffic packets in order to avoid DDoS attack before it reaches the cloud network.

SMC redirects malicious traffic through the paths with the most minor used links in terms of bandwidth and memory consumption of the SDN switch flow tables. However, our solution does mitigate DDoS attacks on bandwidth consumption and packet wait times in the controller queue. The path selected to transmit malicious flow should not be the shortest path in the network reserved

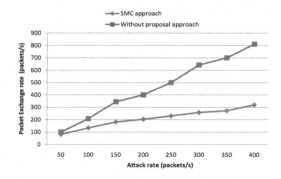

Fig. 5. Number of packet-in messages exchanged between controller and switch under DDoS attack

for legitimate traffic. However, it ensures the minimal impact of the attack on the performance of legitimate flow. At the same time, malicious traffic will reach the destination (which is essential in false-positive alarms). In our solution, malicious traffic will not be blocked or removed to ensure that false-positive malicious flow have the chance to reach the cloud server, even with higher delays. By using this concept, we can reduce the impact of malicious traffic without taking the risk of blocking it. For legitimate flow, they are always routed by the shortest paths between source and destination to ensure minimum round trip delay and ensure good service quality (QoS) for legitimate traffic in the network.

5   Conclusion

SMC offers a reliable and adaptable solution that resolves the considered problems and maintains Cloud server's acceptable performance during a DDoS attack. Our solution is based on the fast entropy algorithm and SDN for the detection of attacks and the identification of flow. In addition, it uses the SDN architecture to analyze the traffic and decide the degree of threat for each flow entering the network. SMC approach consists of three phases which are: the statistics collection, the timeout management and the flow routing. These modules work together to make the appropriate decision for each flow and help the controller assign forwarding rules for each flow to be passed through the data plane switches. There are many promising directions that we can pursue in the future. We plan to evaluate the performance of SMC for more realistic and large-scale deployments.

References

1. Chaudhary, D., Bhushan, K., Gupta, B.: Survey on DDoS attacks and defense mechanisms in cloud and fog computing. In: Cloud Security, pp. 1927–1951. IGI Global (2019)

2. Guesmi, H., Kalghoum, A., Ghazel, C., Saidane, L.A.: FFED: a novel strategy based on fast entropy to detect attacks against trust computing in cloud. Clust. Comput. **24**(3), 1945–1954 (2021). https://doi.org/10.1007/s10586-021-03233-3

3. Guesmi, T., Kalghoum, A., Alshammari, B.M., Alsaif, H., Alzamil, A.: Leveraging software-defined networking approach for future information-centric networking enhancement. Symmetry **13**(3), 441 (2021)

4. Jeon, H., Cho, C., Shin, S., Yoon, S.: A CloudSim-extension for simulating distributed functions-as-a-service. In: 2019 20th International Conference on Parallel and Distributed Computing, Applications and Technologies (PDCAT). IEEE, December 2019

5. Mohammadi, R., Javidan, R., Conti, M.: SLICOTS: an SDN-based lightweight countermeasure for TCP SYN flooding attacks. IEEE Trans. Netw. Serv. Manage. **14**(2), 487–497 (2017)

6. Sahay, R., Blanc, G., Zhang, Z., Debar, H.: Towards autonomic DDoS mitigation using software defined networking. In: Proceedings 2015 Workshop on Security of Emerging Networking Technologies. Internet Society (2015)

7. Schaller, S., Hood, D.: Software defined networking architecture standardization. Comput. Stand. Interf. **54**, 197–202 (2017)

8. Singh, M.P., Bhandari, A.: New-flow based DDoS attacks in SDN: taxonomy, rationales, and research challenges. Comput. Commun. **154**, 509–527 (2020)

9. Srilatha, N., Sravani, M., Divya, Y.: Optimal round robin CPU scheduling algorithm using Manhattan distance. Int. J. Electr. Comput. Eng. (IJECE) **7**(6), 3664 (2017)

10. Tandon, R.: A survey of distributed denial of service attacks and defenses. https://arxiv.org/abs/2008.01345 (2020)

11. Velliangiri, S., Karthikeyan, P., Kumar, V.V.: Detection of distributed denial of service attack in cloud computing using the optimization-based deep networks. J. Exp. Theoret. Artif. Intell., 1–20 (2020)

12. Wang, H., Xu, L., Gu, G.: FloodGuard: a DoS attack prevention extension in software-defined networks. In: 2015 45th Annual IEEE/IFIP International Conference on Dependable Systems and Networks, pp. 239–250 (2015)

13. Wei, L., Fung, C.: FlowRanger: a request prioritizing algorithm for controller DoS attacks in software defined networks. In: 2015 IEEE International Conference on Communications (ICC). IEEE, June 2015

Graph Attention Network Based Object Detection and Classification in Crowded Scenario

Guangyuan Xu and Shaungxi Huang[✉]

Tsinghua University, Beijing, China
xugy18@mails.tsinghua.edu.cn, huangsx@tsinghua.edu.cn

Abstract. Non-maximum Suppression (NMS) is an essential post-processor for most detectors, responsible for merging excessive detections from detector. The standard NMS is a crude greedy algorithm that is not accurate enough sometimes and even fail entirely in crowded scenario, which results from making inadequate use of information of detection. We regard the detection set as the data of the graph structure, and adopt the Graph Attention Network (GAT), which fits the data structure very well, as the backbone to perform NMS. In addition, our algorithm is aware of the density of objects and therefore can handle partly crowded scenario. The result of our algorithm is better than the traditional algorithm, which shows the superiority of performing NMS based on global information.

Keywords: Graph attention network · Non-maximum suppression

1 Introduction

Object detection is to recognize objects in the image and present them with locations and classes. In order to avoid missing objects as much as possible, all detectors are designed to output a set of excessive detections rather than a single detection per object. This strategy of generating multiple responses for an image to ensure a high recall proves to be effective because redundant detections can be eliminated and missed cannot be remedied. As a result, it is necessary to attach a post-processing procedure after the detector to merge these excessive detections.

The original as well as the standard algorithm for merging detections is non-maximum suppression (NMS), which is a simple greedy algorithm and hence named Greedy-NMS [7]. Its assumption is very simple: the more two detections overlap, the more likely they correspond to the same object. Based on this assumption, Greedy-NMS will iterate a suppression process several times, each of which will retain the raw detection with the highest classification score and delete its neighbors who overlap it too much. In the above process, the intersection-over-union (IoU) can measure the overlap and the IoU above the given threshold means overlapping too much. As seen, Greedy-NMS is concise, rapid and easy to implement, and therefore adopted widely.

However, there are inherent flaws in Greedy-NMS. It is worth noting that the classification score of detections cannot accurately measure the location accuracy, and this

Y. Luo (Ed.): CDVE 2021, LNCS 12983, pp. 150–159, 2021.
https://doi.org/10.1007/978-3-030-88207-5_15

deviation results from the binary labels in training. In Greedy-NMS, selection entirely based on classification scores is not accurate, and suppression has poor resistance to this inaccuracy. Therefore, the inaccuracy of one object during iteration is likely to affect the processing of the next object, especially while the detections sets are not separate. A high threshold can enhance the resistance, but at the same time weakens the suppression of negative samples.

Fig. 1. In crowded scenarios, Greedy-NMS can only either adopt a large suppression deleting nearby true positives mistakenly (such as the left image, threshold = 0.5) or adopt a narrow suppression preserving false positives mistakenly (such as the right image, threshold = 0.4).

More fatally, Greedy-NMS is destined to fail completely in crowded scenarios because their basic assumption does not hold. In crowded scenarios where ground-truths may overlap each other, a nearby ground-truth and a false positive may have a same IoU with the newly selected detection. Faced with these two detections, Greedy-NMS with any threshold cannot differentiate them, as is shown in Fig. 1. This inseparability makes it impossible for Greedy-NMS to gain high both the precision and the recall.

In this paper, we think that the detection set can be regarded in graph data structure, and the graph neural network can be used to perform NMS naturally. We first encode the detection information into graph data, in which the similarity between the detection is modified according to the density information. We chose GAT as the backbone of the model for its strong learning ability. NMS is performed by multiple GAT layers based on global information, which can support more accurate screening.

2 Related Work

2.1 Object Detection and NMS

Almost all current competitive detectors today are based on deep learning and can be roughly divided into two categories: one-stage detector [15–18] and two-stage detector [12–14, 19–21, 22]. As the most classical detector, Faster R-CNN establishes the paradigm of the two-stage detector: the proposed generation and refinement are both based on a neural network. Subsequent two-stage detectors either enrich or strengthen the framework or adjust it to adapt to different application scenarios. All detectors above need NMS. Greedy-NMS selects the raw detection with the highest score preserved and deletes its neighbors whose IoU with it above the given threshold. The process above will be repeated several times until no detections untreated and all detections will be treated only once.

2.2 Improvements for NMS

Soft-NMS [1] replaces the above deletion with reducing scores according to IoUs, slightly increasing accuracy. IoU-Net [2] is a predictor attached into upstream detector in order to predict the IoUs between detections and corresponding ground-truths, which are regarded as location confidences and will replace classification scores to guide the following NMS. Similarly, Softer-NMS [3] regards each detection as a Gaussian distribution and standard deviation as location confidence, and then carries on the weighted sum to the nearby detection for merging. T-net [4] and G-net [5] attempt to perform NMS based on network. T-net makes IoU maps and score maps for the detection set and overlay them as the input of the whole network, each detection corresponding to a grid in map depend on the location of its center. The score maps consist of multiple score maps that updated by the Greedy-NMS with various thresholds. Then, multiple convolution layers will obtain the final score map. G-net adopts an completely different framework where multiple blocks will update the feature vector of each detection pair and concatenate the pair feature with features of the two overlapping detection themselves. And all pair features involving the same detection will be aggregated by max-pooling and then updated as the new features of that detection. In the above process, the pair features are learned from handcrafted features by full connection layer, and the final result is also learned from the final detection features by full connection layer. Adaptive-NMS [6] attaches a predictor into upstream detector to predict the maximum overlap between ground-truths in that position as density. In the subsequent process of NMS, threshold will be replaced with the density when density higher than threshold to avoid the mistaken suppression.

2.3 Graph Neural Network

Graph is a kind of data structure that can model a set of objects and their relationships. Because of great expressive power, graph can be used to describe complex and common systems such as social networks and organic molecules [8]. Compared with traditional methods, the early graphical neural network is not attractive. Recently, the great success of deep learning in computer vision and natural language processing has inspired its attempts at graph structure. However, as a unique non-Euclidean data structure in machine learning, graph structure is difficult to be processed by deep network [9]. It is found that the idea of CNN, containing local connection, shared weights and multilayer processing, also adapts in the processing of graph structure, which is the initial motivation of graph convolutional network. However, the neighbors of each node in the graph are irregular and disordered, which is the biggest obstacle against a convolution. The first attempt is to map the graph structure to the frequency domain through Fourier transform to achieve the convolution [10, 11, 23], but now the mainstream method is spatial-based. Early methods [24, 25] aggregate adjacent information in the form of summation. PATCHY-SAN [26] attempts to sort the neighbors and select a fixed number of them, and then transform the graph convolution into one-dimensional convolution.

Similarly, GraphSage [27] attempt to decomposes the convolution for each node into three steps of sampling, aggregation and updating. GCN [28] is one of the most important graph convolution models, indicating consistency of the two kinds of methods. GAT [29] introduces the attention mechanism into the graph convolution model, which allows summing with weights that has much more powerful ability to learn than simply summing.

3   A Novel NMS Based on Graph Attention Network

We start in this Sect. 3.1 with a discussion on the defect of Greedy-NMS and the requirements for an ideal NMS. In Sect. 3.2, we describe the overall framework of our algorithm and details of upstream detector. Finally, In Sect. 3.3, we propose a NMS based on Graph Attention Network aware of density.

3.1   Discussion of NMS

NMS We believe that the flaw of Greedy-NMS results from exploiting too little information. Firstly, the absence of location confidence forces the algorithm to select according to the classification scores, and the deviation between the two prevents the detection closest to the ground-truth from selected. This deviation comes from the fact that all detections whose IoU with ground-truth above the given threshold are labeled as positive samples during training. Secondly, roughly deleting neighbors discards most of information representing the relationships between detections. We believe that the distribution of all detection is not random, but according to certain regularity. In a detection set, an accurate detection always tends to be in the central area of the set and covers more detections, while a bad detection to be at the edge of the set. But suppression based on roughly deleting discards most useful information from the distribution of all detections and, as a result, is hardly fault-tolerant. Finally, Greedy-NMS does not perceive the density of objects. An ideal algorithm should apply a large suppression in a sparse scenario to delete false positives, while a narrower suppression in a crowded scenario to avoid mistakenly deleting nearby true positives. However, the absence of density makes the Greedy-NMS unable to adjust the threshold to adapt to different scenario, and have no choices but to choose a fixed threshold according to experience to balance the loss in two cases.

All the success of improvements to the NMS comes from the using of more information. IoU-net and softer-NMS introduce the location confidence to guide suppression, beneficial to gain accurate result, especially when the suppression has poor resistance to deviation. G-net and T-net process all detections jointly, capturing key information from the relationships between all detections with powerful network. Their success comes from that the accuracy of a detection is related to its position in the overall distribution as mentioned above. Adaptive-NMS introduces density to suppression, which was never involved by previous algorithms. Introducing density allows the algorithm to adopt different suppression strategies flexibly for various scenarios, such as a narrow suppression to prevent mistakenly deleting nearby true positives in crowded scenario.

For the three defects, we believe that a competent NMS must meet three requirements: 1) measuring detection with location confidence, 2) ability to perceive the density of objects, and 3) suppression based on global information. This requirements guide us design our approach.

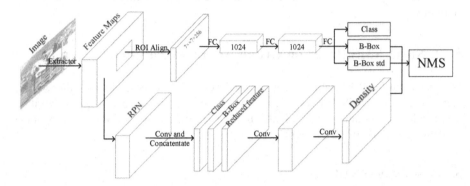

Fig. 2. Our overall framework. Two branches are attached into Faster R-CNN.

3.2 Our Overall Framework

We adopt Faster R-CNN framework as the backbone detector. As the most classical detector, Faster R-CNN proves able to give satisfactory output. Therefore, we focus on other components, instead of trying other more advanced but also more complex detectors. We believe that NMS needs more information from the upstream detector to support distinguishing between retained and deleted detections.

We attach two branches to the upstream detector, the former responsible for predicting the location confidence and the latter for predicting the density of objects. As is shown in Fig. 2, two predictors both obtain image features from the trunk detector. We adopt the idea of [3] to treat a detection as a Gaussian distribution and a ground-truth as a Dirac distribution, and take the KL divergence of the two as the loss function. The added branch is parallel to the regression branch and responsible for predicting the standard deviation of the Gaussian distribution, which we regard as the location confidence. In this way, the detector outputs location confidence at the same time with each detection. Unlike location confidence, predicted density cannot be derived from features of a single detection. Therefore, the density predictor takes the convolutional feature maps of the whole image as one input, which will be reduced first with a 1×1 convolution layer. Then, the feature maps from RPN is captured and then concatenated with the above compressed feature maps. Finally, the predictor applies a large kernel, which can cover nearby objects, at the concatenated maps to get density.

We focus on the third requirement, which is the most important. We think the relationship between detections is valuable, but difficult to utilize. Encouraged by the powerful learning ability of neural networks, we attempt to design a learning-based algorithm instead of manually designing features and classifiers. The data from the upstream detector includes the respective information of each detection and the relationship between overlapping detections, so it is not regular, which is also the reason why it is difficult to process. We think that the data is of graph structure, the information of each detection as the node feature and between them as the edge feature. Naturally, we choose the Graph Attention Network in a series of graph neural networks models, which is hereafter referred to as GAT-NMS.

3.3 GAT-NMS

The core of our GAT-NMS is the GAT layers, with coding module and matching module auxiliary. As shown in the figure, the encoding module takes the original detection sets with from upstream detector as input, and then generates graph data including node features and edge features. The graph is updated by multiple GAT modules, and the final score is obtained by three full connection layers. The above process is the whole process of GAT-NMS. Additionally, the training process requires matching module to assign labels to the detection set, and the loss is computed based on logistic loss function that is weighed in order to balance positive and negative samples (Fig. 3).

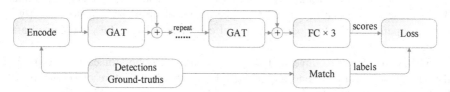

Fig. 3. The backbone of a GAT-NMS is made up of multiple GAT layers.

The emphasis of coding module is to introduce density into the graph. Our motivation for introducing density is to enhance the ability of algorithm to distinguish between nearby true positives and duplicate detections in crowded scenario. The basic assumption of Greedy-NMS is that the more two detections overlap, the more likely they correspond to the same object. This assumption is not true for two pairs of detections in two scenarios with different density: a pair in sparse scenario may have a higher probability of belonging to the same object than a pair in crowded scenario, though they have the same IoU. In other words, the degree of correlation between the IoU and the likelihood of belonging to the same object varies with density, and high density will devalue the IoU. Therefore, our idea is to take the density as an adjustment coefficient and reduce the value of IoU in crowded scenario to offset its depreciation. In addition, it should be noted that the above elaboration focuses on reducing the similarity between detections belonging to different objects, and we should try to avoid reducing the similarity between detections belonging to same objects too much at the same time. We express this requirement as reducing the IoUs between classes more than within classes. Therefore, we use formula (4) to modify the degree of overlap.

$$c_i = \left(\sum_{j=1}^{4} \frac{1}{std_{ij}}\right) \frac{1}{\max(c_i)}. \tag{1}$$

$$a_i = log\left(\frac{w_i}{h_i}\right). \tag{2}$$

$$NF_i = concat(c_i, s_i, a_i, den_i). \tag{3}$$

$$IoU_{ij} = IoU_{ij} - IoU_{ij} \cdot \min(den_i \cdot s_i, den_j \cdot s_j). \tag{4}$$

$$EF_{ij} = concat\left[IoU_{ij}, log\left(\frac{w_i}{w_j}\right), log\left(\frac{h_i}{h_j}\right), log\left(\frac{a_i}{a_j}\right), d_{ij}\right]. \tag{5}$$

In formulas above, std_i, w_i, h_i, s_i, den_i denote respectively the standard deviation, width, height, classification score, density belonging to one detection while IoU_{ij} and d_{ij} denote the IoU and the normalised distance in x and y direction between two detections. These values above can be gained from the output of upstream detector, directly or after computing. And the node feature and edge feature NF_i, EF_{ij} are gained after concatenating.

The key of one GAT layer is the aggregation of neighbors of each node. Before the aggregation of a node and its node neighbors, the node feature of neighbors will be concatenated with edge features between them and center node, as the temporary features participating in the aggregation of this center node. In order to ensure the feature dimension of the node itself participating in aggregation consistent with its neighbors, the feature of the node will also be concatenated with an edge feature between itself and itself. The features of all nodes participating in the aggregation are weighted and summed after linear transformation, while the weight is attention and the dimension of output of all linear transformations is 64. Linear transformations and weights are learned by the GAT layer from graph data. There are eight of the above aggregation processes, which are parallel to each other, and their results are averaged as the final updated feature of the center node. There are 10 GAT layers in our model, where the input of each will be added to its output as the input for the next one, this design inspired by ResNet [30].

The matching module is responsible for generating labels for all detections according to ground-truths. The matching algorithm is determined by the evaluation algorithm, which matches the detection to the ground-truths in descending order of scores and each object can only be matched once. Similarly, the matching algorithm only matches the only best detection for each object as a positive sample, and all other tests are negative samples no matter how close to the best detections. We adopting this strategy is because our model itself is supposed to perform NMS (Fig. 4).

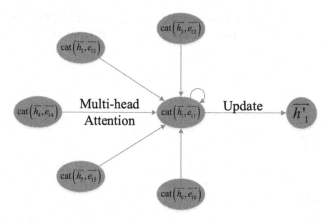

Fig. 4. The features concatenated by node features and edge features will be aggregated with multi-head attention mechanism.

4 Experiment

We tested the performance of our algorithm on VOC data set. We first train the detector with two datasets respectively. As is detailed above, the detector is based on Faster R-CNN framework that adopts pre-trained VGG-16 as backbone. The two training parameters are the same, following the original setting. We train the detector with SGD (stochastic gradient descent) for 80k iterations while the batch size is 1, starting with a learning rate of 10-3 and decreasing it to 10-4 after 50k iterations. Two trained detectors are responsible for generating detections with location confidence and object density, which act as dataset for the training and testing of our NMS. It's worth noting that the detections will be filtered by Greedy-NMS with a threshold 0.85. This very loose filtering is designed to remove almost identical detection, leading to damage that able to be almost completely ignored. All results are measured in average precision (AP), which is the area under the recall-precision curve. The overlap threshold (for matching detections to objects) is traditionally 0.5 IoU (as for Pascal VOC).

4.1 Object Detection on VOC

Dataset VOC dataset including annotated objects of 20 classes is an early general dataset in the field of computer vision and the touchstones for many classic models for classification, detection and segmentation. This dataset contains two subsets of VOC2007 and VOC2012, among which the test set of VOC2012 is not public. We choose both train set and val set of both VOC2007 and VOC2012 as train set including 16551 images with 40058 objects while the test set of VOC2007 as test set including 4952 images with 12302 objects. The two sets for the upstream detection and GAT-NMS are the same, either for training or testing. The generation of detections is detailed above. In addition, detections belonging to different class in a same image will be encoded into graphs respectively but allocated to a same training set. We train our GAT-NMS with ADAM (Adaptive moment estimation) for 40k iterations, starting with a learning rate of 10-3 and decrease it by 0.1 after 20k iterations.We compare our GAT-NMS to the most classic Greedy-NMS with several various thresholds (Fig. 5 and Table 1).

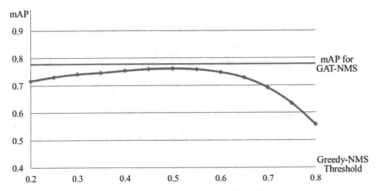

Fig. 5. The result of our GAT-NMS is better than Greedy-NMS with any threshold. Moreover, it should be pointed out that NMS is not easy to get the optimal threshold in practice.

Table 1. The result of our GAT-NMS is better than the best result of Greedy-NMS.

Greedy-NMS	>0.3	>0.4	>0.45	>0.5	>0.55	>0.6	>0.7
mAP	74.09	75.39	75.95	**76.14**	75.84	74.78	69.08
GAT-NMS				**77.54**			

4.2 Analysis of Experiment

As is shown in tables and figure above, our GAT-NMS is more powerful than traditional Greedy-NMS, which can be reflected from the results of two experiments. This success results from GAT-NMS making full use of global information, assisted by the indication of object density. In general terms, less information cannot support more accurate distinguishing. Therefore, it is correct to introduce more information as long as can be utilized effectively, which is proved by our model.

Acknowledgement. This work was supported by National Key R&D Program of China under Grant No. 2018YFB1402902.

References

1. Bodla, N., Singh, B., Chellappa, R., Davis, L.S.: Soft-NMS: improving object detection with one line of code. In: ICCV 2017 (2017)
2. Jiang, B., Luo, R., Mao, J.: Acquisition of localization confidence for accurate object detection. In: Ferrari, V., Hebert, M., Sminchisescu, C., Weiss, Y. (eds.) ECCV 2018. LNCS, vol. 11218, pp. 816–832 (2018). https://doi.org/10.1007/978-3-030-01264-9_48

3. He, Y., Zhu, C., Wang, J.: Softer-NMS: rethinking bounding box regression for accurate object detection. In: CVPR 2019 (2019)
4. Hosang, J., Benenson, R., Schiele, B.: A convnet for non-maximum suppression. In: GCPR 2016. LNCS, vol. 9796, pp. 192–204. Springer, Cham (2016). https://doi.org/10.1007/978-3-319-45886-1_16
5. Hosang, J.H., Benenson, R., Schiele, B.: Learning non-maximum suppression. In: CVPR 2017 (2017)
6. Liu,S., Huang, D., Wang, Y.: Adaptive NMS: refining pedestrian detection in a crowd. In: CVPR 2019 (2019)
7. Neubeck, A., Van Gool, L.J.: Efficient non-maximum suppression (2006)
8. Zhou, J., et al.: Graph neural networks: a review of methods and applications (2018)
9. Wu, Z., et al.: A comprehensive survey on graph neural networks. IEEE Trans. Neural Netw. Learn. Syst. **99**, 1–21
10. Bruna, J., Zaremba, W., Szlam, A., LeCun, Y.: Spectral networks and locally connected networks on graphs. In: Proceedings of ICLR (2014)
11. Henaff, M., Bruna, J., LeCun, Y.: Deep convolutional networks on graph-structured data. arXiv preprint arXiv:1506.05163 (2015)
12. Girshick, R., Donahue, J., Darrell, T.: Rich feature hierarchies for accurate object detection and semantic segmentation. In: CVPR 2014 (2014)
13. Cai, Z., Vasconcelos, N.: Cascade R-CNN: Delving into High Quality Object Detection (2017)
14. Ren, S., He, K., Girshick, R.: Faster R-CNN: towards real-time object detection with region proposal networks. IEEE Trans. Pattern Anal. Mach. Intell. **39**(6), 1137–1149
15. Redmon, J., et al.: You only look once: unified, real-time object detection. In: 2016 IEEE Conference on Computer Vision and Pattern Recognition (CVPR). IEEE 2016 (2016)
16. Liu, W., et al.: SSD: single shot multibox detector. In: Leibe, B., Matas, J., Sebe, N., Welling, M. (eds.) ECCV 2016. LNCS, vol. 9905, pp. 21–37. Springer, Cham (2016). https://doi.org/10.1007/978-3-319-46448-0_2
17. Redmon, J., Farhadi, A.: YOLO9000: better, faster, stronger. In: CVPR 2017 (2017)
18. Redmon, J., Farhadi, A.: YOLOv3: an incremental improvement (2018)
19. Girshick, R.: Fast R-CNN. In: 2015 IEEE International Conference on Computer Vision (ICCV). IEEE 2016 (2016)
20. Lin, T.Y., et al.: Feature Pyramid Networks for Object Detection (2016)
21. Liu, S., et al.: Path Aggregation Network for Instance Segmentation (2018)

Collaborative Filmmaking: Extending the Modes of Working Together by a Digital Platform

Ursula Kirschner[1]([⊠]) and Martin Kohler[2]

[1] Leuphana University Lüneburg, Universitätsallee 1, 21335 Lüneburg, Germany
kirschner@uni.leuphana.de
[2] University of Applied Sciences Hamburg, Berliner Tor 7, 20099 Hamburg, Germany
martin.kohler@haw-hamburg.de

Abstract. This paper reflects the conceptualization, implementation and use of a virtual server platform for urban documentary filmmaking in different teaching environments, ranging from immediate on-site recording to remote collaboration between scholars over longer periods. The platform is part of an on-going series of workshops, courses, summer and spring schools as well as individual research and production work on urban frontier zones.

In addition to a SWOT analysis, we derived a strategy for future use in the context of international workshops as action research design. This should facilitate analysis of the film material and open a discourse about "Frontier Zones" on a broader level, with insights by experts from various parts of the world and coming from different academic disciplines, sharing their thoughts by visual means and narrative analyses. The material from the schools should be available for all participants in the long term in order to enable the schools to carry out new methodological experiments in the post-production.

Keywords: Cooperative visual analytics and communication · Virtual server platform · Collaborative filmmaking

1 Introduction

In urban research, the term "Urban Frontiers" refers to spaces in and around a city on the cusp of larger transformations [1], often due to capital investment, racialized political struggle or technological innovations. The frontier is as much a spatial zone as it is a state of mind and a less verbalized communicative process on the shaping of the urban outcome and hitherto its belonging and identity structure. Discovering "Frontier Zones" in urban areas and examining them from a variety of perspectives applies the language of documentary filmmaking as an exploratory way to analyze urban areas and get closer to social realities than would be possible with text-based empirical social research. The interdisciplinary spring school in 2020 in Tunis was the third one on the topic of "Frontier Zones." The first two summer schools took place in São Paulo in 2015 and 2017. At the end of each session, students completed two online surveys,

© Springer Nature Switzerland AG 2021
Y. Luo (Ed.): CDVE 2021, LNCS 12983, pp. 160–171, 2021.
https://doi.org/10.1007/978-3-030-88207-5_16

evaluating the different methodologies of the field studies. We focused on four skills: collaboration, urban exploration, documentary filmmaking and creativity. Based on the evaluation results in 2015, we changed the schedule and the way of our collaboration to include more non-hierarchical collaboration modes, because the participants expressed clearly more autonomy in their contributions that honor their skills and expertship. In 2017, the evaluation overall was rather positive, but there was still the demand to provide more time for discussions [2]. Based on these outcomes and learnings from the preceding collaborations the concept of a supporting digital environment was developed and in 2020 we were able to install such a system by the support of a funding scheme of the German academic exchange institution (DAAD). This collaboration platform complemented the educational environment and physical site of workshops with a digital environment (see the corresponding section later) providing workflows for open groups and external contributors around rich media documents and offered access to film and sound material from these Brazilian summer schools. The collaboration platform gave teachers and students the possibility to collaboratively store, view and process media data regardless of their physical location, even in environments with a poor digital communication infrastructure. Every component is virtualized and can run on-site or in a remote data center. Thus we can tailor a collaboration suite for different working environments and adapt to the availability of resources. With this platform, we were able to offer a more comfortable digital environment, which in turn freed up time for more in-depth discussions.

In general, the digital platform offers virtual "spaces" either as projects or as processes in which people organize themselves on certain topics and occasions. This is where people communicate, research, collect information, edit and just think out loud. As the software of the collaborative editing targets film production and editing, the spaces support the collaborative editing of meta-data, commenting, time-markers (cues) and process workflows. All members can be contacted individually or in groups. Documents and materials are available to everyone and can be used for new creations and can be discussed. In this sense, the virtual spaces are not isolated, but are part of the entire group of participants of this type of workshops. Content from one space can easily be shared amongst all members on the same or other spaces. Clips can be downloaded and viewed. When new projects are created, they are linked directly to the workspace.

2   Research Framing "Frontier Zones"

Richard Sennett, sociologist, defines two different manifestations of edges - namely borders and boundaries. The dualism border-boundary enables an analysis of the openness of a city. In order to achieve this goal, we as urbanists are responsible for creating and designing places of encounter, which in turn work against a continuous opening of the city [3]. Sennett asked himself when and how this would be possible, which is a focus of his studies. A possible answer to this problem, i.e. a certain property of the city that is suitable as a prerequisite and possible starting point, are border areas or edges [4]. The edge condition means the transition area between different entities inside urban spaces. These transitions can be of a physical nature. Sennett defines the main difference between borders and boundaries as follows: Boundaries are closed, lifeless, relatively unnatural spaces, while borders are open, natural and alive. He takes a critical view of the trends in modern urban development in the sense that "we [urban planners] nowadays mostly create closed boundaries and we have lost the art of designing open border zones" [5].

As Sassen describes: "[A] Frontier Zone is a space where two actors from different worlds encounter each other. The actor could be a firm, an individual, a project, a civil society, an organization. [...] They encounter each other but there are no established rules governing that encounter" [6].

The term urban frontier was quickly adapted for urban settlements and got serious attention as lens for processes of gentrification that offered a more complex theory to understand the dynamics and contributions of processes of gentrification for urban change [7–9] and the structuring of insides and outsides within a city.

"In spatial terms, a paranoid style establishes a solid and hypertrophic line of separation between inside and outside. This hypertrophic line of separation we call border, as opposed to the more permeable organization of the limit in neurosis that we term frontier" [10]. It is therefore not only a question of a clear physical dividing line, but also of boundaries in people's thinking and ideas that are not clearly tangible. In general "the frontier is [...] a 'state of mind', rather than a legal, material and institutional concept: 'it is not so much a line where one stops, but rather an area that works as an invitation to access'" [11].

Discovering "Frontier Zones" in urban areas and examining them from a variety of perspectives, we used the language of documentary filmmaking as an exploratory way to analyze urban areas. This method is based on the thesis posed by the media scientists Horwitz, Joerges and Potthast. They propose that, by using images, film allows one to get "closer" to social realities than would be possible with text-based empirical social research [12]. We used this medium in the above-mentioned summer school sessions as well.

We understand "Frontier Zones" as "[...] a methodology, a set of tools and concepts to analyze emerging and contested urban spaces by observation and creative practice" [13]. The overall aim of the project "Frontier Zones" is not to take the perspective of a neutral observer, but rather to emphasize the different cultural and personal backgrounds and perspectives of the authors. Therefore, the captured and edited material is authentic and valuable and should remain accessible for further analysis by different scientific communities in the future.

3 Analyzing the Work Process

This research uses the results of the SWOT analyses of the different workshop scenarios to increase the added value of the server environment with action research. Action research is described by Kurt Lewin as "a comparative research on conditions and effects of various forms of social action and research leading to social action" [14].

We used for the SWOT analysis, the online evaluations with the software EvaSys during and after the Springschool and excerpts of the subsequently created student assignments. The two online workshops are evaluated by the findings from participant observations, as well as the examination results submitted as clips and papers.

4 The Collaborative Platform

A digital collaboration platform has to support many authors and editors (up to 100 persons at a time) and engage users in linking material, notes and insights with other authors, enabling the users to collaborate in producing richer agglomerated data while still maintaining the visibility of the original sources.

The collaboration platform includes a commercial content-management system optimized for rich media data (mainly film) (Kollaborate© TV), an encoding platform for the processing of audio-visual data, a web-based collaboration suite to access and manage this data and a file server. Each of these services is implemented as a virtual machine in a separate docker container that can be run on a mobile server platform (including all essential technical functionalities such as wireless networking, file storage, processing power) or hosted partially or entirely in data centers.

Together they provide services like editing, commenting, cataloging and tagging of video and audio files in the browser for collaborative and ethnographic documentary filmmaking. To adapt to different work scenarios all components can be hosted on a mobile NAS system with a dedicated graphic adapter for the media encoding and later re-transferred to more performative systems.

The mobile server (less than 10 kg) proved suitable as a mobile device for the smooth realization of workshops and spring schools like the one in Tunis.

Depending on the available networking and computing environment, additional learning scenarios can be realized, such as online workshops working on the same material with students on site or with students connected remotely to the server.

5 Case Studies

5.1 Case Study I: Spring School Tunis

Case study Tunis/Manouba: Manouba is a suburb in the western part of Tunis with a high proportion of disadvantaged social groups in the population, where the Future Lab Tunisia established a partnership between the local school Ibn Khaldoun Middle School and the Tunisian National Orchestra. Based on a model in Bremen, musicians from the Tunisian National Orchestra work in Manouba with the students from Ibn-Khaldoun Middle School [15]. The spring school was intended to grant the participants multi-perspective access to the public space of Manouba: the pupils, who were able to contribute not only their local expertise, but also their creative skills and musical interest. The program, which ran until December 2019, has developed a new dynamic in the district. The spring school examines these latent changes with the means of collaborative documentary. On the one hand, new dynamics are made visually describable and explored by a collaborative working method as multi-perspective spatial description; on the other hand, aspects requiring improvement are revealed and can be pointed out to urban planners. Urban developments were visually describable and explored with the support of various methods of sound and image recordings.

The goal of this spring school was an audio-visual documentary narration of urbanity in the context of previous international "Frontier Zones" summer schools.

Fig. 1. "Farming in Manouba is no longer profitable." Interview. Present and Future of Urban FRONTIER ZONES in Tunis – International Spring School 2020a: Urban Agriculture. Tunis. Minute 00:28.

The aim of the documentary was to "focus more on the polyphony of spaces [Manoubas]: the linking of local activities and social relationships with inscriptions through emotions, memory, stories, physical and mental appropriations, mental maps and struggles for meaning - far beyond the mere plot setting." [16] Descriptive words in interviews were the most important key element of the final films, as Figs. 1 and 2 confirm.

We integrated the server into a working area at different places in Manouba during the field research and later while editing the film at the university. In addition to an important research and archiving aspect, the results offer a critical potential for visualizing and dealing with current urban developments.

SWOT Springschool "Frontier Zones" in Tunis, March 2020	
Strength	• We collaborate in a very respectful way. We provide all collected data for every participant
	• We offer all data for further work and streaming. This particularly benefits the teachers' research work
	• We do not lose time by having to share all data from a workshop at the end
	• We do not have the issue compatibility between Mac and PC users

(continued)

(*continued*)

SWOT	Springschool "Frontier Zones" in Tunis, March 2020
Weaknesses	• "The server was not very useful because these few days are simply not enough to view all of the footage. Uploading things wasted even more time." (student's comment) • It took time to implement the server platform every time in a new environment • Sometimes we lost data • We waste time, because everyone has to be shown how to use the platform
Opportunities	• Create a community of all Frontier Zones participants • Find new creative ways to collaborate with this platform • Provide an archive for further - especially international – workshops • Learning by doing from different users • Ability to enhance our research capability • Use the feedback tool for a better understanding of the interpretations of urban challenges
Threats	• Participants can distribute the files and the links without knowing for what purpose • Participants can mistakenly delete or move files • Participants do not always have access to the platform due to connection problems and speed; this is frustrating and leads to giving up

5.2 Case Study II: Online Courses

The two online workshops that we will examine were carried out during the Covid-19 pandemic. The first one is a workshop on methodology in the master program and the second one is a workshop embedded in a cooperation with the Universidade de São Paulo, Escola da Cidade in São Paulo, HafenCity University Hamburg and Leuphana University Lüneburg. The workshop in the master course reflected the empirical field research methods that were applied in the context of two summer schools on the topic of "Frontier Zones" in an urban area of São Paulo. For the self-hosting we made use of Kollaborate©, which supports a wide range of operations like editing, commenting, cataloging and tagging of video and audio files in the browser. In both online workshops, the participants started from a critical observer perspective and moved to the role of a film producer. In order to test the methodology, master students from different fields were introduced to the topic "Frontier Zones" and then to the sequences-based film analysis.

Based on this knowledge, they were asked to produce new clips with the provided audio-visual material from São Paulo on new "Frontier Zones" topics. They were to convey their content without explanatory words, using only the captured urban sound and video material, as the participants did in São Paulo. Some groups began by creating a topic but were then not successful in finding material related to the specific topic. Just to get inspired by the material was a big challenge for most of them.

Fig. 2. Playground as a meeting point for the neighborhood. Present and Future of Urban FRONTIER ZONES in Tunis – International Spring School 2020b: Playground. Tunis. Minute 04:29.

Fig. 3. One screenshot with the comment "protagonist is getting into contact with the viewer," master course 2020. Film "Urban_Frontier_Loneliness." Minute 3:54.

In every workshop, some clips are chosen several times by different groups for various topics, for example the one from Fig. 3. It is always interesting to observe the different meanings the sequences could have. The menu on the right shows the information that users assign to the clip. Figures 3 and 4 are from the clip "Loneliness," in which the viewer becomes in a way an actor. In Fig. 3 the protagonist is talking with you and in Fig. 4 the protagonist is yourself, like an avatar.

SWOT Online workshop Escola da Cidade/Leuphana Lüneburg 2020	
Strength	• The large pool of authentic material is like a sociological treasure chest. "It can be assumed that not only the use of images as a component of films allows one to get closer to a social reality, but that auditory perception and reproduction make an essential contribution, too." (student comment) • Working online in groups by using Zoom, students are able to watch the clips individually and then discuss the selected clips in breakout sessions

(continued)

(*continued*)

SWOT Online workshop Escola da Cidade/Leuphana Lüneburg 2020	
Weaknesses	• The quality of the clips when watching in Zoom sessions was worse • Each student has to collect clips according to their own association to the topic. "As the full content of the rough recorded material was unknown, a lot of time had to be dedicated to becoming familiar with it. We had to look over all the material a couple of times, not knowing exactly what to expect to see." (Student comment)
Opportunities	• Viewing authentic footage enabled students to grasp an unfamiliar space and to form their own opinion. In some cases, it could serve as a substitute for an excursion • Instead of the usual text-based work, students gain experience in researching with audio-visual material. Implementing this kind of methodology in their own research field, like sustainability, economics, political science, etc. could be an enrichment
Threats	• The raw recorded material is overwhelming for the viewers, so they may lose interest and get lost on the platform • Representatives of some disciplines could reject this methodology, because they assume it does not correspond to the scientific standard

In the second online workshop with bachelor students, the focus was on looking for "Frontier Zones" topics in the given Kollaborate© environment and finding similar scenarios in Hamburg. They conducted experiments using the provided material in combination with their own recorded film material. This time the group started by using the feedback tools but later worked without them; it was easier for them to figure out a suitable topic.

Fig. 4. The protagonist like an avatar. Masters course 2020. Film "Life in the fabric" Minute 2:10

Fig. 5. Framed view of São Paulo (left) and of Hamburg (right) from the film "Frontier Zones Rough Cut," bachelor course 2020; second 05:14; 17:00

Fig. 6. Two protagonists from the film "Frontier Zones Rough Cut" (left São Paulo, right Hamburg), bachelor course 2020; minute 2:35; 2:06

Figures 5 and 6 show images of the two cities from the same perspective, but with a different atmosphere. The images from Fig. 6 present the same protagonists; in São Paulo, the person is sitting in the middle of the pedestrian zone and in Hamburg in front of a shop window. This observation can open a discussion on e.g. how the interaction between society and the protagonists in the different cultures differs.

SWOT Online workshop with BSc students, Leuphana Lüneburg, 2020	
Strength	• The provided material inspired the students • To combine film sequences from two different cities makes on one hand the differences and on the other hand the similarities between single topics more visible. Students become more and more aware of these aspects
Weaknesses	• Not everybody chooses to provide comments on the clips. Normally they prefer to select clips and then to work with them • Sometimes the server is unavailable for various reasons
Opportunities	• The films could give impulses for the discussion of special topics and to deepen some research fields • By using the feedback tools, the group provides for the individuals easier access to the material and opens discussions on the different perspectives und perceptions

(continued)

(continued)

SWOT Online workshop with BSc students, Leuphana Lüneburg, 2020	
Threats	• If students use the material without having studied it and combine it with foreign material, strong alienations or disassociations could arise • All users are invited to act as administrators of the platform. In this role they can design their own file structure, which may not be compatible with other file structures

6 Use Cases

For further, more analytical workshops, it could be useful to preselect clips according to given topics. They could be ranked by the significance of the issue, e.g. using colors. To deepen the discussion on urban Frontier Zones, more time should be spent on the interpretation, e.g. in a hermeneutic way [17, 18]. Therefore, other visual material could be used either from the platform or from the internet, without studying text-based analysis. Furthermore, interpretation modes could be "iconological" and "iconic" interpretation as well as criteria of the formal aesthetics.

Another conceivable use case is as an international hybrid workshop, where people from different countries record audio-visual material on a chosen topic and in similar areas of different cities, such as near the main railway station. After uploading, the whole group could first study the footage individually and then collectively. The next step is collaboratively editing and discussing the different approaches to the research fields, the perception and the findings.

7 Reflection on the Results

Documentaries are often made by journalists and filmmakers, without "scientific" background. The textual bias in society and the habit of relying on written, text-based material contribute to the underrepresentation of visual documentaries in research [19].

The use of audio-visual media is increasing rapidly in our society, and it is also starting to play a greater role in scientific methods and research. Particularly sciences that research social contexts - such as Frontier Zones - could present their research results to a broader audience outside of science using audio-visual media [20].

Rooms are characterized by their multi-dimensionality and the possibility of change in which physical and atmospheric moments take place, which are grasped and perceived differently by different recipients. Text-based methods alone cannot capture or map this complexity and plurality.

The platform with the audio-visual raw material serves as third eyes for a view into foreign places and situations. It takes time to deepen the content. The consequent focus of the DAM on collaborative working processes (shared annotation, synced media-presentation, adaptable workflow models for collaborative video editing, group resources) did improve the integration of foreign material in the participants work and created denser connections between the captured perspectives than have been observed in previous workshops. But for impromptu situations as the workshop in Tunis the encoding response and uploading performance did not satisfy the participants and was perceived a hindrance in their work. This can be technically solved by increasing the processing and storage resources.

Inspired by attending the spring school in Tunis, two Tunisian participants, supported by the Kamel Lazaar Foundation, submitted an application for the HOUMTEK program at the Goethe Institute, which has been approved. Since October 2020, they have been working with pupils and residents to develop concepts for upgrading public spaces, especially a playground in Manouba/Boustil. They will have the opportunity to develop ideas from the field research of the spring school. Some teachers from the spring school are accompanying this project.

Follow-up projects similar to this one signal the interest and sustainable impact of the spring school: The Goethe Institute itself referred our methodology for the concept of a climate radio project. The Kamal Foundation conceptualized public streaming of the final films.

8 Conclusion

The three case studies present different research and teaching concepts on how to implement the server platform. In Tunis we used it in a real laboratory to collect experiences and to gain insight into where the limits are and how we could optimize the structure and the availability. In order to optimize the full capabilities and features of the system, it is advisable to repeat spring schools in comparable situations and environment, in the sense of action research.

The practical applications in the context of the online workshop have shown how valuable this server can be. For the interaction of the workshop participants with physical distance, the server is a prerequisite. Individual and collective work can thus be carried out optimally. Ultimately, the server was successfully used during the pandemic. Only the non-permanent access requires a new system setting.

In addition to the technical use each time, the teachers have to be aware that students need thorough preparation and should be sensitized to the content.

Acknowledgments. We would like to thank all students in the spring school in Tunis 2020 and the co-teachers and the students of the seminars at Leuphana University Lüneburg. The International Summer/Spring Schools are sponsored by the German Academic Exchange Service (DAAD), with funding from the Federal Ministry of Education and Research (BMBF).

References

1. King, C., Burt, S.: Urban frontiers (2019). https://doi.org/10.1002/9781118568446
2. Kirschner, U.: Urban transdisciplinary co-study in a cooperative multicultural working project. In: Luo, Y. (ed.) CDVE 2018. LNCS, vol. 11151, pp. 145–152. Springer, Cham (2018). https://doi.org/10.1007/978-3-030-00560-3_20
3. Sennet, R.: Aufruhr. Lessingtage. Thalia Theater, Hamburg (2015). https://www.youtube.com/watch?v=AkIP-FZuTdY. Accessed 20 June 2020

4. ibid
5. ibid, min. 37–55
6. Sassen, S.: 1/6 - Global Cities as Today's Frontiers - Leuphana Digital School (2015). https://www.youtube.com/watch?v=Iu-p31RkCXI, min. 0:28–0:44. Accessed 03 Apr 2021
7. Wade, R.C.: Cities in American Life, Selected Readings. Houghton Mifflin, Boston (1971)
8. Smith, N.: The New Urban Frontier: Gentrification and the Revanchist City. Routledge, London, New York (1996)
9. Colomb, C.: Pushing the urban frontier: temporary uses of space, city marketing and the creative city discourse in 2000s Berlin. J. Urban Aff. **34**(2), 131–152 (2012). https://doi.org/10.1111/j.1467-9906.2012.00607.x
10. King, C., Burt, S.: Urban frontier. In: The Wiley-Blackwell Encyclopedia of Urban and Regional Studies (2019)
11. Schiavone, A.: La Politica Dei Confini Dell'Impero Romano. In: Politiche e mitologie dei confini europei, pp. 27–39. Foundazione Collegio San Carlo, Modena (2008)
12. Horwitz, M., Joerges, B., Potthast, J. (eds.): Stadt und Film. Versuch zu einer "Visuellen Soziologie". Discussion Paper FS-II 96-503. Wissenschaftszentrum, Berlin (1996). (Translated by the author). http://bibliothek.wz-berlin.de/pdf/1996/ii96-503.pdf. Accessed 29 Apr 2020
13. Kohler, M.: Frontier Zones – International Summer School (2017). https://www.youtube.com/watch?v=wR3o5WwrdCU, min. 1:11. Accessed 20 May 2021
14. Lewin, K.: Action research and minority problems. J. Soc. Sci. **2**, 35 (1946)
15. See. JAOU Kamel Lazaar Foundation org.: Future Lab Tunisia. https://www.kamellazaarfoundation.org/project/futurelab-tunisia. Accessed 04 May 2020
16. Bachmann-Medick, D.: Cultural Turns. Neuorientierungen in den Kulturwissenschaften. 3. Auflage, p. 304 (2009). (Translated by the author)
17. Herbrik, R.: Hermeneutische Wissenssoziologie (sozialwissenschaftliche Hermeneutik). In: Akremi, L., et al. (eds.) Handbuch Interpretativ forschen, Weinheim, pp. 636–659 (2018)
18. Kirschner, U.: A hermeneutic interpretation of concepts in a cooperative multicultural working project. In: Ibaceta, M.R. (Hrsg.) SIGraDi 2017: XXI Congreso de la Sociedad Ibero-Americana de Gráfica Digital, Blucher, pp. 610–615 (2018)
19. Belk, R.: Examining markets, marketing, consumers, and society through documentary films. J. Mark. **31**(3), 403–409 (2011)
20. Abstiens, L., Hierse, L.: Bewegte Räume: Potenziale von Videographie und Film als Methoden der qualitativen Sozialforschung. In: sozialraum.de (2017). https://www.sozialraum.de/bewegte-raeume-potenziale-von-videographie-und-film-als-methoden-der-qualitativen-sozialforschung.php. Accessed 20 July 2020

Building a Big Data Oriented Architecture for Enterprise Integration

Le Hoang Nam and Phan Duy Hung$^{(\boxtimes)}$

FPT University, Hanoi, Vietnam
nam19mse13037@fsb.edu.vn, hungpd2@fe.edu.vn

Abstract. Digital transformation is happening across all industries and affecting all facets of our daily life. However, in many corporations, this important process is fragmented and is undertaken without a farsighted plan to take advantage of an invaluable resource: data. This can be due to a variety of reasons, for example, lack of funding, poor business vision, inappropriate consulting or deployment. Digital transformation is a considerable investment since it will determine the system's ability to grow and adapt to the company's changing requirements. To achieve that end, the architecture must be flexible both in development and deployment and must also be able to harness the ever-increasing data of the corporation. Among the widely used information system architectures being used in the world, Microservice is a standout with many advantages. The adaptation of this architecture to work with Big Data, as well as to tackle different aspects of a data system such as load-balancing, file handling and storage, etc. is a very practical area of research. This paper presents such an enterprise integration solution for a mega-corporation client in Vietnam, the An Pha Petrol Group Joint Stock Company, including the architecture and technologies used to build a comprehensive system that brings novel experiences to its 2,000 internal users. It consists of building the information infrastructure and system, super applications for both desktop and mobile devices to enhance the work performance and quality. The approaches and results of this paper are applicable to similar large enterprise solutions.

Keywords: Enterprise integration · Architecture · Big Data · Microservice

1 Introduction

Digital transformation is not just a trend among big corporations, but it is becoming a necessity for all companies in the age of Industry 4.0. Many are aware of the requirement but do not understand all the advantages or the know-hows. An information system requires 3 separate parts that must be tackled simultaneously: digital infrastructure, digitalized management system and digitalized production data. However, many companies are using fragmented and inefficient pieces of software to manage accounting, production, warehousing, etc., without the ultimate aim of controlling their biggest asset in this process: data. Meanwhile, they should have "started small" but always keep the "big picture" in mind. The small start may include things such as digitizing documents to

Y. Luo (Ed.): CDVE 2021, LNCS 12983, pp. 172–182, 2021.
https://doi.org/10.1007/978-3-030-88207-5_17

keep printing down, digitalize tasks assignment and progress tracking. These works will gradually make using software part of the company's culture. At the same time, using the data gathered with new technologies such as Big Data, Artificial Intelligence, Machine Learning, Blockchain, etc. to achieve the big picture of data-driven decision making in building a smart management system that can bring about better customer satisfaction, shorter time-to-market, increased efficiency and more.

Such a "big picture" information system, of course, requires a similarly grand vision from the directors of the company. And they too need an architect that can build an optimized and flexible system that can adapt to the growing demand of the company in both business and data.

Among the widely used information system architectures, Micro-service is one with many advantages. The microservice architecture is style that structures a system as a collection of services. It enables the delivery of large and complex systems by frequently adding loosely coupled, independent applications. The flexibility and high maintainability are the key features that make Micro-service extremely suitable for large systems.

Regarding building and deploying information system solutions for corporations, as well as optimizing solutions to the integration of different modules in a system, several related studies were found.

In chapter "Microservice Architecture" [1], Bob Familiar introduce an approach of designing microservices using Separation of Concern (SoC). SoC is a design principle for separating implementation into distinct layers corresponding to separate concern. Microservices architecture uses SoC to identify business concerns. Then the business & data layer of 3-Tier Architecture or Layered Architecture is vertically sliced into isolated & bounded context services, each with its own domain model and API.

Alexis Henry and Youssef Ridene in [2] state that the trade-off is essential in order to successfully migrate your business applications toward microservices. The work aims to drive readers through a journey by presenting a roadmap and methodology which has been used successfully in several projects. They guide readers through the typical microservice migration project by using migration patterns for managing service decomposition and data isolation and replication. Those patterns may be used iteratively in any order, therefore authors defined a reference architecture to sequence the building of your microservice architecture. Eventually they conclude with a use case from the real world.

Following previous work on the automated deployment of component-based applications, Mario Bravetti et al. present a formal model specifically tailored for reasoning on the deployment of microservice architectures [3]. The authors present a formal proof of decidability of the problem of synthesizing optimal deployment plans for microservice architectures, a problem which was proved to be undecidable for generic component-based applications. Then, given that such proof translates the deployment problem into a constraint satisfaction problem, they present the implementation of a tool that, by exploiting state-of-the-art constraint solvers, can be used to actually synthesize optimal deployment plans. The work evaluates the applicability of the tool on a realistic microservice architecture taken from the literature.

The above studies have shown the deployments of Micro-service for many different corporations. However, they have yet explored how to combine this architecture with a

Big Data processing business. They also have not gone into details about the technical requirements that are frequently needed for integration and information management solutions.

This paper gives a Micro-service architecture as implemented for large organizations with a Big-data oriented approach. In the different modules, the sub-modules that are frequently used and play an important role in the overall performance of the system are presented and analyzed in details. For example, the load-balancing, dockerization, file size optimization, specialized file handling, archiving, storage.

This paper presents the general architectures and technologies with a case study on a mega-corporation client of ours in Vietnam, the An Pha Petrol Group Joint Stock Company.

An Pha Petroleum Group JSC. [4] is a large corporation with many member companies. The expansion and merger that happened during the development process made it extremely difficult to manage internal information and an urgent concern. The whole corporation and its companies do not have a common platform to handle processes, procedures and paperwork. Internal tasks are either not digitized or are on different heterogeneous software platforms. That leads to difficulty in management and statistics for the company directors, as well as presents challenges in expanding the business in the future.

The paper describes the specific implementation applied to build a comprehensive system that brings new experiences to all of its 2,000 employees. It consists of building the information infrastructure and system, super applications for both desktop and mobile devices to enhance the work performance and quality. The approaches and results of this paper are applicable to similar large enterprise solutions.

With that aim in mind, this paper will introduce the Microservice architecture: the system design and how it is separated into small components. Add-on features that all businesses need are covered and how to integrate them with the system. Software continuous integration and deployment are introduced in the case of an on-premise deployment at An Pha. Database design is also considered here, as a cache layer ready for data mining & big data.

The remainder of the paper is organized as follows. Section 2 describes system requirements. The system design and implementation are presented in Sect. 3. Then, conclusions and perspectives are made in Sect. 4.

2 System Architecture and Requirements

2.1 Architecture Overview

The architecture of whole system is described in Fig. 1.

The whole system is divided into several subsystems, corresponding to a system on the head of group (Corporation Information System) and systems of the member companies (Member Company business system). This will distribute data and operations in each company subsystem located in different geographical locations. Thus, it reduces the latency of business operations on the software. These subsystems are all structurally similar, consists of main components listed as below:

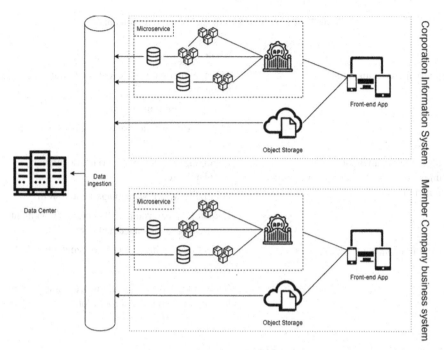

Fig. 1. Architecture overview.

- Front-end app: Applications on different platform (mobile & desktop) that interact directly with end-users. They are used as all-in-one applications with full provided features.
- Object storage: The space for storing all files of employees for paperwork, profiles, reports. The local storage server is used here instead of cloud storage because all files are confidential and need to be saved on premise.
- Microservice: Server side receive front-end request, process & save information in database. Here the microservice architecture is applied, with many services & 1 API Gateway.

The following components are used for mining, analysis data from subsystems:

- Data ingestion: A pipeline is responsible for moving data to the Data Center, where the data can be further enriched and analyzed.
- Data center: A cluster of many servers. Big data analysis and processing are performed here.

2.2 System Requirements

The system focuses on solving digital problems that businesses often encounter, with users being employees of the enterprise and system administrators (also belonging to the enterprise). The functional requirements are described in Table 1.

Table 1. Main categories of functional requirements

Type	Content
Internal communications	Manage internal news, events, activities, job openings
	Communication in groups
	Manage user profiles: roles, avatar, phone, email, etc.
Software modules for units/groups/departments have defined functions	Digitizing production materials: documents, templates, etc.
	Digitizing workflow, management system
	Ex: booking car, room; call center management; retail/wholesale management; etc.
Common management modules	Project management & task assignments
	Request processing
	Send and receive notifications according to the hierarchical model of corporation

3 System Design and Implementation

3.1 Servers

The system consists of many servers configured in Table 2.

Table 2. List of servers used in the system.

No	Configuration			Type	Number	Function	Environment
	CPU (Cores)	RAM (Gb)	HDD (TB)				
1	20	64	8	Physical	1	Database	PRODUCTION
2	20	64	8	Physical	1	Object storage	PRODUCTION
3	32	128	8	Physical	2	Microservice	PRODUCTION
4	20	128	8	Physical	5	Data center	PRODUCTION

3.2 Microservice Applications

The backend application consists of many services. The design, implementation and deployment of a service has the following characteristics:

- A service is an isolated component, performs features of a specific domain. The context, boundary of a domain is divided based on Domain-Driven Design (DDD) [5], closely follow the operations and activities of the divisions in the enterprise.
- The functions provided by a service are independent from that of others. That helps the software implementation to be able to execute in parallel. Thus, the digitization of each department's business in the enterprise can be flexible, depending on the priority of development orientation and their need.
- The implementation of a service is encapsulated as API, so the upgrade, maintenance can be done without affecting client-side.
- A service usually is a stateless application. That is, it doesn't cache any information, such as user's session. That helps the scaling of service into multiple instances, increases the availability of the system and remove the single point of failure.

Services are implemented in Spring boot [6] and are deployed as service instances via containerization [7]. Spring Boot's many purpose-built features make it easy to build and run your microservices in production at scale. And the microservice architecture is completed with the Spring Cloud – easing administration and boosting the fault-tolerance. The containerization technology used here is docker. Source code & dependencies of a service are packaged as a docker image and deployed as docker container.

The microservice architecture is described in Fig. 2:

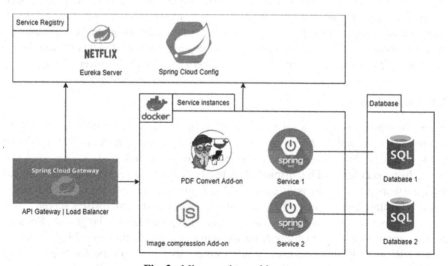

Fig. 2. Microservice architecture.

When creating applications, it's therefore worth optimizing Docker Images and Dockerfiles to help teams share smaller images, improve performance, and debug problems. A lot of verified images available on Docker Hub are already optimized, so it is always a good idea to use ready-made images wherever possible. With some services need to create an image of your own, several ways of optimization it for production is considered, for example: Base image with a smaller footprint, Cleanup commands, Static builds of libraries, Only necessary dependencies, No pip caching, Multi-stage builds, using ".dockerignore" files, dependencies caching. Such intelligent implementation of optimization strategies allowed us to reduce the Docker image size and increase in speed of image building and sharing.

Database architecture is database-per-service [8]. Changing one service's database does not impact any other services. Each service can choose the database type which is best suited for its need (SQL, NoSQL). With SQL database, we are using Microsoft SQL server. SQL table design don't have foreign key constraint, thus increasing flexibility by easily change schema design, data migration without affecting others.

Service registry is an essential component because all other services registered here when deploying. It connects all services & provide communication between them. Hence, API Gateway known the location of service instances on network for routing. API Gateway is a single-entry point of the server side, which receives all requests from client side and proxies/routes to the appropriate services. Thanks to API gateway, a service can be scaled into multiple instances to increase the availability, fault tolerance of system. Here, the technologies we used for Service Registry is Netflix Eureka [9] and API Gateway is Spring Cloud Gateway [10].

In addition to fully satisfying the business operations, other add-on features are also considered. These are normally featuring related to image processing and file processing. We designed each add-on feature as a service in the microservices, rather than SDK or dependencies in front-end apps. It has some advantages: reduction in cost and development time, reduction in the size of front-end applications, using the best libraries for extra requirements. There are various add-ons we have employed in this project for An Pha: Sharp [11] for image compression, Gotenberg [12] for PDF conversion, etc.

3.3 Object Storage

A very common necessity in software service is file storage and transfer. In order to be independent from any third party, to ensure the stability and support for API development and to keep cost down, this service has to be carefully selected.

In the project for An Pha, Minio [13] is used as object storage on system. Minio has the same working concepts as Amazon S3 [14]. Minio is used here instead of S3 because it is open source and can be easily installed on premise at the enterprise's server.

Minio provide an SDK for most commonly used programming languages. Because the files are private, the uploading & downloading is done via pre-signed URLs. A pre-signed URL is a URL that end-users to grant temporary access to a specific object. Using the URL, the user can read and write the object in a specific timeout. By using pre-signed URL, the download/upload files of front-end apps do not go through the backend but connects directly with the Minio, which reduces the load on the backend server, while still ensuring file security (Fig. 3).

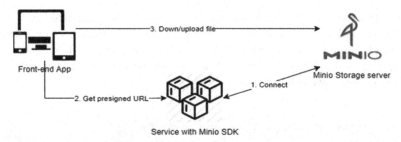

Fig. 3. Working with Minio by presigned URL.

3.4 Data Ingestion and Data Center

The Data Center & Data Ingestion is built as Hadoop Ecosystem. It consists of many elements to solve the big data problems, such as: HDFS, YARN, Spark, Pig, Hive, Kafka, etc. [15].

The data center built for An Pha includes 5 physical servers (with configurations shown in Table 1). All servers use RAID 0 for data storage in disk. In the HDFS concept, there are 1 Name node and 4 Data nodes. The HDFS replication factor here is 3. This data center can handle up to 10 terabytes of data. With a Server Cluster running on Hadoop, data center expansion to accommodate the corporation's needs is guaranteed.

Data ingestion is a process that collects data from various data sources, in an unstructured format and stores it somewhere to analyze that data. This data can be real-time or integrated in batches. Real-time data is ingested as soon it arrives, while the data in batches is ingested in some chunks at a periodical interval of time. To make this ingestion process work smoothly, we can use different tools at different layers which will help to build the data pipeline. Apache sqoop and Kafka are used for data ingestion.

Sqoop designed for efficiently transferring bulk data between Apache Hadoop and structured datastores such as relational databases of The Apache Software Foundation.

Apache Kafka have a core component as Kafka Connect API, introduced in version 0.9. It provides scalable and resilient integration between Kafka and other systems. The two options to consider are using the JDBC connector for Kafka Connect, or using a log-based Change Data Capture (CDC) tool which integrates with Kafka Connect. In this project, Sqoop and CDC tool integrated Kafka are used.

3.5 Front-End Applications

Taking up the most effort in company management solutions is usually the desktop application. It is written in JavaFX in order to optimize the human resources as the backend is developed in Java [16]. JavaFX is an open-source application platform for desktop application built on Java. The community, dependencies and libraries is excellent for all enterprise feature needs. JavaFX also support CSS to create a highly customized and desired user interface.

For the mobile application, React Native is selected because it is one of the most stable (release on 2015) and common framework [17]. It is an open-source framework for building cross-platform mobile apps using React, another framework created and developed by Facebook. It uses JavaScript - a very popular programming language and provides a complete set of common view components and dependencies for enterprise app. The choice in React Native also helps in finding developers without maintaining two separate Android and iOS teams. A few screenshots of the desktop and mobile applications are shown below, in Figs. 4, 5 and 6.

Fig. 4. The main screen of the application on the Desktop.

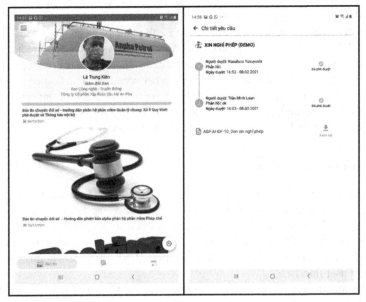

Fig. 5. The main screen of the application on the Mobile (left) and screen of software module "Request Processing" (right).

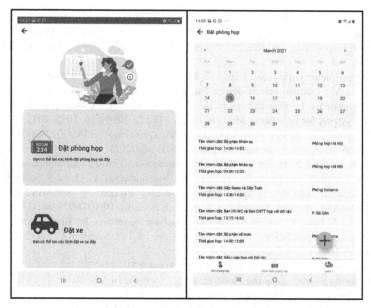

Fig. 6. Two screenshots of software module "Meeting room booking".

4   Conclusion and Perspectives

This research focuses on a practical problem of building a Micro-service architecture with a Big Data oriented approached. At the same time, this research also organizes the best practices to help with the optimization of enterprise integration such as load balancing, services for file transfer, storage, conversion, archiving and optimization of RAM for services.

This paper also presented a case study of a comprehensive digitalization solution and information system for An Pha Petroleum Group JSC, Vietnam.

The microservice architecture is introduced with common solutions as file storage, add-on features. Service design, implementation principles and deployment technologies are also described here. Above all, the database design oriented to the collection and processing of big data is considered.

This solution is also fully applicable for similar large enterprises and is also a good reference for research directions of Software engineering, Information System, etc. [18–20].

References

1. Familiar, B.: Microservice architecture. In: Microservices, IoT, and Azure, pp. 21–31 (2015). https://doi.org/10.1007/978-1-4842-1275-2_3
2. Henry, A., Ridene, Y.: Migrating to microservices. In: Bucchiarone, A., et al. (eds.) Microservices: Science and Engineering, pp. 45–72. Springer, Cham (2020). https://doi.org/10.1007/978-3-030-31646-4_3

3. Bravetti, M., Giallorenzo, S., Mauro, J., Talevi, I., Zavattaro, G.: A formal approach to microservice architecture deployment. In: Bucchiarone, A., et al. (eds.) Microservices: Science and Engineering, pp. 183–208. Springer, Cham (2020). https://doi.org/10.1007/978-3-030-31646-4_8

4. An Pha Petroleum Group JSC. https://anphapetrol.com/. Accessed 01 Mar 2021

5. Khemaja, M.: Domain driven design and provision of micro-services to build emerging learning systems. In: Proceedings of the Fourth International Conference on Technological Ecosystems for Enhancing Multiculturality (TEEM 2016), pp. 1035–1042. Association for Computing Machinery, New York (2016). https://doi.org/10.1145/3012430.3012643

6. https://spring.io/projects/spring-boot. Accessed 01 Mar 2021

7. Yadav, A.K., Garg, M.L., Ritika: Docker containers versus virtual machine-based virtualization. In: Abraham, A., Dutta, P., Mandal, J.K., Bhattacharya, A., Dutta, S. (eds.) Emerging Technologies in Data Mining and Information Security: Proceedings of IEMIS 2018, Volume 3, pp. 141–150. Springer, Singapore (2019). https://doi.org/10.1007/978-981-13-1501-5_12

8. Henry, A., Ridene, Y.: Assessing your microservice migration. In: Bucchiarone, A., et al. (eds.) Microservices: Science and Engineering, pp. 73–107. Springer, Cham (2020). https://doi.org/10.1007/978-3-030-31646-4_4

9. https://spring.io/projects/spring-cloud-netflix. Accessed 01 Mar 2021

10. https://spring.io/projects/spring-cloud-gateway. Accessed 01 Mar 2021

11. https://sharp.pixelplumbing.com/. Accessed 01 Mar 2021

12. https://thecodingmachine.github.io/gotenberg/. Accessed 01 Mar 2021

13. https://min.io/. Accessed 01 Mar 2021

14. https://aws.amazon.com/s3/. Accessed 01 Mar 2021

15. Mrozek, D.: Foundations of the Hadoop ecosystem. In: Mrozek, D. (ed.) Scalable Big Data Analytics for Protein Bioinformatics: Efficient Computational Solutions for Protein Structures, pp. 137–150. Springer, Cham (2018). https://doi.org/10.1007/978-3-319-988 39-9_6

16. Chin, S., Johan, V., James, W.: The Definitive Guide to Modern Java Clients with JavaFX, Cross-Platform Mobile and Cloud Development (2019)

17. Akshat, P., Abhishek, N.: React Native for Mobile Development, Harness the Power of React Native to Create Stunning iOS and Android Applications (2019)

18. Hai, M.M., Hung, P.D.: Centralized access point for information system integration problems in large enterprises. In: Luo, Y. (ed.) CDVE 2020. LNCS, vol. 12341, pp. 239–248. Springer, Cham (2020). https://doi.org/10.1007/978-3-030-60816-3_27

19. Tae, C.M., Hung, P.D.: A collaborative web application based on incident management framework for financial system. In: Luo, Y. (ed.) CDVE 2020. LNCS, vol. 12341, pp. 289–301. Springer, Cham (2020). https://doi.org/10.1007/978-3-030-60816-3_32

20. Chung, N.N., Hung, P.D.: Logging and monitoring system for streaming data. In: Luo, Y. (ed.) CDVE 2020. LNCS, vol. 12341, pp. 184–191. Springer, Cham (2020). https://doi.org/10.1007/978-3-030-60816-3_21

Integrating Chatbot and RPA into Enterprise Applications Based on Open, Flexible and Extensible Platforms

Phan Duy Hung[✉], Do Thuy Trang, and Tran Khai

FPT University, Hanoi, Vietnam
hungpd2@fe.edu.vn, {trangdthe130166,khaithe130197}@fpt.edu.vn

Abstract. The digital transformation is going at break-neck speed in enterprises across all fields. Some of them have chosen to digitalize only essential processes or use ready-made solutions without thinking about system integration or developing application interfaces. Others set out to build a comprehensive digital infrastructure with management, administration, and production systems. However, for a large majority of them, digital transformation is an ever-going process as new business requirements, which will inevitably crop up. In this case, Robotic Process Automation (RPA) is a suitable solution. RPA is a concept in which software robots take over humans in automating iterative business processes with fixed logic that does not have an existing application programming interface (API). Recently, the combination of RPA and chatbots is considered an effective tool for handling many business processes. This research proposes a solution and procedure based on open platforms, which can be readily extended by enterprises as needed. This solution can also be improved with Artificial Intelligence (AI) algorithms. The result is demonstrated through a few selective business processes that have been implemented in an organization and proven effective. The work focuses on the flexibility, ease of deployment, and efficiency of an RPA-chatbot solution targeting business digitalization.

Keywords: Information system integration · Chatbot · RPA · AI

1 Introduction

Investing in technology in businesses has never been more appropriate when new technologies can deliver considerable productivity improvements compared to manual works at very reasonable prices. The year 2020 alone brought about more digital transformations than the whole previous decade combined. As companies do not want to fall behind in the competition, every digitization effort is being accelerated and implemented on a large scale because those who do will inevitably experience a remarkable breakthrough in every aspect [1].

However, there are no common pathways for every company, so each of them has to carve out their own rules regarding estimation of costs, prioritization of high-value works or new services, retraining and transferring redundant workers out of automated

© Springer Nature Switzerland AG 2021
Y. Luo (Ed.): CDVE 2021, LNCS 12983, pp. 183–194, 2021.
https://doi.org/10.1007/978-3-030-88207-5_18

processes, etc. Hence, some businesses have chosen to digitalize only essential management activities while not paying enough attention to the integration process that must happen later. On the other hand, enterprises with large investment budgets can build a unified software solution for their entire digital infrastructure, including management systems and production systems. However, in order to digitize an entire organization, purchasing ready-made software will not be sufficient. In fact, during the operation of businesses, new processes will crop up and demand additional digitation. In these cases, RPA is a viable solution for software systems without proper application programming interfaces. Assigning RPA to tasks with fixed logic will eliminate trivial errors and idle tasks, thus employees will have more time to focus on more important jobs and improve business productivity.

The recent trend of integrating RPA with a chatbot and applying artificial intelligence algorithms has brought about magnificent efficiency gains for automating business activities. Various studies and products of this solution can be listed below:

Object detection in software applications interfaces using an RPA system integrated with the TensorFlow CNN YOLO tool. This application provided an initial solution for robots to simulate human manipulation on frequently changed interfaces. The evaluation tests of this project analyzed and labeled a specific programming software - Eclipse IDE [2].

The research of S. Sutipitakwon and P. Jamsri focused on the effectiveness of using RPA in repetitive tasks. In this case study, the test is performed on filling education workshops forms. The research introduced many supportive platforms of RPA such as Pega, BluePrism, WinAutomation, etc., hence they chose to use UiPath for its advantages. After implementing and testing, the research team got very high satisfaction results (100%) with linear or simple forms RPA and found deficiencies in testing with complex forms for this specific case [3].

An application of RPA in supporting systems for government administrative management processes was presented by Raissa et al. This case study indicated the effectiveness of RPA in improving the performance and reducing costs of executing operations [4].

A case study in communication tools for the elderly was introduced to emphasize the essential aspect of implementing RPA applications into consumer services [5].

A method for software testing automation using RPA was provided by N. Yatskiv, S. Yatskiv, and A. Vasylyk. The solution was improved by combining with computer vision for object detection [6].

The development of chatbot technology recently proved its significant effect on various areas, such as in the research of deploying a chatbot in the airport to support customers. This research proposed a chatbot solution to enhance client experience in gathering information in the airport. The chatbot can answer users' questions immediately, and it supports multiple languages, which human employees can hardly do [7].

The research of Gajra, Lakdawala, and Bhanushali focused on the integration of chatbots and RPA to automate multiple processes in the Student Information Management system. This research proved that the combination of a chatbot and RPA technology is possible, and it could bring significant advantages to the Student Information Management sector [8].

Oza et al. not only implemented a chatbot along with RPA bots, but they also included AI modules in Insurance Claim Processing for automating the process, such as legitimating user claims and sending emails about claims amount [9].

The above research and solutions mainly focus on a specific application without consideration of the organizations' existing IT team or the cost of short-term development. This paper proposes a flexible system based on open platforms that are easy to develop. It also has the ability to integrate AI applications quickly and easily.

The remainder of the paper is organized as follows. Section 2 describes system architecture, analyzes the extensibility for business operations, and integration of AI applications. A concrete example is shown in Sect. 3. Then, conclusions and perspectives are illustrated in Sect. 4.

2 System Architecture and Extensibility

2.1 Architecture Overview

2.1.1 Chatbot Flow

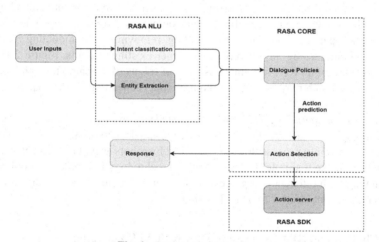

Fig. 1. Design of chatbot flow.

Figure 1 shows the design process of chatbot flow using Rasa Framework. As can be seen from the figure, the first part that will handle the user's input is Rasa NLU (Nature language understanding). In this stage, Rasa NLU will extract essential knowledge such as the user's intents, entities, and other structured information [10]. In order to obtain this knowledge, the Rasa pipeline comprises different components, which are defined by developers, for instance, language models, tokenizers, and intent classifiers. Then, the extracted information will be fed to the dialogue policy to predict appropriate actions to perform from a predefined list of actions. An action could be a direct response to the user, an executable function, or API calls from the action server. For the purpose of writing custom actions or API callings, rasa provides an action server, which is Rasa SDK Action Server.

2.1.2   RPA Flow

What is RPA and how to implement it? *"RPA is a form of business process automation that allows anyone to define a set of instructions for a robot or 'bot' to perform"*, says Aaron Bultman, director of product at Nintex [11]. Thus, to set up an automation process, we first need to specify the process steps, the desired input and obtained results. The complete and detailed scenario will be given to robots as an instruction set. The size of the indicator set will depend on the size of the automated process. However, with support from open source frameworks like the RPA framework and built-in (mostly code-free) platforms such as UIPath, Blue Prism, or Pega, the procedure of creating these sets will become straightforward [10]. Figure 2 shows the general flow of the RPA system. As can be seen from it, after fully setting up the process and providing input (if any), the robot activated by the user will follow the scenario with a guarantee of low error rate, before returning the results to the user.

RPA typically focuses on automating individual operations that perform repetitive mundane tasks, so rule-specific business actions are excellent candidates for RPA [8]. An RPA system can consist of many automated robots that perform various operations with predefined process rules. Besides, the incorporation and expansion of the RPA system are often affordable. An enterprise can effortlessly refactor and expand its RPA system without having to replace the old one completely. Moreover, since the robots in a system are separated from each other, adding, removing, or re-modeling robots can be done without causing any disruptions to other existing systems. Figure 2 shows a simple overview of an RPA system, consisting of robots of the same level that perform separate tasks, which may or may not require input (depending on the requirements of the process).

Moreover, for upgrading, RPA can be integrated with high-consciousness recognition (AI) technologies for tasks that require knowledge and decision-making. AI applications can be embedded into process flows and handled by robots as part of themselves. These combinations make it simpler to incorporate AI technology into practical applications, yet achieving high efficiency in processes that require awareness and decision-making abilities that are not inferior to using human resources [2].

2.1.3   Chatbot and RPA Integration Flow with AI Embedding

Figure 3 shows the flow of chatbot integrated with the RPA system and embedded with AI processing. At the first step, the chatbot will receive the input sentences from users and extract their intents. If the chatbot classifies users' intent as triggering an RPA process, it will check the required information for the process and request additional information from the user if needed. After ensuring that the given information is sufficient, the chatbot will utter a response sentence of confirmation to users and activate the RPA process as a fire-and-forget request by using system commands. When the RPA process is activated, it will access input files to get the necessary data for the process. In some cases, the RPA robots might input this data into an embedded AI model and run this model as a part of the RPA process. When the process finishes, the task's status and output will be logged into a specific folder for reviewing and further activities.

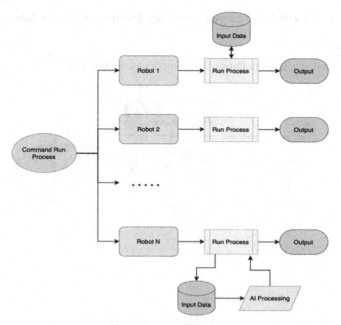

Fig. 2. Design of RPA flow.

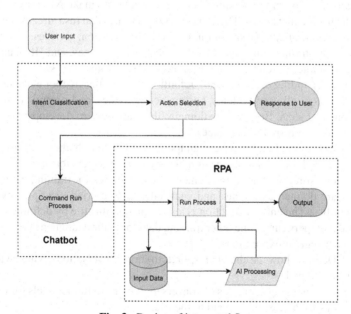

Fig. 3. Design of integrated flow.

2.2   System Extensibility Analysis According to Source Code Architecture

2.2.1   Chatbot

The chatbot code system contains main components below (Fig. 4):

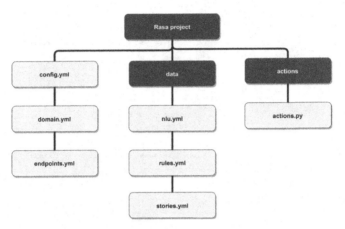

Fig. 4. Chatbot system tree.

- *config.yml*: Defining pipeline components and policies to make NLU predictions and predict the following actions. There are myriad pipelines that rasa already supports for entity extraction, intent classification, or response selection. Besides, rasa also supports many pre-trained language models such as Mitie, Spacy, and HF Transformers NLP. Furthermore, developers can write their custom components.
- *domain.yml*: Including every name of definitions, which the chatbot will use. This file contains labels of all user's intents, custom action names, and several configurations for sessions and slots. Besides, the domain file is also where developers define their entities, slots, and response sentences.
- *endpoints.yml*: Containing different endpoints which the chatbot will use, such as action server endpoints or conversation history store (tracker store).
- *nlu.yml*: Consisting of data of user sentences as examples for training data. Training examples are defined as intents, and each intent has myriad examples, which can contain entities. The entity extraction is also trained in this file by defining examples. Besides, developers can define other training data for natural language processing like synonyms or regular expressions.
- *rules.yml*: Defining how the chatbot responds to short conversations, which will always follow the same path.
- *stories.yml*: Composing examples of conversation paths to train models for predicting which actions to do next to respond to the user.
- *actions.py*: Including custom actions written in python for various purposes such as data querying and API callings. This file helps rasa projects to communicate with other technologies.

According to the architecture of the chatbot's source code, the rasa project could be extended by adding more definitions of intentions, stories, or actions. Therefore, Rasa chatbots are very flexible in scaling, which would significantly benefit enterprise demand to extend the system gradually. Besides, the custom action file makes Rasa chatbot extremely simple to interact with other technologies. For example, in this project, the research team utilizes this function to integrate the Rasa chatbot with RPA technology.

2.2.2 RPA

The basic structure of an RPA system will include many test cases, where each test case corresponds to a small process performed by a robot. Figure 5 shows the source code architecture of the RPA system demonstrated in this work, including 2 test cases: Send Mail Report & Assemble Mail. In which, each test cases will include:

- *Input*: The *folder* contains the necessary input data for the robot to perform the process (may or may not concluded depends on the problem requirement)
- *Output*: The folder contains the output of the process, include:

  - *log.html* (default): contains details about the executed test cases in HTML format. They have a hierarchical structure showing test suites, test cases, and keyword details. Log files are needed nearly whenever test results are to be investigated in detail.
  - *report.html* (default): contains an overview of the test execution results in HTML format. They have statistics based on tags and executed test suites, as well as a list of all executed test cases.
  - *output.xml* (default): contains all the test execution results in machine-readable XML format.
  - The output file corresponds to the process output. In test case 2, the additional output is 2 excel files: *Mail_Classify.xlsx* containing ham (not spam) mail information; *Spam_Classify.xlsx* containing spam mail information.

- *TC.robot*: The robot's run file consists of predefined rules that correspond to the regulations of the procedure. The called robot will activate this file and follow the available commands.

One of the outstanding features that could elevate RPA into the main workforce in the future is its ability to replace humans in several tasks that previously required human intelligence and discernment. To provide RPA with cognitive and decision-making capabilities, AI models can be embedded into systems [2, 6]. For example, in test case 2 of this study, classifying spam emails requires human readability, however, integrating an appropriate NLP AI model for analyzing and classifying email content can also yield equivalent results. Besides, it is rather straightforward to integrate AI into the system to expand or upgrade it. As Fig. 4 shows, an AI model can be embedded directly into the RPA system without the support of any APIs. Robots can use predefined libraries via the RPA Framework to run the classifying process using the provided AI model. Especially in the above example, the Spam Model folder contains the necessary parameters of an

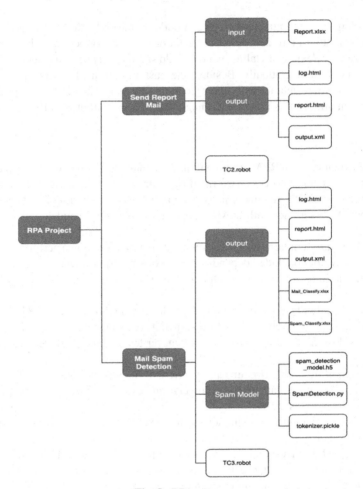

Fig. 5. RPA system.

AI model (*model.h5, tokenizer.pickle*) and the file to run the email classification. This folder can then be imported into the robot as a library, and the execution function will be called by the robot as part of the procedure. In the same way, it is indeed easy to extend and upgrade this RPA system. Depending on the quantity and requirements of the process, the system can be expanded by adding several robots or integrating with cognitive models. Also, as aforementioned, adding, removing, or modifying a robot script of any test cases will not affect the other because of their parallel and independent structure.

3 Case Study

3.1 Problem Introduction

In today's world, companies have to cope with an overwhelming number of manual tasks, which cost a considerable amount of time and budget to deal with. In this paper, the research team tried to use RPA and chatbot technology to solve two common problems for most companies: sending attendance checking emails and checking mailbox to gather important information (Fig. 6).

Firstly, most companies have to send attendance checking emails to employees at the end of every month to confirm their attendance in that month. Tiresome and time-consuming as it is, but this email-sending task plays an indispensable role in almost every company. Therefore, to reduce the amount of work for the Human Resources Department of companies, the research team applied RPA technology to automate the process. This automation process can decrease the amount of time spent on idle works and help the Human Resources Department free up more time for other significant tasks. As a result, tedious operations such as sending attendance emails can be done with an even higher efficiency and accuracy.

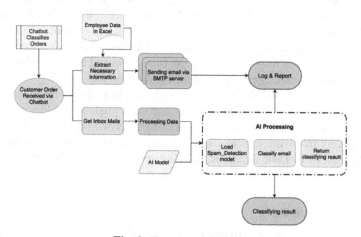

Fig. 6. Test cases flowchart.

Another such tedious and time-consuming task is reading through mailboxes and sorting out every important emails due to the immense number of emails companies receive every day. Emails often contain an enormous amount of information, and they are one of the best ways to communicate with other companies. However, various kinds of spam emails, advertisement emails, and other meaningless emails make managing important emails more complicated and time-consuming. Hence, the research team applied RPA technology to reduce the amount of work for companies' employees and employers by reducing the number of unimportant information of email they have to read. Even though most email service providers applied anti-spam solutions to their service, the number of spam emails remains excessive. Therefore, in this project, the research team implemented a machine-learning model for spam email detection to minimize junk and advertisement emails.

Moreover, to improve user experience, the research team created and trained a chatbot for convenient communication with the project system and RPA process. The chatbot will classify the intents and relevant data of users. Then, it triggers the RPA process to complete the required tasks. With the chatbot implementation, employees can access and activate the RPA process even when they work far from the office without any difficulty. Besides, with the chatbot working as a front-layer of the process, users can have a more friendly experience and human-like conversation.

3.2 Test Cases

3.2.1 Sending Monthly Attendance Checking Emails

This test case takes input as an excel file containing the content of the month's attendance report in a predefined format, including the employee's information such as employee's name, employee ID, email address, rank, the number of working days in the month, the number of days off and off, as well as the reason for taking leave, etc. When a user sends a request to trigger this process through the chatbot, the robot will be activated and start the process. First, the robot will achieve employee information through an excel file. Then it connects to Gmail Server via IMAP protocol with the default business (or personal) email account that is approved. Next, the robot will compose an existing mail form with the information extracted from the excel file and send it to each employee via their email address. The results of the process can be checked as an overview through a report file including *output.xml*, *report.html*, and *log.html* files.

This case demonstrated the effectiveness of RPA in reducing manpower requirements, increasing the accuracy of the process. For many predefined rule processes (such as sending attendance mails), RPA can work smoothly with no monitoring required. Also, by merely following indicator sets, RPA applications can reduce manual errors [3]. Besides, for many basic functions, RPA Framework supports a handful deployment methods, which simplify the setting up of the process.

3.2.2 Email Classifying

In order to improve business performance, automated processes can be integrated with AI models. In this case, an NLP model will be combined with the RPA application to classify spam emails. The purpose of this operation is to "clean" the mailbox and help users achieve important information faster and easier.

In this test case, a model for email spam classification will be integrated as an RPA library. When activated by the user's request through the chatbot, the robot will access the user's email address (or the default email address of the business) and retrieve data of unread emails. The data is then preprocessed and fed into the AI model for categorization. After the classification is complete, RPA will use the collected data to aggregate it through two excel files named *Mail_Classify.xlsx* and *Spam_Classify.xlsx* consecutively. Both of them contain email information such as title, content, sender information, and send date. Therein, *Mail_Classify.xlsx* contains information of all ham (not spam) emails, and *Spam_Classify.xlsx* includes details of spam mails. Besides these outputs, the process will export three detailed report files as *output.xml*, *report.html*, and *log.html*.

The practical significance of this case is speeding up the retrieval of user information (through the elimination of junk mail containing unhelpful information and aggregation of important emails) and increase productivity while also reducing staffing requirements. For other complex processes including flexible operations, the combination of RPA and AI will also yield many promising results [2]. Similar to the above case, the integration is suitable for jobs that require the human ability to make decisions before initiating the process, such as monitoring cameras, identifying dynamic conditions to perform specific operations, etc. Certain cognitive models will be used for the particular tasks. Hence the efficiency of an RPA system partly depends on the performance of the AI model [12]. Despite that, normally, this integration can significantly reduce the need for human resources. Also, it can increase the speed of execution and the accuracy of the process.

4 Conclusion and Perspectives

The attraction of businesses worldwide in implementing RPA technology has been increased considerably due to the significant advantages it offers, especially when the digital transformation process is occuring everywhere around the world. RPA can handle repetitive mundane tasks with ease, and it would be the perfect bridge between applications, which lack appropriate APIs to connect with others. The integration of a chatbot with RPA also helps improve user experience in using the system. Besides, the success of implementing AI applications in the system might provide myriad profits to businesses. Moreover, one of the most important benefits of this solution is that it is rather simple to deploy for companies that have their developer teams or a low budget. Furthermore, this work is not only available for enterprises to enlarge their project according to their demand, but it is also available for smaller scale companies because of its open platforms base.

The technology of automating mundane processes has a promising future, and because of the flexible cost of implementation, the RPA technology gains greater attention from the perspective of businesses [13]. Additionally, with the ability to integrate with other technologies, it might have several effects on certain areas such as Banking, Medical, Economic Management, and many other sectors. Therefore, further research on this technology and its impacts on different sectors should be invested.

References

1. Top 10 Digital Transformation Trends for 2021. https://www.forbes.com/sites/danielnewman/2020/09/21/top-10-digital-transformation-trends-for-2021/. Accessed 30 Mar 2021
2. Martins, P., Sá, F., Morgado, F., Cunha, C.: Using machine learning for cognitive Robotic Process Automation (RPA). In: Proceedings of the 15th Iberian Conference on Information Systems and Technologies (CISTI), Seville, Spain, pp. 1–6 (2020)
3. Sutipitakwong, S., Jamsri, P.: The effectiveness of RPA in fine-tuning tedious tasks. In: Proceedings of the 6th International Conference on Engineering, Applied Sciences and Technology (ICEAST), Chiang Mai, Thailand, pp. 1–4 (2020)
4. Uskenbayeva, R., Kalpeyeva, Z., Satybaldiyeva, R., Moldagulova, A., Kassymova, A.: Applying of RPA in administrative processes of public administration. In: Proceedings of the IEEE 21st Conference on Business Informatics (CBI), Moscow, Russia, pp. 9–12 (2019)
5. Kobayashi, T., Arai, K., Imai, T., Tanimoto, S., Sato, H., Kanai, A.: Communication robot for elderly based on robotic process automation. In: Proceedings of the IEEE 43rd Annual Computer Software and Applications Conference (COMPSAC), Milwaukee, WI, USA, pp. 251–256 (2019)

194   P. D. Hung et al.

6. Yatskiv, N., Yatskiv, S., Vasylyk, A.: Method of robotic process automation in software testing using artificial intelligence. In: Proceedings of the 10th International Conference on Advanced Computer Information Technologies (ACIT), Deggendorf, Germany, pp. 501–504 (2020)
7. Carisi, M., Albarelli, A., Luccio, F.L.: Design and implementation of an airport chatbot. In: Proceedings of the 5th EAI International Conference on Smart Objects and Technologies for Social Good, pp. 49–54 (2019)
8. Gajra, V., Lakdawala, K., Bhanushali, R., Patil, S.: Automating student management system using chatbot and RPA technology. In: Proceedings of the 3rd International Conference on Advances in Science & Technology (ICAST) (2020)
9. Oza, D., Padhiyar, D., Doshi, V., Patil, S.: Insurance claim processing using RPA along with chatbot. In: Proceedings of the 3rd International Conference on Advances in Science & Technology (ICAST) (2020)
10. Bocklisch, T., Faulkner, J., Pawlowski, N., Nichol, A.: RASA: open source language understanding and dialogue management. arXiv:1712.05181 (2017)
11. How to explain Robotic Process Automation (RPA) in plain English. https://enterprisersproject.com/article/2019/5/rpa-robotic-process-automation-how-explain. Accessed 30 Mar 2021
12. Romao, M., Costa, J., Costa, C.J.: Robotic process automation: a case study in the banking industry. In: Proceedings of the 14th Iberian Conference on Information Systems and Technologies (CISTI), Coimbra, Portugal, pp. 1–6 (2019)
13. Chuong, L.V., Hung, P.D., Diep, V.T.: Robotic process automation and opportunities for Vietnamese market. In: Proceedings of the 7th International Conference on Computer and Communications Management, pp. 86–90. Association for Computing Machinery, New York, NY, USA (2019). https://doi.org/10.1145/3348445.3348458

Supporting Undo and Redo for Replicated Registers in Collaborative Applications

Eric Brattli and Weihai Yu$^{(\boxtimes)}$

UIT - The Arctic University of Norway, Tromsø, Norway
`weihai.yu@uit.no`

Abstract. A collaborative application supporting eventual consistency may temporarily violate global invariant. Users may make mistakes. Undo and redo are a generic tool to restore global invariant and correct mistakes. A replicated register allows a collaborative application to concurrently read and write at different sites. Currently, there is very little undo and redo support of eventually consistent replicated registers. We present an approach to undo and redo support for eventually consistent replicated registers. We also present a work-in-progress implementation in a popular open-source library for collaborative applications.

Keywords: Data replication · Optimistic concurrency control · Eventual consistency · Undo · Redo

1 Introduction

Most collaborative applications replicate data at different sites and apply optimistic concurrency control that supports eventual consistency [12]. A system with eventual consistency may temporarily violate some global invariant, such as overbooking of resources. For applications such as online shopping and collaborative editing, human users make tentative updates and introduce additional mistakes. Undo and redo are a generic tool to restore global invariant and correct human mistakes.

Register is one of the simplest and most fundamental data types. An application writes a value to a register and later read the value that it has written. For example, the font type of a document's title could be a register. An *eventually consistent replicated register*, or *EC register* for short, allows different sites to independently reads and writes their local register instances. The values of the instances converge when the sites have applied the same set of write updates to their local instances.

Undo and redo in collaborative applications are generally well understood and supported for immutable data elements that an application can insert into or delete from a composite data collection, such as a set or a document [2,7,11,13,15]. Undo and redo support for EC registers, however, has not been very well understood and supported.

In this paper, we first discuss the issues and requirements of undo and redo support for EC registers. We then present an approach to supporting undo and redo for EC registers. The approach is based on the causality of the write updates and their undo and redo updates. We also present a work-in-progress implementation of the approach in a popular open-source library for collaborative applications.

© Springer Nature Switzerland AG 2021
Y. Luo (Ed.): CDVE 2021, LNCS 12983, pp. 195–205, 2021.
https://doi.org/10.1007/978-3-030-88207-5_19

2   Technical Issues

There exist two types of EC registers. LWW (last-write wins) register [5, 8] is the mostly used EC register. Each write update of the register is associated with a timestamp (or priority in general). For two concurrent updates to the register, the one with the greater timestamp value wins. The resolution to the conflict is thus lossy. The concurrent update that loses the competition gets lost.

Multi-value register [1, 9] makes lossless resolution among concurrent updates at the cost of application complexity. All concurrent updates are preserved and presented to the application. It is up to the application to decide a new value based on the multiple presented values.

When the updates to a register are sequential or serializable, such as in a single-user editor or an ACID (atomicity, consistency, isolation and durability) database, the system can maintain the history of the updates as a linear sequence of values. If the system knows the current position in the sequence, it performs an undo or redo by simply setting the register with the appropriate previous or next value in the sequence.

Under concurrent write updates, the update history is no longer linear. Unless we restrict what can be undone, for instance, by only allowing the undo or redo of the updates that were originated locally, finding a unique previous or next value is no longer trivial.

In addition to the normal write updates, undo and redo updates can also be performed concurrently at different sites. Neither do these undo and redo updates follow a linear order.

Essentially, we must address two issues. First, what is the current undo-redo status of the register? Second, given the current undo-redo status, what should be the appropriate value after the undo or redo?

Researchers count the number of undos and redos to figure out the current undo-redo status of an update [11, 13, 15]. We use undo length [15] for this purpose. For immutable values that are inserted into or deleted from a data collection, it is sometimes sufficient to perform an undo or redo when we are able to figure out the current undo-redo status. For EC registers, there has not been a solution for the second issue yet.

3   Requirements

An eventually consistent system must allow a site to independently perform updates to a register. The updates should include not only normal write updates but also undo and redo of any previously performed update.

When the sites are connected, they must be able to merge concurrent remote updates without any coordination. For example, they must be able to independently resolve conflicting updates without collecting votes from a quorum of sites.

The state of the register instances at different sites must be convergent. That is, when the sites have applied the same set of updates, even though the order of the applications might be different, the instances must report the same register value.

The behavior of the register should be the same as a sequential system when the updates are sequential. As a special case, when we only make undo and redo on locally

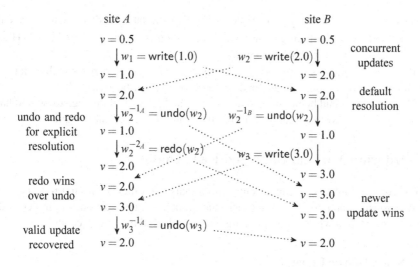

Fig. 1. A scenario of concurrent register updates

originated updates, the behavior should be the same as existing systems that only allow undo and redo of local-only updates.

The system should combine the benefits of current best practice, i.e. LWW and multi-value registers. On the one hand, the system should be able to resolves conflict among concurrent updates, with existing commonly applied conventions, such as LWW. On the other hand, while the system resolves conflict on behalf of the application or user, the application or user should still be able to make an explicit choice.

We illustrate the requirements with an example scenario. In Fig. 1, there are two instances of the same register at sites A and B. The instances have the same initial value 0.5. The sites independently write a new value with write updates w_1 and w_2. Suppose the priority (such as a timestamp value) of w_2 is greater than the priority of w_1. When receiving the update from the remote site, each site independently resolves the conflict and the update w_2 wins. The register instances at both sites have the same value 2.0.

Now, suppose the application at the two sites do not agree with the automatic resolution that the system has made, they can independently make an explicit resolution by undoing the update of w_2 with $w_2^{-1_A}$ and $w_2^{-1_B}$. The new value of the register now becomes 1.0.

Of course, the system must allow any undone update to be redone. If the application at site A regrets the undo and redoes w_2 with $w_2^{-2_A}$, the register at the site is restored back to value 2.0. Moreover, the redo $w_2^{-2_A}$ wins over the concurrent undo $w_2^{-1_B}$ (even though $w_2^{-1_B}$ arrives at site A after $w_2^{-2_A}$ has finished), because $w_2^{-1_B}$ has the same intention as $w_2^{-1_A}$ and site A had already seen the intention of $w_2^{-1_A}$ when it performed $w_2^{-2_A}$. In other words, we say that site A has now figured out that the current undo-redo status of w_2 is "redone", or the update of w_2 is "effective".

Now, site B performs a new write update w_3. It is critical that the sites can independently resolve the conflict between the new update w_3 and the concurrent undo and redo updates $w_2^{-1_A}$, $w_2^{-1_B}$ and $w_2^{-2_A}$. It makes sense that the latest update w_3 wins over the previous update w_2, including its undo and redo updates $w_2^{-1_A}$, $w_2^{-1_B}$ and $w_2^{-2_A}$. Hence the new value of the register becomes 3.0.

If site A now undoes w_3 with $w_3^{-1_A}$, the system restores the register with update w_2, which is currently redone. So the final value of the register becomes 2.0.

Note that if w_2 had been originated at site A, the behavior of the register would have been the same as a system that only allows undo and redo of locally originated updates.

4   Ordering Normal, Undo and Redo Updates

To resolve the conflicts of concurrent write updates and their undo and redo updates, the sites must be able to decide an order among them. In this section, we first consider the order of normal write updates and then take undo and redo into account.

4.1   Normal Write Updates

Two write updates are either concurrent or one of them is causally dependent on the other. For two write updates w and w', we write $w||w'$ if they are concurrent and $w \rightarrow w'$ if w and w' apply to the same register and w happens before w' (or w' causally depends on w).

The causality of updates on a register forms a partial order. We can draw a DAG (directed acyclic graph) where the vertices are the write updates on a register, and there is an edge from update w to update w' if $w \rightarrow w'$ and there does not exists an update w'' on the same register such that $w \rightarrow w''$ and $w'' \rightarrow w'$. That is, there is a direct (or immediate) causal dependency from w to w'.

Given a DAG of write updates on a register, we call an update w a *head* update in the DAG if there is no update w' in the DAG such that $w \rightarrow w'$. Clearly the head updates of the current DAG determine the current value of the register. The head updates are concurrent with each other and are originated from different sites.

A LWW register uses a priority to resolve the conflicts among the head updates, whereas a multi-value register present all head updates to the application which then makes a new update based on the presented updates. We propose that the system uses LWW to resolve the conflict, but an application can still explicitly choose a different concurrent update by undoing the current winning update.

4.2   Undo and Redo Updates

A commonly accepted semantic (or effect [10]) of an undo is that undoing an update w on a register has the same effect on the register where the update w has never occurred. This semantic should apply to concurrent undos of the same write update. When a write update w is undone, the causality of the still-effective updates that was established before the undo remains the same.

The redo of a write update w may have two alternative semantics. The first alternative is that w has never occurred (due to the undo) and a complete new update is applied. The second alternative is that the undo of w has never occurred and the effect of w is restored. We found the second alternative more natural and therefore choose that alternative. The effect of restoring w is that we have restored the DAG that was established before the undo of w.

Based on the discussion so far, we propose the following way to determine the order among the updates. We first build the DAG according to the causality of the normal write updates. Undoing an update does not change the DAG. Instead, we mark the vertex for that undone update as ineffective. When the update is redone, we mark the vertex back to effective. The current value of the register is determined by the effective head updates.

A site usually only undoes the last effective update, since it does not make sense for an application to undo an update that is not currently in effect. The reader should not confuse this with selective undo [10, 13, 14] where an application can undo or redo any update in the history which contains the updates on all data objects (including different registers).

5   Undo Lengths

Now that we are able to maintain the order among the updates on a register, the remaining task is to figure out whether a particular write update is effective at present. Here we adopt *undo length* [15] to figure out the current undo-redo status of a write update.

Notice that in Fig. 1, we used $w_2^{-1_A}$ and $w_2^{-2_A}$ to denote the undo and redo of the normal write update w_2 that site A performed. In general, we can use w^{l_s} to denote an undo or redo of update w that site s performs. Here the l in w^{l_s} (where $l > 0$) is called the undo length of w. w^{l_s} is an undo of w if l is an odd number. Otherwise, it is a redo. In other words, the undo-redo status of a write update is only dependent on its current undo length. That is, the undo-redo status is independent of the site s that has performed the undo or redo update. It is even independent of the number of sites that have concurrently performed the same (i.e. the same l) undo or redo update.

6   High-Level Algorithms

For an EC register, a site maintains a set G of write updates. An update w is a 6-tuple $\langle o, k, p, l, v, D \rangle$, where o is the unique identifier of w, k is the vector clock [3] value, p is the priority, l is the undo length, v is the register value and D is the set of the write updates which w immediately depends on. For a write update w, we use k_w, p_w etc. to denote the k and p elements of w.

The set G represents the DAG of updates described in Sect. 4.1. Unlike traditional graph data structures, the links of the DAG are maintained backward, through the immediate causal dependencies (starting from the head updates). For a set G of write updates, we also maintain $H_G \subseteq G$, the head updates of G.

Initially, the set G is empty.

```
w ← ⟨newId(), readClock(G), getPriority(), 0, v, H_G⟩
G ← G ∪ {w}
H_G ← {w}
return w
```

Algorithm 1: Local update write(v)

When writing a new value v to the register (Algorithm 1), we generate a globally unique identifier, a new vector clock value and a priority for the new write update w. For any write update w' in G, the new vector clock value $k_w > k_{w'}$. Furthermore, for any write update w'' that is currently not in G, $k_w \not> k_{w''}$. The new update w depends immediately on the head updates in H_G. The initial undo length of w is 0. We insert w into G. The new head of G consists only of this new write update w.

$w \leftarrow G.\text{find}(o)$
if $w \wedge \text{even}(l_w)$ **then**
$\quad l_w \leftarrow l_w + 1$
$\quad$ **return** $\langle o, l_w \rangle$

Algorithm 2: Local undo undo(o)

We can only undo an effective update. An update is effective when its undo length is an even number. To undo an effective update, we simply increment its undo length with 1 (Algorithm 2).

$w \leftarrow G.\text{find}(o)$
if $w \wedge \text{odd}(l_w)$ **then**
$\quad l_w \leftarrow l_w + 1$
$\quad$ **return** $\langle o, l_w \rangle$

Algorithm 3: Local redo redo(o)

Similarly, we can only redo an ineffective update, whose undo length is an odd number. To redo the update, we simply increment its undo length with 1 (Algorithm 3).

A site broadcasts the representation of local updates returned by Algorithms 1, 2 and 3 to remote sites.

A site merges an incoming remote update only when the update is causally ready, i.e. when the site has applied all the updates which the incoming update depends on.

$G \leftarrow G \cup \{w\}$
$H' \leftarrow \{w' \in H_G | k_{w'} < k_w\}$
$H_G \leftarrow (H_G \setminus H') \cup \{w\}$

Algorithm 4: Merge update w

To merge a new write update w (Algorithm 4), we insert w into G. Since update w may have already seen some of the head updates of this site, we remove from H_G the updates that w has seen (with clock values less than k_w), and then add w as a new head update.

$w \leftarrow G.\text{find}(o)$
$l_w \leftarrow \max(l_w, l)$

Algorithm 5: Merge undo or redo $\langle o, l \rangle$

To merge an undo or redo update (Algorithm 5), we update the undo length of the write update. The new undo length is the greater one of the incoming undo length l and the undo length l_w that has been locally recorded.

```
00 H ← H_G
   while H ≠ ∅ do
        H_e ← {w ∈ H | even(l_w)}
        if H_e ≠ ∅ then
            return resolve(H_e)
        D_H ← ∪_{w∈H} D_w
        D_{D_H} ← {w ∈ D_H | ∃w' ∈ D_H : k_w < k_{w'}}
        H ← D_H \ D_{D_H}
   return UNDEFINED
```

Algorithm 6: Query current value *read*()

To get the current value of the register (Algorithm 6), we must obtain the head updates of the current effective sub-graph of G. We do this in a loop that starts with the head updates of G. In the loop, H is the set of updates that are the current candidates of effective head updates. We first get the effective updates $H_e \subseteq H$, the updates whose undo lengths are even numbers. If H_e is not empty, we get the register value with the resolve function which resolves the conflicts among the effective updates in H_e using the priorities of the updates. That is, the resolve function returns value v_w of update w in H_e such that for all w' in H_e, $p_w \geq p_{w'}$.

If none of the current head updates in H is effective, we try to obtains a set of new head updates from the sub-DAG $(G \setminus H)$. To get the new head updates, we first get D_H, the set of updates that the updates in H depend immediately on. We then eliminate the updates in D_H that some other update in D_H depends on.

We iterate over the sets of head updates of the sub-graphs until we get an effective write update. If no write update in G is effective (i.e. all write updates are undone), the query returns a special UNDEFINED value.

7 A Work-In-Progress Implementation

In Sect. 6, we presented the algorithms for EC registers at a rather high and abstract level. In this section, we report our work-in-progress implementation in Automerge[1], a popular open source library for collaborative applications. Briefly, Automerge is a Javascript library of a JSON CRDT [6]. A CRDT (conflict-free replicated data type) [9] is a data abstraction specifically designed for data replicated at different sites. The sites can independently query and update the local CRDT instances. A CRDT guarantees that when all sites have applied the same set of updates, the states of the instances at these sites converge.

A JSON[2] document is a tree of nodes. A branching (or intermediate) node is either a key-value map (also known as an "object" or "name-value pairs") or a sequential list.

---

[1] https://github.com/automerge/automerge.

[2] https://www.json.org/json-en.html.

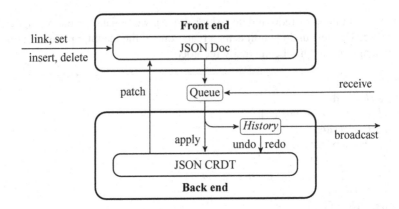

Fig. 2. Structure of a site

In a map, a key is, at any given time, associated with a value. A key in a map is basically a register. In what follows, we will restrict our discussions on setting (i.e. writing) and fetching (i.e. reading) the value of a given key.

Up till the latest release 0.14.2, Automerge only allows a site to undo and redo the latest updates that are originated locally at the site[3]. To achieve this, a site maintains an undo stack and a redo stack. When the site performs a local update, it generates a reverse update and pushes it to the undo stack. To perform an undo, it pops and performs an update from the undo stack, and also pushes the corresponding original update into the redo stack.

In our current implementation, we have removed the undo and redo stacks from Automerge. Figure 2 shows the revised software structure of a site. Instead of using the undo and redo stacks, we now maintain the information necessary for undo and redo in the *history* of updates.

A site consists of a front end and a back end (Fig. 2). A collaborative application updates and queries the JSON document in the front end. The update operations include linking a new node to the JSON tree (including linking a new key to a key-value map), setting a new value to a key in a map, inserting a data element into a list and deleting an element from the list.

The JSON CRDT is stored in the back end. When the front end has performed a local update, it inserts an update for the CRDT in the queue. The queue also contains the remote updates the site has received.

The back end performs the updates in the queue that are causally ready. After it has performed a remote update, it generates an update (called a patch) for the front end. Basically, we can regard the front-end document as the cache of the query result on the latest back-end CRDT state.

The back end also maintains a history of updates that it has performed. One purpose of the history is for the site to synchronize its local updates with remote sites. Now, we in addition use the history for the purpose of undo and redo.

---

[3] While we were preparing the camera-ready version of this paper, we noticed that undo/redo had been removed from the latest unreleased version of Automerge.

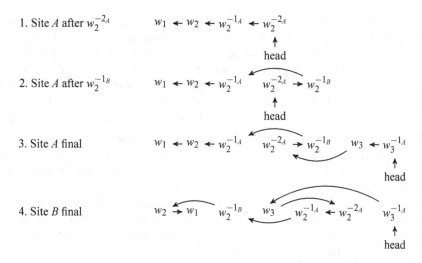

Fig. 3. Histories of updates

The representation of an Automerge update (an *update object*) for the JSON CRDT contains some meta data, including the unique identifier of the site (known as actor-id) that originally performed the update, the sequence number of the update at the original site, the updates that this update immediately depends on, the unique identifier of the data element, etc. An update is uniquely identified with the (actor-id, sequence number) pair. Automerge uses actor-ids as priorities to resolve conflicts between concurrent write updates.

In order to implement the high-level algorithms presented in Sect. 6, we augmented the update objects with additional meta data. More specifically, an update object in the history contains now an additional link to a previous update object as well as the undo length of the update. The update objects of a register are now linked sequentially in a total order that respects both the partial order of the DAG (Sect. 4.1) and the priorities of the concurrent updates. In other words, the links now encode different types of relations between updates, namely, the immediate causal dependencies, priority order, and undo and redo updates. A site only maintains the links locally and does not include them when it sends update objects to remote sites.

Figure 3 shows the update histories at the two sites for the scenario illustrated in Fig. 1. When the back end has performed an update, it appends an update object to the end of the history. If the register happens to be updated in causal order or in the order in which the conflicts are resolved (Figs. 3-1), we link the new update object to the last update object of the register in the history. If a new remote update loses the competition with a concurrent update (Fig. 3-2), we re-arrange the links so that the linked list respects the order for conflict resolution. Figure 3-3 and Fig. 3-4 show the final histories at sites A and B.

To perform a remote update, we first check if the register exists using the identifier of the updated data element. If it does not exist, we simply perform the update, append the update object to the end of the history and mark this object as the head update. If the register exists, we append the update object to the history and scan the history backward until we find the head update of the register. We re-arrange the links and set the new head update using the meta data in the update objects. Then, we start from the new head update and follow the links until we reach an effective update. We generate a patch according to that effective update and send patch to the front end. While traversing through the links, when we have visited an ineffective update, we skip over all the objects of that update. For example, in Fig. 3-3, when we have visited $w_3^{-1_A}$, we skip w_3 and visit $w_2^{-2_A}$, which is effective. So we generate a patch that writes the register with value 2.0. Notice that because $w_2^{-1_A}$ and $w_2^{-1_B}$ have the same effectiveness, their order in the sequential list does not play any role. Therefore the final histories at sites A and B are in fact equivalent.

In summary, the update history maintains two different orders. The physical order in the history allows the different sites to synchronize with each other when they get connected. The linked list of the update objects of the same register allows the sites to independently determine the current value of the register.

8   Related Work

Supporting undo and redo for concurrent updates has been an active research topic, both in the area of collaborative editing [10, 11, 13, 14] and CRDTs for general-purpose collaborative applications [15]. At present, there is no general support for undo and redo of concurrent updates on eventually consistent replicated registers.

In [15], we presented an approach to generic undo and redo support for CRDTs. An update is represented with a join-irreducible state of the (state-based) CRDT where the states form a join-semilattice [4]. Defining appropriate join-irreducible states for replicated registers is non-trivial. For example, LWW registers [5, 8] use timestamp values as the order of the join-semilattice, but timestamp values may not sufficiently capture the causality of the updates. For multi-value registers [1, 9], it is not clear what a previous value should be when we apply an undo to a write update. We address the issues by combining different orders on the updates: the causal order of the normal write updates (similar to multi-value register), the priority order of concurrent write updates (similar to LWW register), and the order of undo and redo updates of a particular write update (via undo length [15]). We then presented the high-level algorithms for maintaining and using these different orders. Finally, we presented an implementation that combined these different orders into a single total order.

9   Conclusion

We have first discussed the issues and requirements of undo and redo support for eventually consistent replicated registers, and then presented a new approach. The new approach is based on the causality of the write updates and their undo and redo updates. The approach addresses the issues and meets the requirements, and it embodies the existing best practice of replicated registers. When the system automatically resolves conflicts among concurrent updates, the new approach falls back to LWW registers. The application using this approach is able to explicitly resolve conflicts through undo and redo, surpassing the capability of multi-value registers. When undo and redo are restricted to locally originated updates, the approach behaves the same as existing systems with such restriction. However, this new approach is not just an ensemble of the current best practice. It allows an application to undo and redo any update, which no existing system supports.

References

1. DeCandia, G., et al.: Dynamo: amazon's highly available key-value store. In: Proceedings of the 21st ACM Symposium on Operating Systems Principles (SOSP), pp. 205–220 (2007)
2. Ferrié, J., Vidot, N., Cart, M.: Concurrent undo operations in collaborative environments using operational transformation. In: Meersman, R., Tari, Z. (eds.) OTM 2004. LNCS, vol. 3290, pp. 155–173. Springer, Heidelberg (2004). https://doi.org/10.1007/978-3-540-30468-5_12
3. Fidge, C.J.: Logical time in distributed computing systems. Computer **24**(8), 28–33 (1991)
4. Garg, V.K.: Introduction to Lattice Theory with Computer Science Applications. Wiley, Hoboken (2015)
5. Johnson, P., Thomas, R.: The maintamance of duplicated databases. Internet Request for Comments RFC 677, January 1976
6. Kleppmann, M., Beresford, A.R.: A conflict-free replicated JSON datatype. IEEE Trans. Parallel Distrib. Syst. **28**(10), 2733–2746 (2017)
7. Ressel, M., Gunzenhäuser, R.: Reducing the problems of group undo. In: GROUP, pp. 131–139. ACM (1999)
8. Shapiro, M., Preguiça, N. M., Baquero, C., Zawirski, M.: A comprehensive study of convergent and commutative replicated data types. Rapport de recherche 7506, January 2011
9. Shapiro, M., Preguiça, N., Baquero, C., Zawirski, M.: Conflict-free replicated data types. In: Défago, X., Petit, F., Villain, V. (eds.) SSS 2011. LNCS, vol. 6976, pp. 386–400. Springer, Heidelberg (2011). https://doi.org/10.1007/978-3-642-24550-3_29
10. Sun, C.: Undo as concurrent inverse in group editors. ACM Trans. Comput. Hum. Interact. **9**(4), 309–361 (2002)
11. Sun, D., Sun, C.: Context-based operational transformation in distributed collaborative editing systems. IEEE Trans. Parallel Distrib. Syst. **20**(10), 1454–1470 (2009)
12. Vogels, W.: Eventually consistent. Commun. ACM **52**(1), 40–44 (2009)
13. Weiss, S., Urso, P., Molli, P.: Logoot-undo: distributed collaborative editing system on P2P networks. IEEE Trans. Parallel Distrib. Syst. **21**(8), 1162–1174 (2010)
14. Yu, W., André, L., Ignat, C.-L.: A CRDT supporting selective undo for collaborative text editing. In: Bessani, A., Bouchenak, S. (eds.) DAIS 2015. LNCS, vol. 9038, pp. 193–206. Springer, Cham (2015). https://doi.org/10.1007/978-3-319-19129-4_16
15. Yu, W., Elvinger, V., Ignat, C.L.: A generic undo support for state-based CRDTs. In: 23rd International Conference on Principles of Distributed Systems (OPODIS 2019), vol. 153, pp. 14:1–14:17. LIPIcs (2020)

Collaborative Design of a Synchrotron Ontology

Julia Szota-Pachowicz$^{(\boxtimes)}$ ⓘ

Jagiellonian University, Łojasiewicza 11, Kraków, Poland
`julia.szota@uj.edu.pl`

Abstract. The paper presents an approach to collaborative analysis and design of the synchrotron ontology. The ontology building process requires the analysis of the subject of conceptualization, the definition of goals and tasks that ontology is to fulfill as well as the way of implementation of an ontology in the appropriate logic language. It often needs cooperation of many specialists: domain experts, analysts and engineers who implement the ontology. In this paper, the use of competency questions defined in cooperation with many specialists from different domains and usage of use cases to develop the synchrotron ontology, is presented. The competency questions are used to define the subject of conceptualization to be represented by the ontology, while collaborative analysis of requirements facilitates specification of use cases and implementation phases. The presented approach enables the cooperation of many engineers in defining ontology design patterns that could be reused in many domains. It is applied to build a prototype high level ontology that could be used to develop ontologies for specific synchrotrons.

Keywords: Ontology analysis · Collaborative ontology design · Synchrotron control system

1 Introduction

The aim of the paper is to present the approach of collaborative analysis and design of a synchrotron ontology that captures knowledge about relations between number of devices and can be used as a roadmap for synchrotron control system architecture design. The considered ontology requires specialistic knowledge of many engineers from different domains and synchrotrons. The ontology building process is a multi-stage process. It requires the analysis of the subject of conceptualization, the definition of goals and tasks that ontology is to fulfil as well as the way of implementation of an ontology in the appropriate logic language and evaluation of existing ontologies. The ontology building process often needs cooperation of many specialists: domain experts, analysts and engineers who implement the ontology.

In the literature there are many methods and methodologies of building ontologies that have common goal – improve and simplify the ontology development process regardless of the complexity of the subject of conceptualization [1]. In this paper, in order to simplify the ontology design process, using the competency questions in defining the subject of conceptualization to be represented by the ontology, and collaborative analysis of requirements in specifying use cases, are proposed.

© Springer Nature Switzerland AG 2021
Y. Luo (Ed.): CDVE 2021, LNCS 12983, pp. 206–212, 2021.
https://doi.org/10.1007/978-3-030-88207-5_20

The presented approach is used to build a prototype high level ontology that could be used to develop ontologies for specific synchrotrons. The ontology design patterns defined in cooperation with many engineers could be reused in many domains.

2 Ontology Building Process

2.1 Synchrotron – A Collaborative Environment

In the case of ontologies used directly in information systems, the process of creating them requires the cooperation of domain specialists and engineers. A synchrotron is a device, in which electrons are accelerated to a very high energy in order to produce electromagnetic radiation of a high intensity and a wide range of energy [2]. Production of synchrotron radiation is a complex process which is possible due to the cooperation of a great number of devices implementing a set of specific tasks. Experts with knowledge in a given field are responsible for the supervision of individual devices. Members of the synchrotron team are specialists from various disciplines such as physics, mechanics, electronics and computer science.

One of the main goals of a synchrotron ontology is to capture knowledge about relations between number of cooperating devices, and their state and attributes controlled by the control system, so it can allow inference about the processes that should be implemented in order to properly control the synchrotron machine. This translates directly to the architecture of the control system and can be used as a roadmap for synchrotron control system architecture design.

Working on building a synchrotron ontology takes place in a collaborative environment, which means cooperation of people who are experts in particular subject areas and distributed control systems responsible for managing synchrotron devices. Therefore in this paper a collaborative approach to analysis and design of a synchrotron ontology is presented.

2.2 Collaborative Ontology Analysis – Competency Questions and Use Cases

The big effort has been made to develop an approach to the analysis of a synchrotron domain, so the final output would contain concepts, attributes and relations, using which, goals and tasks specific for the considered domain could be described by the created ontology. It is important to ensure that all the goals specified within the competency questions can be expressed by the ontology. An ontology meet all requirements if all the competency questions can be answered [3].

As the competency questions are independently defined and gathered from many domain experts responsible for different tasks/subsystems, specifying the ontology only on the basis of the competency questions, without analysis of relations between them, can lead to inaccuracies and numerous gaps. To overcome these problems we apply use cases (requirements) that group competency questions. Thus similar competency questions are answered in the same way. As the use case represents the problem that can be applied to different domains and interpreted in the same way by different domain experts, this approach simplifies the verification process and leads to optimalization of an ontology. The concept of the use case (UC) in Ontology Engineering is equivalent to the concept of the requirement (Req), defined as a non-empty set of CQ competence questions that are not contradictory or incompatible, but may overlap [4]. Thus, a given design pattern solves the design problem represented by the requirement. At the same time, a set of competence questions relating to a given issue is a specific instance of a requirement that in theory represents a use case.

$$Req = \{CQ1, \ldots, CQn\} \tag{1}$$

The following steps have been taken to develop use cases/requirements:

- Preparing competence questions in collaboration with many domain experts;
- Grouping of competence questions into requirements;
- A collaborative verification of requirements;

2.3 Defining Implementation Phases

The process of building an ontology is iterative. In presented approach the iterations (phases) are defined at the beginning in the result of the requirements analysis.

In Requirements Engineering first, business goals and high level requirements, called business requirements, are defined. Then, they are spitted into more detailed functional requirements describing how exactly a solution should met business goals. In our approach to ontology analysis we made analogous steps. Requirements assigned to an iteration are analyzed in more detail, in order to:

- Identify concepts and relations between concepts;
- Find common solutions and potential existing ontology design patterns that could be used to resolve design problems;
- Identify and use existing ontologies;
- Review the requirements by many experts.

In the proposed approach, after defining requirements, relations between them are specified, and each requirement is linked with a subdomain(s) it relates to. To specify these relations subdomains of an ontology domain are used, where the help of at least one expert from a given subdomain is required, as this step requires appropriate level of knowledge about analyzed domain. Determining relations between requirements gives us information about high level relations between requirements and about the order in which the ontology should be built. First, requirements which concern a common subdomain and have the lowest possible correlation with requirements related to other subdomains should be implemented. They are prerequisites for the implementation of requirements related to other subdomains.

3   Analysis of Synchrotron Ontology

3.1 Characteristics of the Subject of Conceptualization

Synchrotrons accelerate electrons to a very high energy, however, they are not able to accelerate particles with zero kinetic energy. Therefore, schemes for injecting pre-accelerated particles into a synchrotron have been developed. Preacceleration can be implemented by a chain of other accelerator structures, such as a linear accelerator. Therefore synchrotrons can consist of several types of accelerators: linear and cyclic i.e., the booster ring, storage ring. The beam, produced by an electron gun and accelerated in a linear accelerator, is introduced into the storage ring (or in the first place into a booster ring, in which it is further accelerated to a higher energy). The purpose of the storage ring is to keep the particles circulating in it with a certain energy in order to generate synchrotron radiation. The generated radiation goes to the beamlines. At the ends of the beamlines there are end stations, or laboratories where experiments are carried out [5]. In Fig. 1 a high-level synchrotron model with marked basics elements is presented.

Fig. 1. General synchrotron model with marked basics elements: 1 – electron gun; 2 – linac; 3 – booster ring; 4 – storage ring; 5 – beamline; 6 – end station [6]

The control system is an integral part of the synchrotron machine. It is responsible for managing the radiation production process. It controls and monitors the devices which the accelerator is built of, and synchronizes their operation with accuracy to microseconds.

Production of synchrotron radiation is a complex process which is possible due to the cooperation of a great number of devices implementing a set of specific tasks. Synchrotrons are built of cooperating devices and differ in terms of construction, equipment used, IT technologies used, and radiation properties that they produce. Conceptualization of the synchrotron domain should include:

- Synchrotron components: accelerators that make up the synchrotron machine; devices which accelerators are built of;
- Objects related to operation, i.e. machine work and synchrotron machine states;
- Distributed synchrotron control system;

Based on above characteristics we can distinguish three basic subdomains of the synchrotron domain: devices that make up the accelerator, the control system and concepts related to machine operation.

3.2 Requirements Specification - Grouping Competency Questions and Define Iterations

Competency questions for a synchrotron domain were developed on the basis of interviews with synchrotron SOLARIS experts, documentation and control system analysis.

Based on competency questions gathered from SOLARIS synchrotron, a questionnaire was created taking into account the requirements and knowledge of the experts from various 8 synchrotron centers that differ in the solutions used.

In Table 1 four selected competency questions developed as part of the work on the synchrotron ontology are presented.

Table 1. Selected competency questions.

No	Competency question	Expected answer
cq15	What is the energy of the booster ring?	Number [GeV]
cq25	Which devices make up the storage ring?	List of devices
cq46	To which group does the device belong?	Device group
cq63	What devices are controlled by the control system?	List of devices

Interviewing the great number of people led to numerous gaps and inaccuracies in the vocabulary of devices and technologies that build up a synchrotron. To minimalize these problems we grouped questions into requirements. The requirements in ontology engineering are identical with the use cases on the basis of which we define the components of ontologies. We group competence questions due to the problem they concern, and due to concepts and type of relationships they concern.

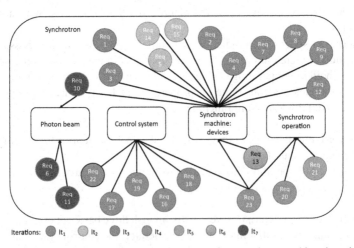

Fig. 2. Requirements assigned to domains they refer to and grouped into iterations.

22 requirements have been determined. The results obtained after specifying relations between requirements and linking them with the subdomains they relate to, are presented in Fig. 2. This structure determines the order in which the requirements should be implemented. Seven phases of implementation have been distinguished.

1. Components of synchrotron
2. Devices that make up the synchrotron machine
3. The synchrotron control system
4. The production process of synchrotron radiation
5. Synchrotron work schedule
6. Information on the synchrotron
7. Particle Beam

Table 2 presents one of the requirements that should be implemented in the first phase (Components of synchrotron). This requirement groups six competency questions.

Table 2. An example requirement including six competency questions.

No	Problem	Competency question	Description
Req8	Listing objects	cq24, cq25, cq26, cq27, cq28, cq29	For each component of the synchrotron you can read the list of devices from which the component is built

As shown in Fig. 2, the requirements R1, R2, R3, R4, R7, R8, R9 and R12 should be implemented in the first phase because they are all related with one subdomain, and the specification of this subdomain is a prerequisite to define other subdomains and requirements related to them. Requirements R6, R10 and R11 are implemented in the last phase as the full specification of a Synchrotron machine is required to capture knowledge about the beam accelerated in the synchrotron.

4   Conclusions

In this paper the usage of competency questions and use cases to develop a synchrotron ontology and determine the phases of its implementation process has been presented. The design of such an ontology takes place in a collaborative environment, as it requires cooperation of many specialists: domain experts, analysts and engineers. The subject of conceptualization to be represented by the ontology has been defined using competency questions gathered from many domain experts. Then the analysis of requirements enabled us to define use cases shared between multiple subdomains and ambiguously interpreted by all users. The presented approach allows to optimize the way of ontology implementation, and to define ontology design patterns that could be reused in other domains.

References

1. Genesereth, M., Nilsson, N.: Logical Foundations of Artificial Intelligence. Morgan Kaufmann, San Francisco (1987)

2. Presutti, V., et al.: A library of ontology design patterns: reusable solutions for collaborative design of networked ontologies. NeOn Project (2007)
3. Gangemi, A.: Ontology design patterns for semantic web content. In: Gil, Y., Motta, E., Benjamins, V.R., Musen, M.A. (eds.) ISWC 2005. LNCS, vol. 3729, pp. 262–276. Springer, Heidelberg (2005). https://doi.org/10.1007/11574620_21
4. Blomqvist, E., Sandkuhl, K.: Patterns in ontology engineering: classification of ontology patterns. In: Proceedings of the 7th International Conference on Enterprise Information Systems (2005)
5. Szota-Pachowicz, J.: Building synchrotron ontology: the analysis of synchrotron control system in collaborative environment. Comput. Sci. **18**, 53–69 (2017)
6. http://www.odec.ca/projects/2005/shar5a0/public_html/how_does_a_synchrotron_work.htm. Accessed 30 Dec 2017

Designing Plots for Multiplayer Games with the Use of Graph Transformation Rules

Wojciech Palacz$^{(\boxtimes)}$ (iD), Iwona Grabska-Gradzińska(iD), Leszek Nowak(iD), and Ewa Grabska(iD)

Faculty of Physics, Astronomy and Applied Computer Science,
Jagiellonian University, Kraków, Poland
{wojciech.palacz,iwona.grabska,leszek.nowak,ewa.grabska}@uj.edu.pl

Abstract. The paper presents a new application of the graph model of the game world and graph rules describing players' actions in this world. This time, this model and rules are used to design storylines in multiplayer role-playing games. The proposed model is suitable for collaborative plot design, as the set of rules describing game actions can be divided into subsets corresponding to particular quests, which are then assigned to different plot writers. The main contributions of this paper are: firstly, a new type of graph transformation rules for construction of storylines in games that require competition or collaboration between multiple players, and secondly, a prototype networked application to validate the proposed ideas and to serve as a playtesting tool for the designed sets of rules. In the presented application, the graph world model is stored in a Neo4j graph database server. Application instances running on players' computers communicate with this server. The paper presents the application's operation on an example of a simple two-player game.

Keywords: Multiple user gaming · Collaborative game plot design · Graph transformation rules

1 Introduction

Classic role-playing games (RPGs) are played with dice on a tabletop. Invented in the 70s, they differ from other games of that time by their collaborative storytelling nature. In an RPG, every player is a character in a game world, a member of an adventuring party. Characters (in reality: players) discuss what the party should do, then take actions which hopefully will let them achieve their goals. Action outcomes are determined by game rules and dice rolls.

Computerized RPGs followed almost immediately, and soon evolved into several subtypes. Action RPGs lost the storytelling aspect, retaining only the dice-based mechanism of resolving actions. Any plot they have is usually just an excuse for killing ever stronger monsters. Narrative RPGs kept the emphasis on

Y. Luo (Ed.): CDVE 2021, LNCS 12983, pp. 213–224, 2021.
https://doi.org/10.1007/978-3-030-88207-5_21

a story, which develops according to the choices made by the player's character. Of course, these choices cannot be completely free—the game presents the player with a finite set of possible actions. On the multiplayer front there are massively multiplayer online RPGs (MMORPGs), in which players can team up. Plots of MMORPGs are usually rather basic, but the players can develop their own additional plot threads by chatting among themselves.

Developing a substantial plot for an RPG is a complex task [7]. The plot should be non-linear, with many branching points, and provide several alternative ways of achieving any given goal (or at least a majority of goals). This allows every player to complete the game in their own way, creating their own story. It also makes the game replayable. If, during the previous gameplay, the hero went to a lonely mountain and learnt a dragon-killing punch from the martial arts master living there, then maybe this time he can join a holy order of dragon-hunting knights in order to acquire a fireproof armor?

In some RPGs such choices have consequences long after the hero killed the dragon. Making outcomes of specific events depend on actions taken in the past can lead to unforeseen interference between game elements and a deadlocked plot [1,3]. To eliminate this risk, plot writers have to consider all characters and items which are present in the game world, and take into account their possible interactions.

An ability to unambiguously describe subplots, also known as quests, is necessary when designing a complex plot (this includes describing in what situation a quest may be started, which parts of the game world are affected by it, and what events must happen to complete it) [6,10]. Game companies which make story-based RPGs use specialized software, which is nearly always proprietary and often tightly coupled with a single game. Therefore, the ways used in the game industry to represent and develop plots often remain unknown.

In our previous work [4,5], we have proposed representing the game world as a graph, with locations, characters and items represented as its nodes. Player's actions modify this graph. To describe these changes, we have employed graph transformation rules. This ensures that the game world and its evolution are represented in a mathematically precise way.

The proposed approach also allows plot writers to design and visualize quests as rule chains. Each chain is a sequence of actions which will let the player's character complete the given quest. During the gameplay these chains aren't followed step-by-step; the story constructed by the player's actions can interleave events taken from many chains. This is a very important aspect of this approach, because it automatically makes the plot design process collaborative.

As reported in [4], during a collaboration project a group of 36 students (divided into teams of world designers, plot designers and art asset creators) created a plot for an adventure game, as well as animations corresponding to locations and actions appearing in it. Plot was represented by graph rules stored in JSON files, animations were implemented using the Godot game engine. Next year, another project was completed, in which a refined version of the JSON format was used [8]. This new rule format can represent preconditions and allows the writers to derive more specific rules from general ones.

1.1 Exploration of the Multiplayer Case

Classic RPGs always have multiple player characters. They also have non-player characters (NPCs), for example bandits attacking travellers on a forest road or shopkeepers selling items in a city. NPCs are controlled by a game master, that is, by a person who creates and controls the environment in which players' actions take place.

Digital RPGs have no human game master, and thus NPCs have to be computer-controlled. In our approach their actions can be described by graph rules, in the same way as actions of a player-controlled hero. Similarly, when a multiplayer game is considered, creating a set of rules shared by all player-controlled characters and, optionally, extra rules specific to particular PCs seems to be an obvious choice.

This paper investigates changes required to make our approach suitable for multiplayer plots. It also describes an application which has been written in Python for the purpose of plot playtesting. For the ease of implementation, the graph world model is stored in an off-the-shelf Neo4j graph database server. Application instances running on players' computers communicate with this central server to query the current state of the world and issue modification requests.

These queries and requests need to be made in the Cypher Query Language. Because of that, the application stores rules not in the JSON format, but in an alternate textual format introduced in [9]. This alternate format allows us to easily translate a given graph transformation rule into a corresponding Cypher update query.

2 Graph Model of an RPG World

Graphs are well-known and widely used data structures. They consist of nodes, which are connected by edges. When a graph is employed as a model of some object's inner structure, node labels are used to specify which components of this object are represented by which nodes, and edges represent relations between these components. Edge labels are used when there is a need to express more than one relation type. For example, in a social graph a person may like another person, but also live in the same city as them, be a child of, have the same birth date, etc. A pair of nodes may then be connected by multiple edges with different labels, thus making this graph a multigraph.

There are many kinds of graphs: simple or with multi-edges, directed or undirected, attributed, planar, bipartite, with edges connecting more than two nodes (hypergraphs), and so on. This allows for choosing the most appropriate kind depending on the type of objects we are trying to model: social networks, room layouts, structures of computer programs, etc.

In our approach, the current state of an RPG world is represented by a layered graph with sheaf-shaped subgraphs. Layered graphs partition the set of their nodes into several distinct subsets. In RPG worlds, there are four layers which contain, respectively, nodes representing locations, characters, items, and narrative elements. Relations between nodes from different layers represent belonging: every character is in a specific location, items are either in a location or in a possession of a character, etc. Additionally, location nodes can be connected by edges representing travel paths.

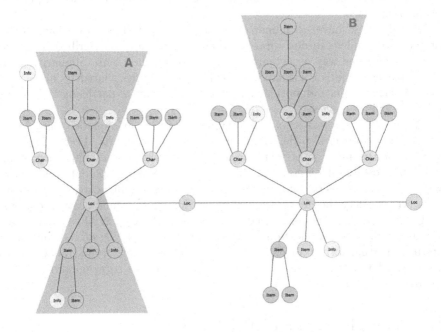

Fig. 1. An example of a world graph

An example of such a graph, taken from [5], is displayed in Fig. 1. Two subgraphs are highlighted in red: "A" is a sheaf corresponding to a location and its contents, while "B" is a half-sheaf representing a character and all things which are held, carried in a backpack, or associated in any other way with this character.

3   Graph Rules Representing RPG Actions

A story is defined by a sequence of actions undertaken by player- and computer-controlled characters, who interact with each other and with their environment. The set of possible actions is, for a given game, fixed and known in advance. Some actions are generic, like traveling between connected locations, picking up items or attacking encountered enemies. Others can be executed only in the context of a specific location or an item. For example, pouring holy water over the blade of an ordinary sword will produce a holy sword, but it must be done in a temple.

The actions change the state of the game world, which means changing the graph model. This can be described by graph transformation rules, also known as graph productions. Each rule consists of two graphs known as its left- and right-hand side. A rule matches a graph if that graph contains a fragment identical to the left-hand side of the rule. The matched fragment can then be replaced by the right-hand side of the rule—this is known as applying the rule at the matched subgraph.

The way an RPG is played corresponds closely to a graph derivation process in which one of the rules is applied to a starting graph, then the resulting graph is transformed by another rule, and so on. In our case, the starting graph represents an initial state of the game world, and the process continues until players manage to win the game or to lose it.

There are many competing formal definitions of what a rule is and how it is applied (in particular, how the inserted copy of the right-hand side is connected to the rest of the graph). Some of them are meant only for specific kinds of graphs, others consider so-called context or interface graphs in addition to the left- and right-hand side graphs, etc. A review of different approaches can be found, e.g., in [11].

In our preliminary papers player actions were represented by rules which, from the formal point of view, were single-pushout rules. An example of such a rule is presented in Fig. 2.

Figure 3 shows its textual representation [9]. The ASCII-art diagrams of its sides include not only node labels, but also additional node identifiers (because labels, in the general case, need not be unique).

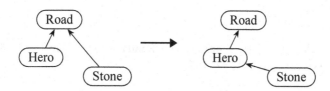

Fig. 2. An example graph transformation rule

```
LEFT HAND SIDE
(a:Hero) --> (b:Road) <-- (c:Stone)
RIGHT HAND SIDE
(c:Stone) --> (a:Hero) --> (b:Road)
```

Fig. 3. Textual representation of the rule from Fig. 2

4 Property Graphs and Cypher Queries

An application for playtesting plots with multiple players has to be network-enabled. Instead of implementing the necessary communication modules on our own, we have decided to use an off-the-shelf graph database server. There are several choices available, both commercial and open source. We have chosen Neo4j Graph Database, which is probably the most popular native graph database at the moment.

The kind of graphs used by Neo4j are known as "property graphs". They are graphs with directed edges, where both nodes and edges can be labelled (labels are text strings). A node can have many labels, an edge must have exactly one (which is known as the type of an edge). Nodes and edges can have zero or more properties, that is, pairs consisting of a key and a value associated with this key. Clients retrieve and modify information stored in a Neo4j database by issuing queries in the Cypher Query Language [2].

Layered graphs with sheaf subgraphs, which are used to model the game world, must be converted to property graphs before they can be stored in a Neo4j database. Hierarchical relations between nodes belonging to the same sheaf are converted to edges of the *parent* type. Edges between locations, which in the original graph model are unlabelled, get the *accessible* type.

Neo4j does not have a concept of a graph rule with a left-hand and a right-hand side. It has update queries, which have a matching clause followed by an update clause. This clause is a list of basic operations which should be applied to the matched part of the graph (delete a matched node and its incident edges, add an edge between two matched nodes, etc.).

The playtesting application, whose instances are started by the players on their computers and connect to the Neo4j server, needs to convert graph rules to appropriate update queries. An example result of such conversion is presented in Fig. 4.

```
MATCH (a:Hero) -[e:parent]-> (b:Road) <-[:parent]- (c:Stone)
CREATE (c) -[:parent]-> (a)
DELETE e
```

Fig. 4. A Cypher update query corresponding to the rule from Fig. 3

5 Rule Adaptations for the Multiplayer Case

Typical graph transformation systems, like those described in [11], do not have a concept of a user. They implicitly assume a single user, which can select and apply any rule, as long as the left-hand side of this rule matches the current state of a graph model. In our case, this assumption does not hold.

The set of rules describing an RPG plot is divided into subsets representing actions which can be undertaken by specific PCs and NPCs. When it is time for a particular character to act, only rules which belong to this character's action set are considered. These subsets cannot be automatically determined. Therefore, annotations pointing out which character should be regarded as the performer of the action had to be added to our rules.

Additional annotations were used to mark game-finishing rules. It is worth noting that in many multiplayer games, winning or losing is an event which applies only to a single player character, and does not prevent other players from continuing the game.

In most RPGs, there are actions which can be executed by many characters, e.g., walking or fighting. A rule representing such an action has to be included in all its potential performers' rule subsets. To obtain this result, a rule could be duplicated and each copy annotated with the name of one of the performers, but this would greatly increase the number of rules and be inconvenient for plot writers.

The fact that Neo4j property graphs can have multiple labels assigned to a node enabled a more elegant solution. In the proposed approach, every node in the graph model has labels representing its identities on different abstraction levels. For example, let us assume that the node representing Bob the Barbarian has five labels: *Bob*, *Swordsman*, *HorseRider*, *PlayerCharacter* and *Character*. Let us also assume that the rule for a "saddle your horse" action has nodes labelled *HorseRider*, *Saddle* and *Horse* on its left-hand side, and is annotated as performed by the *HorseRider*. This rule can be applied by Bob and by any other character with the *HorseRider* label, no duplication required.

The last proposed adaptation concerns not only multiplayer games, but all games where an action can have several different, luck-based outcomes. Rules with multiple right-hand sides are used to represent such actions. For now, we assign to each right-hand side the same probability of being chosen when its rule is applied.

6   An Example Game

The plot described in this section and its representation in the form of transformation rules and an initial world state graph were created to validate the multiplayer plot representation proposed by this paper. They also have allowed us to conduct functional testing of our application.

There are two player characters (Black Spy and White Spy) and five items (three coins, a stick of dynamite and a lighter). The characters and items are placed in a palace park which consists of 15 locations (Fig. 5). One location corresponds to a small square with an exit gate, but the gate is locked. A spy can escape from the park by bribing the gatekeeper (who is sleeping in a chair next to the gate) or by blowing the gate up, and thus win the game.

Players walk around the park, pick up encountered items, and go to the exit when they have completed a set of required items. If they are feeling abnormally merciful they can also drop items which turned out to be unnecessary, thus giving the other spy a chance to win the game, too.

Since relying on an enemy mercy is a losing proposition, spies can attack their opponents. An attack can succeed, killing the enemy and allowing the attacker to loot his opponent's pockets, or it can fail, in which case the attacking spy dies and instantly loses the game.

```
(p1:BlackSpy:PlayerCharacter),
(p2:WhiteSpy:PlayerCharacter),
(i1:GoldCoin:Coin:Item),
.....
(loc1:Exit:Location),
(loc2:Location),
.....
(p1) -[:parent]-> (loc3),
(p2) -[:parent]-> (loc8),
(i1) -[:parent]-> (loc4),
.....
(loc1) -[:accessible]-> (loc2), (loc2) -[:accessible]-> (loc1),
.....
```

Fig. 5. Selected fragments of an initial world state graph

This plot required seven rules to describe all possible actions. Having multiple labels assigned to graph nodes allowed us to create rules which are fully generic (see Figs. 6 and 7) as well as rules which are more specific (see Fig. 8, that rule can be applied in only one location when a spy has two specific items).

Figure 9 displays a rule with two right-hand sides, corresponding to two possible outcomes of picking a fight with the enemy spy. This rule and rule in Fig. 8 have game-ending annotations.

A game has to provide its user with a way of executing actions. It has to display the current location of the player's character, objects which are nearby, and somehow indicate which actions can be attempted at this moment. In the case of our playtesting application, it simply displays a text menu of possible actions.

This menu is constructed by going over the set of rules and trying to find matches such that the actor of the rule corresponds to the player's character. Every menu item represents a distinct match for the left-hand side of a particular rule. A generic rule may generate more than one item, e.g., the "walking" rule from Fig. 6 will match three times if the current location is connected with three other locations.

Transformation rules, as they are presented in the previous examples, do not provide any way of generating human-readable names for menu items. For the sake of playability we had to manually prepare appropriate descriptions, like

```
ACTOR p
LEFT HAND SIDE
(p:PlayerCharacter) -[e1:parent]-> (loc1:Location),
(loc1) -[e2:accessible]-> (loc2:Location)
RIGHT HAND SIDE
(loc1) -[e2]-> (loc2) <-[:parent]- (p)
```

Fig. 6. A rule for walking between locations

```
ACTOR p
LEFT HAND SIDE
(p:PlayerCharacter) -[e1:parent]-> (loc:Location)
    <-[e2:parent]- (i:Item)
RIGHT HAND SIDE
(i) -[:parent]-> (p) -[e1]-> (loc)
```

Fig. 7. Picking up an item

```
ACTOR p
LEFT HAND SIDE
(p:PlayerCharacter) -[e1:parent]-> (loc:Exit),
(i1:Dynamite) -[e2:parent]-> (p),
(i2:Lighter) -[e3:parent]-> (p)
RIGHT HAND SIDE
(loc)
GAME WIN
```

Fig. 8. Escaping from the park by blowing up the gate

```
ACTOR p1
LEFT HAND SIDE
(p1:PlayerCharacter) -[e1:parent]-> (loc:Location),
(p2:PlayerCharacter) -[e2:parent]-> (loc)
RIGHT HAND SIDE
(p1) -[e1]-> (loc),
(p2:DeadSpyBody) -[e2]-> (loc)
ALTERNATE RIGHT HAND SIDE
(p1:DeadSpyBody) -[e1]-> (loc),
(p2) -[e2]-> (loc)
GAME LOSS
```

Fig. 9. Attacking the other spy (two different outcomes)

```
Welcome to the game!

R. Reset the world and start a new game.
J. Join a game which is already in progress.
Your choice: r

Location:
You are at a forest crossroad among conifer trees.

1. Take the path leading out of the forest.
2. Go towards the sound of splashing water.
3. Follow the path going deeper into the forest.
R. Refresh info.
Q. Quit game.


Your choice: 1

Location:
You are in the fountain square. There is a signpost here.

Items and characters in this location:
- a silver coin

1. Follow the 'Gazebo' arrow.
2. Follow the 'Waterfall' arrow.
3. Follow the 'Exit' arrow.
4. Follow the 'Tennis court' arrow.
5. Pick up a silver coin.
R. Refresh info.
Q. Quit game.

Your choice: 5

Location:
You are in the fountain square. There is a signpost here.

Your inventory:
- a silver coin

1. Follow the 'Gazebo' arrow.
2. Follow the 'Waterfall' arrow.
3. Follow the 'Exit' arrow.
4. Follow the 'Tennis court' arrow.
5. Drop a silver coin.
R. Refresh info.
Q. Quit game.
```

Fig. 10. A screenshot from the playtesting application

"walk towards the fountain" or "enter the forest", and store them as properties of location-connecting edges. Nodes, too, were assigned properties with their descriptions in the English language. Then rules were augmented with a mechanism which generates menu item names based on property values in the matched fragment of the world state graph.

Another mechanism, which works in a very similar way, displays contents of the current location. Figure 10 shows descriptions and menus generated by these mechanisms. In this example, a user playing as the White Spy (who starts the game at the forest crossroad) executed two actions: moving to a different location and picking up an item.

7 Conclusion

This paper proposes an extended definition of a graph transformation rule which is suitable for describing characters' actions in a multiplayer RPG plot. This proposal is a continuation of the authors' work on a system for collaborative design of plots for story-based games and for storyline generation. Lessons learned while designing the example multiplayer plot and implementing the playtesting application will be used to further develop the main system, which is based on the Godot Engine.

References

1. Champagnat, R., Delmas, G., Augeraud, M.: A storytelling model for educational games: hero's interactive journey. Int. J. Technol. Enhanc. Learn. **2**(1–2), 4–20 (2010). https://doi.org/10.1504/IJTEL.2010.031257
2. Cypher query language. http://www.opencypher.org/. Accessed 1 Apr 2021
3. Georges, R.A.: Toward an understanding of storytelling events. J. Am. Folklore **82**(326), 313–328 (1969). https://doi.org/10.2307/539777
4. Grabska-Gradzińska, I., Grabska, E., Nowak, L., Palacz, W.: Towards automatic generation of storyline aided by collaborative creative design. In: Luo, Y. (ed.) CDVE 2020. LNCS, vol. 12341, pp. 47–56. Springer, Cham (2020). https://doi.org/10.1007/978-3-030-60816-3_6
5. Grabska-Gradzińska, I., Nowak, L., Palacz, W., Grabska, E.: Application of graphs for story generation in video games. In: Proceedings of the 2021 Australasian Computer Science Week Multiconference (ACSW 2021), pp. 27:1–27:6. Association for Computing Machinery, New York (2021). https://doi.org/10.1145/3437378.3442693
6. Kubiński, P.: Videogames in the light of transmedia narratology and the concept of storyworld. Tekstualia 4(43), 23–36 (2015). https://doi.org/10.5604/01.3001.0013.4243
7. Nobaew, B., Ryberg, T.: Interactive narrator in ludic space: a dynamic story plot underneath the framework of MMORPGs storytelling system. In: Felicia, P. (ed.) Proceedings of the 6th European Conference on Games Based Learning (ECGBL 2012), pp. 600–608. Academic Conferences and Publishing International (2012)

8. Nowak, L., et al.: Graph rules hierarchy as a tool of collaborative game narration creation. In: Luo, Y. (ed.) CDVE 2021. LNCS, vol. 12983, pp. 225–231. Springer, Cham (2021)

9. Palacz, W., Grabska-Gradzińska, I.: Textual representation of pushout transformation rules. In: Luo, Y. (ed.) CDVE 2020. LNCS, vol. 12341, pp. 75–80. Springer, Cham (2020). https://doi.org/10.1007/978-3-030-60816-3_9

10. Putzke, J., Fischbach, K., Schoder, D.: Power structure and the evolution of social networks in massively multiplayer online games. In: ECIS 2010 Proceedings – 18th European Conference on Information Systems, pp. 159:1–159:12 (2010). http://aisel.aisnet.org/ecis2010/159

11. Rozenberg, G. (ed.): Handbook of Graph Grammars and Computing by Graph Transformation. Volume 1: Foundations. World Scientific Publishing, Singapore (1997). https://doi.org/10.1142/3303

Graph Rules Hierarchy as a Tool of Collaborative Game Narration Creation

Leszek Nowak[2]([✉]) [iD], Iwona Grabska-Gradzińska[1] [iD], Ewa Grabska[3] [iD],
Wojciech Palacz[3] [iD], Mikołaj Wrona[1,2,3], Agnieszka Konopka[1,2,3],
Krzysztof Mańka[1,2,3], Michał Okrzesik[1,2,3], Dominik Urban[1,2,3],
Karolina Szypura[1,2,3], Andrzej Mikołajczyk[1,2,3], and Jakub Kuligowicz[1,2,3]

[1] Department of Games Technology, Faculty of Physics, Astronomy and Applied, Computer
Science, Jagiellonian University, Krakow, Poland
`iwona.grabska@uj.edu.pl`
[2] Department of Information Technologies, Faculty of Physics, Astronomy and Applied,
Computer Science, Jagiellonian University, Krakow, Poland
`leszek.nowak@uj.edu.pl`
[3] Department of Design and Computer Graphics, Faculty of Physics, Astronomy and Applied,
Computer Science, Jagiellonian University, Krakow, Poland
`{ewa.grabska,wojciech.palacz}@uj.edu.pl`

Abstract. This paper presents a computer tool for collaborative narration creation
based on graph rules hierarchy that was developed and tested with collaboration
of students of Jagiellonian University in Poland. The tool is made of two modules:
internal representation of game world graph model and animation system: The
former describes the narration points and story arcs and the latter uses basic animations and blends them together to create animated sequences. The opportunity
to develop the system as a group effort allowed to identify and address workflow
bottleneck and proved that using layered graph representation of the functional
elements of the story, characters, locations, and objects is viable method to design
plots and quest for video games. Dynamically changing graph can be visualized at
any stage and helps to perceive the story as animated sequences. This on the other
hand if used for video games story design enables to observe character actions,
possible paths the player can take and quickly iterate on the story components.
The contribution of this paper is to propose an innovative tool which allow the
designers and animators to work together within one platform.

Keywords: Decision support · Collaborative design · Graph transformations ·
Procedural storytelling

1 Introduction

Linear literary plots are usually the work of one author, but in the game industry the
story driven Role-Playing games (RPG) plots are mainly a team effort, especially the
games with the open world and multiple endings [1]. There are many strategies how to
collaborate with creating the story [2, 3].

© Springer Nature Switzerland AG 2021
Y. Luo (Ed.): CDVE 2021, LNCS 12983, pp. 225–231, 2021.
https://doi.org/10.1007/978-3-030-88207-5_22

The real challenge of collaborative plot creation is to allow the individual writers to express their ideas but without disturbing the whole story coherent. The usual way to deal with the problem is to make the team structure hierarchical, with the small group of decision makers and large group of helpers, who implement the leaders' ideas as the working elements of the system. In the formalized graph-based model the team structure can be flat, because the plot is being hierarchically designed.

In our research we have proposed the formal graph-based system to for computer-aided game plot generator [2]. In this paper the hierarchy of graph rules is discussed to make the collaboration flexible and coherent. The mechanism of preconditions, which makes the design process more flexible has been implemented and is described and the application production order in the context of Godot implementation modularity is shown.

2   From Game Mechanics to Graph Productions

In the RPG games there are the game world and the events, which can be performed by the player or are automatically performed by the non-player characters (NPC-s). The event types are derived directly from the game mechanics, but the plot dependencies added by designer cause that many different actions can be derived from one element of game mechanics.

In the sake of formalization there are proposed the following structure [4]:

World State Graph – layered and hierarchical graph model of the game world and its current state. Every graph node stands for one object in the game world and belongs to one of four layers: layer of locations, layer of characters, layer of items or layer of narrative elements. Defined vertex types correspond with different functions of elements in the game world. Graph edges represent dependencies between objects: spatial dependencies, ownership, affiliation etc. Node attributes represent object properties. The layered graph used in the system is formally defined in [5].

Gameplay Graph – graph built dynamically during the gameplay representing the chains of actions available for the player.

2.1   Event Design

Available events and action in the game are represented by graph rules. Every rule, called "graph production" consist of following elements:

- **Left hand side of the production (LHS)** – the subgraph which can be matched to the world state graph. This matching is the first condition to apply the production;
- **Right hand side of the production (RHS)** – the resultative subgraph which replaces the subgraph found by matching function of the left side match;
- **Preconditions** – dependencies between values of attributes which are necessary to apply production;

- **Instructions** – the transformation from the left to the right side of the production is defined as a set of instructions. Moreover, the instructions correspond with the process of embedding the new subgraph into the World Game Graph.

Preconditions allow to make productions more flexible and not only match the attribute values, but also calculate range of the accepted values on the given conditions, see Code sample 1 and 2 to compare the difference.

Code sample 1. Attributes vs. preconditions. Attribute of explicit specified value.

```
"Left_Side": {
    "Locations:": [ {
        "Characters: [ {
            "Name": "Main_hero",
            "Attributes": {"IsHigh": true} } ] } ] },
    "Preconditions":[ ]
```

Code sample 2. Attributes vs. preconditions. Using preconditions for checking the value.

```
"Left_Side": {
    "Locations:": [ {
        "Characters: [ {
            " Name": "Main_hero",
            "Attributes": {"Height": null} } ] } ] },
    "Preconditions":[ { "cond": "Hero. Height >= 180" }]
```

3   Hierarchical Structure of Graph Rules

While playing the game user thinks of the actions concerning the currently available characters, their items and the specified values of attributes. During the plot designing process, especially the non-linear ones, the more general and abstract mechanisms should be created, and the names and attributes are used only for plot twist. This relation between general and detailed productions can be formalized as a generic and detailed productions.

A production can be designed for the specific World State Graph nodes, but also can be designed with the generic nodes "any item", "any location", "any character" (layer name as the only identifier of the node). Generic nodes are the same structure as detailed nodes but have temporary "Id" not a specific "Name".

Generic productions are derived from the implemented game mechanics. Then, there defined common activities available for all characters in any circumstances, e.g., changing their location, fight, items manipulation. Then, the more details can be added to the production until the last "Id" will be changed for the "Name" in the detailed production. The tree of the productions: from the most general ones to the detail productions is shown in Fig. 1. The production can be derived from the generic production by the designer, often with some additional contextual elements added, or automatically during the fitting process in the gameplay.

3.1 Application Production Order

For the current state of the World State graph, the list of both the generic and detailed productions is searched for fitting ones. For the current world state there is always a set of fitting ones. The rules of production application is essential for the gameplay.

There are in general three guidelines:

1. If there are two detailed fitting productions, the player has to decide, which to choose.
2. If there is detailed production and general one and they fit both (general production always fits if the derived detailed production fits), we apply the more detailed one.
3. The generic production fits and there is no derived detailed production.
4. If there is fitting generic production but any of detailed production derived from it does not fit, there are two possibilities:

   a. We use the generic one after automatic conversion to the fitting detailed one.
   b. The derived detail production prohibits the usage of the generic one.

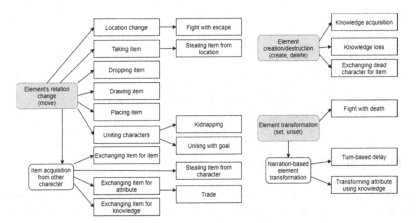

Fig. 1. The illustrative set of generic productions. The position into hierarchy is indicated.

Let us involve a little bit in the design process:

We start from the generic production "Location change". The designer derived the next level production: "Escape from the prison" from the previous one. The temporal identifier is changed to the name "Prison" but also the additional condition is added: the picklock in the character inventory. Then he derived from the first one another production: "Escape the prison when the guard is dead".

Let us track the gameplay: Main hero is in the prison. If both the guard is dead and hero has the picklock, he can choose what to do. If one of them is the only fitting one, the escape is just applied. If none of them fits, there usage of the generic one is blocked (variant B). Why blocked? Let us imagine the opposite situation where after the failure of escaping from the prison with picklock – character just uses the general production: "Location change" and just walked out the prison.

Unfortunately, this solution is not always right. For example: the derived production "Change location as a running away after the fight" should not block the generic one, because we want to change location in any circumstances not only after the fight. If so, the "Change location as a running away after the fight" production should be marked as "unblocking". In this situation the engine converts the generic "Location change" into the detailed one and applied.

The crucial advantage of the system is that only few plots twist are to be designed by humans, the other ones are converted into the detailed productions automatically.

4   The Modularity of Godot Implementation

All above decision making and fitting process is created using the Godot Engine. It is free and open-source engine for making games, well suited for collaborative development of the narration creation tool. Using Godot Engine allowed us to create modular system that consist of three parts. First is the system described earlier that handles graph notation and representation of plot points, arcs, actions etc. The graph representation is using built in graph node system to visually communicate structure of actions/situations that happen in the plot. This graph representation allows us to modify the state of the story and visualize it using second module of the system. The second module is made of granular animations that are based on generic productions. Those granular animations illustrate base actions that can happen in the world e.g., changing a location, interacting with items, trading, dialogue. Those animations are created by a team of animators working in parallel and utilize art assets made by team of artists according to story specifications. The visualization of the system is shown on Figs. 2 and 3.

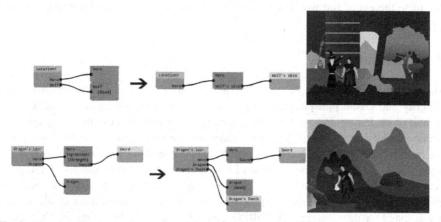

Fig. 2. The visualization tools use: from left graph representation by graph transformation to final animation.

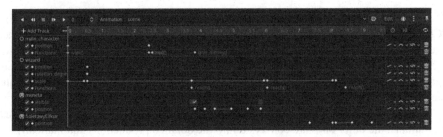

Fig. 3. The move sequence which stand for the one production shown in the tool panel.

Third and final part of the system is the scene animations that visualize lists of actions creating clips that can be played in series creating animated movie. Those scene animations are created from granular animations and are joined based on productions list representing story arc. Some of the more specific productions require dedicated animations in that case we either display text describing the action or craft the needed animation accordingly. The system is meant as narration visualization tool so specific animations that are unique or used rarely are not prioritized. Additionally, the main character is using inventory system like those known form adventure games. This inventory system helps to track items from scene to scene and help create animations faster.

The quests and animations were created with cooperation with the computer science students of Jagiellonian University in Krakow. Three groups of coworkers were assumed: world designers, story writers and artists, including 2D art designers and animators. The first group defines the world: objects, relations among them, restrictions and world structure. The second team prepares plot twists: quests, minor events etc. Graphics designers works on visualizations of world elements and animating the storylines. To complete the cycle, the world designers add connections between the quests and add world events.

5   Conclusion

The design process is complex, and any additional co-workers can disturb the world integrity and create plot paradox. In our paper we propose the complex hierarchical system of designing and applying the smallest plot events, represented by graph productions. The usage of formal graph system and the hierarchical tool structure allow the team to be highly egalitarian. The additional advantage of such a approach is the saving time and money: first because of the mechanism of automatically creating the detail production form generic ones. Second is possible easy way of prototyping and visualizing the story narration. The presented tool can be answer for these challenges, as it was tested for the prototype MMORPG game (12 quests, 20 locations, 36 characters) and the different types of games, especially serious games evaluation is in progress.

References

1. Achterbosch, L., Pierce, R., Simmons, G.: Massively multiplayer online role-playing games: the past, present, and future. Comput. Entertain. **5**, 4 (2007)

2. Putzke J., Fischbach, K., Schoder D.: Power structure and the evolution of social networks in massively multiplayer online games. In: 18th European Conference on Information Systems (ECIS 2010), 159 (2010). https://aisel.aisnet.org/ecis2010/159
3. Khaliq I., Watson Z.: The Omni framework: a destiny-driven solution to dynamic quest generation in games. In: 2018 IEEE Games, Entertainment, Media Conference (GEM), Galway, 2018, pp. 306–311 (2018)
4. Grabska-Gradzińska, I., Grabska, E., Nowak, L., Palacz, W.: Towards automatic generation of storyline aided by collaborative creative design. In: Luo, Y. (ed.) CDVE 2020. LNCS, vol. 12341, pp. 47–56. Springer, Cham (2020). https://doi.org/10.1007/978-3-030-60816-3_6
5. Grabska-Gradzińska, I., et al.: Graph-based data structures of computer games. In: Annual International Conference on Computer Games, Multimedia & Allied Technology (2013)

Calligraphic Drawing for Collaborative Virtual Whiteboard Systems

Yalmar Ponce Atencio[1]($\boxtimes$)(iD), Manuel J. Ibarra[2]($\boxtimes$)(iD),
Julio Huanca Marín[1]($\boxtimes$)(iD), Richard Flores Condori[1]($\boxtimes$),
Fidel Ticona Yanqui[3]($\boxtimes$)(iD), and Juan Oré Cerrón[1]($\boxtimes$)

[1] Universidad Nacional José María Arguedas, Andahuaylas-Apurímac, Peru
{yalmar,juliohuanca,rflores,jore}@unajma.edu.pe
[2] Universidad Nacional Micaela Bastidas de Apurímac, Abancay-Apurímac, Peru
[3] Universidad Nacional del Altiplano, Puno, Peru
fidelticona@unap.edu.pe

Abstract. Interactive whiteboards have become more popular and also essential tools for teaching and learning, especially in basic education classrooms. Studies have been reported on high levels of student motivation, teacher enthusiasm and whole-school support associated with these technological tools. Many researches have reported about the potential of interactive whiteboards (IWBs) to improve the quality of teaching and learning processes by enhancing levels of interaction, communication and collaboration. However, even nowadays, these IBWs suffer some difficulties at drawing time, in other words, are not suitable for freehand drawing, since they require more precision than the traditional input devices like mouse. Meanwhile, it is the preferable form and direct style to use at the teaching or explaining time. These difficulties are inherent to the input device, since the mouse still is the most used and the vast majority of people have no possibilities to get more expensive devices with support to stylus pen. Thus, considering that the mouse is the input device to draw, to do a freehand draw in any popular software is very tedious and frustrating experience. In this research work, we present the incorporation of the old well know DynaDraw drawing technique, into a online collaborative drawing application, which is able to produce drawings in a similar way to do with a pen, using the mouse. The results, on freehand style drawing, compared to other current software, are very satisfactory considering nor special software neither additional hardware are needed. For the implementation, traditional coding frameworks like node.js, express.js, io.js and MongoDB were used, since the main goal is share a drawing work collaboratively. Finally, our implementation is easy to install in other popular teaching and learning platforms like Moodle.

Keywords: Collaborative application · Interactive whiteboard ·
Freehand drawing · Dynadraw

© Springer Nature Switzerland AG 2021
Y. Luo (Ed.): CDVE 2021, LNCS 12983, pp. 232–239, 2021.
https://doi.org/10.1007/978-3-030-88207-5_23

1   Introduction

Over the last years, and more recently with the COVID-19 pandemic, interactive whiteboards have become essential tools for teaching and learning in many contexts, from basic education to graduate teaching in virtual classrooms. In all the cases, the most important resource is to use a freehand drawing in order to replace the whiteboard marker. However, freehand drawing is still limited nowadays, even with stylus pen devices, since they are very expensive and neither them can solve the problem completely, in many cases requires an specialized software or only works in a limited set of applications. On the other hand, the most cheapest input device is the mouse, but to do a freehand drawing is dreadful to do, in particular write text, mainly because have no precision with the drawn lines or curves.

Currently, there are an increasingly demand for creating virtual whiteboard, since many tasks were virtualized and most of them require to use freehand drawing. Certainly, in order to achieve better results, there are some solutions like to use optical pens with specific boards or monitors, which are a little bit expensive. Drawing is one of the most interesting hobbies that can be seen, even in a professional way, in many cases it is done using certain art forms such as calligraphy and graffiti art and are often the result of skillful and expressive movements that require years to master [2]. Surely it could not be possible to achieve good results using the computer mouse in traditional applications, but there is a relatively old technique called Dynadraw [8], which allows to draw strokes close to a freehand style using the mouse, and it was used on the solution proposed in this research work. On the other hand, in the current context of the COVID-19, has had an huge increase of demand for interactive and collaborative applications for drawing. Mainly in virtual teaching and learning systems. In that sense, applications to express your ideas by fast drawing there are few and maybe the most popular by its simplicity could be the Google Jamboard.

The main difficulty in creating a tool to draw quickly using the computer mouse is, how to simplify the strokes made by dragging the mouse, since the mouse is an input device exclusively to position its pointer on elements of the graphical interface of user (GUI), and it doesn't matter how you bring this to each of these elements. Another common interaction with the mouse is dragging and dropping elements from the GUI, and again, no matter how you do it, as long as the action taken has been successful. Is well know that even nowadays, the mouse is one of the most important input devices, and for many users is mandatory, clearly during the last decades there isn't exists another input device to replace it, neither the laptop mouse touch nor mobile devices touchscreen. Only on the last decade, was introduced to market most evolved equipment, like high-end portable computers equipped with touchscreen and optical pen, but we only referring to high-end, since middle or low-end are not useful, because the freehand experience is painful and sad on these. Considering the issues related above, in this research work, we present the implementation of a online collaborative application for sharing drawing documents, which aims to help teaching and learning in many situations and contexts, from basic education to college, since it will be possible to interact between teachers and classmates.

The rest of the document is organized as follows: related works are presented in the follow section, the third section describes the implementation details of the proposed application, the fourth section presents some experiments and results, finally, the fifth section presents the conclusions and some suggestions for future works.

2   Related Work and Background

While in the past teaching was dominated by chalk and whiteboard marker, in the last two decades this was progressively evolving to use virtual whiteboards, and after the COVID-19 it becomes something like mandatory in all levels of education and in many workjob contexts. Although there are many different tools which have the purpose to simulate a real whiteboard, only a few are really useful. Among the difficulties we find are complications in the installation or some requirements that are difficult to provide as in the case of Microsoft Whiteboard or Microsoft OneNote which need an email account. Thus, there are a lot of proposals in order to improve the drawing experience in a computer, using the classical mouse. Perhaps Haeberli [8] pioneered in this field, implementing his DynaDraw system, a computer program that allows the user to interactively generate strokes evocative of calligraphy by simulating a mass attached to the mouse position. In this context we can also cite the work presented by Berio et al. [2], where they present a survey on calligraphy techniques for drawing and describes in detail their proposal. Typically, freehand drawn curves are interactively specified by using a sketch based interface, in which a user traces a curve with a pen tablet, mouse or touchscreen tablet, and the trace is then processed to remove discontinuities and imperfections caused by the digitizing device. In many fields, calligraphy and typography are very requested to do freehand on a computer. There a lot of research works dedicated to do that, and much of them are incorporated into many commercial software [4,12,17]. Hand-draw techniques are become more popular, but in the past it was very limited due to there are not good input devices, and in that sense proposed research works were limited too, that is the case of the proposal presented by Foster and Wartig [7], where their proposal consists in use some predefined GUI elements to express ideas replacing a real whiteboard in meetings, but it not allows to do creations by using freehand. Recently more sophisticated devices have been evolving like stylus pen but this devices are very expensive. On the other hand, recently with the popularization of virtualization, there is an increasing demand for create tools to help collaborative interaction in different settings, in education, at work and other activities [9–11,16]. From a large list of existing collaborative systems, drawing attracts a special attention to developers and software creators, since it helps to many fields, from teaching and learning to professional design [1,3,5,13–15]. The present research work aims to contribute in that direction, creating a collaborative online system for fast freehand drawing. It might be useful for sign documents, since it need a calligraphy style, in addition, this simplifies the mouse interaction for rapid drawings, even is able to do straight strokes easily which is highly used in math and physic teaching.

3   Implementation

The proposed implementation consists in to prepare a collaborative application environment for sharing documents. We essentially have used the same implementation as described in [13–15], where a MongoDB database is used and sockets for real time input/output interaction.

In this work, we have ported the original drawing method Dynadraw [8] to the JavaScript (ES6) language, since it is easy to incorporate in a collaborative application environment online.

An important aspect to consider is the interaction experience, since the original proposed DynaDraw technique was ported to some languages and platforms, but in some cases the interaction was very slow, so it is necessary to improve the implementation to allow a greater dynamic response and achieve real-time interaction as if we were really writing on the screen.

We have used the code ported from the original Dynadraw paper and re-implemented by Claudio Esperança in his Observablehq notebook page [6]. He implements two main classes: Brush and BrushedStroke.

In order to draw smooth calligraphic strokes, it is necessary store many small stroke segments, and this is as this class allows to do. Next, the BrushedStroke implementation allows to manage the list of segments created by the Brush class and allows to render on a HTML canvas context. In other words, the important thing is allows trace all the points where the mouse have passed and simplifies the curve in order to draw a as simple as possible representation for the curve.

Finally, the most important thing is the implementation of mouse interaction. This is done in three different times, when the mouse is pressed, when the mouse is pressed and simultaneously is moved (dragging process) and when the mouse button is released (mouse-up).

Additionally, a basic 2D Vector implementation is needed. All the implemented classes are simple to understand and easy to use.

In order to test the presented implementation, it could be copied back into any HTML JavaScript environment, or alternatively clone (fork) it from the Esperança's notebook site [6]. Although this implementation is easy to port to other platforms, like pure HTML Javascript, incorporate this to an existing platform like Moodle is a little hard, since we need treat with sessions and other properly platform functionalities. The Fig. 1 shows our implemented collaborative application inside the Moodle platform.

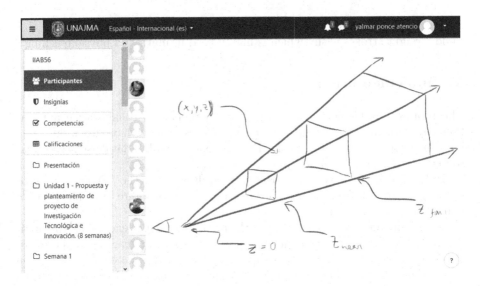

Fig. 1. Our collaborative application installed on the Moodle platform.

4   Results

In order to demonstrate the advantages of the proposed drawing method we conducted two experiments. The first consists of draw a signature using three popular collaborative drawing software. In the Fig. 2 are presented the results. Clearly, the strokes done in the proposed implementation look more similar to a real signature done in a paper.

Fig. 2. A signature drawn in Heyhi (left). The same signature drawn in Google Jamboard (middle). The same signature drawn using the proposed drawing system (right).

Another experiment was to draw a simple diagram, done entirely with strokes. In the same way as in the first experiment, we have drawn this in three applications in order to compare the produced strokes. Again, the diagram drawn by the proposed system has produced better strokes compared to the other applications (see Fig. 3).

Fig. 3. An example drawing done in three applications: Heyhi (left), Jamboard (middle) and our proposed application (right).

As a third experiment, we have tested another web application, close similar to the proposed in this paper. MyScript web application allows to draw math formulae, and additionally is able to recognize what is writing in a freehand mode with the mouse. In counterpart, we want to show that the strokes generated by our proposed application are even more readable than the MyScript and easy to write with the mouse, and for consequence could be also suitable for applying in a recognition process too (see the Fig. 4).

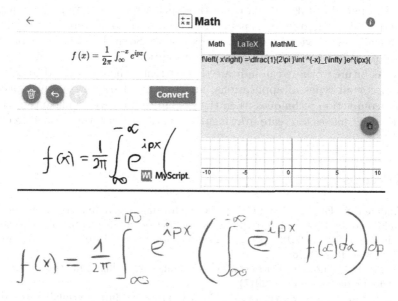

Fig. 4. An example drawing a math formula. The application MyScript was used (top) and also our proposed application (bottom).

Finally, we present an example where a calligraphic text is written, using the mouse in a freehand mode, in four different systems (see the Fig. 5). It's possible to compare and notice that the freehand calligraphic draw done in our application has a slightly better aspect than the others, and also we can notice that the worst was by using Google Jamboard.

Fig. 5. An example of writing freehand text in four different applications. Using the Microsoft Paint (a), using our implementation (b), using Google Jamboard (c) and using Microsoft Whiteboard (d).

5   Discussion

Although there are currently various freehand drawing applications, many have evolved achieving excellent results, such is the case of Microsoft Whiteboard, and in Microsoft's trend towards the free software market, its Whiteboard application is very good since it currently integrates with other platforms like Google. However, we can still notice that his strokes are not quite good as what we would like, especially when we want to make a signature. Regarding the implementation of a drawing system as exposed in this research work, a really important aspect is the interaction with the drawing, this must be really dynamic and in real time, since today there are many low-cost touch devices, however they require an optical pencil to take advantage of the touch screen, but even having a good optical pencil the interaction is not satisfactory, so the only appropriate solution is high-end touch devices that are very expensive. So in that sense, our proposal aims to provide a low-cost and easy-to-use solution for these types of tasks and needs. As future work we can indicate that currently there is a trend to use deep learning for all types of applications, and this could be very useful especially in auto-completion techniques, then the system could learn to make the strokes that the user makes to create drawings automatically with the learned freehand style.

References

1. Andiana, S., Fauziah, P.Y.: Collaborative drawing: Upgrading creativity for early childhood. In: Proceedings of the International Conference on Special and Inclusive Education (ICSIE 2018), pp. 293–298. Atlantis Press (2019). https://doi.org/10.2991/icsie-18.2019.53
2. Berio, D., Calinon, S., Fol Leymarie, F.: Generating calligraphic trajectories with model predictive control (2017)
3. Blazhenkova, O., Kozhevnikov, M.: Creative processes during a collaborative drawing task in teams of different specializations. Creative Educ. **11**, 1751–1775 (2020). https://doi.org/10.4236/ce.2020.119128
4. Buckingham-Hsiao, R.: Collaborative calligraphy: an Asemic writing performance. Liminalities J. Perform. Stud. **13** (2017)
5. Delgado Meza, J., Castro Castro, M., Jaime, R., Rueda, A.C.: Collaborative learning tools used in virtual higher education programs: a systematic review of literature in iberoamerica, pp. 1–7 (2020). https://doi.org/10.23919/CISTI49556.2020.9140901

6. Esperança, C.: Dynadraw (2020). https://observablehq.com/@esperanc/dynadraw. Published 19 November 2020

7. Forster, F., Wartig, H.: Creativity techniques for collocated teams using a web-based virtual whiteboard, pp. 7–11 (2009). https://doi.org/10.1109/ICIW.2009.9

8. Haeberli, P.: Dynadraw. Grafica OBSCURA (1989)

9. Ignat, C.L., Norrie, M.: Draw-together: graphical editor for collaborative drawing, pp. 269–278 (2006). https://doi.org/10.1145/1180875.1180917

10. Northcote, M., Mildenhall, P., Marshall, L., Swan, P.: Interactive whiteboards: interactive or just whiteboards? Aust. J. Educ. Technol. **26** (2010). https://doi.org/10.14742/ajet.1067

11. Owhadi-Kareshk, M., Nadi, S., Rubin, J.: Predicting merge conflicts in collaborative software development. CoRR abs/1907.06274. arXiv:1907.06274 (2019)

12. Turgut, Ö.P.: Calligraphic forms in contemporary typographic design. Procedia - Social and Behavioral Sciences, vol. 122, pp. 40–45. 2nd World Conference on Design, Arts and Education (DAE-2013) (2014). https://doi.org/10.1016/j.sbspro.2014.01.1300, https://www.sciencedirect.com/science/article/pii/S1877042814013172

13. Atencio, Y.P., Ibarra, M.J., Baca, H.H.: Collaborative application for rapid design of paintings in vector format. In: Luo, Y. (ed.) CDVE 2020. LNCS, vol. 12341, pp. 322–331. Springer, Cham (2020). https://doi.org/10.1007/978-3-030-60816-3_35

14. Ponce, Y.: A collaborative ide for graphics programming. J. Critical Rev. **7**, 1570–1577 (2020). https://doi.org/10.31838/jcr.07.15.209

15. Atencio, Y.P., Cabrera, M.I., Huaman, L.A.: A cooperative drawing tool to improve children's creativity. In: Luo, Y. (ed.) CDVE 2019. LNCS, vol. 11792, pp. 162–171. Springer, Cham (2019). https://doi.org/10.1007/978-3-030-30949-7_19

16. Quiñones, G., Ridgway, A., Li, L.: Collaborative drawing: a creative tool for examination of infant-toddler pedagogical practices. Aust. J. Early Childhood **44**, 183693911985521 (2019). https://doi.org/10.1177/1836939119855219

17. Sun, D., Zhang, J., Pan, G., Zhan, R.: Mural2sketch: a combined line drawing generation method for ancient mural painting. In: 2018 IEEE International Conference on Multimedia and Expo (ICME). pp. 1–6 (2018). https://doi.org/10.1109/ICME.2018.8486504.

Large-Sized Tablet-Based Live Mobile Learning System with a Large Whiteboard Area

Jang Ho Lee(✉)

Department of Computer Engineering, Hongik University, Seoul, Korea
janghol@hongik.ac.kr

Abstract. Most existing live mobile distance learning systems lack support for the simultaneous view of both a presentation slide and a whiteboard, which makes it difficult for students to understand a lecture. Thus, we had previously developed a tablet-based live learning system with a whiteboard shown together with a presentation slide on a 9.7-inch tablet. However, the limited size of the tablet and the small size ratio of the whiteboard area still made it difficult for an instructor to draw a sophisticated figure that can help students to understand a difficult subject. Therefore, we propose a large-sized tablet-based live learning system with a large size ratio of a whiteboard area that allows students to watch lecture video, chat, presentation slide with annotation, and figures being drawn on a whiteboard area simultaneously on a 12.9-inch tablet in real time. The results of our preliminary evaluation suggest that students' perception of the proposed system is significantly better than our previous one in terms of lecture understanding, sophistication of a lecture, and the feedback to a question.

Keywords: Live mobile learning · Tablet · Whiteboard · Synchronous collaboration

1 Introduction

The benefit of allowing students geographically apart to participate in a class via the internet had made researchers interested in the field of distance learning. Over the last decade, the idea of mobile learning attracted their attention since it enables distant students to participate in a learning session just with their mobile devices such as smartphones or tablets from anywhere avoiding the hassle of seating in front of a computer [1]. Then, as the recent pandemic has significantly changed the way people live their lives around the world over a year, distance learning including mobile learning has become virtually the only way students participate in their classes.

Classroom Presenter [2] and MLVLS [3] are early examples of live mobile learning system. Although Classroom Presenter provided support for sharing of slides and annotation between a teacher and students on a tablet, students had to be in the same classroom with the teacher to watch him/her and ask questions. MLVLS enabled students from a distance to watch a lecture video and slides with annotation on their Symbian

Y. Luo (Ed.): CDVE 2021, LNCS 12983, pp. 240–245, 2021.
https://doi.org/10.1007/978-3-030-88207-5_24

smartphone in real time. However, its display is too small for a slide with complex content and it lacks support for interaction between a teacher and students. Cisco Webex [4] allows students to watch a lecture video, slides with annotation and a whiteboard as well as to interact with a teacher on a mobile device in real time. However, since it does not simultaneously show a slide and a whiteboard, the instructor is not allowed to draw figures on the whiteboard and refer to the slide at the same time, which often makes it difficult for students to understand a difficult subject. This is different from an offline classroom environment where an instructor can draw figures on a blackboard beside a projection screen showing a slide. Therefore, we had previously developed a tablet-based live mobile learning system [5] that enables students to watch an instructor to give an explanation on a slide, make an annotation on it, and draw figures on the whiteboard at the same time on a 9.7-inch iPad. They can also ask questions via chat. Later, however, we found out that a whiteboard shown with a slide in parallel is not useful enough if the whiteboard is not large enough. An instructor had difficulty in drawing a sophisticated figure on the small whiteboard, which made it difficult for students to understand the lecture. We also noticed that the slide area was not large enough for a detailed annotation on a 9-7-inch display.

Thus, we present a large-sized tablet-based live learning system that allows students to watch lecture video, a slide and annotation along with an ample whiteboard shown simultaneously in real time as well as to ask questions via chat. We improved our previous system in two ways to address the problems mentioned above. Firstly, we increased the size ratio of the whiteboard area on the full screen of a tablet display. Secondly, we adopted a tablet equipped with a larger display hardware, which is 12.9-inch iPad. As a result, the large whiteboard area allows an instructor to comfortably draw large complex figures, which helps students better understand a lecture. We also present the result of a preliminary evaluation of the prototype of the proposed system.

2   Large-Sized Tablet-Based Live Mobile Learning System with a Large Whiteboard Area

Figure 1 shows the run-time communication architecture of the proposed system.

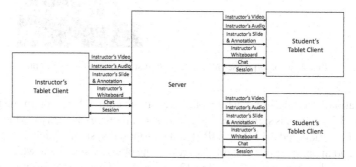

Fig. 1. Communication architecture of the proposed system

The system consists of a server and tablet clients. The main function of the server is to broadcast data from the clients, which are of two types: instructor's tablet and student's tablet. The video, audio, slide with annotation, and whiteboard drawing data are only generated by the instructor's client and sent to the server, which multicasts them to students' clients. The video and audio are encoded in H.263 and G.723.1 respectively by the instructor's client, and sent to the server, which multicasts them to students' clients for encoding. These data do not flow from the students' clients to the server to reduce the server overload and network congestion. On the other hand, a chat message and session control such as join a session, can be generated by any type of clients and sent to the server, which broadcast them to the other clients.

Figure 2 shows the prototype user interface of an instructor's 12.9-inch iPad client app. An instructor can explain the presentation slide (in the upper left) by voice and gesture via video (in the lower right) as well as make an annotation on the slide in real time. The instructor can also draw figures on the large whiteboard area (in the upper right) in order to help students better understand a complex concept. These actions are supported by the UI controls including arrows (for previous slide and next slide), pencil, eraser, Open (a file), and Clear (a whiteboard) as can be seen at the top. The list of participants are shown at the lower left. The instructor can receive questions from students via chat (in the lower middle).

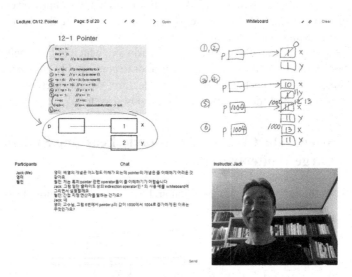

Fig. 2. Prototype user interface of an instructor's iPad client app

The ratio of the size of the whiteboard area to the entire client app in the proposed system is 23.7% which is significantly bigger than our previous system [5] which is 8.4%. In addition, we adopted a 12.9-inch iPad in the proposed system, which is larger than a 9.7-inch iPad in our previous system. As a result, the physical size of the whiteboard area of the proposed system has increased to 121.9 cm^2 (12.7 cm × 9.6 cm) which is much larger than 24.5 cm^2 (5.7 cm × 4.3 cm) of our previous system. And the presentation slide area of the client app in the proposed system has also increased to 121.9 cm^2 (12.7

cm × 9.6 cm) which is also larger than 87.5 cm^2 (10.8 cm × 8.1 cm) of our previous system.

Figure 3 shows the prototype user interface of a student's 12.9-inch iPad client app. A student can watch the lecture video and the presentation slide with annotation being made on it as well as figures being drawn on a whiteboard area by an instructor in real time. The students ask questions in real time via chat, which can then be answered by the instructor through voice, gesture, annotation on the slide, chat or by drawing a figure on the whiteboard area. The previously mentioned UI controls for the instructor's app are not provided for the student's app.

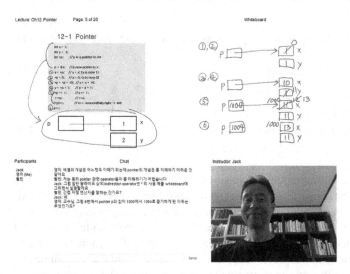

Fig. 3. Prototype user interface of a students' iPad client app

We are currently in the development of the prototype. The hardware for client is a 12.9-inch iPad Pro running iOS 14 [6]. Regarding the development platform, the iOS client apps for instructor and student are being implemented in Swift using Xcode integrated development environment on macOS Big Sur. The server application is being developed in C++ language with GNU compiler on Linux.

3 Preliminary Evaluation

For a preliminary evaluation, a paired sample t-test was conducted to compare student's perception of our previous system [5] and the proposed system in terms of three aspects of a lecture: (1) how easy the lecture was; (2) how sophisticated the lecture was; and (3) how good the feedback to a question was. First, we asked ten undergraduate students in our department of Computer Engineering to participate in two short lecture sessions: one session using our previous system and the other using our proposed system. Then, we conducted a survey on the participants perception in terms of three aspects described above. The results are shown in the following three tables. In these tables, ten students were numbered from 1 to 10. The perception score for both systems given by a student ranges from 1 to 10.

Table 1 shows students' perception of how easy the lecture was. The paired sample t-test shows that there is a significant difference between the students' perception of easiness of understanding a lecture with the previous system (Mean = 6.4, SD = 1.58) and the one with the proposed system (Mean = 7.4, SD = 1.17) (two-tailed, $p < .05$). The result suggests that students felt that the lecture was easier to understand in the proposed system equipped with a large whiteboard than in the previous one with small whiteboard. The students said that it was easier to understand an explanation that was made by an instructor on a ample whiteboard of the proposed system.

Table 1. Students' perception of easiness of lecture comprehension

| Tested system | Student | | | | | | | | | | Mean | SD |
	1	2	3	4	5	6	7	8	9	10		
Previous system	6	7	4	8	5	7	8	4	8	7	6.4	1.58
Proposed system	8	8	6	9	6	7	8	6	9	7	7.4	1.17

Table 2 shows students' perception of how sophisticated the lecture was. The paired sample t-test shows that there is a significant difference between the students' perception of the degree of detail of the lecture with the previous system (Mean = 6.1, SD = 1.29) and with the proposed system (Mean = 7.5, SD = 1.35) (two-tailed, $p < .001$). The result suggests that students felt that an explanation was made in more detail with the proposed system than with the previous system. The students said that the ample space of a large whiteboard allowed the instructor to draw a large sophisticated figure in more detail. The large whiteboard area allowed an instructor to rely less on speaking and gesture but more on drawing a complex figure in explaining a sophisticated concept, which seemed to help students better understand it.

Table 2. Students' perception of sophistication of a lecture

| Tested system | Student | | | | | | | | | | Mean | SD |
	1	2	3	4	5	6	7	8	9	10		
Previous system	6	6	8	7	6	4	6	4	7	7	6.1	1.29
Proposed system	7	9	8	9	7	6	7	5	9	8	7.5	1.35

Table 3 shows students' perception of how good a feedback to a question was. The paired sample t-test shows that there is a significant difference between the students' perception of the quality of a feedback to a question with the previous system (Mean = 5.9, SD = 1.66) and the one with the proposed system (Mean = 6.9, SD = 1.97) (two-tailed, $p < .001$). The result suggests that students was more satisfied with the feedback to a question using the proposed system than with the one using the previous system. Students said that the instructor was able to answer to a student's question by quickly drawing a delicate figure on the large whiteboard, which helped them better understand the instructor's answer.

Table 3. Students' perception of a feedback to a question

Tested system	Student										Mean	SD
	1	2	3	4	5	6	7	8	9	10		
Previous system	5	8	7	6	4	3	5	6	8	7	5.9	1.66
Proposed system	6	9	8	8	5	4	4	8	8	9	6.9	1.97

Therefore, our results described above suggest that the proposed system is more useful to students than the previous one in three aspects: easiness of understanding a lecture, sophistication of a lecture, and feedback to a question.

4 Conclusion

We proposed a large-sized tablet-based live mobile learning system with a large whiteboard area. It allows students to watch lecture video and a presentation slide with annotation, along with a large whiteboard as well as ask questions via chat on their 12.9-inch tablet in real time. An instructor can explain a complex subject on a slide by drawing a sophisticated figure on the large whiteboard shown simultaneously with the slide on the tablet. Preliminary evaluation results suggest that students' perception of the proposed system is significantly better than our previous system in terms of easiness of lecture comprehension, sophistication of a lecture, and feedback to a question. We are currently working on the prototype implementation of the proposed system. When it is completed, we plan to conduct an in-depth empirical study.

Acknowledgements. This work was supported by 2018 Hongik University Research Fund.

References

1. Wains, S.I., Mahmood, W.: Integrating M-learning with E-learning. In: 9th ACM SIGITE Conference on Information Technology Education, pp. 31–38. ACM (2008)
2. Anderson, R., et al.: Classroom presenter: enhancing interactive education with digital ink. IEEE Comput. **40**(9), 56–61 (2007)
3. Ulrich, C., Shen, R., Tong, R., Tan, X.: A mobile live video learning system for large-scale learning-system design and evaluation. IEEE Trans. Learn. Technol. **3**(1), 6–17 (2010)
4. Cisco Webex. https://www.webex.com
5. Lee, J.H.: Design of tablet-based live mobile learning system supporting improved annotation. In: Park, J.J., Fong, S.J., Pan, Y., Sung, Y. (eds.) Advances in Computer Science and Ubiquitous Computing. LNEE, vol. 715, pp. 221–226. Springer, Singapore (2021). https://doi.org/10.1007/978-981-15-9343-7_30
6. iOS 14. https://developer.apple.com/ios/

The Potential of Campus Business and Estimated Cost of In-Class Advertising

Kanata Itoh[✉] and Takayuki Fujimoto[✉]

Graduate School of Information Sciences and Arts, Toyo University, Tokyo, Japan
{s3B102000037,fujimoto}@toyo.jp

Abstract. In conducting "Research on the Use of Educational Space as an Advertising Medium," we investigate corporate advertising activities that are currently taking place in schools and attempt to estimate the fees for in-class advertising, assuming that it is put to practical use. From there, we will calculate the distribution of incentives for professors and reduced tuition fees in detail.

Keywords: Advertising · Information · University lecture

1 Background

In recent years, the advertising market has undergone a major transformation. Internet advertising expenditures have surpassed television advertising expenditures, and this momentum is being further strengthened by the impact of COVID-19, which began in 2020. However, Internet advertising as a whole is becoming saturated, and it is becoming more difficult to secure effective advertising media. In the future, it will be necessary to find a new advertising medium on the Internet. For example, 'digital signage', which displays digital advertisements on displays in real space rather than on the Web, is an advertising medium that is expected to expand in the future as "interactive billboards." Of course, digital signage is not new, but with faster communication environments and higher performance devices, a variety of expressions and possibilities are expected.

The authors have been conducting research focusing on the use of educational spaces and school classrooms as a new advertising medium targeting the young generation. Specifically, in recent years, in higher education, computers are often connected to projectors and class materials and slides are presented on large displays and screens. Displays used in class are much more likely to be viewed intently by students than television or the Internet. Classes are also divided by grade level, subject, and specialty, making it easier to target marketing. Educational spaces can be extremely effective as an advertising medium targeting young people, but there have been no examples of such use to date. The three reasons for this are as follows:

① Resistance to bringing business into the field of education.
② Interfering with teaching and learning by including advertisements that have nothing to do with the class.
③ The contradiction of forcing advertising on tuition-paying students.

© Springer Nature Switzerland AG 2021
Y. Luo (Ed.): CDVE 2021, LNCS 12983, pp. 246–255, 2021.
https://doi.org/10.1007/978-3-030-88207-5_25

In other words, it is a violation of the desirability for an educational space and a violation of the students' right to learn. Of course, there will be legal issues that need to be resolved to make this happen. On the other hand, if the introduction of advertising can be linked to a reduction or exemption in school fees, the right to learn can be extended. In recent years, the rising cost of higher education has become a social problem in developed countries. It is not uncommon for the cost of education to consume a large portion of a parent's annual income. Currently many students are barely able to attend university on scholarships. In addition, Japan's university and junior college advancement rate is 61%, ranking 32nd in the world, low among developed countries. In the ranking of average tuition fees for universities, Japan ranks third in the world for both private and public universities. This shows that Japan has a low advancement rate and high tuition costs. Therefore, it is expected that there will be a high need for a system that links the introduction of advertising into the educational space with the reduction or exemption of school fees for Japan's university enrollment rate and scientific research, which has been lagging in recent years.

2 Purpose

In order to conduct "Research on the Use of Educational Space as an Advertising Medium," this paper clarifies campus businesses and how in-class advertising is currently used. We then calculate the advertising fees, assuming that in-class advertising is put to practical use. In-class advertisements are advertisements that are displayed on the edge of the class materials and slides that are projected on the screen and are used by the professor during the class. These are expected to be similar to the banner advertisements seen on Google or Yahoo!! We will use a 'term contract type' as the method of calculating the fees for in-class advertising, in which the fees will be based on the period of time the advertisement is posted. We will make a trial calculation assuming the use of a pure advertising banner advertisement. The 'term contract type' was chosen because, while it has the disadvantage that advertising fees will still be incurred even if there are few impressions or clicks, it also has advantages, such as:

① No unexpected costs.
② Low set-up fees.
③ Advertising material will always be displayed for the duration of the contract.

In addition, in-class advertisements are the most cost effective and suitable type of advertisement because the audiences that watch them are closely matches to the target group of the advertising company. A pure advertising banner advertising means 'purchasing an advertising space in a particular medium and posting a banner on it'. It is an advertising method used on the Yahoo!! top page for the purpose of increasing awareness and sales promotions. The advertising fee is estimated impressions × $0.0096. This comes to approximately $631,000/week. In addition, incentives for professors and reduced tuition fees from the expected advertising revenue to the school will be mentioned.

3   Examples of Existing In-School Advertising

We will first describe how advertising activities are currently conducted in schools before calculating the fees for in-class advertising, A review showed many examples of in-school advertising. The five main ones are:

3.1   Digital Signage

The multi-language switching function allows the display to be switched to multiple languages. In recent years, the number of foreign students who are unfamiliar with the Japanese language has increased and this medium is rapidly growing. There are various types of digital signage, such as displays hanging from the ceiling and embedded in the wall. It is expected to have a high degree of visibility because there are more ways to display them than other advertising media. Digital signage is widely used in cafeterias, school buildings, office buildings, and etc.

Advertising Fee: from approximately $5,000 (15 s × 2 weeks).

Size: various sizes (Fig. 1).

Fig. 1. Digital signage, URL [12]

3.2   Tadakopi

Free photocopying services are provided by including advertising space on the back of the photocopy paper. This is an information medium that eliminates the costs borne by the user. Black-and-white photocopies cost $0.096 but using photocopy paper with a corporate advertisement pre-printed on one side of the paper allows photocopying services to be provided free of charge. Universities can also rent photocopy machines for free.

Advertising fee: unknown.

Size: A4 size.

3.3 Cafeteria Lunch Trays

Advertisements are placed on cafeteria lunch trays in university cafeterias with stickers. This is a medium that has a very long contact time, because it is always in view from the time users are waiting for their order, while they are eating, until they return their tray. In addition, many students use the school cafeteria every day. So the advertisement can be repeatedly imprinted and the high visibility rate is a major feature. As an advantage, it is expected to have a high advertising effect as it may be a topic of conversation among university students. On the other hand, it has the disadvantage of being a little more expensive than other forms of advertising because of the stickers on the trays. This is the most popular type of advertising in schools.

Advertising fee: approximately $9,000/30,000 person plan (1,000 copies).

Size: A4 size (Fig. 2).

Fig. 2. Cafeteria lunch trays, URL [13]

3.4 Eco Chopsticks

The advertisement is placed on the packaging of chopsticks used in university cafeterias and stores. Chopsticks are used during every meal, so word-of-mouth effects can be expected. However, the disadvantage is that the advertisement is smaller than cafeteria lunch tray and only catches the user's eye for a moment.

Advertising fee: $0.13 Minimum lot 10,000 sets or more.

Size: 32 mm (width) × 190 mm (length) (Fig. 3).

3.5 On-Campus Posters

This is the most orthodox type of advertising but there is a decreasing trend in its use for corporate advertising. However, there are many advantages, such as not being limited in where they can be posted. On-campus posters are often used to advertise school events.

Advertising fee: approximately $500 per location per month, minimum lot of 5.

Size: various sizes (Fig. 4).

Fig. 3. Eco chopsticks, URL [14]

Fig. 4. On-campus posters, URL [15]

From the above, we can see that various types of advertisements, from classic print media to the latest electronic media, continue to be used together in universities. Many of the paper medias are reasonably priced. Digital signage costs about approximately $2,000 per month in advertising fees. We can assume that there is a large demand for advertising in schools. All of these media are expected to induce a word-of-mouth effect from conversations among students and have a high visibility rate. On the other hand, even with high visibility, all of the above-mentioned advertising mediums are only seen 'a few times', for 'a few minutes'. Moreover, it is not something that users see when they are committed to looking, but something that they see unconsciously for an instant. Therefore, it can be said that these do not provide a sufficient advertising effect. In-class advertisements are embedded in the edge of the screen of the class slides which the students stare at for 90 min, so they can be expected to attract the intentional gaze of the students many times over a long period of time.

4 Calculating the Cost of In-Class Advertising

In order to calculate the fees for in-class advertisements, reference will be made to the fee rates for banner advertisements. There are three types of banner advertisements: the guaranteed period method, the impression-based method, the pay-per-click method, and the performance-based method. Since in-class advertisements are always displayed during classes, the guaranteed period method was adopted.

In general, the market rate for the guaranteed period method is.

'estimated number of times displayed × $0.0048 ~ $0.019'

Looking at the example of a pure advertising banner advertisement placed on the top page of a major advertising medium, Yahoo!!

- Payment method: period contract method
- Weekly PV number: 17.5 billion PV
- Advertising fee: approximately $631,000 per week

This translates to about $2.53 per 1PV.

In this estimation, the numbers will vary widely depending on how the expected number of displays is calculated. In-class advertisements have a very high visibility rate because they are seen many times over the course of 90 min so a trial calculation will be made as follows:

- Estimated number of views (one lesson) × $0.019
- Estimated number of views (one lesson) × $0.096

Using the example of a pure advertising banner ad placed on the top page of.

Yahoo!!, a calculation is made upon the condition as follows; Weekly PV: 17.5 billion PV, Advertising fee: 66 million yen (approximately $631,000)/week, approximately $2.53 per PV.

- Estimated number of views (one lesson) × $2.53.

In this estimation, the same students will take multiple lectures by the same professor. The same advertisement will be displayed for all 30 sets of lessons throughout the year. For the purpose of this calculation we will not consider whether users will get bored of the advertisement.

① [Calculating the number of expected views (one lesson) × $0.019 from each professor]

If we consider this as an in-class advertisement, it will be assumed that an average of approximately 200 people attend each lesson, and that $3.83/lesson will be received from each advertisement. The below is an estimate based on the number of classes taught by Professor Takayuki Fujimoto's class in Toyo University. This does not include seminars, which are attended by a small number of students.

4 lessons × $3.83/lesson = $15.32/week.

There are 15 sets of 4 lessons (per week) per semester.

$15.32 × 15 = $229.

In other words, an annual advertising income of approximately $459 can be expected for each professor's class.

There are 429 professors in Toyo University,

so, this will equal 48,000 × 429 = approximately $197,000.

As a matter of course, there are some professors who are not popular, therefore this number is the maximum value.

② 【Calculating the number of expected views per student (one lesson) × $0.019】

Assuming that a student attends eight-lessons (per week) 15 times during a semester, each student will have attended a total of 240 lessons in a year.

Therefore, the advertising fee per student is $4.59/year.

Considering the university as a whole, Toyo University has 32,000 students,

so, this will equal 32,000 × 480 = approximately $147,000.

③ 【Calculating the number of expected views per professor (one lesson) × $0.096】

Assuming that an average of about 200 people attend a lesson, $19.13/lesson will be received from each advertisement.

4 lessons × $19.13/lesson = approximately $77/week.

And, since there are 15 sets of 4 lessons (per week) per semester,

$77 × 15 times = approximately $1,148.

In other words, an annual advertising income of approximately $2,296 per professor per class is expected. There are 429 professors in Toyo University.

$2,296 × 429 = approximately $985,000.

④ 【Calculating the number of expected views per student (one lesson) × $0.096】

Assuming a student attends eight-lessons (per week) 15 times in a semester, each student will attend a total of 240 lessons per year.

Therefore, the advertising fee per student would be approximately $23/year.

Considering the university as a whole, Toyo University has 32,000 students, so.

32,000 × $23 = approximately $735,000.

⑤ 【Considering about $2.53 per PV from each professor. 】

Assuming that an average of about 200 people attend a lesson, equaling 200 PV, and approximately $507/lesson will be received.

4 lessons × $507/lesson = approximately $2,000/week.

In addition to this, there are 15 weeks per semester,

so, $2,000 × 15 times = approximately $30,000.

In other words, up to approximately $60,000 in advertising revenue is expected to be generated per year per professor per lesson. There are 429 professors in Toyo University as a whole,

So $60,000 × 429 = approximately $25M.

⑥ 【Considering about $2.53 per PV from each student】

Assuming that a student attends eight-lessons (per week) 15 times during a semester, each student will have attended a total of 240 lessons in a year.

Therefore, the advertising fee per student is approximately $6,100/year.

Considering the university as a whole, Toyo University has 32,000 students, so.

32,000 × $6,100 = approximately $195M.

5 Expected Incentives for Schools and Professors and Reduced Tuition

In this chapter, we will examine two patterns of incentives for schools and professors and how reduced tuition can be distributed. In order to eliminate errors in the values calculated in Sect. 4, the average values will be used to calculate incentives for schools/professors and reduced tuition fees.

① 【Calculating the number of expected views (one lesson) × $0.019 from each professor】
② 【Calculating the number of expected views per student (one lesson) × $0.019】
　　The average advertising fee for the above two calculations is approximately $172,000.
③ 【Calculating the number of expected views per professor (one lesson) × $0.096】
④ 【Calculating the number of expected views per student (one lesson) × $0.096】
　　The average advertising fee for the above two calculations is approximately $851,000.
⑤ 【Considering about $2.53 per PV from each professor. 】
⑥ 【Considering about $2.53 per PV from each student】

The average advertising fee for the above two calculations is approximately $11M.
　　The incentives for professors and the reduced tuition fees are calculated from the above. Since the primary purpose of this study is to reduce tuition fees, the liberty has been taken of setting the ratio as incentive: tuition reduction = 2:8.

In case of ① and ②,
the average advertising fee is approximately $172,000,
so incentives for professors = approximately $34,000.
Therefore, since there are 429 professors, each professor will receive an incentive of about approximately $80/year.
Reduced tuition = approximately $138,000.
Therefore, since there are 32,000 students, a reduction of about approximately $4.30/year per student can be expected.

In the case of ③ and ④,
the average advertising fee is approximately $851,000.
Incentives for professors = approximately $170,000.
There are 429 professors, therefore, each professor will receive an incentive of about approximately $400/year.
Reduced tuition = approximately $679,000.
There are 32,000 students, therefore, a reduction in tuition of about approximately $21/year per student can be expected.

In case of ⑤ and ⑥,
the average advertising cost is approximately $11M.

Incentives for professors = approximately $27M.
There are 429 professors, therefore, each professor will receive an incentive of about approximately $64,000 /year.
Reduced tuition = approximately $92M.
There are 32,000 students, therefore each student can expect a reduction of about. approximately $2,800/year in tuition fees.

6 Discussion

We calculated the cost of in-class advertising and incentives for professors and reduced tuition for students as described above. The figures above are all based on the maximum possible value, however, different values may be arrived at if variations in the average number of students per lecture, the number of hours of a lecture (the number of lessons), exam dates and popularity of lectures are taken into account. As shown in Sect. 5, in the example of a pure advertising banner ad on the top page of Yahoo!!, a major advertising medium, each time the banner ad is displayed, even for an instant, is counted as one PV. Despite this, the advertising fee is expensive at about $2.53 per PV. In comparison, in-class advertisements that students will view for 90 min seem to have a reasonable value as media. This is the most suitable medium for meeting advertisers aim to strongly and deeply imprint the company or product name on the user. The ratio of the distribution of advertising fees in Sect. 6, incentive: tuition reduction = 2:8, is not well explained. This ratio is the result of roughly calculating a figure for all professors as a single group and the ratio was determined, based on the idea: due to the overwhelming difference in the number of professors and students, it is impossible to distribute the share equally in a defined ratio.

As another model, this example may be easier to understand: the method of applying 60% of the 'Advertising revenue of approximately $2,300 per year per professor per class' to the university in the form of a top-up fee and $2,300 × 6/10 × 429 = approximately $573,000 for tuition reduction and exemption. In any case, the distribution method warrants further consideration in the future. In addition, the term contract method was used to make the calculations easier, however, the impression-based method, click-based method, and performance-based method should also be tested. It is clear that it is important for advertisements to make people aware of the product, but the final goal is for people to jump from the banner ad to the sales website and purchase the product.

In this case, we made the calculations based on the assumption that the same ad would be displayed for all 30 lessons throughout the year, but this method will not actually be implemented. An influential university professor who is active in the mass media is expected to receive a flood of offers from companies, The calculation should be subdivided into more complex cases, such as the case of showing different ads for different lectures and the case in which a different ad is displayed for Xth lesson of a lecture. With this in mind, we would like to aim for a more concise calculation method. Also, it goes without saying that lectures by unpopular professors will not be sponsored. Thus, it is expected to improve the quality of lectures.

7 Conclusion

In this paper, we analyzed the current status of campus business and roughly calculated the incentives for in-class advertising and reduced tuition fees. As economies around the world stagnate due to the COVID-19, more active purchasing power of young people will be needed. Because this medium of advertising is new, the appropriate method and pricing for practical use and social demand is not yet known. We aim to make this research contribute to society by leading to a reduction in tuition fees, and an increase in the percentage of students who go to university.

References

1. Itoh, K., Fujimoto, T.: A research of the utilization of educational space as an advertising medium. Lect. Notes Netw. Syst. **182**(1), 342–347 (2020)
2. Fujita, H., Sennosuke, K., Nose, T., Kubo, S.: Study on the effect of advertising on the internet. Trans. Japan Soc. Manage. Eng. **51**, 6 (2001)
3. Fujita, A.: Advertising model on the web. J. Japan. Soc. Inf. Knowl. **16**, 4 (2006)
4. Amano, E.: In-school Marketing of Food and Beverage Companies in the United States: Schools as 'Markets' and Children as 'Consumers. Kanto Gakuin University Economic Association, vol. 251 (2012)
5. Kato, T., Tsuda, K.: Difference in purchasing behavior between web advertisement induction and spontaneous web search. In: National Research Presentation for Management Information Society, pp. 95–98 (2018)
6. Wakae, M., Mori, R., Yoshii, H.: Current status of tracking in online advertising and its legal consideration. J. Inf. Commun. Policy. **2**, 2 (2019)
7. Syouda, T.: Website as an ad and interactivity. Ad. Sci. **44**, 127–143 (2003)
8. Arai, T.: Role of internet advertising in the media planning. Aichi Gakuin Daigakuronso. Shogakukenkyu **6**, 1 (1958)
9. Sakata, T.: Instagram Marketing Strategy: An Advertising Communication for Instagram User Engagement. Takachihoronso, vol. 52 (2016)
10. Wakimoto, K., Kawamoto, S., Zhang, P.: Keyword-based text generation for internet advertisement. In: National Conference of AI Conference, vol. 34 (2020)
11. Okada, M., Kinoshita, T.: Effects of transition on late of click in banner advertisement-on the effect of over-lap and wipe. Yamaguchi Univ. Facult. Eng. Res. Report **62**, 2 (2012)
12. RUNEXY Homepage. https://www.runexy.co.jp/solution/digitalsignage/
13. AllWIN Homepage. https://allwin-inc.co.jp/case/collage/tray
14. ecobashi Homepage. http://www.ecobashi.com/wordpress/
15. YOU CAN PASS Homepage. https://www.youcanpass.net/business/view/4

Loan Default Prediction Using Artificial Intelligence for the Borrow – Lend Collaboration

Ngo Tien Luu and Phan Duy Hung[✉]

FPT University, Hanoi, Vietnam
luu18mse13018@fsb.edu.vn, hungpd2@fe.edu.vn

Abstract. In the lending industry, such as banks or finance companies, investors provide loans to borrowers in exchange for the promise of repayment with interest. This two-way collaboration has many potential risks that need to be assessed. If the borrower repays the loan, then the lender would make a profit from the interest. However, if the borrower fails to repay the loan, then the lender loses money. Therefore, lenders face predicting the risk of a borrower being unable to repay a loan at any step of the credit process. Many financial institutes calculate FICO scores of a customer based on some factors such as the Payment History (35%), Amounts owed (30%), Length of credit history (15%), Credit mix (10%), and New credit (10% of the total point) of the customer, that score qualifies how risk customers are, how repayment ability of the customer. FICO score (Fair Isaac Corporation) is a traditional approach used broadly in finance fields to estimate risks and give a worthy credit amount to the customer. In this study, a new way is to use Artificial intelligence to predict the above problems. It bases on credit information and more personal information of the customers to predict its repayment ability. The data collected from VietCredit Finances used for training several Machine Learning models to determine if the borrower can repay its loan. Some linear, nonlinear models involved are Logistic Regression, Linear Discriminant Analysis, K Nearest Neighbors, Decision Tree, Naïve Bayes, Support Vector Machine. The algorithm turning and Boosting and Bagging ensemble methods were also used to determine the best model. As a result, the Gradient Boosting model was the outperform and optimal predictive model (PR-AUC metric = 0.957).

Keywords: Borrow – Lend Collaboration · Artificial intelligence · Machine learning · Micro-finance · Risk management · Credit risk · Credit score · Credit loan assessment · Loan repayment ability

© Springer Nature Switzerland AG 2021
Y. Luo (Ed.): CDVE 2021, LNCS 12983, pp. 256–270, 2021.
https://doi.org/10.1007/978-3-030-88207-5_26

1 Introduction

The size of Vietnam's consumer finance market has continued to have stable growth in recent years. According to the State Bank of Viet Nam (SBV) 16 finance companies are licensed to provide consumer lending with their total charter capital worth more than VND22 trillion (US$948 million) as of the end of 2020 [1]. Along with the development of telecommunications infrastructure, internet, shopping habits on digital platforms of consumers, plus more than half of the population of Vietnam has never used credit through banks, so the amount of consumer finance market is still huge for companies, financial institutions to exploit. From an economic perspective, finance companies play an essential role in the transition of an export-dependent economy to one that depends on domestic consumption. In terms of social aspects, finance companies meet the needs of people to borrow money for consumption, mainly low and middle-income people, who have difficulty accessing bank loans. It helps them have the opportunity to borrow money from a more reliable address, thereby reducing black credit activities, contributing to economic development, and improved quality of life [2, 3].

The consumed loan is one significant product of any financial institutes. All financial companies are trying to figure out effective business strategies to persuade more customers to apply for their loans [4]. With simple loan procedures, no need for collateral, an easy approval process, and quick disbursement cause the number of consumed loan applications at financial companies increases, taking a lot of time and resources to process promptly [4, 5]. On the other hand, to minimize credit risks leading to bad debts, ensure financial safe for customers and organizations, loan appraisal is always the most critical stage in the credit approval process [6, 7]. The purpose of the appraisal is to answer the question Are customers eligible to receive a corresponding loan? If received, what is the limit? There are some customers not able to pay off the loan after their applications are approved. Therefore, many financial institutions take several input variables (such as personal information, monthly income, expenses, credit history) into account before approving a loan and determining whether a given borrower will fully pay off the loan or otherwise [8–10]. If the lender is too strict, fewer loans get approved, which means there is less interest to collect. However, if they are too lax, they end up approving loans that default.

Some positive results are achieved by many researchers who conducted studies on the loan default prediction.

No	Authors	Title	Source Dataset	Imbalanced Dataset	Classifiers	The Best Model	Metric	Score
4	Aslam, U., Tariq, A., Hafiz, I., Sohail, A., Batcha, N.K	An Empirical Study on Loan Default Prediction Models	UCI		Support Vector Machine, Logistic Regression, Decision Trees, Neural Nets	LR	AUC	0.74
5	Turkson, R.E., Baagyere, E.Y., Wenya, G.E	A machine learning approach for predicting bank creditworthiness	UCI		ExtraTree, RandomForest, AdaBoost, GradientBoosting, RandomTreesEmbedding, Voting, LogisticRegression, SVM, CART, NearestCentroid, Kneighbors, GaussianNB, Neural networks, LinearDiscriminantAnalysis, Bagging	AdaBoost	F1	0.9
6	Sheikh, M.A., Goel, A.K., Kumar, T	An Approach for Prediction of Loan Approval using Machine Learning Algorithm	Kaggle		Logistic regression, SVM, KNN	LogisticRegression	F1	0.811
7	Pandey, T.N., Jagadev, A.K., Mohapatra, S.K., Dehuri, S	Credit risk analysis using machine learning classifiers	UCI		Bayesian classifier, Naive-Bayes, Decision tree, KNN, K-means, MLP, SVM, ANN	ELM	Accuracy	0.96

(continued)

(continued)

No	Authors	Title	Source Dataset	Imbalanced Dataset	Classifiers	The Best Model	Metric	Score
8	Shiv, S.J., Murthy, S., Challuru, K	Credit Risk Analysis Using Machine Learning Techniques	UCI		LR, RF, NN	LR	Accuracy	0.81
9	Qiu, W	Credit Risk Prediction in an Imbalanced Social Lending Environment Based on XGBoost	Kaggle	x	KXGB, XGB, LR, RF, GBDT	XGB	Accuracy	0.92
10	Chen, S., Wang, Q., Liu, S	Credit Risk Prediction in Peer-to-Peer Lending with Ensemble Learning Framework	Kaggle		GBDT_AE_LR, Logistic Regression, Decision Tree, GBDT_LR	Gradient Boosting Decision Tree (GBDT)	ROC AUC	0.858
11	Alexandru, C., Maer-Matei, M.M., Albu, C	Predictive Models for Loan Default Risk Assessment		x	LightGBM, XGBoost, RF, LR	Random Forest optimal	ROC AUC	0.89

(continued)

(continued)

No	Authors	Title	Source Dataset	Imbalanced Dataset	Classifiers	The Best Model	Metric	Score
12	Zhu, L., Dafeng, Q., Daji, E., Cai, Y., Kuiyi, L	A Study on Predicting Loan Default Based on the Random Forest Algorithm	Lending Club	x	Random Forest, Decision Tree, SVM, Logistic Regression	RandomForest	ROC AUC	0.983
13	Soares, L.M.J, Nardini, F.M., Renso, C., Fernandes, J.A.M	An Empirical Comparison of Classification Algorithms for Imbalanced Credit Scoring Datasets	UCI	x	kNN, ELM, SVM, LOGR, TREE, ANN, FUZZ, QDA, GNET, LDA, GNB, RNDF, XGB, ADAB	Random forest, extreme gradient boosting	ROC AUC	0.932
14	Shoumo, S.Z.H., Dhruba, M.I.M., Hossain, S., Ghani, N.H., Arif, H., Islam, S	Application of Machine Learning in Credit Risk Assessment: A Prelude to Smart Banking	Lending Club	x	LR, SVM, RF, XGB	SVM + RFE	PR AUC	0.99
15	Lawi, A., Aziz, F., Syarif, S	Ensemble GradientBoost for increasing classification accuracy of credit scoring	UCI		Logistic Regression, Bagging, GradientBoost	GradientBoost	Accuracy	0.884

(continued)

(continued)

No	Authors	Title	Source Dataset	Imbalanced Dataset	Classifiers	The Best Model	Metric	Score
16	Ferreira, L.E.B., Barddal, J.P., Gomes, H.M., Enembreck, F	Improving Credit Risk Prediction in Online Peer-to-Peer (P2P) Lending Using Imbalanced Learning Techniques	Lending Club	x	DT, GNB, LG, AdaBoost, Bagging, RF,	LG + RU	ROC AUC	0.66
17	Chen, Y., Zhang, J., Ng, W.W.Y	Loan Default Prediction Using Diversified Sensitivity Undersampling	Lending Club	x	ROS + LR, ROS + RF, ROS + XGB, RUS + LR, RUS + RF, RUS + XGB, SMOTE + LR, SMOTE + RF, SMOTE + XGB, DSUS	DSUS	PR	0.6884
18	Barboza, F., Herbert, K., Edward, A	Machine Learning Models and Bankruptcy Prediction	North American		LDA, LR, NN, SVM, Boosting, Bagging, RF	Bagging	ROC AUC	0.914
19	Namvar, A., Mohammad, S., Fethi, R., Mohsen, N	Credit Risk Prediction in an Imbalanced Social Lending Environment	Lending Club	x	RF-RUS, LDA-SMOTE, LR-Tomek, Logistic Regression, Random forest	LR-RUS	ROC AUC	0.703

It is no doubt to say that most of the studies mentioned above aim to try various machine learning techniques to predict loan default and credit risk. Many supervised algorithms are tested, such as linear: Logistic Regression, Linear Discriminant Analysis, Nonlinearity: KNN, Naïve Bayes, Decision Tree, SVM, combined methods are also tested such as Bagging, Boosting, Voting. The data using model training was mainly collected from sharing communities such as UCI, Kaggle, Lending Club. Some authors mention the data imbalance problem as a challenge in building a classification model. The results print out most of the studies have found good models on the data sets collected. However, some studies on imbalanced data using Accuracy or ROC AUC metric lead to excessive optimism in the evaluation results. On the whole, all machine learning methods for this problem are heavily dependent on the data, the features extracted from the data, and the data preparation process.

This study uses several machine learning models to analyze the loan approval process. The dataset in this paper collects from VietCredit Finance, a consumer finance company in Vietnam. This work exploratories data to get more knowledge about the dataset such as data type proportion, input-output variables distribution, check and handle the missing values, outlier detection, correlation input variables with another, between input with output variable, remove redundant variables, and necessary data transformations conducted to process the data. Finally, several suitable machine learning models trained on that data set to predict the loan repayment ability of the customer and propose the best-suited model.

The remainder of the paper is organized as follows. Section 2 describes the collected data. Then, the methodology is analyzed in Sect. 3. Finally, brief conclusions and perspectives are made in Sect. 4.

2   Data Collection and Preparation

The data set used to train loan default prediction models was collected from the following systems at VietCredit: 1.CAS - the system used to circulate and store customer information in the appraisal and approval of loan card registration documents. 2.PCB - the system to query and store customer credit information. 3.CMS - the system to manage card account information and transactions, fees, interest rates. 4.CMR - customer information storage system. 5.Scorecard – credit scoring system.

The data set has the 47750 loan applications (67 features) disbursement by the VietCredit platform from May 2020 to August 2020. Microsoft SQL Integration Service uses application-id attribute as key to join data from five transaction systems into a single CSV file. During the study, we were consulted with some of the official experts of VietCredit and sorted out a wide array of essential variables. From the business perspective of our company, these variables are essential for credit scoring and loan default predictions. However, many of these variables may act differently in other companies in predicting loan defaults due to the difference in economic and business conditions. Table 1 below is a short explanation of each variable in the data set.

Table 1. Variable description

No	Description
1	Outcome variable. Value 0 identity good customer who can pay off the loan. Otherwise, value 1
2	Loan application id
3	Type of company where customer work
4	Job title of customer
5	Type of salary payment
6	Age of customer
7	Residence status
8	Marital status
9	Address type
10	Yes – in Vietnam, No - Foreign
11	Place of issue of ID card
12	Number of dependents
13	Number of children
14	Education level
15	Type of business
16	Labor contract type
17	Job title
18	Number of year customer work at current company
19	Company operation status
20	Date of company establish
21	Total years of work experience
22	Highest debt group in the last 12 months
23	Monthly payment from other credit institutions (million VND)
24	Total monthly income (million VND)
25	Total other source income/month (million VND)
26	Highest debt group in the last three months
27	Highest debt group in the last six months
28	Highest debt group in the last 12 months
29	Highest debt group in the last 24 months
30	Number of contracts currently borrowed from other credit institutions
31	Total debt balance at other credit institutions
32	Total unpaid amount at other credit institutions

(continued)

Table 1. (*continued*)

No	Description
33	Number of inquiries at other credit institutions
34	The number of installments contracts currently borrowed from other credit institution
35	Total installments debt balance at other credit institutions
36	The total unpaid amount of installments at other credit institutions
37	The number of inquiries installments at other credit institution
38	The number of card contracts currently borrowed from other credit institution
39	Total debt balance of card at other credit institutions
40	The total unpaid amount of card at other Credit Institutions
41	The number of inquiries of the card at other credit institution
42	The highest credit limit is granted at another credit institution
43	Total credit limit of card currently being granted at other credit institutions (Calculated on the valid contract)
44	The highest credit limit of card issued at other credit institutions (Calculated on the valid contract)
45	Request credit limit
46	Salary type
47	Occupation
48	Industry
49	Code of company type (Vietcredit define)
50	Total gross monthly income
51	Total annual net income
52	Total annual gross income
53	Total income from other sources
54	Total monthly payment
55	Total monthly expense
56	Group of income
57	Approve credit limit
58	First withdrawal date
59	How many days from the first borrowing date to Aug 30, 2020
60	The total amount of at first withdrawal date
61	The total amount paid by the customer
62	Latest repayment date
63	How many days from the last repayment date to Aug 30, 2020

(*continued*)

Table 1. (*continued*)

No	Description
64	Number of repayments
65	Debt balance at August 31, 2020
66	Debt balance at the time of the first withdrawal
67	Request card type

The data is further cleaned, such as removing redundancy attributes by experts, removing high correlation attributes in pairwise, correcting data, and removing missing values. The data after cleaning will remain 45670 rows and 45 columns. The data set has both string (category) and numeric (int, float) data type. The way used to convert the category to number data type was one hot encoder. The numeric attributes have different scales going to be rescaled before modeling. After data pre-processing, the dimension of the data set down from (47749, 67) to (45670, 45) in rows and columns. This study uses 80% of the dataset for training model and hold back 20% for testing. The training set is divided into ten folds for cross-validation.

3   Methodology

3.1   Evaluation Metrics

The data set of this research is imbalanced, with 27% target variable values are 1 (bad in repayment), and otherwise is 73%. For imbalanced classification problems, the majority class is typically referred to as the negative outcome, and the minority class is typically referred to as the positive outcome. Both the precision and the recall are focused on the positive class (the minority class) and are unconcerned with the true negatives (majority class). Precision-recall curves and PR AUC are recommended for highly skewed domains, so it is used in this study to evaluate the model's performance. This metric avoids the use of true negative in the calculation, so it avoids an excessively optimistic view of ROC curves' performance.

3.2   Baseline Algorithms for Evaluating

This study selects a suite of different algorithms capable of working on this classification problem. The six algorithms selected include Linear Algorithms: Logistic Regression (LR) and Linear Discriminant Analysis (LDA). Nonlinear Algorithms: Classification and Regression Trees (CART), Support Vector Machines (SVM), Gaussian Naive Bayes (NB), and k-Nearest Neighbors (KNN). The algorithms all use default tuning parameters. The category attribute will transform by using the one-hot encoder. The numeric attributes were original and not transformed. The mean and standard deviation of Precision-Recall AUC on all folds for each algorithm was calculated and used to compare models' performance (Table 2).

Table 2. Precision-recall AUC score baseline

Models	Precision-recall AUC score (Std)
Logistic Regression	0.881988 (0.007399)
Linear Discriminant Analysis	0.875218 (0.007809)
k Neighbors Classifier	0.681097 (0.010216)
Decision Tree Classifier	0.777429 (0.006443)
Gaussian NB	0.634776 (0.001324)
SVC	0.839620 (0.008465)

Table 2 shows the mean score values, and it suggests that both Logistic Regression and LDA may be worth further study.

The differing distributions of the raw data may be negatively impacting the skill of some of the algorithms. Let us evaluate the same algorithms with a standardized copy of the dataset. Evaluate Algorithms Standardize Data is where the data transformed such that each attribute has a mean value of zero and a standard deviation of one or the same scaler. It helps seeing how algorithms improve when all number attributes are the same scaler. The results is in Table 3.

Table 3. Precision-recall AUC score with standardized data.

Models	Precision-Recall AUC Score (Std)	
	Baseline	Standardized data
Logistic Regression	0.881988 (0.007399)	0.923708 (0.004893)
Linear Discriminant Analysis	0.875218 (0.007809)	0.914196 (0.006199)
k Neighbors Classifier	0.681097 (0.010216)	0.748866 (0.015157)
Decision Tree Classifier	0.777429 (0.006443)	0.854862 (0.006187)
Gaussian NB	0.634776 (0.001324)	0.634795 (0.001276)
SVC	0.839620 (0.008465)	0.916982 (0.004754)

Table 3 shows that both Logistic Regression, Linear Discriminant Analysis, and Support Vector Machine are still doing well, even better than before. The results suggest digging deeper into the LR, LDA and SVM algorithms. Configuration beyond the default may likely yield even more accurate models.

3.3 Improve Results

Algorithm Tuning

This section of the study investigates tuning the parameters for the Logistic Regression algorithm that show promise from the spot-checking in the previous section. The algorithm can start by tuning three parameters are Solver, Penalty, and C values. The 10-fold cross-validation on the standardized training dataset was used for turning.

```
Best: 0.877440 using {'C': 100, 'penalty': 'l2', 'solver': 'newton-cg'}
0.877440 (0.006770) with: {'C': 100, 'penalty': 'l2', 'solver': 'newton-cg'}
0.876230 (0.006852) with: {'C': 100, 'penalty': 'l2', 'solver': 'lbfgs'}
0.877390 (0.006797) with: {'C': 100, 'penalty': 'l2', 'solver': 'liblinear'}
0.876635 (0.006771) with: {'C': 10, 'penalty': 'l2', 'solver': 'newton-cg'}
0.876210 (0.007250) with: {'C': 10, 'penalty': 'l2', 'solver': 'lbfgs'}
0.876665 (0.006801) with: {'C': 10, 'penalty': 'l2', 'solver': 'liblinear'}
0.871355 (0.007534) with: {'C': 1.0, 'penalty': 'l2', 'solver': 'newton-cg'}
0.871290 (0.007476) with: {'C': 1.0, 'penalty': 'l2', 'solver': 'lbfgs'}
0.871396 (0.007486) with: {'C': 1.0, 'penalty': 'l2', 'solver': 'liblinear'}
0.859313 (0.007166) with: {'C': 0.1, 'penalty': 'l2', 'solver': 'newton-cg'}
0.859313 (0.007166) with: {'C': 0.1, 'penalty': 'l2', 'solver': 'lbfgs'}
0.859208 (0.007321) with: {'C': 0.1, 'penalty': 'l2', 'solver': 'liblinear'}
0.846978 (0.006480) with: {'C': 0.01, 'penalty': 'l2', 'solver': 'newton-cg'}
0.846991 (0.006509) with: {'C': 0.01, 'penalty': 'l2', 'solver': 'lbfgs'}
0.846908 (0.006519) with: {'C': 0.01, 'penalty': 'l2', 'solver': 'liblinear'}
```

Fig. 1. Results of tuning LR on the scaled dataset.

Figure 1 prints out the configuration that resulted in the highest accuracy and the accuracy of all values. The result shows that the optimal configuration is C = 100, Penalty = L2, and Solver = newton-CG, but PR-AUC does not improve.

Ensemble Methods

Another way that we can improve the performance of algorithms on this problem is by using ensemble methods. This section will evaluate four different ensemble machine learning algorithms, two boosting and two bagging methods. Boosting Methods: AdaBoost (AB), Gradient Boosting (GBM), and LGBMClassifier. Bagging Methods: Random Forests (RF) and Extra Trees (ET). The experiment pipeline will use the same approach as before, 10-fold cross-validation. The results say that all ensemble techniques methods provide strong accuracy scores in the low 90s (%) with default configurations. Table 4 below identifies the mean and distribution of PR-AUC across the cross-validation folds.

Table 4. Output of evaluate ensemble algorithms

Models	Precision-Recall AUC Score (Std)
AdaBoostClassifier	0.933243 (0.005047)
GradientBoostingClassifier	0.945025 (0.004562)
RandomForestClassifier	0.916121 (0.006834)
ExtraTreesClassifier	0.902806 (0.006040)
LGBMClassifier	0.957052 (0.004170)

The results suggest that LGBM is the best model on the data set, reaching a high 0.957 PR-AUC score. Therefore, it is the final model for loan default prediction in this study. Using LGBM for making predictions for the hold-out validation dataset to confirm the final findings.

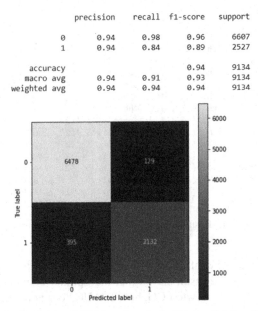

	precision	recall	f1-score	support
0	0.94	0.98	0.96	6607
1	0.94	0.84	0.89	2527
accuracy			0.94	9134
macro avg	0.94	0.91	0.93	9134
weighted avg	0.94	0.94	0.94	9134

Fig. 2. Evaluating LGBM on the standardized validation dataset

Figure 2 shows that the result achieves an accuracy of nearly 94% on the held-out validation dataset. That score matches closely to the expectations of the study. With good predictive results, this research can confidently be used to predict the loan default on VietCredit's loan data set.

4 Conclusion and Perspectives

In this study, the loan application data set was collected from five transaction systems of our company VietCredit. After the data set was analyzed and summarized to expose the best structure of the data before modeling, the data set was pre-processed as cleaning and transforming. The strategies to deal with missing values and imbalanced data sets were covered; the category attributes transformed using the one-hot encoder, while the numeric attributes transformed using a min-max scaler. Then algorithm evaluation metrics were investigated base on characteristics of the data set. Precision-recall curve and PR AUC score recommended for highly skewed domains, so it is used in this study to evaluate and compare the performance of each model. After tuning algorithms and improving by ensemble methods, the LGBM ensemble method becomes the best classifier with a high PR-AUC score of 0.957. On the held-out test data set, the mean accuracy of prediction archives 94%, and that matches closely to the expectations of the research. So The LGBM is the best-suited model for predicting loan default problems.

In future, researchers in this field may apply the resampling techniques to the datasets. This technique helps to reduce the imbalance ratio of datasets which in turn produces better classification results. The number of machine learning algorithms is perhaps more than a hundred, so the study will test more algorithms to find out better ones in the future.

We will also try to conduct experiments on larger data sets or try to tune the ensemble model to achieve the state-of-art performance of the model.

1. References

1. https://vietnamnews.vn/economy/898552/three-companies-dominate-consumer-lending-market-in-vn.html. Accessed 4 Apr 2021
2. https://thelawreviews.co.uk/title/the-lending-and-secured-finance-review/vietnam. Accessed 4 Apr 2021
3. https://your.fitch.group/rs/732-CKH-767/images/Fitch_10079224.pdf. Accessed 4 Apr 2021
4. Aslam, U., Tariq, A., Hafiz, I., Sohail, A., Batcha, N.K.: An empirical study on loan default prediction models. J. Comput. Theoretical Nanosci. 16(8), 3483–3488 (2019). https://doi.org/10.1166/jctn.2019.8312.American Scientific Publishers
5. Turkson, R.E., Baagyere, E.Y., Wenya, G.E.: A machine learning approach for predicting bank creditworthiness. In: Proceedings of the third International Conference on Artificial Intelligence and Pattern Recognition (AIPR), Lodz, pp. 1–7 (2016). https://doi.org/10.1109/ICAIPR.2016.7585216
6. Sheikh, M.A., Goel, A.K., Kumar, T.: An approach for prediction of loan approval using machine learning algorithm. In: Proceedings of the International Conference on Electronics and Sustainable Communication Systems (ICESC), Coimbatore, India, pp. 490–494 (2020). https://doi.org/10.1109/ICESC48915.2020.9155614
7. Pandey, T.N., Jagadev, A.K., Mohapatra, S.K., Dehuri, S.: Credit risk analysis using machine learning classifiers. In: Proceedings of the International Conference on Energy, Communication, Data Analytics and Soft Computing (ICECDS), Chennai, pp. 1850–1854 (2017). https://doi.org/10.1109/ICECDS.2017.8389769
8. Shiv, S.J., Murthy, S., Challuru, K.: Credit risk analysis using machine learning techniques. In: Proceedings of the 14th International Conference on Information Processing (CIPRO), Bangalore, India, pp. 1–5 (2018). https://doi.org/10.1109/ICINPRO43533.2018.9096854
9. Qiu, W.: Credit risk prediction in an imbalanced social lending environment based on XGBoost. In: Proceedings of the 5th International Conference on Big Data and Information Analytics (BigDIA), Kunming, China, pp. 150–156 (2019). https://doi.org/10.1109/BigDIA.2019.8802747
10. Chen, S., Wang, Q., Liu, S.: Credit risk prediction in peer-to-peer lending with ensemble learning framework. In: Proceedings of the Chinese Control And Decision Conference (CCDC), Nanchang, China, pp. 4373–4377 (2019). https://doi.org/10.1109/CCDC.2019.8832412
11. Alexandru, C., Maer-Matei, M.M., Albu, C.: Predictive models for loan default risk assessment. Econ. Comput. Econ. Cybern. Stud. Res. 53(2). Bucharest 149–165 (2019). https://doi.org/10.24818/18423264/53.2.19.09.University of Economic Studies
12. Zhu, L., Dafeng, Q., Daji, E., Cai, Y., Kuiyi, L.: A study on predicting loan default based on the random forest algorithm. Proc. Comput. Sci. 162, 503–513 (2019). Elsevier B.V. https://doi.org/10.1016/j.procs.2019.12.017
13. Soares, L.M.J, Nardini, F.M., Renso, C., Fernandes, J.A.M.: An empirical comparison of classification algorithms for imbalanced credit scoring datasets. In: Proceedings of the 18th IEEE International Conference on Machine Learning And Applications (ICMLA), Boca Raton, FL, USA, pp. 747–754 (2019). https://doi.org/10.1109/ICMLA.2019.00133
14. Shoumo, S.Z.H., Dhruba, M.I.M., Hossain, S., Ghani, N.H., Arif, H., Islam, S.: Application of machine learning in credit risk assessment: a prelude to smart banking. In: TENCON 2019 - IEEE Region 10 Conference (TENCON), Kochi, India, pp. 2023–2028 (2019). https://doi.org/10.1109/TENCON.2019.8929527

15. Lawi, A., Aziz, F., Syarif, S.: Ensemble GradientBoost for increasing classification accuracy of credit scoring. In: Proceedings of the 4th International Conference on Computer Applications and Information Processing Technology (CAIPT), Kuta Bali, pp. 1–4 (2017). https://doi.org/10.1109/CAIPT.2017.8320700

16. Ferreira, L.E.B., Barddal, J.P., Gomes, H.M., Enembreck, F.: Improving credit risk prediction in online peer-to-peer (P2P) lending using imbalanced learning techniques. In: Proceedings of the IEEE 29th International Conference on Tools with Artificial Intelligence (ICTAI), Boston, MA, pp. 175–181 (2017). https://doi.org/10.1109/ICTAI.2017.00037

17. Chen, Y., Zhang, J., Ng, W.W.Y.: Loan default prediction using diversified sensitivity under-sampling. In: Proceedings of the International Conference on Machine Learning and Cybernetics (ICMLC), Chengdu, pp. 240–245 (2018). https://doi.org/10.1109/ICMLC.2018.8526936

18. Barboza, F., Herbert, K., Edward, A.: Machine learning models and bankruptcy prediction. Expert Syst. Appl. **83**, 405–417 (2017). https://doi.org/10.1016/j.eswa.2017.04.006

19. Namvar, A., Mohammad, S., Fethi, R., Mohsen, N.: Credit risk prediction in an imbalanced social lending environment. Int. J. Comput. Intell. Syst. **11**(1), 925–935 (2019). https://doi.org/10.2991/ijcis.11.1.70

Identifying Human Factors for Remote Guidance on Physical Tasks

Hai Chau Le[1]([✉]), Weidong Huang[1], Mark Billinghurst[2], and Eng Hwa Yap[1,3]

[1] University of Technology Sydney, Sydney, NSW 2007, Australia
`HaiChau.Le@student.uts.edu.au, Weidong.Huang@uts.edu.au`
[2] University of South Australia, Adelaide, SA 5001, Australia
`Mark.Billinghurst@unisa.edu.au`
[3] Xi'an Jiaotong-Liverpool University, Suzhou 215123, China
`EngHwa.Yap@xjtlu.edu.cn`

Abstract. Remote collaboration is becoming increasingly crucial, especially currently when travel is restricted because of the Covid-19 pandemic. People are looking for real-time and no-travel solutions to enable remote collaboration with colleagues and experts. A lot of research has been conducted on how to support remote guidance on physical tasks. However, these studies have mainly focused on development of technical components to support collaboration, while less attention has been paid into exploring and evaluating human factors that could influence remote collaboration. The aim of this paper is to identify human factors including culture, language, trust and social status for their possible effects on remote collaboration by reviewing their effects on computer-supported collaboration. This review adds more critical views of human perspectives into the current research mostly-focused on the technical side of remote guidance.

Keywords: Remote guidance · CSCW · Physical task · Human factors · Culture · Language · Trust · Social status

1 Introduction

A remote guidance system uses computer interfaces and a network to connect a local worker with a remote helper. The system typically allows the helper to see through the worker's eyes and guide him to perform physical tasks as if they were at the same place such as remote maintenance [12]. Remote guidance on physical tasks has many applications in several industries including health and manufacturing. Examples include a remote mechanic who helps a field worker to repair complex machinery [19], a scenario where a radiologist can offer real-time diagnostic imaging, read the images remotely and instruct the technician [45], and a technician remotely guiding a user to set up a new device [38]. During the current Covid-19 pandemic remote guidance is expected plays a even more important role in industries where people are looking for a no-travel, real-time, and cost-effective solution for remote expert assistance.

© Springer Nature Switzerland AG 2021
Y. Luo (Ed.): CDVE 2021, LNCS 12983, pp. 271–283, 2021.
https://doi.org/10.1007/978-3-030-88207-5_27

(a) Remote helper   (b) Local worker

Fig. 1. Illustration of a remote guidance system which has devices allowing distributed users to work collaboratively on physical tasks

Figure 1 illustrates the interfaces of a typical remote guidance system. Panel (b) presents the local worker unit with a headed camera and a microphone which enables the worker to freely discuss with the helper and stream video to the helper's monitor presented in Panel (a). This system allows the remote helper to easily see what the worker is working on and provide visual feedback to help him complete the physical task.

A significant amount of research has been conducted on remote guidance [23], especially on designing and evaluating collaborative systems. For example, Kuzuoka et al. investigated the design of a SharedView system that supports spatial work-space collaboration [32]. Alem et al. developed a range of systems that support remote collaboration using hand gestures, smart devices, and Augmented Reality (AR). These systems include 3DHelpingHands [41], HandsOnVideo [4], HandsInTouch [18,22], HandsIn3D [20,21], MobileHelper [39], ReMoTe [33]. A recent research by Bai and coauthors presented a Mixed Reality system supporting remote instructions that allows workers to share their surroundings in a live 3D panorama with remote experts [5].

A remote guidance session involves human-computer and human-human interaction. Therefore, the factors affecting the remote guidance session could come from either the computer side or the human aspect. The majority of existing user studies focus on the effects of the factors regarding technical issues. For example, Donovan et al. examined how network performance affects the user experience of remote guidance [12]. Alem and Li conducted a study to evaluate the impacts of overlaying hand gesture and cursor pointing on the collaboration performance [3]. Results revealed that there is no difference between those gesture representations regarding task performance. Focusing on the effects of different configurations of shared gaze between instructors and workers, Akkil et al. showed that the gaze helps improve both the task performance in terms of time consumed and the perception of the collaboration [1]. Similarly, Gupta and colleagues confirmed that sharing the eye gaze significantly improved the task completion performance [15].

However, little attention has been paid into exploring the effects of factors affecting the success of a remote guidance session that are from the human side.

Motivation

A typical *Remote Guidance* system requires the instructor and the worker to collaborate via computer-supported tools. Since human factors for remote guidance have not been well researched, we decided to conduct a review of human related factors in the field of Computer Supported Collaborative Work (CSCW) that could be applied in the context of *Remote Guidance*.

CSCW is a research area focusing on how to incorporate computing and networking technologies to facilitate cooperation and collaboration among physically distributed users [14] which overlaps with the field of Human-Computer Interaction (HCI) [10]. The collaboration includes two aspects: collaborators interacting with computers and interacting with other collaborators using computers [10,42]. These aspects could be strongly affected by human related factors such as culture, language, social status, and trust between collaborators [42].

The rest of this paper is presented as follows: the next section presents the methodology used to conduct the research. Section 3 presents a literature review on how human factors could affect the Computer-Supported Collaboration. Section 4 discusses how the influences of those factors could be applied in the context of *Remote Guidance*. Section 5 includes conclusions and directions for future work.

2   Research Methodology

2.1   Research Questions

Our original research question was *How human factors could affect remote guidance task performance and user experience?*. However, given the lack of research in the remote guidance literature on this question, we instead turn our attention to the general field of computer-supported cooperative work to identify some human factors and discuss how these factors could be applied in the context of *Remote Guidance*.

2.2   Source and Searching

We follow the guidelines introduced by Kitchenham et al. [31] and Moher et al. [11] to conduct a survey on the effects of human factors on CSCW.

The sources used for initial search include:

- ACM Digital library (http://dl.acm.org)
- IEEE (http://ieeexplore.ieee.org)
- Scopus (https://www.scopus.com/home.uri)
- Springer (http://link.springer.com)

These sources contain the comprehensive database and full-text of publications including books, conference proceeding, journals, magazines, and newsletters focused specifically on *Human-Computer Interaction (HCI)*.

Table 1. Searching terms and Keywords

Primary terms	CSCW, computer-supported collaboration, collaborative, collaboration, cooperative, cooperation, remote guidance, remote instruction, remote assistance, remote guiding
Secondary terms	Human factors, human personalities, culture, language, trust, social status
Tertiary terms	Distributed, virtual, remote, physical task

The terms and keywords in Table 1 are used to search for the publications. The initial search teams in those databases included the words: Remote Guidance/Remote Instruction/Remote Assistance/Remote Guiding, Physical Task, Human Factors. However, this search gave us a very low number of publications. In order to widen the span of the search, we then decided to search for articles in the field of CSCW. Since Remote Guidance is part of the CSCW field, findings from CSCW could also be applied to Remote Guidance. Besides, we included in the search several keywords representing the human factors such as culture, language, trust, social status, cognitive load. In addition, we decided to search those keywords both in metadata and full-text of the publications.

The searched results were then manually scanned to exclude the irrelevant studies. We excluded the research on the technical aspects of the system and/or on co-located groups because we are interested in the remote collaboration. The exclusion also involves publications that i) are not aiming at the human related factors; ii) are focusing on the design of collaborations; and iii) are not involving computer-supported tools.

By reviewing the selected publications, we also included other relevant studies cited by those publications and listed on the bibliography section that meet our criteria. We then reviewed those found ones and repeat this process. As a result, 15 publications were selected for having identified human factors. We present a further discussion of these in the next two sections.

3   Effects of Human Factors

The search results showed that *Culture, Language, Trust and Social Status* have indeed been researched in CSCW. The emergence of computer-aid collaboration with remote guidance gives rise to greater diversity within each group of collaborators, whose diverse cultural, language, and social background are contributing factors that shape the outcome of the group's tasks. At the same time, the importance of trust – a traditional factor that acts as a foundation of human-human relationships should not be downplayed.

Culture

Researchers have adopted experimental designs to investigate how cultural diversity affects the collaboration processes and how culturally enriched modifications to collaborative working affect the attitudes, performance and behaviour of learners. Studies have found a significant interaction between culture and working outcome in a computer-mediated environment, and that giving consideration to cultural diversity enhances participants' learning experience and performance.

The majority of prior studies examining the effect of cultural diversity referred to culture as the national culture that differentiates the citizens of one nation from another [37]. The research by Lim and Liu [34] presented the its impact on collaborative learning processes in computer-aided environment. The authors designed an experiment involving 40 subjects assigned to different online groups. The results show that members in groups with diverse culture are more likely to have different opinions, disagreements between each other, and feelings of annoyance [35] that lead to high chance for negative attention to happen and hence the distrust between them.

Examining the similar cultural attribute of national diversity, a study by Vatrapu and Suthers showed that the difference in nationality significantly affects the performance of a distributed group [42]. In this research, 60 participants were paired into three groups of dyads of Chinese, American, and Chinese-American inter-cultural conditions and were given the same challenge in a computer-assisted collaborative learning environment. The results revealed that American pairs took significant less time to complete the task, compared to the Chinese dyads and Chinese-American dyads. The Americans are more task-oriented, while Asian people are more relationship-oriented [30]. Perhaps going directly to the task and focusing on finding the solution helped American dyads perform better than the others.

Group of collaborators, despite coming from the same country still face great differences in terms of culture. Swigger and colleagues conducted a study to evaluate the effects of five cultural dimensions including activity, human nature, relationship, relation to nature, and time on Computer-Supported Collaboration [40]. The authors researched on 55 distributed pairs of computer sciences students at two universities using computer-supported tools to virtually solve the tasks provided. The result of this two-year research proved that the hierarchical attribute of culture negatively affected the pair's performance. The more hierarchical score a pair has, the less accurately and efficiently they performed. The high-hierarchical person seems inflexible when facing a difficulty, making them less capable of tailoring the issue and finding the solution, hence hindering the pair to collaborate efficiently. Similarly, groups consisting of low destiny-predetermined and/or low future-oriented members are more likely to perform poorly. Their disagreement in the predetermination of the events' outcomes and non-worrying about its future consequences hinders their ability to manage unexpected issues.

Language

Members of a distributed group might come from different countries all over the world. They may speak different languages, leading to communication issues. In a collaborative group, this could lead to the group's poor outcome as a consequence of misunderstanding. It gives rise to another challenge of remote groups, in which language is a barrier to the distributed collaboration [43].

Speaking different languages could obviously be one of the biggest concerns for researchers. A study by Quin and Ming proved that speaking the same language positively influences the pair-work's performance [44]. To explore the effects, the authors grouped 118 undergraduate students who speak English and their native language into 54 pairs to collaboratively solve two given tasks. They found that pairs speaking the same languages beside English performed significantly better than the other ones. They took less than half the time to complete the task. This may be because speaking the same language helps team members easily to communicate, taking them less time to understand each others, while the other group needed more time to clarify their partner's ideas. Even when all group members speak the same language, the difference in proficiency could be a big concern, especially when it come to the task involving the technical terms. The study by Quin and Ming [44] revealed that the smaller the difference in English proficiency, the more participants collaborated within pairs. It is much easier for an individual to understand what the partner is trying to express and it engenders positive feelings which greatly contributes to the pair performance. Tsedal and colleagues confirmed that uneven proficiency negatively influences collaboration in the global team although they all speak English [6] as a result of a qualitative analysis in a global tech giant headquartered in Germany. Even though the German staff spoke English proficiently, they were not confident with their language proficiency, making them feel anxious when talking in English. As a consequence, they tended to withdraw from the communication, exclude colleagues from meetings. Also, they may not present their own ideas and switch to discuss in German. Consequently, the native English members felt disrespected and responded with negative emotions.

Similarly, He and colleagues explored how the difference of language fluency between native and non-native speakers affect group collaboration [17] in a study of 16 distributed groups consisting of two native English speakers and one non-native speaker. They were required to complete several tasks using the computer-supported tools. The results showed that the difference in language proficiency caused significant mismatches between native and non-native speakers [17], leading to less accurate and efficient outcomes of the collaborations. Non-native speakers spoke less and hesitated to ask for the clarification due to their feeling of anxiety when not speaking in their mother-tongue. They were unable to detect accurately the emotional valence of native speakers [16]. They tended to show strong neutrality and negativity effects, thus could lead to low connectivity between members and then the rejections of each others [9].

When all group members speak the same language at the same proficiency level, what other language aspects could affect the collaboration? Jeong's study proved that the conversational language positively affected collaboration [26]. The conversational language includes asking questions, greetings, acknowledgements, "I-agree-but". In the research, 30 graduate students participated in eight weekly online group debates. The results clearly showed that conversational language significantly affected the collaboration when it helped arguments to elicit 41% more challenges and three-to-eight times more explanations. It helps build the relationship between members, making them feeling friendlier towards group members, and removing the barrier between them, thus encouraging them to actively collaborate and more confidently express their own ideas.

Trust and Social Status

Trust is a foundation of human-human relationships and is the key point in the efficiency of group work [28]. It plays an important role in a distributed team where members may come from different culture and language backgrounds, be in different locations, and communicate through computer-supported environments [2,24]. It can help with managing the uncertainty and promoting open information sharing between distributed members [24]. Trust has been widely proved to have a strong relationship with the virtual collaboration [24,29]. The more a member believes in their partners, the less wasted efforts and process losses they need to collaborate [25]. They require less time, and evidence to clarify the ideas of each other. Thus the collaboration would go more smoothly and efficiency.

Bos and colleagues conducted a study to test the hypothesis that trust positively affects group performance [8]. In the research, participants were assigned to groups of three to play a social dilemma game allowing them to virtually discuss on the play's strategy after each five rounds of the game. The study results confirmed that the more trust exists, the larger payoffs the groups earned and the payoffs increased over time. Over time the group members built a stronger level of trust and hence performed better and better. The group's outcome was significantly higher in the round right after the discussion than the other rounds. Since they just recently communicated, the level of trust and cooperation was higher, hence they better understood and believed more in their team members.

Similarly, Ban and David confirmed that establishing trust in virtual teams can increase the effectiveness and efficiency of the group's collaboration [2]. Trust engenders the comfortable feeling of individuals when remotely collaborating with colleagues, thus making them more open to share their own insights. It helps members to grow more confident and to overcome the fears or concerns about the risks of the consequence when expressing their ideas.

When applied into an industry, trust plays an integral part in the use of computer-supported environments. Jirotka et al. [27] confirmed this in the context of the health care industry, particularly in breast-cancer screening requiring clinicians to collaborate with geographically distributed colleagues. Turning data into a "common" good brings huge benefits, but also requires strict security measures to ascertain trust, especially when a novice clinician seeks help from experts. Due to ethical and the strict security requirements of the system, the junior clinicians are guided by experts only when they trust each other. Without trust, the instructions would not be performed, thus seriously affecting the mammogram's detection and possible treatment.

However, these effects of trust depend on the surrounding conditions [25]. Javenpaa et al. have proved that the impacts of trust on task performance are decreased in the groups who share information between members during the early stage of the collaboration [25]. In this study, the 6-student groups remotely worked together to solve a research task over a eight-week period. During the first stage of the task, half of the teams were required to do exercises of introducing themselves with team members and discuss with each other about how to collaborate successfully. The remaining teams didn't do this exercise. The results clearly showed that trust had significant impact on the outcome of the group who did not complete the team building activities, while its effects on the other groups were very small. The exercises helped to reduce the uncertainty one felt about teammates since they knew about their background and ability as well as agreed on the goals and process to complete the task. Hence, the process of interpretation is not necessary, decreasing the role of trust.

Members of a distributed groups would collaborate more effectively if they shared a common ground [36]. Working together in the past, or just sharing a common expertise, previous experience if they have never worked together would assist collaborators to save a lot of time for task clarification, thus making them collaborate more efficiently. Bos and colleagues proved this relationship [7] in a study where groups of collaborators virtually solved a task. There were two types of groups in which members were total strangers or knew each other before. The study results showed that stranger groups performed significantly worse than the ones who were not strangers, getting a lower score. Players in groups who knew each other were more motivated by the goals of the whole group, instead of their own incentives.

Similarly, Swigger et al. observed the same relationship between sharing common ground and group performance [40]. In this research, the groups spending time for members to communicate with each others during the early stage of the project performed more accurately and more efficiently than those who not. By communicating with colleagues, members clearly understood about expertise of each other and what they were good at, thus helping increase the awareness of members and the group task and decreasing uncertainty about the group's future events.

Being in different geographic locations hinders the coordination and performance of groups [13]. Olson and Olson observed this pattern in a giant global automotive firm when some junior engineers ignored the expertise of their German senior fellows. However, a study by Espinosa and colleagues proved that understanding colleagues' presence and status information could mitigate that negative effect and boost a team's collaboration and performance [13]. The authors qualitatively studied a distributed team which had team members located in England and Germany. Almost all participants in the study confirmed that the more familiar they were with their distributed colleagues, the better work they performed as a group. If team members knew what the others know, they could easily develop a suitable work strategy for the team and then collaborate more efficiently.

4 Discussion

Our research has presented a review of the studies which found several human factors affecting computer-supported collaboration. Further insights are discussed in this section with regards to the context of remote guidance.

Speaking the same language plays an important role in the performance of computer-supported collaboration [44]. In the context of remote guidance, a remote helper might take less time to convey ideas and instructions with a worker who shares the same language than the one who does not and vice versa. Even though when they can speak and understand the same language (e.g. English), language proficiency does have big impacts on the performance of the remote system [6,17,44], especially when it comes to technical terms in specific fields such as health. A difference in language proficiency leads to mismatches and misunderstandings between native and non-native speakers [17]. In the specific field of health, there are numerous medical terms specialized for health system which may be difficult for experts to explain to users. Likewise, users could find it more difficult to ask questions or express necessary concerns with suitable medical terms. Conversational language may elicit and help workers to overcome their shyness or fear to communicate more effectively by asking questions or confirming accurate understanding with the helper [26].

The diversity of people from different nationality and cultural backgrounds is determined to increase the informational influences, while reducing normative influences in computer-supported cooperative learning process and it is closely related to the group's outcomes [34]. Correspondingly, there would likely be more questions, and informational evidence needed for different-nationality pairs of workers and helpers. Being of different nationality could make it more difficult and time consuming for the pair to reach the same level of understanding and to successfully complete the guidance session. In addition, Western people seem to collaborate more efficiency than Eastern people in terms of time consumed for task completion [42]. Cutting the time wasted on talking about things non-related to the task and being straight to the point would help a remote session of the worker and the helper to run smoothly and more quickly. Finally, the cultural personalities of individuals are found to have strong effects on the outcome of virtual group collaboration, even when they come from the same country [40]. The pair who believes in a rigid power structure or have a disagreement in the predetermination of the event's output experiences less accurate performance because they may be inflexible in facing an unexpected issue. Perhaps learning about a partner's culture before joining in a remote guidance session and spending the early stage of the conversation to express individual personality and sharing expectations could help workers and experts perform better [40].

Similarly, the pair sharing the same background would lead to a better collaboration outcome [7]. Sharing the same working experience or common expertise would allow the expert and worker to save a lot of time for clarification and explanation during the session, leading to a successful collaboration. Even if they do not have any common identity, understanding about the colleagues' status would be a valuable contribution to the success of a remote instruction session [36]. The expert would be able to more easily develop an appropriate strategy to guide the worker to fix a physical object if he knows what the worker knows about the object. Sharing is the key for remote collaboration. It helps establish the trust between members, thus improving the task performance of the pair [8]. The more trust that exists in the pair, the better payoffs they will gain in the outcome. It would also enrich the comfortable feeling of workers towards the situation, making them grow more confident and be more open to ask for clarifications when needed [2]. Trust is obviously important in a situation requiring a high level of security [27]. Junior workers may not be able to learn advanced knowledge from their senior fellows without establishing trust with them.

However, there are a significant difference in the mechanism between two contexts of CSCW and remote guidance. Existing research on human factors in CSCW focused mainly on the online groups remotely working together over a period of time and members met several times to discuss the task. In addition, members do not know how to tackle the problem in the beginning and they all have similar role in the project. These are different compared to the mechanism in remote guidance when the helper and the worker meet once during the task time. The helper knows how to use or fix the device but has no access to it, while the worker has the access but does not know how to use it. Furthermore, the helper knows how to solve the problem and instructs the worker to complete the task. These make us believe that there are potential differences in the effects of human factors between remote guidance and CSCW.

5 Concluding Remarks and Future Research

In this paper, we identified several human factors that may have impact in remote guidance by doing research from the wider Computer-Supported Collaboration literature. Speaking the same language positively influences the performance of remote collaborations, while the effect of uneven language proficiency is negative. Similarly, conversational languages help improve the performance of remote guidance. Regarding the cultural aspects, the difference between people coming from different countries or culture backgrounds leads to the increase of the informational influence and decrease of the normative influence in remote collaboration. Moreover, Western people seem to collaborate more efficiently than the Eastern people, and pairs who believe in rigid power structures perform more accurately than the ones who do not. Finally, having a common ground or sharing identity helps establish the trust between the pair's members and thus improves their task performance.

For future research, we plan to validate and explore the effects of these factors in the context *Remote Guidance*:

– Designing experiments for remote guidance with participants coming from different cultural and language backgrounds, and social status.
– Evaluate and validate effects of the above mentioned human factors on task performance and collaboration experience.
– Developing design recommendations with consideration of human factors to support remote guidance.

This further research would help improve and optimize the design of the system as well as provide valuable insights for organizations when organizing remote collaboration, especially in this period of time during the Covid-19 pandemic where restricted travel leads to a significant increase in demand for remote solutions.

References

1. Akkil, D., Poika, I.: Comparison of gaze and mouse pointers for video-based collaborative physical task. Inter. Comput. **30**, 524–542 (2019)
2. Al-Ani, B., Redmiles, D.: In strangers we trust? Findings of an empirical study of distributed teams. In: Proceedings of the 2009 Fourth IEEE International Conference on Global Software Engineering, pp. 121–130, August 2009
3. Alem, L., Li, J.: A study of gestures in a video-mediated collaborative assembly task. Adv. Hum.-Comput. Inter. **20111**, 987830 (2011)
4. Alem, L., Tecchia, F., Huang, W.: HandsOnVideo: towards a gesture based mobile AR system for remote collaboration. In: Alem, L., Huang, W. (eds.) Recent Trends of Mobile Collaborative Augmented Reality Systems, pp. 135–148. Springer, New York (2011). https://doi.org/10.1007/978-1-4419-9845-3_11
5. Bai, H., Sasikumar, P., Yang, J., Billinghurst, M.: A user study on mixed reality remote collaboration with eye gaze and hand gesture sharing. In: Proceedings of the 2020 CHI Conference on Human Factors in Computing Systems (CHI 2020), pp. 1–13. Association for Computing Machinery (2020)
6. Beyene, T., Hinds, P., Cramton, C.: Walking through jelly: language proficiency, emotions, and disrupted collaboration in global work. Harvard Business School, Harvard Business School Working Papers, June 2009
7. Bos, N., Buyuktur, A., Olson, J., Olson, G., Voida, A.: Shared identity helps partially distributed teams, but distance still matters. In: Proceedings of the 16th ACM International Conference on Supporting Group Work, pp. 89–96, January 2010
8. Bos, N., Olson, J., Gergle, D., Olson, G., Wright, Z.: Effects of four computer-mediated communications channels on trust development. In: Proceedings of the SIGCHI Conference on Human Factors in Computing Systems, pp. 135–140, January 2002
9. Byron, K.: Carrying too heavy a load? The communication and miscommunication of emotion by email. Acad. Manag. Rev. **33** (2008)
10. Chang, C., Zhang, J., Chang, K.: Survey of computer-supported collaboration in support of business processes. Int. J. Bus. Process Integr. Manag. **1** (2006)
11. Moher, D., Liberati, A., Tetzlaff, J., Altman, A.G.: Preferred reporting items for systematic reviews and meta-analyses: the PRISMA statement. J. Clin. Epidemiol. **62**(10), 1006–1012 (2009)

12. Donovan, A., Alem, L., Huang, W., Liu, R., Hedley, M.: Understanding How network performance affects user experience of remote guidance. In: Baloian, N., Burstein, F., Ogata, H., Santoro, F., Zurita, G. (eds.) CRIWG 2014. LNCS, vol. 8658, pp. 1–12. Springer, Cham (2014). https://doi.org/10.1007/978-3-319-10166-8_1

13. Espinosa, J., Slaughter, S., Kraut, R., Herbsleb, J.: Team knowledge and coordination in geographically distributed software development. J. Manag. Inf. Syst. **24**, 135–169 (2007)

14. Grudin, J.: Computer-supported cooperative work: history and focus. Computer **27**(5), 19–26 (1994)

15. Gupta, K., Lee, G.A., Billinghurst, M.: Do you see what i see? the effect of gaze tracking on task space remote collaboration. IEEE Trans. Visual. Comput. Graph. **22**, 2413–2422 (2016)

16. Hautasaari, A., Yamashita, N., Gao, G.: How non-native English speakers perceive the emotional valence of messages in text-based computer-mediated communication. Discourse Process. **56**, 1–17 (2017)

17. He, H.A., Yamashita, N., Hautasaari, A., Cao, X., Huang, E.M.: Why did they do that? Exploring attribution mismatches between native and non-native speakers using videoconferencing. In: Proceedings of the 2017 ACM Conference on Computer Supported Cooperative Work and Social Computing (CSCW 2017), pp. 297–309. Association for Computing Machinery (2017)

18. Huang, W., Alem, L.: Gesturing in the air: supporting full mobility in remote collaboration on physical tasks. J. Univ. Comput. Sci. **19**, 1158–1174 (2013)

19. Huang, W., Alem, L., Nepal, S., Thilakanathan, D.: Supporting tele-assistance and tele-monitoring in safety-critical environments. In: The 25th Australian Computer-Human Interaction Conference: Augmentation, Application, Innovation, Collaboration (OzCHI 2013), pp. 539–542. Association for Computing Machinery (2013)

20. Huang, W., Alem, L., Tecchia, F.: HandsIn3D: supporting remote guidance with immersive virtual environments. In: Kotzé, P., Marsden, G., Lindgaard, G., Wesson, J., Winckler, M. (eds.) INTERACT 2013. LNCS, vol. 8117, pp. 70–77. Springer, Heidelberg (2013). https://doi.org/10.1007/978-3-642-40483-2_5

21. Huang, W., Alem, L., Tecchia, F., Duh, H.B.L.: Augmented 3D hands: a gesture-based mixed reality system for distributed collaboration. J. Multimodal User Interf. **12**, 77–89 (2018)

22. Huang, W., Billinghurst, M., Alem, L., Kim, S.: Handsintouch: sharing gestures in remote collaboration. In: Proceedings of the 30th Australian Conference on Computer-Human Interaction (OzCHI 2018), pp. 396–400. Association for Computing Machinery (2018)

23. Huang, W., Kim, S., Billinghurst, M., Alem, L.: Sharing hand gesture and sketch cues in remote collaboration. J. Vis. Commun. Image Represent. **58**, 428–438 (2019)

24. Jarvenpaa, S., Knoll, K., Leidner, D.: Is anybody out there? antecedents of trust in global teams. J. Manag. Inf. Syst. **14**, 29–64 (1998)

25. Jarvenpaa, S., Shaw, T., Staples, D.: Toward contextualized theories of trust: the role of trust in global virtual teams. Inf. Syst. Res. **15**, 250–267 (2004)

26. Jeong, A.C.: The effects of conversational language on group interaction and group performance in computer-supported collaborative argumentation. Instruct. Sci. **34**, 367–397 (2006)

27. Jirotka, M., et al.: Collaboration and trust in healthcare innovation?: The diamond case study. Comput. Support. Cooper. Work **14**, 369–398 (2005)

28. Jones, S., Marsh, S.: Human-computer-human interaction: trust in CSCW. ACM SIGCHI Bull. **29**, 36–40 (1997)
29. Kauffmann, D., Carmi, G.: E-collaboration of virtual teams: the mediating effect of interpersonal trust. In: Proceedings of the 2017 International Conference on E-Business and Internet, pp. 45–49. Association for Computing Machinery (2017)
30. Kim, K.J., Bonk, C.: Cross-cultural comparisons of online collaboration. J. Comput-Med. Commun. **8** (2002)
31. Kitchenham, B., Charters, S.: Guidelines for performing systematic literature reviews in software engineering. Tech. Rep. EBSE 2007-001, Keele University and Durham University Joint Report (2007)
32. Kuzuoka, H.: Spartial workspace collaboration: a sharedview video support system for remote collaboration capability. In: Conference on Human Factors in Computing Systems, pp. 533–540, June 1992
33. L. Alem, F.T., Huang, W.: Remote tele-assistance system for maintenance operators in mines. In: 11th Underground Coal Operators' Conference, pp. 171–177. University of Wollongong and the Australasian Institute of Mining and Metallurgy (2011)
34. Lim, J., Liu, Y.: The role of cultural diversity and leadership in computer-supported collaborative learning?: a content analysis. Inf. Softw. Technol. **48**, 142–153 (2006). https://doi.org/10.1016/j.infsof.2005.03.006
35. Nguyen, D.T., Fussell, S.R.: How did you feel during our conversation? retrospective analysis of intercultural and same-culture instant messaging conversations. In: Proceedings of the ACM 2012 Conference on Computer Supported Cooperative Work (CSCW 2012), pp. 117–126. New York, NY, USA (2012)
36. Olson, J., Olson, G.: Bridging distance: Empirical studies of distributed teams, April 2011
37. Popov, V., Biemans, H.J.A., Fortuin, K.P.J., Vliet, A.J.H.V., Erkens, G., Mulder, M.: Learning, culture and social interaction effects of an interculturally enriched collaboration script on student attitudes, behavior, and learning performance in a CSCL environment. Learn. Cult. Soc. Inter. **21**, 100–123 (2019)
38. Re'Flekt: Remote support tool with live video and augmented reality, August 2020. https://www.re-flekt.com/reflekt-remote
39. Robert, K., Zhu, D., Huang, W., Alem, L., Gedeon, T.: Mobilehelper: remote guiding using smart mobile devices, hand gestures and augmented reality, November 2013
40. Swigger, K., Alpaslan, F., Brazile, R., Harrington, B., Peng, X.: The challenges of international computer-supported collaboration. In: 34th ASEE/IEEE Frontiers in Education Conference, pp. 13–18. Savannah, October 2004
41. Tecchia, F., Alem, L., Huang, W.: 3D helping hands: a gesture based MR system for remote collaboration. In: The 11th International Conference on Virtual Reality Continuum and Its Applications in Industry. Singapore, December 2012
42. Vatrapu, R., Suthers, D.: Intra- and inter-cultural usability in computer-supported collaboration. J. Usab. Stud. **5**(4), 172–197 (2010)
43. Vinaja, R.: Major challenges in multi-cultural virtual teams. In: Proceedings: Southwest Case Research Association, January 2003
44. Yow, W.Q., Lim, T.Z.M.: Sharing the same languages helps us work better together. Palgrave Commun. **5**(1) (2019)
45. Zennaro, F., et al.: Real-time tele-mentored low cost "point-of- care us" in the hands of paediatricians in the emergency department: diagnostic accuracy compared to expert radiologists. PLoS ONE **11**, e0164539 (2016)

Building a Remote Laboratory Based on NVIDIA GeForce Experience and Moonlight Streaming

Tran Khanh Linh and Phan Duy Hung$^{(\boxtimes)}$

FPT University, Hanoi, Vietnam
`linh20mse13065@fsb.edu.vn, hungpd2@fe.edu.vn`

Abstract. Innovations in Internet technology have led to new forms of teaching and learning. Online education is one of the most exciting innovations. In the current period, the COVID-19 pandemic has made the need for online learning more prominent and essential to avoid contact and gather many people. In online courses, students can not only do distance learning but also conduct experiments using a remote lab. The implementation of remote experiments that use hardware or have high requirements for real-time has been studied recently. However, there is still a lack of a flexible, easy-to-deploy and effective solution. This article presents a new case study for remote labs utilizing a combination of labs and NVIDIA GeForce Experience and Moonlight Streaming. On the server-side connected to the practical KITs, NVIDIA GeForce Experience enhances video quality. It reduces image rendering latency by using the GPU to encode streaming video, while the client is custom programmed software based on Moonlight PC - an open-source NVIDIA Gamestream Client. Furthermore, this work set up a prototype to illustrate the entire proposed system.

Keywords: Remote laboratory · NVIDIA GeForce Experience · Moonlight streaming

1 Introduction

According to a summary from Giusti, A.D. [1], the COVID-19 pandemic has created the most extensive disruption of education systems in history, affecting nearly 1.6 billion learners in more than 190 countries and all continents. The "social distancing" policy leading to closures of schools impacted 94 percent of the world's student population, up to 99 percent in low and lower-middle-income countries. From that fact, education has been changed forever [2], and remote learning becomes an urgent need. Many online learning platforms offer free access to their services, including platforms like BYJU'S, Tencent classroom, DingTalk, etc.

There are many solutions to build a remote laboratory. Remote desktop software is a choice for a student to connect remotely to a computer in the university's laboratory. TeamViewer, Chrome Remote Desktop [3], Microsoft Remote Desktop are some popular applications. Another solution is using a live-streaming platform, such as Apple

Y. Luo (Ed.): CDVE 2021, LNCS 12983, pp. 284–292, 2021.
https://doi.org/10.1007/978-3-030-88207-5_28

HTTP Live Streaming, YouTube Live, Facebook Live, or a commercial provider such as Wowza, Ant Media, Agora. But in practice, it needs to customize the platform to adapt to different learning scenarios, for example, when a booking and access control must be integrated. However, they are proprietary, and their architectures and sources are closed. This limitation makes them difficult to be used for learning and research purposes. Capture-render delay is another issue with a relatively high delay of at least several seconds in the mentioned solutions.

Throughout this research, some related works are found. In [4], the authors propose an Open and Scalable Web-Based Interactive Live-Streaming architecture with a Redis cluster layer as its main component. Data from the input sources layer (webcams) can stream into the Redis at a high FPS (generally at 30 FPS). The stream data from Redis will be served to each user, using a web browser, by CamServers layer, using a simple image-refreshing scheme or an H.264 streaming scheme. An architecture based on Matlab and WebSockets [5], with the Matlab Server uses the MatlabWebSocket library. Then the client can be realized in JavaScript. These authors do not use cameras but visualize the remote laboratory in 3D on the client size by the Three.js JavaScript library. The advantage of the 3D animation is the view from different angles and the fact that it can stress some essential details, but it takes time to build the visualization. In other work [6], the authors use a dedicated solution for IoT, the Blynk IoT platform, to create a server and a mobile application that controls an SEDC motor. Dr. May et al. [7, 8] present a ready-to-use remote laboratory in electronics called Virtual Instrument System In Reality (VISIR). The work is a case study and the connected evaluation using VISIR to adapt an existing circuits course over one semester in the College of Engineering at the University of Georgia. The VISIR Open Lab Platform provides a virtual interface enabling students to build a circuit board and monitor the result. A study that focuses on one particular e-Learning area is Computer-Aided Design [9]. The authors propose grouping average CAD laboratory workstations in pairs to create remote stations capable of performing required CAD graphics processing for remote users while streaming it over the network for a near real-time experience.

The above studies all have a case-based approach. At any rate, some methods can be applied to other situations. However, there is still a gap in integrating practice lessons using hardware, especially with low latency requirements, into online lectures.

This paper proposes a solution to build a remote laboratory. This solution is very suitable for experiments that require very low capture-render delay. It's easy to implement and flexible to customize. A prototype system is also implemented, with an investigation that controls a robot in real-time. The latency was measured to make sure of the near-real-time requirement.

The remainder of the paper will be organized as follows: Sect. 2 describes the system architecture, system implementation presented in Sect. 3, and finally, conclusions and perspectives are made in Sect. 4.

2   System Architecture

With the goal of building a system to support online exercises, such as practice exercises for embedded systems programming, embedded software programming, which can be expanded as needed, the system architecture is proposed as follows (Fig. 1):

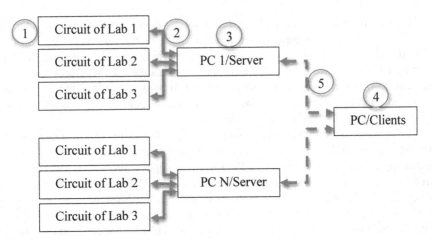

Fig. 1. System architecture.

The system consists of principal components as below:

- **Circuit of Lab (1):** practice circuits are pre-assembled electronic circuits managed with servers. The number of exercises can be expanded as needed. Their content can also change dynamically with the subject or student.
- **Wire/Cable (2):** the electrical wires or cables connect between the circuit and the Server.
- **Server (3):** The computer is equipped with NVIDIA's GeForce GPU and installed with the Geforce Experience software, an application produced by NVIDIA to assist users in optimizing the computer. A webcam captures images of devices and displays them on the screen. After students finish their session, the system will be reset automatically to its original state.
- **Clients (4):** Learners' computers with software reprogrammed based on Moonlight software are suitable for the organization and management of exercises and learners. Moonlight is an open-source implementation of NVIDIA's GameStream protocol. The GameStream protocol combined with the optimization of the GeForce GPU has made the delay when working on the Server screen at the Client machine is very small [10]. The latency in this work is about 10 ms in this work.
- **Streaming over the Internet (5):** Moonlight Internet Hosting Tool provides some options to stream over the Internet, such as Pairing, VPN, Manual port forwarding [11].

3   System Implementation

This section presents some remote experiments to evaluate the proposed system (Fig. 2). These experiments are required as part of an IoT course for college students.

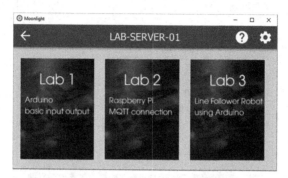

Fig. 2. Screen of the experiment list

3.1   Lab 1: Program on Arduino Board to Interface with Sensor and LCD

In the first experiment, students write a program for Arduino to read temperature and humidity data from the DHT11 sensor and display the two values on the LCD screen. Students will observe the actual circuit through the image taken from the Webcam on the server's screen (Fig. 3). Students write the source code and verify the results displayed on the LCD instantly (Fig. 4). The information for Lab 1 is described to the students as shown in Table 1.

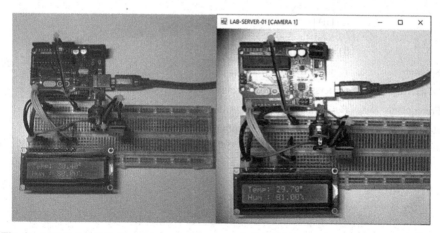

Fig. 3. Actual circuit (left) and images are captured via Webcam on the server's screen (right).

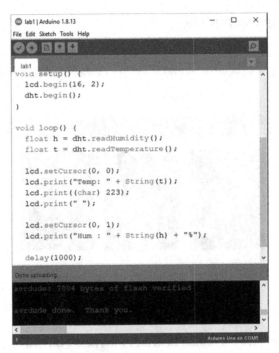

Fig. 4. Software interface for writing code.

Table 1. Information of Lab 1

Title	Program on Arduino board to interface with sensor and LCD
Devices	01 Arduino Uno 01 LCD 16x2 01 DHT11 sensor 01 Resistor 330 Ω 01 Potentiometer 10 KΩ
Software	Arduino IDE
Objective	Understand how to program with LCD1602 and with DHT11 sensor
Prerequisite	Basic knowledge about Arduino
Result	Read temperature and humidity data from DHT11 sensor Display measured values on the LCD

3.2 Lab 2: Programming on Raspberry PI Embedded Computer with Control and Monitoring via Web Using MQTT Protocol

In the experiment, students write a Web site in Python language. The program integrated with the website reads temperature and humidity data displayed on the website and saves it to a file (monitoring and storage function). On the server's screen, the website has additional buttons. These buttons turn on or turn off the LEDs on the circuit board (control function) (Figs. 5 and 6). The information for Lab 2 is described to the students as shown in Table 2.

Fig. 5. Actual circuit (left) and images are captured via Webcam on the server's screen (right).

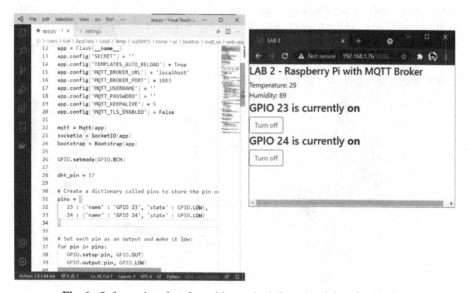

Fig. 6. Software interface for writing code (left) and web interface (right).

Table 2. Information of Lab 2

Title	Programming on Raspberry PI embedded computer with control and monitoring via Web using MQTT protocol
Devices	01 Raspberry Pi 02 LED 01 DHT11 sensor 02 Resistor 330 Ω
Software	Python3 mosquitto MQTT broker Visual Studio Code IDE
Objective	Understand MQTT Protocol Know using Flask Framework to build a web page that can interact with GPIO pins of Raspberry Pi
Prerequisite	Basic Python programming skill Program web application using Flask MQTT broker
Result	Web application has the following functions: monitoring, control and data storage

3.3 Lab 3: Programming on Raspberry PI Embedded Computer with Control and Monitoring via Web using MQTT Protocol

Students write programs on the Arduino IDE in the third experiment and upload the code to the robot remotely via Bluetooth connection. The algorithm will be adjusted from the control results to meet the requirements that the robot follows the black line (Figs. 7 and 8). The information for Lab 3 is described to the students as shown in Table 3.

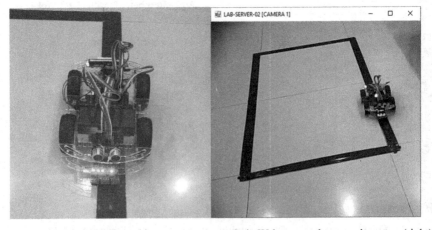

Fig. 7. Actual circuit (left) and images are captured via Webcam on the server's screen (right).

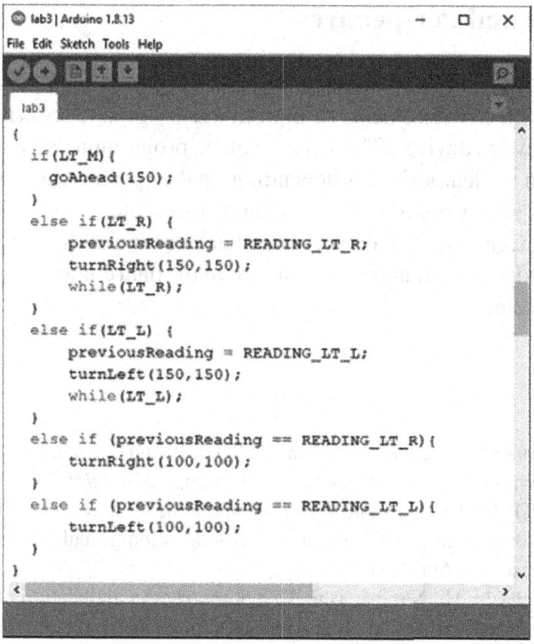

Fig. 8. Software interface for writing code.

Table 3. Information of Lab 3

Title	Line follower robot
Devices	01 Four wheels Arduino-based robot + 04 independence wheels + 01 Arduino board + 03 infrared modules + 01 HC-06 Bluetooth module
Software	Arduino IDE
Objective	Understand how to use sensors data to control motors
Prerequisite	Basic knowledge about Arduino Basic programming skill
Result	The robot follows the black line

4   Conclusion and Perspectives

This study introduces a method of designing and implementing a remote laboratory. In particular, it meets the requirements of high transmission latency with experiments for lessons using hardware devices. The system can be programmed to customize the application software on the learner's side depending on the specific case to add management functions such as: access control, learner management, etc.

The system design allows scaling the number of exercises flexibly. The lecture content can also be updated without much influence of the data communication management method in the system.

References

1. Giusti, A.D.: Policy brief: education during COVID-19 and beyond. Rev. Iberoam. Tecnol. en Educ. y Educ. en Tecnol., no. 26, p. e12 (2020). https://doi.org/10.24215/18509959.26.e12
2. Li, C.: The COVID-19 pandemic has changed education forever. This is how. https://www.weforum.org/agenda/2020/04/coronavirus-education-global-covid19-online-digital-learning/. Accessed 10 Apr 2021
3. Tran, T.V., Takahashi, H., Narabayashi, T., Kikura, H.: An application of IoT for conduct of laboratory experiment from home. In: Proceedings of the IEEE International IOT, Electronics and Mechatronics Conference, pp. 31–34 (2020). https://doi.org/10.1109/IEMTRONICS51293.2020.9216375
4. Rodriguez-Gil, L., Garcia-Zubia, J., Orduna, P., Lopez-De-Ipina, D.: An open and scalable web-based interactive live-streaming architecture: The WILSP platform. IEEE Access **5**, 9842–9856 (2017). https://doi.org/10.1109/ACCESS.2017.2710328
5. Bistak, P.: 3D three-tank remote laboratory based on matlab and websockets. In: Proceedings of the 5th Exp. International Conference, pp. 85–89 (2019). https://doi.org/10.1109/EXPAT.2019.8876585
6. El-Hasan, T.S.: Internet of Thing (IoT) based remote labs in engineering. In: Proceedings of the 6th International Conference Control Decision Information Technology, pp. 976–982 (2019). https://doi.org/10.1109/CoDIT.2019.8820591
7. May, D., Reeves, B., Trudgen, M., Alweshah, A.: The remote laboratory VISIR - Introducing online laboratory equipment in electrical engineering classes. In: Proceedings of the IEEE Frontiers in Education Conference, pp. 1–9 (2020). https://doi.org/10.1109/FIE44824.2020.9274121
8. May, D., Trudgen, M., Spain, A.V.: Introducing remote laboratory equipment to circuits - concepts, possibilities, and first experiences. In: Proceedings of the American Society for Engineering Education's 126th Annual Conference & Exposition "Charged up for the next 125 years" (2019). https://doi.org/10.18260/1-2-33017
9. Besic, I., Hodzic, K., Karabegovic, A.: E-Learning remote laboratory station for computer aided design. In: Proceedings of the International Symposium on Electronics in Marine, pp. 127–130 (2019). https://doi.org/10.1109/ELMAR.2019.8918910
10. https://www.nvidia.com/en-us/geforce/forums/shield-tv/9/202365/nvidia-gamestream-and-moonlight-latency-test-wired/. Accessed 10 Apr 2021
11. https://github.com/moonlight-stream/moonlight-docs/wiki/Setup-Guide. Accessed 10 Apr 2021

A Sufficiency Agriculture Learning Platform for the Development of New Agriculturists

Kazuya Komatsu$^{(\boxtimes)}$, Pimlapat Yoothong$^{(\boxtimes)}$, and Pornsuree Jamsri$^{(\boxtimes)}$

Faculty of Information Technology, King Mongkut's Institute of Technology Ladkrabang, Bangkok, Thailand
{60070007,60070066,pornsuree}@it.kmitl.ac.th

Abstract. The agricultural industry has the problem of price reduction of products and market oversupply. The root cause comes from Thai farmers practicing monoculture, plant and cultivation of the same types of products at the identical time in a nearby area. To address this problem our team developed a mobile application "Kueakul". This application serves a sufficiency agriculture platform for a new agriculturist to strengthen a cooperative society of agriculturists. The application is accessible through iOS and Android platforms. It provides eight major features: (1) login; (2) agriculturist profile; (3) preference of users; (4) advising services for basic agriculture; (5) allocation of land and plant model; (6) knowledge for mixed crops (7) crop nourishment (watering); (8) and a discussion forum. The applications "Kueakul" can help Thai agriculturists have better understanding of correct information to best-manage their resources. The application was successfully implemented and evaluated by 2 groups—target users and an expert. The results and evaluation found three most useful features: land allocation, watering scheduling and discussion forum with significant potential for sufficiency agriculture.

Keywords: Cooperative farmer · Sufficiency agriculture · Mobile application · Agricultural platform · Integrated agriculture

1 Introduction

For the agriculture situation in Thailand, most farmers still practice monoculture. This means growing a large number of one kind of plants during one period at a time [1]. Studies have shown that monoculture has a low yield but a high risk ("high-risk, low return"), so farmers have to bear higher production costs yet lower incomes [2]. Statistical data shows that 2 out 3 farming households use monoculture as researched by Puey Ungphakorn, Institute for Economic Research in 2019 [3]. However, the new approach proposed by King Rama IX sparked farmers to undertake a variety of mixed farming. The research by Babatunde and Qaim (2019) [4] discovered that mixed farming that is integrated offers an increase in income compared to monoculture farming.

Technology helped farmers in terms of access to agricultural information through the use of various media, easy-to-access and low-cost channels, for example, social

© Springer Nature Switzerland AG 2021
Y. Luo (Ed.): CDVE 2021, LNCS 12983, pp. 293–306, 2021.
https://doi.org/10.1007/978-3-030-88207-5_29

media (Chaokaset) that farmers are already using currently [5]. Chaokaset is a mobile application that guides farmers in the right way of cultivating at the right time. It has a vital function–crop tracking, which helps farmers know what daily activities to do for a particular crop. Nevertheless, there is still a lack of land allocation for planting missing in this platform. This important function is needed to introduce farmers to manage land for planting on a selected area appropriately.

The researcher, therefore, has created a mobile application, "Kueakul", suitable for those farmers who are newly interested in farming but lacking in multi-crop knowledge [6]. The application provides 8 parts including system registration and login, watering schedule, plant information, land allocation and management including prototype models, user information, record interested users, and a chat room. This paper consists of 6 sections: 1) Introduction, 2) Related Work, 3) Research Design, 4) Kueakul Application, 5) Results and Evaluations, 6) Conclusions and Future Research.

2   Related Work

The studies and related theory in agriculture and agricultural technology are vital background information to study and analyze for design and development assistance to achieve a successful mobile application.

2.1   Agricultural System in Thailand

Initially, farming in Thailand had aimed to produce sustainability for farmers. Since the Bowring Treaty [7], the farming situation shifted resulting in a situation called "The Green Revolution" [8] which used agricultural machinery instead of human labor and work animals. Chemical fertilizers were discovered, and various kinds of agricultural chemical products applied in farming such as pesticides. Consequently, the agricultural system in Thailand, changed from a variety of subsistence farming to commercial agriculture. Farmers depended on monoculture to meet the needs of agricultural production leading to mass planting of one type of crop to facilitate harvesting [8]. However, growing a vast number of one crop over a long period of time has had a negative impact on the environment, reduction in work animals by gasoline machine replacements, pesticide residues that impact negatively on natural resources and increased risks in insect and plant diseases [9]. All together this situation contributed to the causes of unstable price of agricultural products.

2.2   Alternative Agriculture

Traditionally, an alternative agriculture focuses on the use of compost, manure and mulch to reduce the use of synthetic chemicals. An alternative agriculture is subsistence agriculture that has as its main goal to produce food and other essential elements of life rather than commercial trade by overuse of natural resources. There are many groups of alternative agriculture with commitments to similar principles of farming methods such as sustainable agriculture, integrated agriculture, new theory agriculture, natural agriculture and organic agriculture [7]. Integrated agriculture is especially well-known today in agriculture [8].

Integrated Agriculture: Significantly, this is a form of agriculture that grows two or more types of plants or agricultural activities during the same period in the same area by relying on the combination of plants, animals, and the environment. All activities are mutually beneficial in one way or another to reduce production costs, reduce dependence on external factors. such as water and fertilizers, to reduce the risk of product price fluctuation in a single agricultural system. By using available resources in the area efficiently and appropriately. an integrated agriculture is essential in creating diversity of plants, animals, and biological resources and natural compost and manure as fertilizer [8].

New Theory of Agriculture: New Theory of Agriculture has concepts and theories in development based upon "The Royal Initiative of His Majesty King Rama IX", [10] This theoretical framework has been thought and calculated according to the academic principles of natural resource management methods that optimizes the social condition of community. Basically, both concept and the technical aspects must entail reasonable time consumption to be able to solve problems for actual benefit. The major aim is for sustainable development that is suitable for a small area of 10 - 15 rai. Various agricultural activities are undertaken in order to gradually utilize resources on a slow basis [11]. With a ratio of 30:30:30:10 the area used can be adjusted as appropriate with a basic ratio for the real sufficiency economy and self-sufficiency. The first part of 30% is for a pond of cultivation. The second part of 60% is an agricultural area where crops are grown and divided into 2 sections: 1) 30% of rice farming and 2) 30% for growing crops or horticulture. The third part of 10% is allocated for a residence.

2.3 Target Area

The research team studied a specific area based on research information and analyzed the population of the province [12] and the number of farmers in the province [13] to determine the percentage of the number of farmers [14]. The selected criteria correspond to the agricultural situation–number of monocrop farmers ratio to multi-crop farmers. The selected province is located in the Northeast of the country (Thailand) with high potential to practice multi-crop agriculture as shown in Table 1 for 2019.

Table 1. The table shows the percentage of the number of farmers in major provinces of the Northeast region.

Province	Farmer (%)
Nakhon Ratchasima	19.93%
Ubon Ratchathani	24.93%
Khon Kaen	19.11%
Buri Ram	22.79%
Surin	24.93%

Significantly, Ubon Ratchathani province is one of Thailand's seventy-six provinces that is ranked highest together with Surin in terms of farmers in its region. Ubon Rajathani province is divided into 25 districts. The districts are further divided into 219 subdistricts and 2,469 villages. This province has a population totaling 1,878,146 persons and agricultural population of 468,289 persons [14]. The province has the potential to continue growing plants and moving farming from one generation to another generation as the majority of farm owners are local people [13].

3 Research Design

3.1 System Architecture

Nowadays, the majority of farmers practice monoculture agriculture to meet the demands of agricultural products. But this comes at a high risk, when the product is exported to the market at the same time, because it causes product oversupply. Product prices, thus, are reduced with less commercial negotiating power. Studies have shown that Integrated Farming or growing two or more types of crops helps diversify risks [1].

The research team realizing the importance of hybrid cropping, land allocation and other features, applied this understanding to the most widely used available technology, namely a Smartphone that allows easy access to information. Using React Native that can be developed in two platforms, iOS and Android, allows ease of development and using Firebase to manage databases allows speed of data readability. See Fig. 1 for System Architecture.

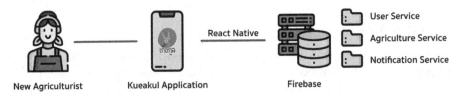

Fig. 1. System architecture

New Agriculturist: The application is available for the farmer (novice user) to interact with the system. The farmer can choose plants to grow, view watering schedules, exchange knowledge among users and community, and query for interested user information. Then, the system will show the results relevant to the user's needs.

Kueakul Application: This is the central operating part of platform that communicates between user and database. It is called "Kueakul" application, to contact the database (Firebase) to query information corresponding for each crop, user data, watering table, and exchange knowledge from users and retrieve the results back to user.

Firebase: Firebase is Google's mobile application development platform that mainly carries data storage providing many services that are easy to develop.

3.2 Focus Group

Initially, our research begins with a study of focus groups. To gather initial requirements and bring it into design criteria, the researcher gathered information through an online survey from 26 responders. The survey is about agricultural knowledge and farmer information. The initial survey informed the research team that the target group who participated in the survey had never done farming and lacked multi-crop agricultural knowledge as a large group in the survey. Listing of tasks for participants in the survey was achieved by searching for agricultural information from Google that can return a variety of information from many sources. Expert sources are considered as another source. From this preliminary information, the researcher realized the importance of accessing agricultural information for new farmers by providing an application that can be easily accessed through both iOS and Android operating systems. Both are available channels to help those interested in basic agriculture. They can follow the cultivation of mixed crops, disseminate credible agricultural knowledge and are able to discuss and exchange ideas with agricultural experts. Moreover, this feature includes exchanging knowledge and opinions through the application.

From the above, information gathered assisted in forming clearer goals and reassured the appropriateness of our idea at the initial design and development steps. The focus user is a person who wants to be a farmer. who has little knowledge or does not have any knowledge of agriculture, above 20 years or older, and has done less than 3 years of farming and therefore judged to be the target group.

3.3 System Development

Researcher started system development from the selected planned features. These features came from analyzing requirements and drafting artifacts in the front-end followed by the back-end. The interrelation between back-end and front-end works together until both fit into the concept. The initial design concept drove the research idea into an actual system structure that is developed in 2 major parts.

Back-end: Researchers use Firebase as a NoSQL database, which is suitable for creating mobile applications. Basically, Firebase serves main services–user service, agriculture service, and notification service. There are many services available for developing as Firebase authentication helps manage authentication. cloud Firestore not only provides Firebase cloud function but also handles a multi-platform on a mobile application.

Front-end: Researchers use React Native as a tool to create a multi-platform mobile application that supports both iOS and Android platforms to facilitate farmers with the most access to our application. A React Native creates layouts to follow the system design. Another tool in the front-end, is an Expo application that helps managing things with React Native, such as retrieving images and notifications from the phone. It also allows the developer to interact between the front-end and back-end of the application. The outcomes are expressed while developing and testing in process.

From the data analysis, the researcher found that Ubon Ratchathani province has the highest percentage of farmers up to 24.93% and is equal to Surin province. The researcher chose Ubon Ratchathani province as an area for our focused location. For this study, plants are divided into 3 categories: economic crops, horticultural crops and fruit trees. In order to follow the sufficiency agriculture theory, each farm must consist of these same 3 major categories. There are 10 selected types of plants in this design system that include 1) economic crops: rice, corn, cassava, 2) horticultural crops: red onion, tomato, chili, long green bean pod, 3) fruit trees: durian, longan and coconut.

4 Kueakul Application

Kueakul mobile application provides 8 major features presented in a mobile application. The features contain the following: feature appearance, its components and functions benefits are described together with relevant information. This mobile application is developed in the Thai language only. The example exists in Thai only at the moment. Kueakul Application divides its 8 features into 4 groups: Getting started, Cropping, Plant information and a Chat room.

4.1 Getting Started: Login Page, User Information, and Preference of Users

Login Page: When a user starts the application for the first time, the user is required to register to utilize this application. Users can register in 3 choices 1) Register with our system 2) Login with Facebook Account, 3) Login with Google Account. Then, the user can click "Sign in" to access into the platform (See Fig. 2).

User Information: This page displays the user's personal information, including name, number of likes from other users who have been interested as liked can be selected by clicking the provided icon. After pressing, the system will display a page for user to fill-in individual personal information (See Fig. 3).

Preference of Users: This page will display the list of users that were saved. The owner can be edited by pressing the icon "Edited Saved users" to edit saved users if any (See Fig. 4). This page appears with 4 identified information 1) a name of preference user 2) area size 3) a heart symbol and 4) a number of users who follow this person. Once, the user clicks the preference user's name, the information will pop-up underneath the particular name.

4.2 Cropping: Start Planting and Growing Model

Start Planting: After a user logins successfully, it will show the cropping starts page. To be able to start planting new plants later, the user must insert a deed number. Next, the user can continue to the growing model step.

Fig. 2. Login page

Fig. 3. User information

Fig. 4. Preference of users

Growing Model: This selected area model page in the system will show 2 options of the models that will be presented based on the area size that the user has entered in the previous first step. The user can only select one particular interested model whether a "Plant Model" or a "Custom Model." The user can see the list of plants in the page that is the same as the activated "Next" bottom for confirmation to the next step.

- **Plant Model** is represented for all existing models contained in the system that are shared by other users. The user can duplicate the planting from any selected model. There will be a description of the selected plant that will identify the size of the plots that are planted for each type of plant and are provided within the model (See Fig. 5).

- **Custom Model** is for the owner user who will be the person who identifies area' size and plants by preference in the provided list they created from a list of all available plants. User can select each plant one by one (See Fig. 6). Then, the user determines the area of the plot to be planted for each plant. In addition, the user can adjust the grid size to a suitable area. Some smaller grid sizes can be more suitable for the small area. The selected plant for the area will be shown in the area with each plant's image (See Fig. 7).

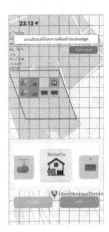

Fig. 5. Plant model   **Fig. 6.** Custom model   **Fig. 7.** Area &
plant allocation

4.3 Plant Information: Plant Information and Watering Schedule

Plant information: This page lists all the plants available in the system. User can see or search for plants in the search box (See Fig. 8). To see details of each plant's information, this page is divided into four topics: planting, caring, plant disease and harvest (See Fig. 9).

Watering Schedule: This is a page showing the watering schedule of each plant in the user's area. It is divided into morning watering and for the evening when applicable. There will be a notification of specific time relevant to a plant's watering period. User can edit the time setting and see the schedule each day of all plants (See Fig. 10).

Fig. 8. Plant name   **Fig. 9.** Plant information   **Fig. 10.** Watering schedule

4.4   A Chat Room

This page represents the exchange of opinion among the agriculturists community. They can ask any question about agriculture, as plants etc. for sharing experiences in agriculture and learning from other agriculturists. The information can be posted in forms of text and images (See Fig. 11–12).

Fig. 11. List menu   **Fig. 12.** A chat room

5   Results and Evaluations

5.1   Testing Scenario

The researcher designed a preliminary test application. For the test, it was divided into two parts: targeted users. and experts. For the first step, a user downloaded an Expo application into a smartphone, which is an intermediary for testing Kueakul Mobile Applications. In the second step, the user read the provided information including the scenario given by the researcher. While the user was trying to complete all tasks during the testing process, the researcher was there to observe and standby for any user's questions. The user answered a questionnaire after the test ended to evaluate the application.

Scenario. The user wants to use the provided Kueakul app, an agricultural application for new agriculturists, to plan their crops in their area. When successfully registered and logged in, the user found that there was no profile picture. The user then wants to change his profile picture and wants to find information about plants' harvest and related plant diseases. To be used for growing crops in their area, a user has some crops that they have a problem with after planting the crop. For example, "Why does the tomato I have grown have yellow leaves and how can I deal with this problem?" Therefore, there is a need to save the user's information because of the relevant crop data that they can view for later references.

5.2 User Results and Evaluations

Test results of a group of 10 users who tested features from the use of Kueakul application are the following. They range from 21–42 years old, 22 years old, 40% and 23 years, 20% and other 40%. Users in an educational institution are 60%. The researcher analyzed the data in score ranges 1–2 is low level, 3 represents moderate level and 4–5 is high level. The evaluations looked at 3 dimensions: 1) Overall usage, 2) Design and decorative display of application, 3) Response speed of application.

Overall for the application usage, it was found that 80% were satisfied and 20% were very satisfied with the application and its components (See Fig. 13). The users demonstrated that they can complete all tasks that are given by themselves with very few questions along the testing process. That implied their confidence and comprehension with this Kueakul Application. Their confidence (ease of use) interacting with the system was shown in that they spent 5–7 min, which is considered a fast pace to accomplish the objectives. The researcher received the information from the user.

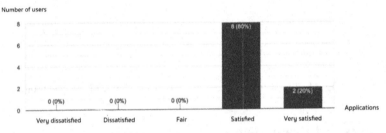

Fig. 13. Application satisfaction

According to the artifact, 50% were satisfied and 40% indicated very satisfied with the attractiveness of the application (See Fig. 14). Most of the users said the design is beautiful, easy to use and comfortable for eyes. As a user stated, "The infographic is beautiful and interesting. Beautiful color application. The color scheme is compatible with the application. The content displayed is suitable for the application." They also gave feedback with application's components as enjoyable and user friendly.

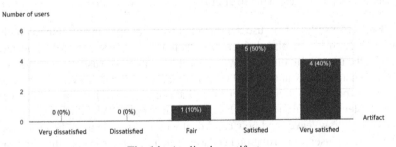

Fig. 14. Application artifact

Due to the responsiveness, 50% of those thought they had a moderate response (See Fig. 15). As researcher found that users were informed, they were getting some feature work done in a slow response than they expected, for example, the chat room feature has a slow performance while downloading a discussion to display on their device compared to other features responded in real time. It took approximately 5 s longer depending on the amount of conversation in that chat room and content type (text and images).

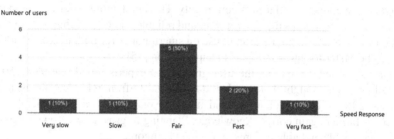

Fig. 15. Response speed of application

5.3 Expert Results and Evaluations

After the completed implementation of this mobile app, the research team tested the application with an expert, a former professor of the Faculty of Agriculture at one well-known public university. The overall feedback was positive that it has potential to be useful for new agriculturists as stated in their feedback, "The application is useful, beautiful, and if adding plant tracking function will be even better." Moreover, there are some suggestions from this expert. Test results of the application found that the plant information in the app could be more accurate when adding a larger number of a variety of plant data into the system. This app's features could benefit new agriculturists more as the expert emphasized. "If the system adds more plant's information. It will be beneficial to farmers by choosing up-to-date plant information." When a system could monitor plants in the area with data of numbers of days that have been growing, time to fertilize and harvest the expert suggested "If the system had a crop tracking function, it would be even more useful, because this lets farmers know what we should do to increase production." These comments could be included in future development. Another suggestion is that the specific section for searching expert's name be in the list for easy access. There is also a section to store preferred agriculturists who count as experts. The expert also suggested that a person's name can be searched on the user page to make it easier and faster to access that specific person's information.

6 Conclusions and Future Research

6.1 Conclusions

This mobile application, Kueakul app, was successfully implemented and offers 8 useful features of 4 main group functions as stated in its development for new agriculturists.

The novice farmer can use the app for utilizing multiple types of crop knowledge and to promote cultivation of hybrid crops. In corresponding to the sufficiency agriculture theory, new agriculturists are able to allocate their agricultural areas to grow with their intent to grow more than one type of crop in one area is counted as practicing and following the sufficiency agriculture principles of King Rama IX [7]. Likewise, this app assists new agriculturists to allocate areas suitable for growing plants of specific types, Moreover, it allows farmers to exchange ideas with other farmers as the way to strengthen the cooperative farmers community. This app facilitates farmers to have easy access to useful resources that are relevant and reliable and free of charge. The research team chose to create an application to use on smartphones for both iOS and Android so it would be easier for farmers to use the application [15].

For results and evaluation, the user groups and experts found that 90% (50% and 40%) of the users thought that the plant data was taken from reliable sources, and 70% (50% and 20%) thinks that planting, land allocation planning is most beneficial to novice farmers as farmers gain correct knowledge. Planning to grow in their own areas makes them more visible and able to foresee the actual outcome.

The awareness of some limitations in forms of data resources and system development can be acknowledged and created for future research. For instance, the performance of the app can be solved by using Lazy Load. It is one of the techniques to make the website display faster by not sending requests to retrieve all files at the same time while loading. The application's back-end would be adjusted to send requests only when the user wants to use them. This method will improve performance in terms of response speed that we learned about as a limitation during the evaluation process.

When analyzing and comparing the applications of "Kueakul" with "Chaokaset" developed by the National Center for Electronic and Computer Technology, or NECTEC, [9] as studied in the related study it was found that the difference in features are considered as *distinctive* features that include area allocation for growing plants, watering schedule and notification, interested agriculturists, chat rooms and prototype models, yet track cropping feature is in this development while the agricultural application, Chaokaset, does not support these Kueakul features as track cropping (See Table 2).

However, there are some limitations into 3 categories 1) Data has some outdated agricultural information from reliable sources. Available resources in multiple online sources have inconsistent information and need updated information. This makes research difficult to double check for consistent information among sources. 2) System development has many parts that are complicated in terms of use that can cause confusion to user. There is a chat room development technology for improvement that researcher can simplify the feature for future development and research. By changing development technology from MongoDB to Firebase, slows down the overall performance because of sending a request to retrieve all data at the same time since loading, instead of sending the request only when needed. 3) Time consumption with learning new technique and tools by researcher has increased time to spend to research its functionality and how to integrate technology together such as Firebase and Google maps in the platform.

Table 2. The comparison between Kueakul and Chaokaset agricultural applications.

Features	Kueakul	Chaokaset
Register and login	✓	✓
Area Allocation	✓	✗
Growing Plant	✓	✓
Watering schedule and Notification	✓	✗
Plant information	✓	✓
User Profile	✓	✓
Interested Agriculturist	✓	✗
Chat room	✓	✗
Prototype model	✓	✗
Track cropping	✗	✓

Note: ✓ means Available Feature   ✗ means Not Available Feature

6.2 Future Research

There is potential for further development by adding an artificial intelligence system that can recommend the right crops to grow in specific areas that is based on the soil's quality, environment. This would enable the system to suggest increasing the quality of the soil that is suitable for growing crops. Then, this will improve the quality of the soil and minerals if needed. To consider crops, agriculturist needs to decide whether or not a specific area is suitable for the plants they want to grow. If not, what should be done to ensure the quality of the soil is appropriate to plant that type of plant when the soil is in this condition. Using fertilizers might be an option when AI is completely implemented for adding into the existing system. Another potential is to develop in the section of plant disease analysis from photos by using image processing (Image Processing) to analyze the disease in the plant. There are methods of treatment and prevention by collecting data from the Department of Agricultural Extension. Finally, the development of a tracking system for each plant that a new farmer grows in their area is another potential. To know the number of days a crop has been growing, date to fertilize, time for harvest, are suggested additional feature from the expert's evaluation. All of the information can be gathered from the Department of Agricultural Extension.

All three parts of the above additional development could be added into a "Kueakul" application and then further developed accordingly or researcher can develop a separate platform that serves more features to create more benefits for farmers in the future.

References

1. Sommarat, C., Wisanu, A., Bunthida, S.: Thai agricultural microstructures through vehicle registration data and agricultural decks (2018). https://www.pier.or.th/wp-content/uploads/2018/05/aBRIDGEd_2018_009.pdf
2. Sommarat, C., Wisanu, A., Phumsit, M., Kannikar, T., Jirat, J.: Landscapes of the Thai agricultural sector How will it be transformed into sustainable development (2019). https://www.bot.or.th/Thai/ResearchAndPublications/articles/Pages/Article_26Sep2019.aspx
3. Sommarat, C., Wisanu, A., Bunthida, S.: Dynamics of agriculture in Thailand and implications for the returns and risks of agricultural households. From the article, Puey Ungphakorn Institute of Economic Research (2019). https://www.pier.or.th/wp-content/uploads/2019/06/aBRIDGEd_2019_014.pdf
4. Babatunde, R.O., Matin, Q.: Patterns of income diversification in rural Nigeria: determinants and impacts. Q. J. Int. Agricult. **48**(4), 305–320. (2019)
5. Latthaphon, R., et al.: Digital technology to improve the quality of life of Thai farmers (2019). https://rb.gy/snrixx
6. Castro, P.J.M., Caliwag, J.A., Pagaduan, R.A., Arpia, J.M., Delmita, G.I.: A mobile application for organic farming assistance techniques using time-series algorithm (2019). https://doi.org/10.1145/3322645.3322697
7. Office of the Royal Development Projects Board.: New theory, sustainable self-reliance principle. (1st ed.) Publisher, Nakhon Pathom (2009)
8. Department of Lands.: Sufficiency economy elements (2016). https://rb.gy/rvat7g
9. Chiang Mai News: An application for modern Thai farmers that must have. https://www.chiangmainews.co.th/page/archives/1234681
10. New theory: Mixing farms according to the new theory. (2nd ed.) Farm Management Promotion Group Agricultural business promotion division department of agricultural extension (1997)
11. Nature Farming Textbook.: Sufficiency Economy Philosophy. (2nd ed.) Publisher, Bangkok (2011)
12. National Statistical Office of Thailand.: Demographic statistics (2021). statbbi.nso.go.th/staticreport/page/sector/th/01.aspx
13. Office of Agricultural Economics.: Number of farmer households (2021). farmerone.org:9502/analytics/saw.dll Portal
14. Office of Agricultural Economics: Central Farmers Database. http://farmerone.org:9502/analytics/saw.dll? Portal
15. Suen, R.C.L., Chang, K.T., Wan, M.P.H., Ng, Y.C., Tan, B.C.: Interactive experiences designed for agricultural communities (2014). https://doi.org/10.1145/2559206.2574819

Smart, Practical, and Low-Cost Assistant System for Hospital Nutritionists in Times of a Pandemic

Chakkrit Snae Namahoot[1,2](✉) ⓘ, Michael Brückner[3] ⓘ, and Sakesan Sivilai[4] ⓘ

[1] Faculty of Science, Naresuan University, Phitsanulok, Thailand
chakkrits@nu.ac.th
[2] Center of Excellence in Nonlinear Analysis and Optimization, Faculty of Science,
Naresuan University, Phitsanulok, Thailand
[3] Naresuan University International College, Naresuan University, Phitsanulok, Thailand
michaelb@nu.ac.th
[4] Faculty of Science and Technology, Pibulsongkram Rajabhat University, Phitsanulok, Thailand
sakesan@psru.ac.th

Abstract. We report on a research project supporting dieticians. This paper presents the results of field tests carried out in collaboration with nutritionists and medical staff at Naresuan University Hospital in Phitsanulok, Thailand. The aim was to support the daily work of nutritionists by streamlining the processes used to provide the bi-weekly meal plans to reduce time to planning for meals in stressful situations like a pandemic. We designed and developed a low-cost system for assisting the nutritionists with all information they need, including nutritional values of available foods and patients' data with physician's notes if available. The system process involves a MySQL storage component with a Web-based PHP application to address the cost limits of the hospital. The cooperative field tests of the newly designed system showed a faster processing power compared to the old one by a factor of 174. Similarly, sound results could be gained by the user satisfaction survey, which indicated "good" levels of satisfaction with the system in all five categories asked for.

Keywords: Cooperative applications · Diet recommender system · Supporting nutritionists · Hospital management · Cost-benefit-analysis

1 Introduction

The Global Nutrition Report 2020 [1] states warning signs regarding healthy nutrition delivery for large parts of the Thai population. The report states: "Thailand has shown limited progress towards achieving the diet-related non-communicable disease (NCD) targets. The country has shown no progress towards achieving the target for obesity, with an estimated 12.7% of adult (aged 18 years and over) women and 7.0% of adult men living with obesity. Thailand's obesity prevalence is higher than the regional average of 8.7% for women and 6.0% for men. At the same time, diabetes is estimated to affect 8.8% of adult women and 8.3% of adult men."

© Springer Nature Switzerland AG 2021
Y. Luo (Ed.): CDVE 2021, LNCS 12983, pp. 307–316, 2021.
https://doi.org/10.1007/978-3-030-88207-5_30

Appropriate nutrition is one of the major elements for gaining and maintaining good health, especially for patients that receive medical treatment. Consuming beneficial foods can relieve medical conditions and support rehabilitation. Dietary requirements are second only in importance to medical treatment for hospital in-patients. Nutritional principles and suitable ingredients that take into account the patients' medical condition, particular illness, and physical conditions are essential and contribute to the relief of the patient's illness and the patient's continuing rehabilitation.

This is particularly the case for many specific diseases, including diabetes, high blood pressure, coronary artery disease, gallstones, gout, and cancers. Consumption of inappropriate food and foods to which the patient has an allergy will exacerbate and prolong the patient's medical condition. From a public health perspective, correct dietary requirements can also contribute to disease prevention and reducing the cost of medical treatment [4]. The prolongation of patients' medical conditions leads to another common problem in Thai hospitals as far as in-patients are concerned: a shortage of hospital beds due to the unnecessary bed occupancy rate. This is particularly unfavorable in times of a pandemic.

Hospitals have to manage numerous and diverse groups of patients; specific disease conditions and allergies, as well as social, ethnic, and religious food preferences and prohibitions, must be catered for. All of these factors create a complicated and time-consuming process for all staff in hospitals regarding food and dietary planning, purchasing, and distribution, particularly where these planning activities need to be based on each patient's needs. This situation asks for support employing digital means [2, 3].

The system and the process developed and presented here act as a Smart, Practical, and Low-Cost Assistant System for Hospital Nutritionists, called SPL@SH. It was designed within a rapid prototyping project to make the daily workload of local nutritionists at Naresuan University Hospital more efficient. The system applies knowledge representation relating to nutritional data and considers the health conditions and food preferences of individual patients [5]. This system is responsible for managing the ingredient selection for the suitable diet for each particular patient to find and rank the most appropriate nutrients and ingredients. An important aspect of this system is its user-friendliness and provision of timely information to the nutritionists and staff, as well as being sufficiently comprehensive.

This paper presents the cooperative design and development effort taken by the authors and hospital staff. The paper also details the results of field tests involving assistant nutritionists and staff in a hospital in Thailand. The resulting system can be used by hospitals to improve their dietary service processes and improve processing times considerably.

The rest of this paper is structured as follows: Sect. 2 outlines the Methodology of the system design and development with Sect. 3 addresses the Cooperative System Use of SPL@SH. In Sect. 4, the field test results are presented and briefly discussed. In Sect. 5 conclusions are drawn, and the last Sect. 6 indicates further work.

2 Objective and Methodology

This section outlines briefly the objectives and methodology of SPL@SH, the System for Assisting Nutritionists in Hospitals. The main objective of this research was to provide a smart and practical prototype system for selecting the most suitable ingredients for food supply of elderly in-patients with.

- a food ontology for managing the necessary nutritional concepts and data [9], and
- a recommender system using real-time data from the hospital wards for dietary planning regarding elderly patients in the hospital.

From collecting data and studying the food service process of the hospital's nutrition department and analyzing it, the idea was to design and develop a system to help solve the problem of selecting the most suitable ingredients for in-patients as presented in Fig. 1.

As shown in Fig. 1, Step 4, the nutritionist had to look at the number of diets for the patient, such as soft and normal foods in the Naresuan Hospital Imed system, as well as at comments from doctors, such as soft (sterile) food, soft food (postnatal), soft food (after surgery), including food for protein-deficient patients to prepare the right nutrients by avoiding adversary ones. By applying this step, nutritionists need to spend a lot of time looking at individual meals and counting the amount of food in each ward. This is a complex task and has a high chance of missing out on important information. We developed a system to ease this task by calculating the number of patients quickly and conveniently. Step 5 is the process where the system supports the nutritionists' work in a fast and more efficient way compared to the previously used manual calculation method via Excel spreadsheets. Important modules are food item management, ingredients handling, food introduction (choose whether to use the menu all 14 days or from the recommendation of the appropriate ingredients and then lead to the recommendation of the food items), including the calculation of the nutritional values and the cost of ingredient selection.

The research team has cooperatively worked with the staff responsible for the hospital's patient database. It was found that the hospital used a SQL type database, so the researcher agreed to switch to MySQL 8.0 database to achieve results faster than using the ontology. Working with the familiar SQL platform is also easier to maintain for hospital administrators, while the knowledge structure still adheres to the original ontological concepts. The database is designed as shown in the example of the Entity-Relationship Diagram in Fig. 2 and 3.

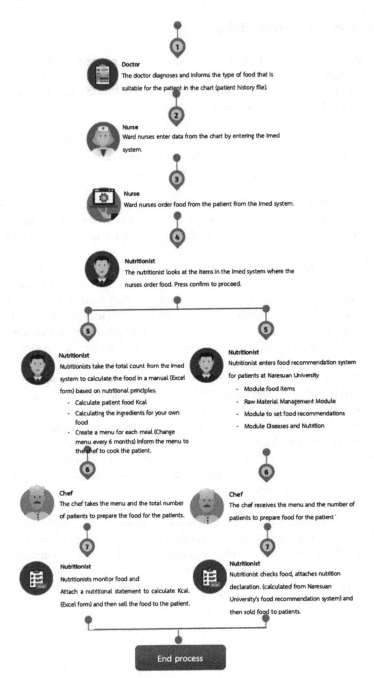

Fig. 1. Working process of the old system, left (and SPL@SH) right

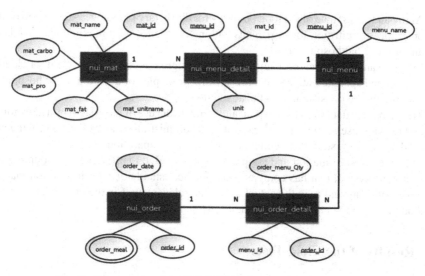

Fig. 2. An example of the SPL@SH Entity-Relationship Diagram

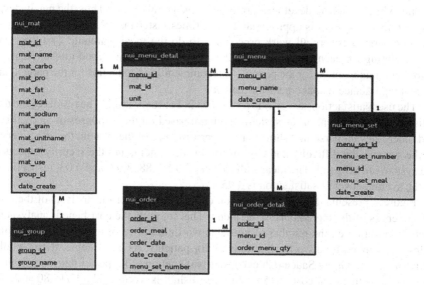

Fig. 3. Example of SPL@SH database correlation table

3 Cooperative Development

The cooperative development process comprises the following elements and steps:

- Analyze the original work system of nutritional dietary planning for in-patients.
- Implement and adjust the dietary planning system for elderly, general and specific patients in the hospital.

- Apply and adjust data of the food ontology for the dietary planning system based on the principles of nutrition for in-patients and in accordance with international standards and use in Thai hospitals [6].
- Integrate and apply the most suitable cooking ingredient selection system for elderly, general and specific patients according to the principles of nutrition in the hospital to support and be consistent with the actual use [7].
- Test using real data from the hospital and evaluate the use of the system by a nutritionist and relevant users, such as medical staff and administrators, as well as improving and modifying the system to be complete for a policy preparation.
- Exchange of information and cooperate in knowledge management by adopting the prototype system that has complete and practical standards with instruction manual to demonstrate and train the actual use of the relevant staff in the hospital.
- Analyze, discuss and summarize the results.

4 Results of the Field Tests

Regarding the time efficiency of the prototype system compared with the traditional working process, we found that the processing time of the original system was 61 min in total, while the newly developed prototype took a total of 21 s. Thus, the newly developed prototype system is approximately 174 times faster than the traditional process. The comparison covers all work procedures to do the meal planning: 1) appropriate food counting for each type of patient, 2) calculation of patient food intake (Kcal), 3) ingredient management for the patient, 4) recommending food items for the patient, and 5) cooking balance management for patients.

The user satisfaction survey was performed in February 2021. The results of the user satisfaction assessment of the system which are based on the responses of 33 dietitians and other relevant personnel show that the performance of the system, the effectiveness of the system, the difficulty and ease of use of the system, and the security aspects of the system are all good. The mean values were 3.92, 3.88, 3.97, and 4.03, respectively, so the average level of satisfaction is 3.95.

Figure 4 presents the recommendation of food items after the analysis of the cost-effectiveness of the ingredients in the menu. This supports the cost-benefit analysis for each food item, i.e., the number of nutrients worth the price of the ingredients, which helps recommend food worthwhile to cook for patients. As an example, Rice Noodles with Chicken in Gravy Sauce (Chicken Rad-Na) contains 43 types of nutrients from all ingredients with a total cost of 15.80 baht per dish, it is worth 2.72 (43/15.80 = 2.72).

Figure 5 is a cost-effective ingredient recommendation screen modified from Fig. 4 based on the value of the number of nutrients to the price of the ingredient to find ingredients that are worthwhile to be formulated into food items. The ingredients and nutritional information are derived from the table of the nutritional value of Thai food. In conjunction with the USDA database, the price uses the middle price of the market ingredients to calculate by using the value equation equal to the number of nutrients divided by the price of that ingredient, such as egg, yolk, contains 42 nutrients and cost 2.00 baht per 1 egg which will have a value of 21.00 (42/2.00 = 21.00).

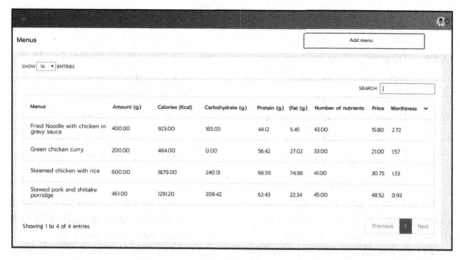

Fig. 4. List of food allocated to a patient

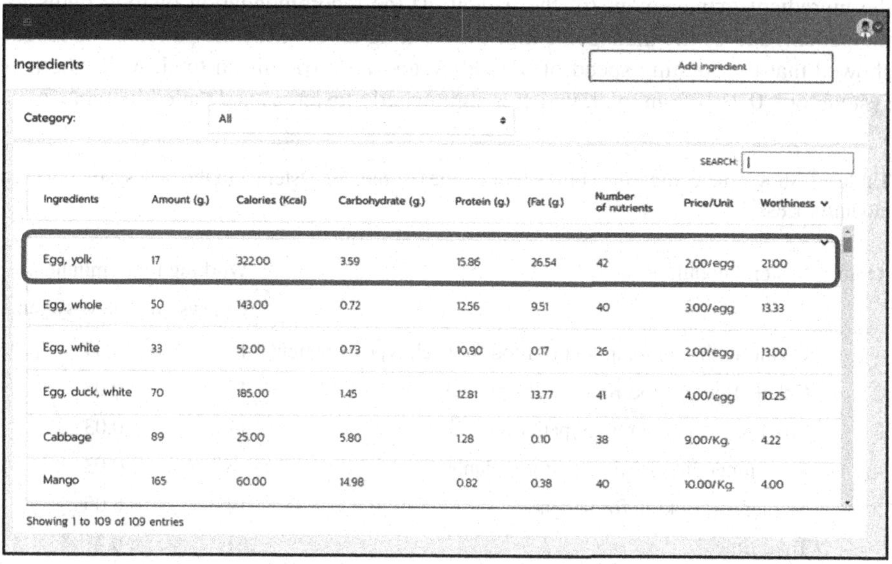

Fig. 5. Ingredients selection by value (example)

The system was tested using real data from the hospital and assessed the results of its use by nutritionists and relevant users. The satisfaction of 33 users was assessed by using questionnaires in 3 parts: 1) general information of respondents, 2) satisfaction in using the system, and 3) evaluation results. Summarized as in Table 1.

Table 1. User satisfaction regarding SPL@SH

Order	The results of the user satisfaction assessment	$\bar{x}$	s.d.	Performance level
1	Performance of the system	3.92	0.60	Good
2	System effectiveness	3.88	0.62	Good
3	The difficulty/ease of using the system	3.97	0.53	Good
4	Information security of the system	4.03	0.55	Very good
	Total average	3.95	0.57	Good

From Table 1, when considering the evaluation results from the overall user group, it was found that the performance of the system, system effectiveness, the difficulty/ease of using the system, and the security of the system's information are good.

To compare the operating speed of the old system and the new system, five modules of the old and newly developed system operating times were performed: 1) the appropriate food count for each type of patient, 2) the calculation of the patient food Kcal, 3) the ingredient management for the patient, 4) the recommendation of food items for the patient, and 5) the management of the cooking amount for the patient. The results showed that the running speed of the old system took 61 min in total, while the new system took 0.21 min in total, which is significantly faster, as is detailed in Table 2.

Table 2. Shows the comparison of operating times of the old system and the new system in each modul/process.

Order	System module/Process	Working time (minutes)	
		Old system	New system
1	Counting the right amount of food for each type of patient	13	0.04
2	Calculation of food Kcal for the patient	11	0.06
3	Providing ingredients for patients	15	0.03
4	Recommending food items for patients	8	0.03
5	Managing cooking for patients	14	0.05
	Total time	61	0.21

5   Conclusions

The conclusions from this work are as follows:

We have presented the cooperative development and field test results regarding a Smart, Practical, Low-cost Assistant System for Hospital nutritionists (SPL@SH), which supports staff in planning the various diets for in-patients in Naresuan University Hospital, Phitsanulok, Thailand.

SPL@SH uses the MySQL platform and a php web-application to store and retrieve knowledge concepts based on a previously constructed food ontology.

SPL@SH can set measures to buy or select raw ingredients for implementing a nutritional dietary plan, both in terms of nutrients and value, including the calculation of the quantity and cost of raw ingredients used in hospitals, both public and private sectors to meet the good health policy.

The field tests indicate that SPL@SH using MySQL performs 174 times faster than its predecessor, which used the food ontology as the knowledge base. This is certainly due to the performance of the SQL environment selected as the data management tool.

Based on a user survey involving 33 dietitians and staff, it can be stated that the overall satisfaction is good. Using five criteria, the average level is 3.95.

6   Further Work

Further work regarding SPL@SH is as follows:

- Promote the application of the system for usage in other hospitals in the region and the country.
- Develop a system to automatically calculate the cost of planning the purchase of recommended ingredients to estimate the cost for the hospital's finance department.
- Develop an application to support the elderly's flexible meal planning, in which they can apply ingredients that are easily available, such as home-grown crops, or buy ingredients comfortably near their homes.
- Furthermore, food item detection [8] can be used in the SPL@SH system to determine good foods for consumption or the ones to avoid.

Acknowledgements. We would like to thank the Faculty of Science, Naresuan University and the National Research Council of Thailand (NRCT) for funding this research. We are very grateful for the good cooperation with the dieters and the administration of the Naresuan University Hospital. Special thanks go to the hospital director, Prof. Sirikasem Sirilak, who effectively supported our work.

References

1. Global Nutrition Report 2020. https://globalnutritionreport.org/resources/nutrition-profiles/asia/south-eastern-asia/thailand/, Accessed on 2 April 2021
2. Abhari S, et al.: A systematic review of nutrition recommendation systems: with focus on technical aspects. J. Biomed. Phys. Eng. **9**(6), 591–602 (2019)
3. Dall'Oglio, I., et al.: A systematic review of hospital foodservice patient satisfaction studies. J. Acad Nutrition Dietetics **115**, 567–584 (2015)
4. Dimosthenopoulos, C.: Malnutrition. In N. Katsilambros et al. (eds.), Clinical Nutrition in Practice. Wiley-Blackwell (2012)
5. Namahoot, C.S., Sivilai, S., Brückner, M.: An ingredient selection system for patients using SWRL rules optimization and food ontology. In: Luo, Y. (ed.) CDVE 2016. LNCS, vol. 9929, pp. 163–171. Springer, Cham (2016). https://doi.org/10.1007/978-3-319-46771-9_22

6. Thai Food Composition Database. https://inmu2.mahidol.ac.th/thaifcd/home.php. Accessed on 20 April 2020
7. Walker, M.: A survey of food consumption in Thailand. Occasional Paper #11, University of Victoria, Victoria, Canada (1996).
8. Namahoot, C.S., Brückner, M., Nuntawong, C.: A Recommender system supporting diet planning in hospitals. ICIC Express Lett. **15**(6), 585–594 (2021)
9. Boulos, M.N.K., Yassine, A., Shirmohammadi, S., Namahoot, C.S., Brückner, M.: Towards an 'Internet of Food': food ontologies for the Internet of Things. Future Internet **7**(4), 372–392 (2015)

Addressing the Constraints of Elderly Tourists in a Recommendation Algorithm

A. Salaiwarakul[✉]

Department of Computer Science and Information Technology, Faculty of Science,
Naresuan University, Phitsanulok, Thailand
anongporns@nu.ac.th

Abstract. In this article, research on elder tourism algorithm that recommend best fit attractions for individual elders with various limitations, is presented and discussed. The algorithm of interest uses three different factors relevant to the elderly tourist and their probable physical limitations. The algorithm being considered categorizes elderly tourists as being entirely self-reliant, partially self-reliant, or are wheelchair reliant, as the important factors to consider when developing a tourism information recommending algorithm. The requirements of elderly tourists in each of these categories will obviously vary, so each of these conditions have been acknowledged and applied in the development of the algorithm. This paper applies descriptive statistics appropriate to each elder category and the constraints, to describe the level of significance of each factor. Empirical studies have demonstrated how significant factors enhance the accuracy of the recommendations in terms of appropriateness related to elderly tourist's constraints.

Keywords: Elder tourism algorithm · Information retrieval · Recommender system

1 Introduction

The number of aging citizens, and the rising ratio of this demographic in society, is becoming an important and even urgent public health consideration worldwide. Thailand is experiencing this demographic phenomenon, with forecasts that Thailand will be considered as an aging society by 2026, given age trends and other population factors. At a time when the aging society is growing dramatically, tourism could be one of the key factors to increase the quality of life for the elderly.

Importantly, the elderly tourist's behavior and travel opportunities have a relationship with their quality of life. The term "Quality of Life (QOL)" indicates the level of personal satisfaction of the individual with current family, social, work and travel circumstances. The study, reported in [3], shows that a satisfactory and enjoyable trip experience can improve the physical and mental health of the elderly which leads to greater quality of life.

Various solutions for information retrieval in the tourism domain have been identified. These include utilizing an ontology as a method for searching tourism information and information retrieval and applying a semantic approach to the task [13, 14].

© Springer Nature Switzerland AG 2021
Y. Luo (Ed.): CDVE 2021, LNCS 12983, pp. 317–328, 2021.
https://doi.org/10.1007/978-3-030-88207-5_31

A semantic approach solves the problem of the ambiguity in meaning when searching the information. Other aspects of tourism information retrieval include users' physical constraints, preferred language, and presentation or appropriate trip recommendations, are also highlighted. Some of these research approaches applied machine learning to solve the problem of language ambiguity [15, 16] which was a significant complication faced by natural language searching algorithms when attempting to recognize and correctly comprehend the intended questions from the users.

However, managing a good travel itinerary that appropriately accommodate the particular traveler's trip requirements and facilities would determine the tourist's satisfaction with the planned leisure trip. A number of recently published research projects relevant to the development of leisure planning algorithms have attempted to arrange tourism itineraries based on user preferences to cope with restricted times to travel, length of travel period, and some of the fundamental real world problems such as local traffic at venues and facilities, time restrictions when visiting attractions, budget, and visit start and end locations [11, 12, 17, 22]. However, consideration of the tourist's physical or mental constraints is generally overlooked which are not included as planning factors, especially for the elderly and disabled tourist demographic which have constraints and limitations that restrict them from many leisure and travel opportunities [10, 23]. Such constraints include physical and mental considerations, as well as cost factors and limitations.

Existing methodologies cannot be applied to include all relevant factors of elderly tourists whose limitations and constraints should be important factors to be considered in order to recommend travel attractions for them. An analysis of the primary research identifies the influencing factors for senior travelers as short travel distances, facilities of transportation to and around venues, and the attractions' facilities, all of which are significant in the selection of a variety of travel routes suitable the elderly. The travel preferences of each individual are different as are the influencing factors for travel planning, especially the limitations specific to each elderly tourist.

However facilities supporting elder tourist are not widely available. Due to the fact as discussed, amenities, facilities and support that assist tourism for elder that provide and suggest information that matched the preference and limitation of individual elder should be studied.

The research presented in this paper demonstrates the factors that affect the tourism interests of the elderly and the constraints that limit the elderly from participating in leisure and tourism activities. The variety of recommended attractions very much depends on the level of self-reliance of the elderly tourist who may be entirely self-reliant, partially self-reliant, or wheelchair reliant. The tourism algorithm that was developed to accommodate the interests of the elderly tourist is illustrated here. The method of the recommendation system that identifies appropriate leisure routes for specific elderly tourists is based upon their tourism preferences, requirements and limitations.

2 Related Works

Elder tourism refers to tourism for elderly people who most often present with special limitations and needs appropriate to the age. One previous study divided the elderly demographic by using age segmentation i.e. younger seniors, age was between 55 and 64 years old, and older seniors, whose age over 65 years old [1]. As well, tourism activities and facilities were categorized as nature based tourism, cultural based tourism, and special interest tourism. Each category offers a different variety of activities as well as presenting limitation on tourists, especially the elderly who more commonly have physical limitations. The literature shows that different tourism categories offer different services and support. For elder tourism, the attraction attributes such as accessibility, amenities, or service are different and can be important constraints [2, 6]. Additionally, the senior's mobility capabilities and health are constraints on the available choices of both transportation modes and types of facilities, and access to them, by elderly tourists [10]. A number of studies revealed that traveling short distances at a sedate pace would be suitable for elderly tourists [8, 9]. As well, attractions and facilities should provide good accessibility and availability of information for the elderly tourist to accommodate their physical condition and health status.

In an aspect of planning travel itinerary, planning travel routes with multiple points of interest (POIs) is challenging for travelers. The user's preferences and restrictions are factors that need to be considered. Several techniques have been applied to generate travel itineraries encompassing multiple places of interest based on user preferences. The Greedy algorithm which improves user' satisfaction with the travel package [18] that offering tour packages based on user preference factors such as maximum places to visit, minimum cost, or maximum popularity weight. The generated tour package could be offered to the tourist by a tour agent. In addition to planning the tourism itinerary based on user's preference, the shortest path calculation should be applied to the planning process. In [19], the algorithm included factors such as available POIs and distances to and between POIs in the web-based information system in order to calculate the shortest path to the planned destinations. In a different direction, the problem of different times and the various times that could be spent at each POI differs between each individual tourist. As well, the probability of repeated visits to popular POI is also addressed [21].

Several personalized based tourism algorithms [4, 6, 7, 20] when recommending points of interest and travel durations based on user's preference, commonly used the factors time, and tourism category in designing the users' model when recommending POIs. Personalized Tourism is an effective recommendation tool for suggesting attractions that fit with user's preference, but research in this area has mostly focused on the user's interests and not on user limitations which are important factors that may restrict or modify recommendations for the elderly tourist. Some of the personalized tourism recommendation algorithms use social media in order to gather user profiles to know their past tourist activities, specific interests or repeat visits made by that user. However, the information available in user profiles in social media does not usually include the constraints of the traveler, such as physical limitations or special needs. One algorithm, published in [5], does however include disability factors in the modelling, but the majority of factors usually available in users profiles are demographic information, interests, and budget considerations. The limiting factors of mobility, disability or special requirements, dues to age or otherwise, are not used to generate the tourism route.

This limited set of factors used in these studies means that the studies are not relevant to, or useful for, tourism planning for the elderly who have disabilities or mobility limitations. To overcome this lack of acknowledgement of the special needs of the elderly tourist, it is this area of tourism planning that was specifically addressed in the current research. Together with the acknowledged fact of the importance of this growing demographic, the development of an algorithm to include those pertinent factors is seen as an important contribution to the field.

3 Research Methodology

In this section the research framework and methodology are elaborated and the essential elements necessary to the development of an appropriate travel algorithm to meet the elderly tourist's constraints and requirement are identified and discussed. The categories of tourism that are suitable for elder tourism are proposed and their inclusion in the developed algorithm is shown.

The scope of the study encompasses the Lower Northern region of Thailand which covers 9 provinces. This area has well developed transport connectivity within those provinces, as well as connection to Bangkok and Chiang Mai, both cities having international air links. This makes travel opportunities for the elder accessible by both public and private transport, and the area offers great variety and combinations of tourist attractions: religious, cultural, environmental and social. Moreover, distance between individual POIs is short. These reasons are suitable for elder choice of selections.

3.1 Research Framework

In this study, the model is concerned with two sets of variables that are significant to the requirements of the elderly tourist: the elder categories of regarding independence and mobility, and the tourism categories of religious, cultural, environmental and social. The level of significance of each set of categories to the elderly tourist's requirements, and the probability of the elder's requirements being factors in decision making are statistically calculated.

In order to study the elderly tourist's requirements and the importance of that to each elder category, a questionnaire was used as the method of data collection. There were 300 questionnaires returned; 100 from respondents in each elderly category. The data were processed and the descriptive statistical data analyzed. That analysis identified the significant factors that were then included in the recommendation algorithm, enabling the algorithm to consider their tourism category preferences together with their physical constraints.

The importance of the factors relevant to influencing the choices of, and recommendations for, tourism attractions appropriate to the elderly, were calculated from the mobility limitations and special facility requirements of the elderly tourist. These limitations and requirements therefore included the independence of the elderly tourist, or their level of dependence on others, and the need for equipment aids.

The facility requirement refers to special aids or assistance needed for individual tourists. This questionnaire was analyzed in order to rank the importance of each limitation factor important to the elderly tourist. Sample data returned 300 respondents was applied to calculate the ranking of tourism attractions that satisfactorily fulfilled the preferences of the elderly tourist.

Information regarding the availability of facilities offered in each tourism attraction category was collected and processed. The derived statistical data were included in the weighting algorithm.

The constraints and requirements of the elderly tourist and the available facilities at each tourism attraction were processed in the weighting algorithm which was then applied in the recommendation system in order to propose appropriate leisure attractions for the elderly tourist, taking into consideration their constraints, mobility category, and preferences. The research framework is shown in Fig. 1.

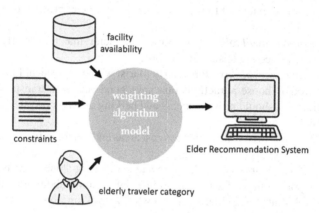

Fig. 1. Elder recommendation system framework

4 Research Methodology

In this research, the factors that are important to choices and decisions made by the elderly tourist for selecting the tourism attractions, were studied. For the purposes of this research the physical limitations of the elderly tourist and their tourism preferences, define the elderly tourist' behavior. Both collaborative filtering and content-based filtering were applied in order to generate the best fit recommendations solution to the elderly tourist's requirements. The collaborative filtering methodology in this study uses the limitations, together with the requirements of, the elderly tourist to calculate the congruence of the requirements and limitations of a particular tourist with the requirements and limitations of other tourists by a weighting algorithm that was developed in this research. In accordance with the content-based methodology used in this article, the algorithm calculates the similarity of the selected tourism category and facilities available at that POI, to the elderly tourist's preferences of tourism categories. The elder tourism algorithm can then suggest the attractions that match the elderly tourist's preferences with full consideration of the appropriateness of that POI to the physical limitations of, and the amenities and facilities requirements of, that tourist.

The three major crucial factors that affect the recommendation system are: *requirement of elderly tourist, elderly traveler category,* and *elder tourism category.*

Requirement of Elderly Tourist

Elder tourism planning requires additional and different information from general tourism. Physical limitations, restrictions on movement and mobility, special aids and assistance requirements differ both generally and between particular individual. This sections discusses the special requirement of the elderly tourist desiring to travel.

1) *Slippery slope route* - Places with slippery routes present special barriers to the elderly, depending on their difficulty in walking and avoidance of falling. This category can also be extended to steps and stairs which can prove problematic to the elderly.
2) *Elderly restroom availability* - an important factor that the elderly tourist will consider when selecting leisure attractions.
3) *Transportation accessibility* - the elderly tourist who has physical limitations when traveling would choose attractions that have good access to transportation. Especially, attractions should provide access and parking areas for private transport, cars, coaches and so forth.
4) *Availability of rest areas and facilities* - rest areas and other facilities such as first-aid rooms.
5) *Availability of support staff* - elderly travelers travelling alone or with a group may require support from staff who can provide information about attractions. This is especially relevant for the elderly traveler who is travelling alone, but also for private, un-guided groups.
6) *Wheelchair accessibility* - for the wheelchair traveler, wheelchair paths and access ramps are important factors that would encourage the elderly tourist to choose a particular attraction.

The elderly tourist's requirements were applied as one of the fundamentals in developing the recommendation algorithm which would correspond to a particular tourists requirements.

Elderly Traveler Category

Different categories of mobility and reliance have different requirements and limitations. To properly include these, in this research, three categories of mobility of elderly tourists were stated in order to develop the algorithm for rankings attractions that suit the preferences of a particular traveler. These categories are:

1) *Entirely self-reliant* - this category refers to elderly tourists who are independent and can travel alone, or without any need for special support, not having any difficulty of movement.
2) *Partially self-reliant* - elderly tourists who fall into this category may be dependent to some extent on a travel partner or other assistant. This category refers to the elderly tourist who can walk but may need to rest frequently.

3) *Wheelchair reliant* - includes elderly tourists who are wheelchair bound. They there-fore, require more special facilities than the other elder categories. Ease of access to facilities, such as having a ramp, is an obvious and important consideration.

Elder Tourism Category

There are many reasons for tourists wishing to visit certain attractions, or go on tours, or partake of leisure attractions. For the individual elderly tourist, the type of tourism is also a significant factor in the recommendation algorithm. The terminology of these various types of tourism is explained as follows:

1) *Natural Tourism* – natural attractions that are protected, curated and maintained by public or private actors, and include scenic waterfalls, mountains, and nature parks and reserves.
2) *Cultural Tourism* – this category refers to the culture of the local people as lived in their daily life and also includes historic sites of cultural significance. This category includes arts and crafts, the production of handicraft products, and local foods, and may include museums.
3) *Recreational Tourism* – includes recreational activities in special locations, such as mountain climbing, trekking and rafting, and boating. As well as man-made attractions such as theme parks.
4) *Agricultural Tourism* – this category of tourism brings the tourist the opportunity to experience farm life or rural living, and participate in such activities as mustering, shearing and other farm activities in a variety of agricultural and farm settings. It also provides educational experience of agriculture or within local communities.

5   Experimental Result and Evaluation

Both the elderly tourist mobility categories, and the tourism style categories, were applied in the recommendation algorithm developed in this study. The importance, or weighting of each was statistically calculated. The data tested in the weighting algorithm was derived from the responses to the research questionnaire returned by 300 participants. The data about the tourism attractions in the Lower Northern area of Thailand were used in the study. The percentage of the requirements that each of the elderly tourist categories demand is illustrated. The descriptive statistics relevant to the elderly tourist reliance attributes that were statistically significant are also shown.

The information shown in Table 1 indicates that the older travelers requires paths and walkways that are not sloping and slippery as the most important factor, due to their physical constraints.

Obviously wheelchair accessibility is important only to the wheelchair bound trav-eler. This factor is included, and its important is shown in Table 1, to wheel reliant tourists only. Although the importance of wheelchair accessibility is only relevant to one category, it is included in the analysis, and in the algorithm, to ensure completeness in considering all appropriate factors and including all tourists.

Availability of rest areas and supporting facilities is an important requirement of the partially self-reliant elders.

Table 1. Descriptive statistical analysis of each elderly tourist mobility category

Individual's limitation attribute	Elder category's percentage (%)		
	1	2	3
Not slippery/easy slope route	99	100	99
Elderly restroom availability	39	32	71
Transportation accessibility	34	89	91
Availability of rest area and facility	53	96	32
Availability of support staff	89	78	91
Wheelchair accessible	0	0	99

Note: Elder category 1 = Entirely self-reliant; 2 = Partially self-reliant; 3 = Wheelchair reliant

For the self-reliant tourist, avoiding slippery paths and difficult slopes is important, but the availability of supporting staff that can provide information for leisure attractions is the most important. This facilitator involves information available relevant to tourism attraction that should be available to all tourists both beforehand and during the tourism activity.

Table 2 summarizes the importance of the requirements applicable to each of the three tourist mobility categories in each tourism category in influencing the choice of tourism activities by the elderly tourist.

Table 2. Descriptive statistical analysis of each tourism category

Individual's limitation attribute	Availability in each tourism category (%)			
	1	2	3	4
Not slippery/easy slope route	63	97	50	79
Elderly restroom availability	26	69	0	36
Transportation accessibility	100	100	100	93
Availability of rest area and facility	53	77	100	43
Availability of support staff	68	28	100	50
Wheelchair accessible	47	74	50	29

Note: Tourism category 1 = Natural Tourism; 2 = Cultural Tourism; 3 = Recreational Tourism; 4 = Agricultural Tourism

Table 2 shows that the wheelchair bound tourist has limited opportunities for travel in the diversity of tourism attractions due to the physical difficulties that may be found at particular locations or attractions, and the limited availability of assistance to those tourists. Cultural tourism is seen to provide more availability of services for all categories of tourist, but particularly the wheelchair bound elderly tourists, than do the other tourism categories. This implies that cultural tourism operators and providers should improve their facilities in order to expand the choices available, and the number of elderly tourists selecting those tourism attractions and experiences. As wheelchair bound tourists are most likely to be accompanied by a companion, or travel in a group, this factor multiplies the benefits to facility providers, especially restaurants and other hospitality and accommodation providers.

The provision and availability of restroom facilities is not extensive in recreational tourism. The facilities and attractions provided by recreational tourism providers are more likely designed for younger tourists. Given this, to encourage the elderly tourist to select this style of tourism, greater attention needs to be paid to the provision of appropriate facilities, thus broadening the appeal of their tourism ventures to the elderly tourist demographic.

One important finding in this study was that the provision of special assistance and facilities to cater for the needs of the elderly tourist has not been of concern to tourism operators, and there is considerable room for improvement of the facilitators identified in the study, to enhance the opportunities available for elderly tourists.

From the derived statistical data, this research developed the weighting tourism algorithm in order to calculate the preferences and requirements of the elderly tourists, applying the facilitators that the elderly tourists' mobility categories require. The algorithm was formulated as (1). Let Aj be the statistical weight of the attraction calculated from the weighted limitation of the elderly tourist category and the weighted availability of the particular actual limitation in each tourism category. The relationship of attraction tourism weight can be donated as (1), where W(ej) is the elder limitation of each elder category, and W(cj) is the availability of the offered facility that each tourism category offers.

$$A_j = \sum ((W(e_j) \times W(c_j), W(e_{j+1}) \times W(c_{j+1}), \ldots, W(e_n) \times W(c_n)) \quad (1)$$

The recommendation system applies (1) as the basis of calculation for suggesting the leisure attraction for a particular elderly traveler. Then the attractions that are most fit to elderly tourist's constraints, tourism attraction category preference, and the level of availability of the facilities that are necessary for individual elder are ranked, using (2).

$$\text{Rank}(A_{(i,n)}) = (A_i, A_{i+1}, \ldots, A_n) \quad (2)$$

The method of evaluation in the real world of tourist activity for the elderly tourist recommendation system uses the information retrieval based metrics as following:

Precision: The proportion of the number of tourism attractions relevant to the elderly tourists' preferences that are retrieved from that tourist's information data store and the total number of tourism attractions that are retrieved.

Recall: The proportion of the number of tourism attractions relevant to the elder' preference that are retrieved and the total number of relevant tourism attractions that are stored in the data store.

F measure: A weighted harmonic mean of precision and recall.

The study has effectively been a simulation of the recommendations likely to be made to the elderly tourist. As yet, no data has been collected based on the experiences of the elderly tourists having accepted and acted upon those recommendations. Further investigation of the level of satisfaction of elderly tourists who have acted upon the recommendations needs to be undertaken to further prove the effectiveness of the algorithm.

6 Conclusion and Future Work

This article discusses the constraints, physical limitations, and facility requirements that restrict the elderly from tourism activities. The potential elderly tourists are grouped into three categories based on their physical limitations and special requirements. Tourism attractions perceived as appropriate and friendly to the elderly tourist are analyzed and studied as to their importance as facilitators provided in each tourism category. The responses to a survey identified the requirements that are significant for each elderly tourist mobility category. The most significant factor that affects the choice of attractions for the elderly tourist is that the tourism route; walkways, paths and so forth, not be difficult to progress due to slope or slipperiness, which would make it difficult or dangerous due to the reduced physical capability of the elderly tourist. Availability of well-maintained rest areas and facilities is another important factor relevant to the partially self-reliant elder. The outcomes of this study identified the importance of the availability of these attributes in each tourism category. The findings from this study show that all of the tourism categories have a high level of the transportation accessibility which is necessary for the older traveler. Although rest areas and support staff are well provided in recreational tourism to a high degree, the availability of other facilities with attributes necessary for the elder tourist in this recreational category are relatively low. The descriptive statistics utilized in the study illustrated areas of improvement that are required to enhance accessibility for elderly tourists.

The proposed algorithm and the recommendation system provided in this research apply the weighting recommendation strategy based on similarity value in each elderly tourist category. Hence, the elderly tourist constraint algorithm for the tourism recommendation that is proposed in this article can generate the best fit solution for elder tourism and promote the recommendation system which serve the requirements, physical limitations, and desired tourism behavior of the elderly traveler.

Compared to previous research [7, 20, 22] which focused on recommending attractions based one POI, types of activities, or tourism preference, this article proposes an algorithm and methodology that should be combined in the recommendation system to promote the efficiency, accuracy, and precision of the retrieved information for the elderly tourist.

For the direction of future work, the algorithm could provide methods to enable a particular traveler to pick his own weighting of the constraints relevant to them rather than the similarity value that is provided in this proposed algorithm. This would give a more exact match for that traveler. However, providing this usage capability requires further steps to provide that information to the system. The adaptive system concept would be one of the things that can be added to the current system. Feedback from the elderly tourist who has previously accepted and acted upon recommendations from the system can enable the system to better fit the needs of each particular elderly tourist.

Such an adaptive algorithm could improve the recommendations made to the user based on the previous access and experience of the user. The collection of that experience and of the attractions, visits and events that the elderly tourist visited would be used as factors in the recommendation algorithm. Another aspect that will be investigated in the a future study is the time aspect, such as length of participation in a particular activity, which would be an important factor given that the elderly tourist is more likely to need slow tourism due to his physical limitation and declined physical conditions. The time interval during their trip should be considered for arranging and recommending the itinerary algorithm which will add to the user's satisfaction.

References

1. Hossain, A., Bailey, G., Lubulwa, M.: Characteristics and travel patterns of older australians: impact of population ageing on tourism. Internat. Sympos. Econom. Theory Econ. **15**, 501–522 (2003)
2. Alén, E., Dominguez, T., Losada, N.: New Opportunities for the Tourism Market: Senior Tourism and Accessible Tourism, Visions for Global Tourism Industry - Creating and Sustaining Competitive Strategies. IntechOpen, pp. 139–166 (2012)
3. Kim, H., Woo, E., Uysal, M.: Tourism experience and quality of life among elderly tourists. Tour. Manage. **46**, 465–476 (2015)
4. Souffriau, W., Vansteenwegen, P., Vertommen, J., Vanden Berghe, G.: A personalized tourist trip design algorithm for mobile tourist guides. Appl. Artif. Intell. **22**, 964–985 (2008)
5. Gavalas, D., Kenteris, M., Konstantopoulos, C., Pantziou, G.: Web application for recommending personalised mobile tourist routes. Softw. IET **6**, 313–322 (2012)
6. Liew, S.L., Hussin, S.R., Abdullah, N.H.: Attributes of senior-friendly tourism destinations for current and future senior tourists: an importance-performance analysis approach. SAGE Open **11**(1), 2158244021998658 (2021)
7. Satria Pamungkas, K.A., Nurjanah, D.: Personalized automated itineraries generator for tourism. In: Silhavy, R., Silhavy, P., Prokopova, Z. (eds.) CoMeSySo 2020. AISC, vol. 1295, pp. 714–727. Springer, Cham (2020). https://doi.org/10.1007/978-3-030-63319-6_66
8. Sangkakorn, K., Boonyanupong, S., Thiensiri, J., Wandee, C.: Tourism development guidelines for the elder tourists. In: The 9th ApacCHRIE Conference (eds), School of Hotel & Tourism Management, The Hong Kong Polytechnic University Hong Kong (2011)
9. Batra, A.: Senior pleasure tourists: examination of their demography, travel experience, and travel behavior upon visiting the bangkok metropolis. Int. J. Hosp. Tour. Adm. **10**(3), 197–212 (2009)
10. Huber, D., Milne, S., Hyde, K.F.: Constraints and facilitators for senior tourism. Tour. Manage. Persp. **27**, 55–67 (2018)
11. Gunawan, A., Lau, H.C., Lu, K.: A fast algorithm for personalized travel planning recommendation. In: PATAT (eds) the 11th International Conference of the Practice and Theory of Automated Timetabling, pp. 163–179. PATAT, Italy (2016)
12. Lim, K.H., Chan, J., Karunasekera, S., Leckie, C.: Tour recommendation and trip planning using location-based social media: a survey. Knowl. Inf. Syst. **60**(3), 1247–1275 (2018). https://doi.org/10.1007/s10115-018-1297-4
13. Daramola, O., Adigun, M., Ayo, C.: Building an ontology-based framework for tourism recommendation services. In: Höpken, W., Gretzel, U., Law, R. (eds.) Information and Communication Technologies in Tourism, pp. 135–147. Springer, Vienna (2009). https://doi.org/10.1007/978-3-211-93971-0_12

14. Salaiwarakul, A.: Thai natural language based cultural tourism ontology. ICIC Express Lett. **12**, 159–165 (2018)
15. Salaiwarakul, A., Khruakong, S.: A hybrid approach for natural language querying segmentation for tourism ontology. JTEC **10**(1–5), 109–113 (2018)
16. Shaikh, A., KulkarniIOSR, S.B.: Natural language processing applications for tourism sector. J. Comput. Eng. **22**, 27–35 (2020)
17. Baizal, A., Lhaksmana, K., Rohmawati, A., Kirom, M., Mubarok, Z.: Travel route scheduling based on user's preferences using simulated annealing. Int. J. Electric. Comput. Eng. **9**, 1275–1287 (2019)
18. Benjamin, A., Aimi, S., Abdullah, Abdul Rahman, S., Bakar, E., Yahaya, H.: Developing a comprehensive tour package using an improved greedy algorithm with tourist preferences. J. Sustain. Sci. Manage. **14**, 106–117 (2019)
19. Afida, A., Musyafa, M., Muhsina, E., Sugiantoro, B.: An implementation of A* algorithm to tourism destination. Int. J. Inf. Dev. **4**, 1–7 (2015)
20. Kesorn, K., Juraphanthong, W., Salaiwarakul, A.: Personalized attraction recommendation system for tourists through check-in data. IEEE Access **5**, 26703–26721 (2017)
21. Zheng, W., Liao, Z., Qin, J.: Using a four-step heuristic algorithm to design personalized day tour route within a tourist attraction. Tour. Manage. **62**, 335–349 (2017)
22. Hsu, F.-C., Chen, P.: Interactive Genetic Algorithms for a Travel Itinerary Planning Problem. TSP, pp. 1–7 (2000)
23. Lee, B., Bowes, S.: A study of older adults' travel barriers by examining age segmentation. JTHM **4**(2), 1–16 (2016)

Automatic Picture-Matching of Crested Newts

Guillaume Magnette$^{(\boxtimes)}$, Yoanne Didry$^{(\boxtimes)}$, and Xavier Mestdagh$^{(\boxtimes)}$

Luxembourg Institute of Science and Technology (LIST), 41, rue du Brill,
4422 Belvaux, Luxembourg
{yoanne.didry,xavier.metdagh}@list.lu

Abstract. This article highlights a group of image processing, deep learning, and pattern matching techniques that can be used together in order to automatically identify different specimens of newts from a single species (Triturus cristatus Laurenti 1768). First, each image of newt will be: augmented, segmented, straightened. Then, patterns of images will be detected and compared between each other, allowing the differentiation of newts living in selected areas.

Keywords: Amphibian · Underwater Camera trap · Transfer learning · Picture-matching · Collaborative Newt Re-identification

1 Introduction

As an endangered species, it is necessary to study the evolution of the great crested newt populations. Previously, the production of field observations of newts allowing individualisation required stressful methods including live traps and specimen handling for taking pictures of their belly or implanting microchips. The NEWTRAP project developed a camera trap automating the production of newt observations in the field [1], and the classification of newt pictures by species [2]. Individualisation is essential to produce accurate population size estimates, but few remaining manual steps in the process of picture-matching software (e.g. AmphIdent[1]) induce time-consuming newt population studies. Thus, we are trying to automatically process different images of newts and automatically identify specimens that were already "photo-captured" at different times in order to obtain an estimation of their population. We also call this process re-identification.

We propose in this paper a set of methods allowing, when being used together, the achievement of this re-identification process in a fully automated way. This pipeline consists of two main parts: handling the preprocessing phase through Deep Learning and Image Processing techniques [2] then realizing the re-identification through the pattern matching technique named SIFT [3].

---

[1] http://www.amphident.de/en/index.html.

© Springer Nature Switzerland AG 2021
Y. Luo (Ed.): CDVE 2021, LNCS 12983, pp. 329–334, 2021.
https://doi.org/10.1007/978-3-030-88207-5_32

A user interface has been developed on which the different participants in this re-identification project can deposit new images of newts. Collaborators can add these images at different times when they wish, and select the area in which their new images were taken, allowing for a long-term collaborative study oriented towards the evolution of this species.

2 Preprocessing

As images of newts have important variability, different steps of preprocessing was necessary. We can see example of newts in Fig. 1 below.

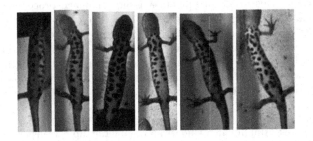

Fig. 1. Samples for the newsts dataset

2.1 Data Augmentation

First step was the augmentation of the dataset through scikit-image[2]. Here is a description of each different augmentation. We can see example of newts augmentation in Fig. 2 below.

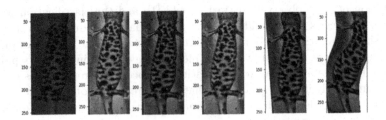

Fig. 2. Original, adaptative contrast enhancement, random lightness, random saturation, random shearning, random swirling (from left to right)

---

[2] https://scikit-image.org/.

2.2   Image Segmentation

The second step was to extract the bodies of the newts from the rest of the images. Different methods were tested for this purpose : Active Contours [4], Color segmentation [5], Saliency Map [6], Mask R-CNN [7] and Unet [8]. This last one was the best by far. We first needed to have images of newts labeled such that the area of interest was delineated with markers. Those markers were made manually clicking all around the belly of a hundred newts, as depicted in Fig. 3 below, using VIA software[3].

Fig. 3. Manually labelled images using VIA software

After using Transfer Learning [9], we obtained very convincing masks of the bodies of newts. Here we can see in Fig. 4 an augmented image as described in the previous section, then the ground truth regarding what we want to extract, and finally the mask output from the Unet.

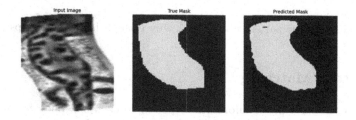

Fig. 4. Masks of newt bodies, obtained after transfer learning

2.3   Straightening

Finally, as individuals might look differently on the different pictures taken, we had to find a way to harmonize them. A straightening method was developed to achieve that. After the segmentation obtained from the previous section, the "Skeletonization" [10] method was applied, as seen in the Fig. 5 below. From these skeletons, a simple straightening method was implemented:

---

[3] http://www.robots.ox.ac.uk/~vgg/software/via/via.html.

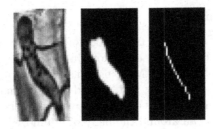

Fig. 5. Skeletonization method applied to the result of the segmentation

– Extract each pixel belonging to the skeleton
– Calculate the distance between each pixel and the center of the image
– Shift this pixel so that it is located in the center of the image
– Repeat until each pixel is centered

We finally obtained images of newts, which were augmented, segmented, straightened and vertically oriented, enabling a better re-identification as seen in Fig. 6

Fig. 6. The pattern is extracted, after each of the previous steps

3   Pattern Matching

In practice, as no a priori information related to each specimen being "photo-captured" is given, a classic supervised learning approach could not be used. We can see below the exploratory work in the field of Deep Learning that has been implemented:

– Counting Classes [11]: Clustering the embedding space obtained from an autoencoder with HDBScan [12] after reducing dimensionality
– Self Labeling [13]: Alternating between a traditional learning phase using convolutional neural networks thanks to pseudo-labels, and an optimization phase based on the resolution of the optimal transport
– Triplet Loss Embedding [14]: 3 Convolutional Neural Networks learning to project images from the same classes near each other while separating images from different classes in an embedding space

However, results were not consistent enough to be usable in a real world scenario. Thus, a more robust method has been found by using SIFT to detect patterns from the different images of newts.

Here is the pipeline enabling the re-identifications:

1. Images of newts were preprocessed like described in the previous section. We now have augmented, segmented, and straightened images of newts.
2. We convert these to grayscale then to binary thanks to an Adaptive Gaussian Thresholding method
3. The SIFT method was applied in order to detect patterns
4. The K-nearest neighbour algorithm was used to match descriptors previously found by SIFT
5. The Lowe ratio test [3] to filter those matches
6. If the average number of matches between a new image and all images of a previously encountered newt is above an empirically found threshold, the re-identification is successful.

Overall performances of this method were satisfying but not perfect. In fact, when using 20 different newts while each of them has different pictures taken at different times, most of the images were correctly re-identified.

4   Conclusion

We can reidentify newts photo-captured at different times and automatically distinguish the different specimens even when they look a lot similar thanks to the combination of different methods presented. This work is useful as it shows non-invasive and fully automatic methods can be used successfully to study the evolution of the population of different animal species. This type of method has been shown to work equally well for different amphibians [15] such as: fire-bellied toad (Bombina bombina), yellow-bellied toad (Bombina variegeta), fire salamander (Salamandra salamandra) or marbled salamander (Ambystoma opacum). Thus, we can envision the possibility of developing an inter-species interoperable framework, where the first step would be to automatically identify the species of each amphibian image, and then apply customized preprocessing methods depending on the species, allowing collaborators studying different species to work together.

Acknowledgement. We would like to thanks Christian Hundt from NVIDIA AI Technology Center, for his very valuable advices throughout the creation of this work. Thanks to Remy Haas and Lionel L'Hoste for retrieving the pictures on the field and annotating them in Newtrap Manager. This work has been financed by the Luxembourg FNR through the POC17 NEWTRAP.

References

1. Didry, Yoanne, Mestdagh, Xavier, Tamisier, Thomas: Newtrap: improving biodiversity surveys by enhanced handling of visual observations. In: Luo, Yuhua (ed.) CDVE 2019. LNCS, vol. 11792, pp. 277–281. Springer, Cham (2019). https://doi.org/10.1007/978-3-030-30949-7_32
2. Didry, Y., Mestdagh, X., Tamisier,T.: Visualizing features on classified fauna images using class activation maps. In: CDVE, pp. 352–356 (2020)
3. Lowe, D.G.: Distinctive image features from scale-invariant Keypoints. Int. J. Comput. Vis. 60(2), 91–110 (2004). https://doi.org/10.1023/B:VISI.0000029664.99615.94
4. Kass, M., Witkin, A., Terzopoulos, D.: Snakes: active contour models. Int. J. Comput. Vis. 1(4), 321–331 (1988). https://doi.org/10.1007/BF00133570
5. Demarty, C-H., Beucher, S.: Color Segmentation algorithm using an HLS Transformation. In: Mathematical Morphology and its Applications to Image and Signal Processing, p. 8 (2000). https://doi.org/10.1007/b117970
6. Hou, X., Zhang. L.: Saliency detection: a spectral residual approach. In: IEEE Conference on Computer Vision and Pattern Recognition, pp. 1–8, Minneapolis, June 2007. https://doi.org/10.1109/CVPR.2007.383267
7. Girshick, R., Donahue, J., Darrell, T., Malik, J.: Rich feature hierarchies for accurate object detection and semantic segmentation. arXiv:1311.2524 [cs], October (2014). http://arxiv.org/abs/1311.2524
8. Ronneberger, O., Fischer, P., Brox. T.: U-Net: convolutional networks for biomedical image segmentation. arXiv:1505.04597 [cs], May 2015. http://arxiv.org/abs/1505.04597
9. Pan, S.J., and Yang, Q.: A survey on transfer learning. IEEE Trans. Knowl. Data Eng. 22(10) , pp. 1345–1359 (2009)
10. Zhang, T.Y., Suen, C.: A fast parallel algorithm for thinning digital patterns. Commun. ACM (1984). https://doi.org/10.1145/357994.358023
11. McConville, R., Santos-Rodriguez, R., Piechocki, R.J., Craddock, I.: N2D: (Not Too) Deep clustering via clustering the local manifold of an autoencoded embedding. arXiv:1908.05968 [cs, stat], June 2020. http://arxiv.org/abs/1908.05968
12. Campello, R.J.G.B., Moulavi, D., Sander, J.: Density-Based clustering based on hierarchical density estimates. In: Pei, J., Tseng, V.S., Cao, L., Motoda, H., Xu, G. (eds.) PAKDD 2013. LNCS (LNAI), vol. 7819, pp. 160–172. Springer, Heidelberg (2013). https://doi.org/10.1007/978-3-642-37456-2_14
13. Asano, M., Rupprecht, C., Vedaldi, A.: Self-labelling via simultaneous clustering and representation learning. arXiv:1911.05371 [cs], February 2020. http://arxiv.org/abs/1911.05371
14. Hermans, A., Beyer, L., Leibe, B.:In defense of the triplet loss for person re-identification. arXiv:1703.07737 [cs], November 2017. http://arxiv.org/abs/1703.07737
15. Matthé, M., et al.: Comparison of photo-matching algorithms commonly used for photographic capture-recapture studies. Ecol. Evol. 7(15), 5861–5872 (2017). https://doi.org/10.1002/ece3.3140

Reproducible Improvement of Images Quality Through Nature Inspired Optimisation

Olivier Parisot[✉] and Thomas Tamisier

Luxembourg Institute of Science and Technology (LIST), 5 Avenue des
Hauts-Fourneaux, 4362 Esch-sur-Alzette, Luxembourg
olivier.parisot@list.lu

Abstract. Transparent and reproducible image processing is fundamental in science and engineering, whether to prove the efficiency of an algorithm or to prepare a new corpus of images. In this paper, we propose a Nature Inspired Optimisation algorithm based on Image Quality Assessment methods to obtain a reproducible sequence of transformations that improves the quality of a given image. Preliminary tests were realized on state-of-the-art benchmarks.

Keywords: Nature inspired optimisation · Image quality assessment · Image processing for cooperative applications

1 Introduction

Image quality improvement is a popular topic in computer vision. New techniques are constantly proposed in the literature to improve the quality of images whether they are blury, noisy, low-light or low-resolution [10]. Applying appropriate transformation to improve the quality of an image requires strong and regularly updated expertise. It is also essential to use metrics to guide the process. In this regard, Image Quality Assessment aims at automatically estimating the quality of an image in a way that corresponds to a human subjective assessment of the same image [18].

Furthermore, in the context of both scientific research or engineering, it is increasingly required to guarantee the reproducibility of experiments by keeping trace of the transformations performed on the images [1]. For example, a recent work has shown that a significant proportion of research papers lacks of transparency regarding image handling and it may compromise their interpretation [8]. We can make an analogy with Machine Learning: data preprocessing should be transparent to lead to meaningful and trustable predictive models [17].

In this paper, we propose a Nature Inspired Optimisation algorithm to obtain a reproducible improvement of image quality by relying on transformations monitored by Image Quality Assessment methods. The rest of this article is organized as follows. Firstly, related works about Image Quality Assessment and Nature

© Springer Nature Switzerland AG 2021
Y. Luo (Ed.): CDVE 2021, LNCS 12983, pp. 335–341, 2021.
https://doi.org/10.1007/978-3-030-88207-5_33

Inspired Optimisation for images are briefly presented (Sect. 2). Then, a new algorithm to improve images quality is described (Sect. 3). Finally, the results of preliminary experiments are discussed (Sect. 4) and we conclude by opening some perspectives (Sect. 5).

2   Related Works

Numerous Image Quality Assessment approaches were developed in recent years and an exhaustive list was already compiled [18]. We can distinguish two main types of techniques: Full-reference (FR) and Reduced-reference (RR) methods are based on a referential of images (raw/distorted) while No-reference (NR) and Blind methods intend to estimate single image quality [6]. In this paper, we focus on NR and Blind approaches because we don't use reference images. Among them, we can mention:

- Classical methods like BRISQUE (Blind/Referenceless Image Spatial Quality Evaluator): a score between 0 and 100 is produced (0 for good quality image, 100 for poor quality) [7].
- Recent Deep Learning methods like NIMA (Neural Image Assessment) – a set of Convolutional Neural Networks to estimate the aesthetic and technical quality of images: a score between 0 and 10 is produced (0 for poor quality, 10 for good quality) [14].

In practice, Image Quality Assessment is widely used in benchmarks to compare the efficiency of image processing algorithms [4].

Nature Inspired Optimization is a family of problem-solving approaches derived from natural processes. Among them, the most popular include evolutionary algorithms and particle swarm optimization [5]. Nature Inspired Optimization is also increasly applied in image processing for various tasks such as blur and noise reduction, restoration and segmentation [2,12]. In particular, [9] enhances optical images with a Genetic Algorithm.

To the best of our knowledge, there are no much contributions about the generation of reproducible images transformations sequences by applying Nature-Inspired Optimisation and guided by Image Quality Assessment techniques.

3   Approach

The cornerstone of our approach is defined as follows:

- An initial image.
- A sequence of transformations applied on the initial image (examples: enhance, dehaze, adjust histogram, deblur, total variation denoise, etc.).
- A quality score is evaluated with the BRISQUE or NIMA Image Quality Assessment methods (aesthetic or technical). This step is critical and drives the algorithm (quality serves here as the *fitness* of the solution, in the terminology used for evolutionary algorithms).

For a given input image (I), by considering a Image Quality Assessment method (M) and a maximum count of epochs (E), the following algorithm computes the transformations sequences leading to an image with a better quality:

- A population is generated with P images: each image is a clone of the initial image I on which a random transformation has been applied or not. In fact, to ensure that the algorithm does not lead to a lower-quality image, it is important to keep at least one unmodified clone of the initial image in the population: at worst, it will remain the best solution.
- During E epochs:
  - The current best image or an other randomly selected image is cloned, and then a random transformation is applied: the newly created image is evaluated with M and added into the population.
  - An other image is randomly selected in the population and is stacked with the initial image (with a random weight): the newly created element is evaluated with M and added into the population.
  - According to the evaluation with M of the images present in the population, the worst images are selected and then removed from the population (to always keep P images in the population).
- The final result is the image of the consolidated population having the best quality estimation. The algorithm output is then an sequence of transformations that leads to an amelioration of the Image Quality Assessment.

To prevent the image from deviating too much from the original one, we have added a test comparing the similarity between the produced image and the initial image: if the similarity is too low (i.e. lower than a predefined threshold T), then the image score is strongly penalised and the last transformation is therefore not retained. The test is based here on the Structural Similarity Index (SSIM): in practice, the value is close to 1 when the two images are similar while the value is close to 0 when the images are really different.

4   Implementation and Experiments

The algorithm has been implemented into a Python prototype. Various well-known open-source packages have been integrated. Images loading and transformations are realized with various dedicated packages like openCV[1] and scikit-images[2]. BRISQUE score is computed through the image-quality package [3] and NIMA scores are provided by a Tensorflow implementation[4].

By using these packages, these potential transformations can be applied:

- Contrast/brighten/sharpness adjustements, Histogram optimisation
- Blurring and deblurring, erosion and dilatation.

---

[1] https://pypi.org/project/opencv-python/.
[2] https://pypi.org/project/scikit-image/.
[3] https://pypi.org/project/image-quality/.
[4] https://github.com/idealo/image-quality-assessment.

- Denoising/restoration: total variation, non local means, wavelets, bilateral.
- Dehazing and details reconstruction with Deep Learning.
- Weighted stacking and subtraction of images.

The prototype was tested on a computing infrastructure with the following hardware configuration: 40 cores and 128 GB RAM (Intel(R) Xeon(R) Silver 4210 CPU @ 2.20 GHz) and NVIDIA Tesla V100-PCIE-32 GB.

(a)   Original   image: (b) Artificially degraded: (c) After our algorithm: BRISQUE = 9.637 and BRISQUE = 14.771 and BRISQUE = 3.134 and NIMA(aesthetic) = 5.166.   NIMA(aesthetic) = 5.071.   NIMA(aesthetic) = 5.160.

Fig. 1. An image of the SpaceX Falcon Heavy rocket (1a), an artificially degraded version (1b) and processed with our algorithm (1c).

The algorithm was applied on numerous images such as Fig. 1[5]; in this case, the following transformations have been applied: *dehaze, stack (weight:0.8), bilateral denoise, increase-contrast, enhance (beta:0.95), increase contrast, bilateral denoise, remove dark, increase contrast, enhance (beta:1.05).*

Several state-of-the-art images benchmarks were considered: TID2013 with 500 randomly chosen distorted images [11] and LIVE with 175 noisy images [13]. Additionally, we tested the approach on CID2013 and LOL benchmarks: the first one contains 475 images captured with consumer devices like smartphones [15] and the second one consists in 485 low-light images [16].

The results of Table 1 have been obtained with the following hyperparameters: NIMA aesthetic as targetted Image Quality Assessment score, an initial population of 20 images, 50 maximum epochs and 0.25 as minimum similarity. According to significant runs, this setting offers the best tradeoff between quality improvement and execution time. BRISQUE score has been computed

---

[5] https://tinyurl.com/falconheavyrocket.

afterwards to check the quality of the algorithm inputs/outputs and Noise Variance [3] has been esimated to highlight the level of noises in the benchmarks.

Table 1. Experiments on images benchmarks: the average Image Quality Assessments metrics (before and after the algorithm execution) are listed.

Images benchmark		BRISQUE	NIMA (aesthetic)	Noise variance
TID2013	Initial	45.271	4.952	97.414
	After	34.168	5.792	89.588
LIVE	Initial	59.309	5.005	2781.754
	After	54.833	5.710	1663.338
CID2013	Initial	13.560	4.778	12.031
	After	28.990	5.277	23.094
LOL	Initial	21.158	4.706	9.228
	After	51.241	5.464	16.543

Based on those first experiments, the quality scores (NIMA aesthetic and BRISQUE) are better for the images coming from the TID2013 and LIVE benchmarks after the execution of our algorithm. Idem for the noise: our algorithm tends to reduce it in transformed images for these benchmarks.

However we note that the results for low-light images are partially satisfying (LOL benchmark). Even if the transformations computed by our algorithm increase the NIMA aesthetic score as desired, it tends to degrade the BRISQUE score and it increases the noise. This issue shows the limitations of NIMA and BRISQUE for the quality evaluation of low-light images: these methods should not be used to guide the transformation of such images.

Finally, a word on performances: the time needed for the experiments was reasonnable on the infrastructure described above (from a few seconds to several dozen seconds per image). Most of the execution time depends of the applied Image Quality Assessment method: for example, BRISQUE evaluation is two to four times slower than NIMA.

5 Conclusion and Perspectives

This paper presented a Nature Inspired Optimisation algorithm to improve the quality of a given image from a reproducible sequence of transformations. A prototype based on Image Quality Assessment methods was implemented and tested on various state-of-the-art images databases.

Thanks to various academic and operational partners, we will set-up real-world use-cases to validate the approach. In parallel, we will improve the prototype by automatically generating the Python source code to transform the image as it is done in Automated Machine Learning for classifications and regressions.

Moreover, the future use-cases will also be used to improve the benefits of the proposed algorithm on low-light images. Finally, we will work to improve execution performance by distributing calculations via frameworks like Spark.

Acknowledgements. this work was realized by using the LIST Cognitive Pillar, a high performance infrastructure funded by the Data Analytics Platform project (http://tiny.cc/feder-dap-project). Special thanks to A. Hendrick, S. Renault and R. Jadoul for their support.

References

1. Berg, J.: Progress on reproducibility. Science **359**, 9 (2018)
2. Dhal, K.G., Ray, S., Das, A., Das, S.: A survey on nature-inspired optimization algorithms and their application in image enhancement domain. Arch. Comput. Methods Eng. **26**(5), 1607–1638 (2019)
3. Immerkaer, J.: Fast noise variance estimation. Comput. Vis. Image Understand. **64**(2), 300–302 (1996)
4. Li, B., et al.: Benchmarking single-image dehazing and beyond. IEEE Trans. Image Process. **28**(1), 492–505 (2018)
5. Li, H., et al.: Newly emerging nature-inspired optimization-algorithm review, unified framework, evaluation, and behavioural parameter optimization. IEEE Access **8**, 72620–72649 (2020)
6. Liu, Y.H., Yang, K.F., Yan, H.M.: No-reference image quality assessment method based on visual parameters. J. Electr. Sci. Tech. **17**(2), 171–184 (2019)
7. Mittal, A., Moorthy, A.K., Bovik, A.C.: No-reference image quality assessment in the spatial domain. IEEE Trans. Image Process. **21**(12), 4695–4708 (2012)
8. Miura, K., Nørrelykke, S.F.: Reproducible image handling and analysis. EMBO J. **40**(3), e105889 (2021)
9. Pal, S.K., Bhandari, D., Kundu, M.K.: Genetic algorithms for optimal image enhancement. Pattern Recogn. Lett. **15**(3), 261–271 (1994)
10. Parekh, J., Turakhia, P., Bhinderwala, H., Dhage, S.N.: A survey of image enhancement and object detection methods, In: Advances in Computer, Communication and Computational Sciences, pp. 1035–1047 (2021)
11. Ponomarenko, N., et al.: Image database TID2013. Sig. Process. Image Commun. **30**, 57–77 (2015)
12. Ramson, S.J., Raju, K.L., Vishnu, S., Anagnostopoulos, T.: Nature inspired optimization techniques for image processing–a short review. In: NIO Techniques for Image Processing Applications, pp. 113–145 (2019). https://doi.org/10.1007/978-3-319-96002-9
13. Sheikh, H.R., Sabir, M.F., Bovik, A.C.: A statistical evaluation of recent full reference image quality assessment algorithms. IEEE Trans. Image Process. **15**(11), 3440–3451 (2006)
14. Talebi, H., Milanfar, P.: Nima: neural image assessment. IEEE Trans. Image Process. **27**(8), 3998–4011 (2018)
15. Virtanen, T., Nuutinen, M., Vaahteranoksa, M., Oittinen, P., Häkkinen, J.: Cid 2013: a database for evaluating no-reference image quality assessment algorithms. IEEE Trans. Image Processi. **24**(1), 390–402 (2015)
16. Wei, C., Wang, W., Yang, W., Liu, J.: Deep retinex decomposition for low-light enhancement. arXiv preprint arXiv:1808.04560 (2018)

17. Zelaya, C.V.G.: Towards explaining the effects of data preprocessing on machine learning. In: 2019 IEEE 35th ICDE, pp. 2086–2090. IEEE (2019)
18. Zhai, G., Min, X.: Perceptual image quality assessment: a survey. Sci. China Inform. Sci. **63**(11), 1–52 (2020). https://doi.org/10.1007/s11432-019-2757-1

Virtual Learning Tools for Students with Delimited Ability

Eva Pajorová(✉) and Ladislav Hluchý

Institute of Informatics, Slovak Academy of Sciences, Dúbravská 9, Bratislava, Slovakia
utrrepaj@savba.sk

Abstract. Augmented Reality (AR) is a technology that dramatically shifts the location and timing of learning and training, while for students with limited ability it shifts the way of education and learning. This paper describes our research on augmented reality, how it applies to learning and training for students with limited ability, and the potential impact on the future of education. We developed Apps including virtual speaking head, speech synthesis, text to speech and speech to text conversion. We found out that for students with hearing impairments and for those with limited ability it is the best way of learning. Augmented reality is incredibly important as a tool of communication too, because, as a part of scientific gateway it creates a space for communities, collaboration, data sharing and visualization. It is very important for us, researchers to communicate our science to non-scientists. Our paper shows how augmented reality can serve as an important component of the virtual learning process. It enables students to take the courses and workshops online, manage course contents and downloadable resources, to validate courses and so on. In this paper, we present one of our developed tools for students, especially for those with limited ability.

Keywords: Augmented reality · Virtual speaking head · Speech synthesis · Limited ability · Cooperative visualization

1 Introduction

Augmented reality (AR) is the main part of virtual learning, virtual communication and education processes. Augmented reality supplements the real world with virtual objects in such a way that virtual objects appear to coexist in the same space as the real world.

Thomas Holz and col. presented in 2006 a framework for augmented reality agents, i.e. agents that exist in both the real and virtual space [1]. These agents combine the physical presence of a robot with the adaptability and expressivity of a virtual character. The objective is to blur the traditional boundaries between the real and the virtual and to provide a standardized methodology for intelligent agent control specifically designed for social interaction. The architecture may be employed in the context of a mobile collaborative augmented reality environment that is cohabited by both robots and humans. As an example of its application, they applied the framework to a museum virtual presence of the augmented reality agent to convey an individual and personalized learning experience.

© Springer Nature Switzerland AG 2021
Y. Luo (Ed.): CDVE 2021, LNCS 12983, pp. 342–347, 2021.
https://doi.org/10.1007/978-3-030-88207-5_34

AR allows a user to interact with a computer-generated virtual environment and also with three-dimensional model. This environment may be realistic, effective that it is familiar to us at a macroscopic scale, it may be realistic effective that it depicts the physical world as known to science, but which is not usually obscure, or it may be used to visualize a world that is absolutely imaginary. AR is widely applicable and has been applied to many ways of education. We argue here that this experiential nature of AR, together with its other key feature interactivity provides a valuable aid to conventional learning paradigms. In this chapter, we give a brief description of the common AR setups to give an idea of how AR experience is provided. We also consider, from cognitive and sensory psychology points of view why learning may be facilitated by interactive multi-sensory systems and we provide some examples of the use of AR in educational contexts. AR supplements the real world with virtual objects, such that virtual objects appear to coexist in the same space as the real world [2]. Augmented reality is a technology that allows a live real-time direct or indirect real-world environment to be augmented/enhanced by computer-generated virtual imagery information [3].

2   AR as a Main Component for Virtual Learning

AR is a modern technology that replaces sensory input obtained from the real world with sensory input composed by computer simulation. It provides interactivity with a view to movements and the natural behaviors. Therein AR may prove to be an accomplished appliance that can help in process of teaching by providing an environment that allows the student to experience scenarios and situations before imagining them. The experiential nature of AR systems derives from three sources: immersion, interactivity and multisensory feedback. Immersion means being enveloped or surrounded by the environment.

The benefit of immersion is that it protects a sense of presence or the feeling that one is really in the displayed world [4]. Interactivity is the ability to control events in the simulation by using one's own body movements, which in turn initiates responses in the simulation as a result of these movements. Virtual learning enables students to take all courses and workshops online, in a fully customizable and collaborative environment. It enables creating lab experiences with live demos, augmented reality objects that are accessible from anywhere, managing course content and downloadable resources and ensuring interactivity with Q&A and Live sessions. For example, mobile augmented reality is a method for providing a "head-up display" to individual dismounted users. A user wears a miniaturized computer system, tracking sensors, and a see-through graphics display. The system superimposes three-dimensional spatially registered graphics and sounds onto the user's perception of the real world. Because information can be presented in a head-up and hands-free way, such a system has the potential to revolutionize the way in which information is presented to individuals. A mobile AR system can insert friendly, neutral, or enemy computer-generated forces (CGFs) into the real world for training and mission rehearsal applications. The CGFs are drawn realistically and properly occluded, with respect to the real world. The behaviors of the CGFs are generated from two Semi-Automated Forces (SAF) systems: Joint SAF and One SAF. The AR user appears as an individual combatant entity in the SAF system. The AR user's position and orientation are fed into the SAF system, and the state of the SAF entities is reflected in the AR display.

The SAF entities react to the AR user just as they do to any other individual combatant entity, and the AR user interacts with the CGFs in real time. In this paper, we document the development of a prototype mobile AR system for embedded training and its usage in MOUT-like situations. The potential of combining smartphones and AR for education is very big. AR in could in many fields grant students an extra digital information about lots of subjects, and make complex information better understood. Actually, we may find some excellent examples of AR in education environment [5]. Connection of digital and real brings up more options for teachers and students. AR animated content in classroom lessons could catch students' attention in our dynamic day and age, as well as motivate them to study. For example, different data, fun facts, historical data, visual 3D models, would provide students a wider array understanding in lot of problematics. Students receive lesson text, audio or video form from teachers. Within web pages they can find useful information about the lesson, communication between student and teacher is better. AR technology has an ability to render unobtainable objects like are underground objects or astronomy objects and turn them into 3D models, thus making it easier to grasp the abstract and difficult concept. This is especially good for visual learners and practically anyone to translate theoretical material into a real.

Utilization of AR for education and teaching is unlimited. Its features could help also students with limited ability – with augmented tutorials, digital modeling, and simulations, to acquire some experience in the end. Virtual learning enables taking the students with limited ability into normal student environment and may enable them to feel more appreciated and happier. The paper is about our approach to the students and to those with limited ability. We present here some of our developed tools for virtual learning and education.

3   Augmented Reality Apps for Students

We adopted many augmented reality apps for different subjects in the student classes. For example, Elements 4D (Android/iOS) by DAQRI studio is an app for studying chemistry. It allows combining different elements for simulation, to see how they would react in reality. To start it, we have to use special triggers on printed cards. On their website, you can find lessons plans suitable for high school, secondary and elementary school programs.

Anatomy 4D (iOS/Android) is an app suitable for medical students. By scanning printed targets, the application shows 3D models of a human body and allows students to interact with it. Users may change and adjust any part of the human body, learn more about parts, joints, functions etc. Corinth Micro Anatomy, available for Windows Mobile, is another human anatomy application that may be interesting for medical students. Human Heart 3D app is with less content, but more specific – to explore the human heart in detail. 3D model of a heart is there completed with various animations and textual tips. AugThat (Android/iOS), designed by a former teacher, is the application that brings AR into a classroom. AugThat mainly targets students who may be lack of motivation with the help of 360-degree virtual photos and multiple 3D experiences. Google Translate (Android/iOS) is just great for studying foreign languages without a dictionary. By using Google Translate special "AR mode" our students can instantly checkup unknown words.

It works well for both our students and tourists, to navigate in cities. We also found out that some of AR apps that were not developed for educational purposes primarily, but they may serve as tools for creating augmented reality content for various subjects including educational projects. Augment (Android and iOS) has packages suitable for educational purposes in schools and universities. The platform provides options to create 3D models, as well as multiple other useful features. ZVR is a powerful tool by Zspace that comes with an extensive toolkit to create educational materials. Students equipped with special glasses could interact with AR objects, while there may also be used for engineers and designers. Daqri Studio, the application for creating AR projects and experiences, with examples of education apps such as Anatomy 4D, Elements 4D. Blippar (Android/iOS) an AR creation tool already used for many educational projects and integrated with different media outlets. It can visualize objects from printed material turning it into 3D interactive models. Aurasma and Layar, two powerful and popular tools for creating AR content designed by Layar Creator. Both of them have potential in many areas, not just education. Coming with user-friendly constructors, guides and tutorials, YouTube videos, audio tracks, images, https links, 3D models etc.

4 Our Tool for Students with Limited Ability

Combine Spoken Lesson with Text - Students with limited ability, especially hearing, have different learning abilities. Teaching students with various learning abilities involves creativity, time and a desire to understand how a student can learn the best. AR virtual lessons for such students implement all levels of virtual learning. Many tools start with lessons where they combine spoken lesson with text. See Fig. 1.

Fig. 1. Physics lesson for students.

Lip Reading - For students with impaired hearing, we found that the best form of communication is lip reading. In our virtual lessons such students would also be able to learn by lip reading. Education tools for all students, both the normal ability ones and limited ability ones, is building on components as speech phonemes [5], speech visemes, anatomy of virtual head, text, text to speech, speech to text converter, and generator of computer Slovak speech. Based on these components our tool for all students has been built. The communication tool is composed of various modules with different functionality. The usefulness of the speaking virtual head, as well as 3D visualization tools in the new communication form, audiovisual communications software technologies open almost unlimited possibilities for teaching and learning. Currently we are working on creating the final communication and presentation tool for all students, including the deaf, hearing impaired and students with limited ability. See Fig. 2.

Fig. 2. Physics lesson for hearing impaired students

Lots of deaf or hearing-impaired people are using lips reading as a main communication form. They prefer the virtual speaking head in crisis situations, as are fires, floods, bombing, various evacuation situations etc. They prefer using the speaking head for learning speaking, and other education purpose. In our case, a viseme is used for a presentational unit to classify speech sounds in the visual domain. It is helpful to describe the particular facial and oral positions and movements that occur alongside the voicing of phonemes, see Fig. 3. The capability limited students feel as other students with normal ability. This new way of teaching take teacher's expectation for better results.

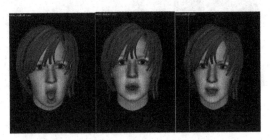

Fig. 3. Examples of the Slovak speech visemesTools's functionality

Development of a Virtual Speaking Head - We use speech synthesis technique in developing our teaching tool. As input data we use both normal audio files and synthesized speech. One of the modules developed by our team is to convert normal speech to synthesized speech. It is able to convert text to speech and speech to text. The second main module is for developing anatomy of faces.

We are working on preparing anatomy of face compound of more points. These two modules basically enable the creation of virtual speaking head. One of the other modules converts all phonemes to visemes. The module is able to develop 17 main visemes and 5 special visemes of Slovak speech. At the end of the process, the module for synchronization is used to synchronize visemes, phonemes and all the face anatomy. This completes the formation of the final virtual speaking head and finally the whole communication tool.

5 Conclusion

The paper describes our project of developing a virtual teaching and learning tool for both normal and ability limited students. The adopted applications, some major modules are briefly described. The major part of the tool has been implemented.

At this stage, we are communicating with the students asking their opinion about what they would like to be improved. We will try to include all these necessary requirements into the modules. In the future, we would like to focus on students with more significant problems in learning, as well as the students with bounded mobility.

Acknowledgements. This work was partially supported by the VEGA project No. 2/0125/20.

References

1. Augmented Reality Agents as Museum Guides, May 2006 in Conference: Agent Base, d Systems for Human Learning (ABSHL) Workshop to be held in conjunction with the Fifth International Joint Conference on Autonomous Agents and Multi- Agent Systems (AAMAS-06) 8th–12th May 2006.
2. Kangsoo Kim, Student Member, IEEE, Mark Billinghurst, Senior Member, IEEE, Gerd Bruder, Member, IEEE, Henry Been-Lirn Duh, Senior Member, IEEE, and Gregory F. Welch, Senior Member, Revisiting Trends in Augmented Reality Research: A Review of the 2nd Decade of ISMAR (2008–2017), IEEE
3. Carmigniani, J., Furht, B.: 2011. Augmented reality: an overview. In: Furht, B., (ed.) Handbook of Augmented Reality, pp. 3–46. Springer, New York. https://doi.org/10.1007/978-1-4614-006 4-61
4. Schuemie, M.J., van der Straaten, P., Krijn, M., van der Mast, C.A.P.G.: Research on presence in virtual reality: a survey. CyberPsychol. Behav. **4**(2), 183–201. https://doi.org/10.1089/109 493101300117884. https://www.researchgate.net/publication/11645364
5. Ezzat, T., Geiger, G., Poggio, T.: Trainable videorealistic speech animation. In: SIGGRAPH '02: Proceedings of the 29th Annual Conference on Computer Graphics and Interactive Techniques, pp. 388–398. ACM Press (2002)

Author Index

Printed in the United States
by Baker & Taylor Publisher Services

Printed in the United States
by Baker & Taylor Publisher Services